The Soul Sleepers

Christian Mortalism
from Wycliffe to Priestley

Bryan W. Ball

James Clarke & Co

James Clarke & Co
P.O. Box 60
Cambridge
CB1 2NT

www.jamesclarke.co.uk
publishing@jamesclarke.co.uk

First Published in 2008

ISBN: 978 0 227 17260 5

British Library Cataloguing in Publication Data
A catalogue record is available from the British Library

Contents

Abbreviations   5

Acknowledgements   7

   Introduction   9

   1. Continental Antecedents   25

   2. English Origins and Developments to 1600   43

   3. The Seventeenth-Century Scene to 1660   69

   4. The Major Seventeenth-Century Advocates   97

   5. Early Eighteenth-Century Debates and Digressions   127

   6. The Ascendancy of Thnetopsychism   149

   7. The World to Come – Realised Immortality   175

Appendix I. The Mortalist Works of Henry Layton   197

Appendix II. Mortalist Interpretation of Biblical Texts   201

Appendix III. The Eighteenth-Century Sussex Baptists   208

Bibliography   210

Index of Biblical References   222

Index of Names and Places   224

General Index   228

Abbreviations

BB	W.T. Whitley, *A Baptist Bibliography*
BL	British Library
BDBR	R.L. Greaves & R. Zaller (eds), *Biographical Dictionary of British Radicals*
CFF	L.E. Froom, *The Conditionalist Faith of our Fathers*
CM	N.T. Burns, *Christian Mortalism from Tyndale to Milton*
CSPD	*Calendar of State Papers Domestic*
DNB	*The Dictionary of National Biography*
DWL	Dr Williams's Library, London
HJ	*The Historical Journal*
HPT	*History of Political Thought*
JEH	*The Journal of Ecclesiastical History*
LW	*Luther's Works,* American edn
ME	*The Mennonite Encyclopedia*
MM	Richard Overton, *Mans Mortalitie*
NCE	*The New Catholic Encyclopedia*
ODCC	*The Oxford Dictionary of the Christian Church*
ODNB	*The Oxford Dictionary of National Biography*
OED	*The Oxford English Dictionary*
RR	G.H. Williams, *The Radical Reformation*
SP	*Studies in Philology*
STC	*Short Title Catalogue 1641-1700*
WER	T. Russell (ed.), *The Works of the English Reformers*

Acknowledgements

That this book, which has been seven years in the making, has finally come to see the light of day is due in no small measure to the interest and assistance of many other people. I am greatly indebted to them all and welcome the opportunity to say so.

Ronald Emmerson, Harry Leonard and Dennis Porter all read an early version of the manuscript and offered many helpful comments and suggestions from their own particular perspectives. They would probably not recognise large portions of it now since much has been added and amended, including a new title. Undisclosed publishers readers made further valuable suggestions which have also been incorporated into the final draft as it appears in the following pages.

My greatly-respected former mentor at the University of London, the late Dr. Geoffrey Nuttall, must also be mentioned. He first drew my attention to the existence of Soul Sleepers and mortalist thought in seventeenth-century England while I was pursuing a doctoral programme under his supervision, and he also read the manuscript in draft. He again made many constructive suggestions and would have been gratified to see it in print. His demise in July, 2007, unfortunately did not allow it.

I am also much indebted to the staff, always courteous and helpful, at several libraries on three continents where I was able to locate and read the writings of the sixteenth, seventeenth, and eighteenth-century authors whose views on mankind, death and the future form the basis of this study. In particular I recall with gratitude assistance given by staff at the Bodleian Library in Oxford, the British Library and Dr. Williams's Library in London, the University of Sydney and University of Newcastle Libraries, and Avondale College Library and the State Library of New South Wales in Australia, and the Andrews University Library in Michigan, U.S.A.

Many of the original writings examined in this study can only be found in libraries in the UK and in North America, and the work could not have been undertaken without several trips to locate and read the material. I must thank Robert Rawson and Robert Lemon and their associates at Silver Spring, Washington for financial assistance which made these long trips possible. I am also most grateful to the Avondale College Council for appointing me as a Senior Research Fellow for the past several years. Hopefully the confidence shown in these gestures is now to some extent justified.

My wife Dawn typed and re-typed the manuscript at the computer keyboard as she has done many times previously, and my two granddaughters, Lara and Katie Kuivisto, helped with the indexes. Lastly, but by no means least, a word of sincere appreciation to Adrian Brink at James Clarke and Co., Cambridge, England, for his interest in the manuscript, and to him and his associates for producing such a clear and readable book. It has been a pleasure to work with them, as it has with all whose names appear above. Remaining errors and omissions are, of course, mine.

Bryan W. Ball
Martinsville, N. S.W.
September, 2007

Introduction

Milton's brief line in *Paradise Regained*, "Much of the soul they talk, but all awry",[1] conceals rather more than it reveals of that mortalist theology which by the middle of the seventeenth century had been circulating in England for 150 years or more and which Milton himself, among others, readily endorsed.[2] It suggests that the soul was a matter of serious discussion in Milton's England, but says nothing about the origin or nature of the soul itself, its relationship to the body, or its condition after death. It testifies to Milton's disagreement with the prevailing majority view, but does not tell us why he disagreed or what he believed instead about the soul, either concerning its status in this present life or beyond the grave.[3] It says nothing about the protagonists on either side of the argument, those who were Milton's theological allies or those who took a different view, and nothing about the long history of mortalist thought reaching back, as it did, to the earliest days of the Reformation, both in England and on the Continent. And, of course, it has nothing to say whatsoever of that long line of mortalists who would succeed Milton, of the considerable body of literature they would generate, or the intensity of the arguments that would flow between those who would, often with some passion, share Milton's theology and those who would with equal passion oppose it. Those who proposed and debated these and related matters from Wycliffe onwards, their reasons and arguments, the questions about human being, the soul, life and death, mortality and immortality, Christ's resurrection and their own, which they raised and attempted to answer, are together the focus of this examination of Christian mortalism in

1. John Milton, *Paradise Regained* (1671), IV, 313. The words are spoken by Christ in Milton's schema, set against the background of Satanic temptations which extolled the "conjectures" and "fancies" of Greek culture, built on "nothing firm", "ignorant of themselves, of God much more", 236-284, 292, 310. It is mortalist thinking, if somewhat condensed.
2. Milton became a "staunch advocate" of mortalist doctrine in later life, even though some of his earlier poetry shows signs of a more orthodox position, *A Milton Encyclopedia* (William B. Hunter, ed.), 5 (1983), 155.
3. Milton's own mortalism, together with comment on the authorship of the *De Doctrina Christiana*, is discussed in ch. 4.

English thought from Wycliffe's time to that of Joseph Priestley at the end of the eighteenth century.

Two facts must be acknowledged at the outset. In the first place mortalism, in either of the two forms in which it was most commonly articulated, was always a minority view. The majority of English Christians from the very earliest days of the Reformation subscribed to the traditional and deeply cherished belief in the separate identity and inherent immortality of the soul, its release from the body at death to immediate heavenly felicity, and its ultimate re-unification with the body at the general resurrection of the dead at the last day.[1]

This had been the essence of Christian hope for centuries, and most English believers during the Reformation and immediate post-Reformation eras, Protestant as well as Catholic, felt disinclined to depart in this particular from the received faith. The moderate Richard Baxter, if we may take him as representative, is at pains to affirm the immortality of the soul and to take issue with the "Somatists" who believed otherwise.[2] The lay scholar William Hodson, whose *Credo Resurrectionem Carnis* was as emphatic an argument for the resurrection of the body as any, and who declared that burial was "an act of hope", nevertheless began his apology by asserting the soul's immortality.[3] This traditional doctrine, preached from pulpits of every persuasion up and down the land, alluded to frequently and with fervency at funerals and in biographies, and published in sermons, treatises and expositions of Scripture, had continued as the believers' chief source of comfort and hope for generations. It was unthinkable to the vast majority of English Christians that any alternative might even be suggested to take

1. The Westminster Confession of Faith (1643), although Presbyterian in character and intent, well represents the broadly accepted eschatology of the day. Article XXXII, 'Of the state of Men after Death, and of the Resurrection of the Dead', reads: 'The Bodies of Men, after Death, return to dust, and see corruption: but their Souls (which neither die nor sleep) having an immortal subsistence, immediately return to God who gave them. The Souls of the Righteous, being then made perfect in holiness, are received into the highest Heavens, where they behold the face of God in light and glory, waiting for the full redemption of their Bodies: and the Souls of the wicked are cast into Hell, where they remain in torments and utter darkness, reserved to the Judgement of the great day. Besides these two places for Souls separated from their Bodies, the Scripture acknowledgeth none.' *The Confession of Faith, Together with the Larger and Lesser Catechisms. Composed by the Reverend Assembly of Divines Sitting at Westminster* (1658), 105. It appears that this Article was intended to protect the faithful from the perceived errors of both mortalism and purgatory.
2. Richard Baxter, *The Reasons of the Christian Religion* (1667), 489ff; *The Life of Faith* (1670), 200ff; and, *contra* Clement Writer, in *The Unreasonableness of Infidelity* (1655). See also N.H. Keeble and G.F. Nuttall, *Calendar of the Correspondence of Richard Baxter* (2 vols., Oxford, 1991), I, 338.
3. W[illiam] H[odson], *Credo Resurrectionem Carnis* [1636], 20-1, 111.

its place. In the view of one well-known expositor of moderate seventeenth-century Puritan theology, they were heretics who asserted "the corruptibility and mortality of the soul as well as the body".[1]

Yet this is precisely what a diverse succession of convinced, energetic and, in the main, able apologists attempted to do for the best part of three centuries and more. Indeed, as the relevant literature testifies, for much of Christian history an alternative had existed to the traditional and deeply held beliefs concerning death and immortality. This study will remind us that, beyond the radicals and the sectaries, some of the most respected names in Reformation and post-Reformation English thought were ardent advocates of another position. Most of them came to believe that the Bible taught that the soul is not a separate entity inherently possessed of immortality, claiming instead that conscious existence ceases temporarily at death, pending the resurrection of the body, when the soul, i.e., the whole person, would live again according to the promises and power of God. Seeking to be true to what they considered to be the whole testimony of Scripture, they asserted with equal vitality that immortality was conditional upon Christ and His resurrection from the dead and upon the believer's faith in Him, culminating in resurrection to eternal life at the last day, and not upon an inherently immortal soul. To them this view was a more cohesive and consistent interpretation of the relevant biblical texts and it provided an equally certain future for the true believer. In the words of one of their more notable eighteenth-century spokesmen, Edmund Law, Professor of moral philosophy at Cambridge, eternal life "is not an inherent property of our original nature". Rather, the resurrection at the end of time "is the grand object of our faith, hope, and comfort", even our "full hope of immortality".[2]

Those who advocated such views have been known variously as mortalists, conditionalists, or more particularly in their own day, as soul sleepers. They were mortalists because, it was said, they believed in the death of the soul as well as the body, although some of them, particularly in the early years of the Reformation, did not quite go that far; conditionalists because they held that immortality derived from the work of Christ, personal faith in Him, and the resurrection at the last day; and soul sleepers because they considered that death was a sleep during which the soul was non-existent or, in the less extreme view, unconscious although still alive. This is, for the present, to leave undefined the nature of the soul, ultimately the most significant single consideration in mortalist dissatisfaction with the traditional doctrine. We

1. John Flavel, *Pneumatologia. A Treatise of the Soul of Man* (1685), Ep.Ded., sig. A3r.
2. Edmund Law, *Considerations on the Theory of Religion* (4th edn, 1759), 341, 355. This edition of the *Considerations* was essentially the same as Law's earlier *Considerations on the State of the World with Regard to the Theory of Religion* (1st edn, 1745), but with an amended title and including, *ad cal, The Nature and End of Death under the Christian Covenant,* and an appendix 'Concerning the Use of the Words *Soul* or *Spirit* in Holy Scripture, and the State of Death there described'.

should also observe that these definitions, even in their own day, were not always precise enough and that further clarification is necessary if the whole spectrum of mortalist conviction is to be understood. This is particularly true of the concept of soul sleeping. Provided we remember that soul sleepers were not always mortalists in the strict sense, the term Christian mortalist seems reasonable enough since all mortalists believed death to result in the cessation or suspension of personal existence, certainly of consciousness, and that it was not the continuation of life in another sphere.[1] That they were also Christian is evident from their insistence on the efficacy of the redemptive work of Christ which culminated in His resurrection from the dead, and on the fact that their own hope of eternal life was vested in Him rather than in themselves. We shall return shortly to the more precise and necessary definitions and distinctions which recent scholarship has proposed.

In the second place, something needs to be said in justification of another historical study of Christian mortalism. Without re-stating again the significance of Reformation and post-Reformation thought *per se*, in England or on the Continent, it may be argued that it is important to see the development of mortalist belief in the sixteenth, seventeenth and eighteenth centuries more as a legacy of Reformation theology than as an outcome of the influence of philosophy or rationalism on the theology of the day. Thus the veins of mortalist thought we shall seek to expose in this study were normally to be found in dogma, theological treatises, biblical commentaries and exegesis of the text, however limited at times that particular exercise may seem to later generations to have been. The status of the biblical text as divine revelation was a fundamental presupposition in the minds of all advocates of the mortalist position throughout the period covered by this study. The fact that mortalism could be found in Scripture, at least in the eyes of those who advocated it, and that it was found there by successive generations of English Christians, is one reason for the present study.

This is not to minimise the debt that the mature mortalism of the late seventeenth and eighteenth centuries owed to philosophical reflection. With hindsight it may be predicated that the forays into neo-Aristotelian anthropology by a small but significant minority in sixteenth-century Italian academic circles foreshadowed in principle later philosophical enquiry in the English tradition. The conclusions reached by Thomas Hobbes and John

1. In addition to N.T. Burns, *Christian Mortalism from Tyndale to Milton* (Cambridge, Mass., 1972) and G. H. Williams, *The Radical Reformation* (3rd edn, Kirksville, MO,1992), both of whom are cited in the following pages, other more recent uses of the term Christian mortalism include G.H. Tavard, *The Starting Point of Calvin's Theology* (Grand Rapids, MI and Cambridge, 2000), 36, 81 and V. Nuovo, *John Locke, Writings on Religion* (Clarendon Press, Oxford, 2002), xxxiii, 289. Wainwright uses the term inclusively of both types of mortalist belief, A.W. Wainwright(ed.), *John Locke, A Paraphrase and Notes on the Epistles of St. Paul to the Galatians, 1 and 2 Corinthians, Romans, Ephesians* (2 vols., Oxford, 1987), I, 54.

Locke in particular were crucial to the development and ultimate establishment in England of thnetopsychism and its continuance beyond their own day as a viable alternative Christian hope. The interdependence of philosophical deliberation and theological argument in the work of both these early advocates of the mortalist understanding of man is itself an important phenomenon, and may reasonably be argued as justification for an examination of this aspect of their thought. Beyond that, as we shall see more than once, many mortalists walked hand in hand with philosophers and with others who emphasised the necessity of reason to a credible faith. It may therefore be proposed that these earlier mortalists have something to say, both to those who currently find the mortalist position of interest in itself, and to those who wish, for whatever reason, to understand the thinking of earlier generations, particularly those, perhaps, who are persuaded of reason's necessary concurrence with belief.

From an historical perspective, the seeds of Christian mortalism had been sown in English religious thought at least as early as the fifteenth century. Mortalism itself first appeared in recognisable form during the sixteenth century, came more fully into the light in the first half of the seventeenth century, and found its fullest expression later in the seventeenth century and throughout the eighteenth century. It has continued as an alternative Christian hope ever since, although its later nineteenth-and twentieth-century advocates are beyond the scope of this present study.[1] Generally speaking, there are more fully-developed expositions of mortalism and more prominent advocates of the doctrine in the eighteenth century than in previous times given, of course, that Thomas Hobbes, John Milton and Locke, *inter alia,* belong to an earlier generation.[2]

There is, as we shall see, both continuity and development in English mortalism from John Wycliffe and his followers in the late fifteenth century to Francis Blackburne and Joseph Priestley in the latter half of the eighteenth century. Perhaps of greater significance is that this continuum of mortalist apologists included representatives from a broad cross section of the theological spectrum – Presbyterians, Independents, Baptists, Unitarians and ultimately Anglicans. While it is incorrect to designate all mortalists as being precisely of the same mind, or to denominate them as a separate sect,[3] there is clearly

1. Prominent nineteenth-century English mortalists and their more notable works include Edward White, *Life in Christ* (1846) and William Gladstone, *Studies Subsidiary to the Works of Bishop Butler* (1896). Twentieth-century advocates include William Temple, *Nature, Man and God* (1934) and H. Wheeler Robinson, *The Christian Doctrine of Man* (1926). The Norwegian philosopher, Jostein Gaarder, claims that in the Judaeo-Christian tradition, "there is nothing in man – no 'soul', for example – that is in itself immortal". Any hope of eternal life that man may have is not through his "own merit nor through any natural, or innate, ability", *Sophie's World* (1996), 134.

2. Milton, as ever, is thorough and articulate, but the *De Doctrina Christiana,* in which his mortalism is set out at length was unknown in his own day. See further, p. 115.

3. E.g., D. Saurat, *Milton, Man and Thinker* (New York,1925), 310-11; C. E. Whiting, *Studies in English Puritanism* (1931), 317.

significant common ground between those of otherwise divergent or even contentious opinion.

It must also be said that previous studies of mortalist thought which have included English advocates of the doctrine have not, for one reason or another, been entirely adequate. Beginning with my own *A Great Expectation*, the inclusion of a short appendix in the published edition of a limited Ph.D thesis, did little more than draw attention to the existence of the mortalist viewpoint,[1] which in any case was at that time already well known from other sources. However, no analysis of seventeenth- or eighteenth-century eschatological thought can be considered complete without adequate discussion of mortalism as a serious alternative to traditional views of death and the afterlife, and its relationship to other aspects of the prevailing eschatology. This present study may therefore be regarded from one standpoint as a late attempt to rectify a major earlier omission and to explore another important dimension of post-Reformation English thought concerning the last things and the *ordo salutis*.

L.E. Froom's comprehensive two-volume *The Conditionalist Faith of Our Fathers*[2] deserves mention as a starting-point and a rich source of information concerning mortalists and their beliefs throughout the Christian era. However, it fails to distinguish between the various strands of mortalism and is thus open to the charge of ambiguity. It also omits or mentions only in passing several important names from the seventeenth-century English scene, including Thomas Browne, Thomas Hobbes, Thomas Lushington, George Hammon and Clement Writer, and Samuel Bold, George Benson, George Clark and John Tottie from the eighteenth century, to mention only a few. More disturbing is Froom's inclusion of several names for whom the evidence of a mortalist stance is, at best, minimal or even refutable, notably Nathaniel Homes, John Tillotson and Peter Sterry in the seventeenth century and Isaac Watts, William Warburton and John Leland in the eighteenth century, none of whom can seriously be regarded as mortalists and most of whom were of another mind altogether.[3]

There is some evidence that in his discussion of the English mortalists, Froom relied on the earlier work of the English writer A.J. Mills, whose brief but helpful *Earlier Life-Truth Exponents* was published in 1925.[4] While noting

1. B.W. Ball, *A Great Expectation: Eschatological Thought in English Protestantism to 1660* (Leiden,1975), 243-6.
2. L.E. Froom, *The Conditionalist Faith of Our Fathers* (Washington, D.C., 1965), II, *passim,* but particularly pp. 49-243 for English mortalists of the sixteenth to eighteenth centuries.
3. For example, Isaac Watts, who wrote against both soul sleep and the death of the soul. His last word on the subject was, "The dead saints are not lost nor extinct . . . we may be assured that they neither die nor sleep", Isaac Watts, *Death and Heaven; or, The last Enemy Conquered, and Separate Spirits made perfect* (Edinburgh, 1749), 154-5.
4. A.J. Mills, *Earlier Life-Truth Exponents* (1925). Mills had participated in conferences of The Conditional Immortality Mission, formed in England in 1878, although he is scarcely acknowledged by Froom.

most of the seventeenth- and eighteenth-century English mortalists, Mills fails sufficiently to analyse or contextualise their theology, or to denominate those whose works can be regarded as seminal to the continuity of the mortalist tradition, or to recognise the distinction between psychopannychism and thnetopsychism, concepts which are crucial to a correct understanding of mortalism as a whole, and to which we shall return shortly. Mills also omits Browne, Hobbes, Hammon and Writer, as does Froom, and while he is not guilty of claiming marginal or improbable names such as Homes, Watts or Warburton, his inclusion of Isaac Barrow, Henry Dodwell (the Elder), and Joseph Hallett III, as thorough-going or representative mortalists is not supported by the original source material.[1]

D.P. Walker's *The Decline of Hell*[2] has justifiably made its mark in the literature concerned with seventeenth-century eschatological thought since its publication in 1964. Certainly the demise of traditional views of hell in many quarters is a significant development of more recent times[3] and Walker's study remains an important contribution to our understanding of this phenomenon. In mortalist understanding, however, hell was contingent upon the soul's traditional immortality and could not exist as a place of torment if the wicked did not have an immortal soul. Strangely there are few references in Walker's text to mortalist doctrine and the index does not list mortalism, soul, soul sleep or related concepts. In fact, having stated that the simplest way to eliminate the idea of eternal torment is "to deny personal immortality", Walker inexplicably decides not to pursue the relationship at all.[4]

The more recent work by N.T. Burns, *Christian Mortalism from Tyndale to Milton*, is by far the best and most scholarly study of early seventeenth-century English mortalism currently available, although it too is rapidly becoming dated. It is thorough, reliable and readable as far as it goes, its chief weakness being that it does not go far enough. As the title indicates, Burns' study concludes with Milton, and therefore does not take into consideration the more developed and mature thought of later seventeenth- and eighteenth-century mortalist writers, and the omission of Locke is surely indefensible in

1. Froom includes Dodwell as a "fringe writer", and notes Hallett's work as a "recognised contribution" to the mortalist debate. The latter is inadmissible, although Hallett from a cursory reading appears at times ambiguous. In *A Collection of Notes on Some Texts of Scripture, and of Discourses* (1729), he states emphatically "The soul is a substance distinct from, and independent on [*sic*] the body. . . . This I firmly believe", 211-12, but allowing that those who deny the soul's immateriality "would not thereby overturn any Article in Religion", 214-15.

2. D.P. Walker, *The Decline of Hell* (Chicago, 1964), *passim*.

3. Confirmed as a major issue for re-consideration, perhaps, by William Temple's call for a radical re-evaluation of the traditional doctrine of everlasting punishment in 'The Idea of Immortality in Relation to Religion and Ethics', *The Congregational Quarterly*, X (Jan. 1932).

4. Walker, *Decline of Hell*, 67.

any serious study of seventeenth-century mortalism. One of Burns' important contributions is his recognition of the distinction between psychopannychists, thnetopsychists and annihilationists and the application of these distinctions to the English mortalist scene. Burns also recognises that English mortalism was "based on a wholehearted belief in the Word of God"[1], rather than deriving solely or even in part from philosophical rationalism, and that the more courageous mortalists saw their doctrine not only as emanating from Scripture, "but also as part of a coherent Christian creed".[2] The present study will attempt to demonstrate, as did Burns, that this mortalist creed was indeed a thoroughly Christian vision, however unorthodox or marginal it may have appeared to its contemporaries.[3] Burns will help us considerably in our analysis of the earlier English mortalists.

One further consideration may be noted as justification for this study – the ease with which early and developing English mortalism continues to be overlooked, despite Burns' attempt more than thirty years ago to bring it to the attention of the scholarly world. Given mortalism's significance to the substance of seventeenth- and eighteenth-century philosophy and also to the study of early psychology and anthropology,[4] as well as its indisputable place in the development of Reformation and post-Reformation Christian dogma, however deviant at times that dogma may have appeared to contemporaries, such disregard is quite remarkable. This phenomenon can be illustrated by three recent studies of major mortalist apologists of the period whose own thought will appear in due course in the following pages, Tyndale and Milton, and by reference to Peter Marshall's recent comprehensive study of death in the Reformation and post-Reformation period.

David Daniell's detailed, readable and justifiably acclaimed life of Tyndale, *William Tyndale, A Biography*, published in 1994 by Yale University Press, is virtually silent throughout four hundred pages concerning Tyndale's mortalism. Admittedly his mortalism is not the most frequently recognised feature of Tyndale's theology, but it is there, at times quite apparent, and it cannot simply be ignored. Yet we do not find it in Daniell's book, especially at the two points where we would most expect it – in his treatment of Tyndale's *Answer* to Sir Thomas More's *Dialogue*, and of the altercation with George Joye over the latter's pirated and substantially changed version of Tyndale's New Testament in 1534.[5] Neither is it mentioned in Daniell's comments on one of Tyndale's last tracts, his

1. *CM*, 3, 4.
2. *Ibid.*, 9.
3. *Ibid.*, 22.
4. For example in the writings of Locke, Hartley and Priestley. Locke's *Essay concerning Humane Understanding* (1689) and Hartley's *Observations on Man* (1749) are two examples. The latter was later abridged by Priestley as the *Theory of the Human Mind* (1775).
5. D. Daniell, *William Tyndale, A Biography* (New Haven and London, 1994), 269-74; 322-26. See ch. 2, pp. 48ff for Tyndale's mortalism.

account of the Gloucestershire gentleman William Tracy's last will and testament,[1] which was mortalist in tone, as well as Lutheran in the wider sense, and which was condemned at the time on both accounts. There are no references to 'soul', 'resurrection', 'mortality' or 'immortality' and only one incidental reference to 'death' in the index. It is, in many respects, a strange silence.

The most recent omission of mortalism in a major study of Tyndale is in Ralph Werrell's *The Theology of William Tyndale* (Cambridge, 2006). It is, actually, not so much an omission as an outright denial. Contradicting Diarmaid MacCulloch's observation that Tyndale shared Luther's belief in soul sleep,[2] Werrell flatly says that this is a "false statement", arguing that Tyndale did not endorse a mortalist theology.[3] A careful reading of Tyndale confirms, however, that MacCulloch is correct, as we might expect, and that Werrell is mistaken. Werrell's analysis of Tyndale's theology, in fact, has virtually nothing to say of Tyndale's eschatology from any perspective, let alone his mortalism. There is one reference to 'soul sleep' in the index to Werrell's book, that referred to above, and one reference to eternal life. There are no references to the soul, death, resurrection, immortality, heaven or hell.[4] While Werrell's study is of interest in other respects, it is surely indefensible to say nothing about eschatology in a work that purports to analyse the theology of one of the great English Reformers, particularly since Tyndale lived and wrote at a time when belief in the life to come and the eternal salvation of the soul were of primary concern to scholars and laity alike.

There is an equally inexplicable silence about Milton's mortalism in the otherwise commendable collection of essays devoted to Milton's divergent theological views, *Milton and Heresy* (Cambridge University Press, 1998). Here, if anywhere, one might legitimately expect to find at least minimal discussion of a 'heresy' that in Milton's time was already well known and regarded with as much apprehension as any other unorthodoxy of the day and which appears in *Paradise Lost* as well as the *De Doctrina Christiana*. Despite the early promise inherent in the assertion that Milton "insists on the common materiality and mortality of body and soul" and passing recognition of his mortalism,[5] the theme is never explored and rarely referred to again, even though Burns, Saurat and Masson had all previously seen it.[6] The few references to monism as such

1. *Ibid.,* 222. See ch. 2, pp. 52-54 for Tracy's mortalism.

2. Diarmaid MacCulloch, *Reformation: Europe's House Divided 1490-1700* (2004), 580-81.

3. Ralph S. Werrell, *The Theology of William Tyndale* (Cambridge, 2006), 7.

4. Werrell's comments on William Tracy also ignore his mortalism.

5. S.B. Dobranski and J.P. Rumrich (eds.), *Milton and Heresy* (Cambridge, 1998), 1, 8.

6. *CM*, ch. 4, *passim;* Saurat, *Milton, Man and Thinker,* ch. 3; D. Masson, *The Life of John Milton,* VI (1880), 833-39, where Masson suggested that mortalism was a late addition to Milton's thinking.

appear to relate as much to the nature of God as to the nature of man,[1] and the phrase "animate materialism", which is used almost entirely in the context of oral functions such as eating, speaking and kissing,[2] is never examined for its wider theological content or its broader implications. It is disappointing to find that one of Milton's more notable 'heresies' is thus marginalised by inattention, if not trivialisation, the more so since clarification of Milton's mortalism undoubtedly would have strengthened the book's central proposition, Milton as heterodox rather than orthodox.[3] Perhaps part of the problem is that the book was written by "bibliographers, feminists, literary historians, Marxists and psychoanalytic critics"[4] without any input from theologians, biblical scholars or specialists in historical theology.

The writings of both Tyndale and Milton contributed materially to the shaping of the English language and, we may suppose thereby, to some extent at least, to the shaping of English thought. The omission of mortalism in very different and unrelated studies, either by accident or design, may be symptomatic of a general unawareness, even neglect, of the mortalist phenomenon and its presence throughout the Reformation and post-Reformation eras and the early modern period as a whole, and of its significance to the development of later and modern thought, particularly the current renewed interest in mortalist thought and doctrine. If that should be the case, it is surely no longer defensible.

The brief account of mortalism's appearance during the English Reformation in Peter Marshall's detailed and quite fascinating study of death, dying and the dead in the late medieval and early modern periods, *Beliefs and the Dead in Reformation England* (2002),[5] is also an incentive for a more thorough analysis of mortalist theology. Marshall recounts the confrontation between Tyndale and George Joye over the issue, and also recognises the later mortalism of "major figures" such as Overton, Milton and Hobbes (but not Locke) in a footnote.[6] Evidence for belief in the resurrection of the body in early English Protestantism, an undeniable fact of some significance that emerges frequently and strongly from the literature, is drawn almost exclusively from early seventeenth-century sources.[7] Yet Tyndale, Frith, Tracy and Latimer, to mention only the mortalists of the early English Reformation who will appear in the following study, all had something to say about it. It must also be noted that the resurrection hope they entertained was certainly not the sole prerogative of these early mortalists, however much they preached and wrote in its favour. This is not intended to

1. Dobranski and Rumrich (eds.), *Milton and Heresy*, 83, 118.
2. *Ibid.*, 118, 129, 133. The title of the chapter which purports to examine Milton's "heretical" monism is "Milton's Kisses".
3. *Ibid.*, 2, 3.
4. *Ibid.*, 16.
5. Peter Marshall, *Beliefs and the Dead in Reformation England* (Oxford, 2002), 223-25.
6. *Ibid.*, 225.
7. *Ibid.*, 226-28.

detract from what is a significant and enlightening investigation of thanatology in the sixteenth and early seventeenth centuries, but merely to underline again the need for a more comprehensive account of mortalist thought as it emerged and developed in Reformation and post-Reformation England respectively.

We must now return to the question of definitions. The distinctions between various strands in European mortalist thought were recognised by G.H. Williams in his definitive *The Radical Reformation*, an indispensable guide to the development of divergent theological views on the Continent in the wake of the mainstream Reformation[1], particularly in its revised, and substantially enlarged, third edition (1992). The work is a rich mine of well-documented information, and we shall find it helpful in the chapter dealing with the Continental radicals. Williams maintains that psychopannychism "may be considered the Italian counterpart of Germanic solafideism and Swiss predestinarianism" in its contribution to the dismantling of the medieval church and its theological hold on the minds of ordinary men and women.[2] It was, indeed, a "recurrent feature of the Radical Reformation",[3] and although Williams does not find psychopannychism as prominent in Reformation and post-Reformation England as he does in Italy, Switzerland and Germany, it nonetheless found vigorous support there, as we shall see. To what extent English mortalism owed its existence to Continental radicalism is not entirely clear, but it is in the context of European radical theology that we can begin to understand the difference between the two major strands of mortalism which eventually also found expression in English mortalist thought.

Williams allows the term psychopannychism, "soul sleep", to describe both the sleep and the death of the soul while awaiting the resurrection,[4] conceding that although psychopannychism thus used is "etymologically ambiguous" it is permissible as "the generic term for the two variants" of soul sleep.[5] These variants may be further defined as psychosomnolence, "the unconscious sleep of the soul" and thnetopsychism, "the death of the soul", both pending the resurrection.[6] Both psychopannychism, more narrowly defined, and psychosomnolence, however, presuppose the existence of a separate immaterial entity, the soul, which may live apart from the body, a position which thnetopsychism was not prepared to endorse. Sleep in the literal sense, indeed, requires existence and the capability of consciousness. Williams' definition of thnetopsychism as "the death of the soul" is permissible and helpful, provided that the soul is

1. *RR*, particularly 64-70, 899-904.
2. *Ibid.*, 70.
3. *Ibid.*
4. *Ibid.*, 64.
5. *Ibid.*, 900. Cf. also Williams' definition of psychopannychism as "the generic term for a complex of sectarian views about the death or sleep of the soul after the death of the body", G.H. Williams, 'Camillo Renato (c.1500 -?1575)' in J.A. Tedeschi (ed.), *Italian Reformation Studies in Honor of Laelius Socinus* (Florence, 1965), 106.
6. *RR*, 902.

not defined in traditional terms, but only as authentic thnetopsychists would allow.

Burns is rather more precise. Psychopannychists believed in a separate, immaterial soul in common with those who held the traditional view of the soul's immortality, but maintained contrary to them that the soul 'slept' until the resurrection. Thnetopsychists did not believe in the soul so defined, maintaining instead that the soul was best understood as the mind, or more usually the person, which existed as the result of the union of breath and body. The soul, therefore, died or 'slept' between death and the resurrection, since the union of breath and body then no longer existed.[1] Burns explains,

> The psychopannychists believed that the immortal substance called soul literally slept until the resurrection of the body; the thnetopsychists, denying that the soul was an immortal substance, believed that the soul slept after death only in a figurative sense. Both groups of soul sleepers believed in the personal immortality of the individual after the resurrection of the body, and so they should not be confused with the annihilationists.[2]

The terms psychopannychism and thnetopsychism will be used throughout this study, under the more general and inclusive term Christian mortalism, as thus defined.[3] Both maintain a 'sleep' of the soul during death, the one literal, the other metaphorical, since psychopannychism's immortal soul could not die when the body died, and since thnetopsychism's 'soul', not being a soul in the accepted sense, could not actually sleep apart from the body. Moreover most, if not all, psychopannychists were mortalist in the sense that the soul, although a separate entity, was not inherently immortal, but derived its immortality from Christ. Annihilationism, which defines those who "denied personal immortality altogether because they believed that the personal soul was annihilated with the body and that neither soul nor body would be resurrected",[4] does not readily fall within the scope of this study, since strictly speaking its advocates cannot be regarded as Christian mortalists, even though during the seventeenth century they were often regarded as one of a kind with others who denied the traditional view.

1. *CM*, 16-18.
2. *Ibid.*,18.
3. *OED*, following the Greek *psuche* and *pannuchios*, defines psychopannychy or psychopannychism as the "all-night sleep of the soul", the state in which "the soul sleeps between death and the day of judgement", and thnetopsychism, after the Greek *thnetos* and *psuche*, as "the doctrine. . .that the soul dies with the body, and is recalled to life with it at the Day of Judgement". Tavard uses the term "anabaptist mortalism" inclusively for both the sleep and the death of the soul, *Calvin's Theology*, 36, 55. 'Mortalism' thus used more generically seems better on balance than risking further confusion by restricting it to being a synonym for thnetopsychism.
4. *CM*, 2.

There were, indeed, those in sixteenth- and early seventeenth-century England who held such annihilationist views, although it is fair to point out that compared to psychopannychists and thnetopsychists, they were relatively few in number, and that annihilationism had all but run its course by the middle of the seventeenth century. If we interpret the later mortalist writers correctly, psychopannychism continued with decreasing momentum to find expression throughout the seventeenth century, until by the latter decades of the century virtually all mortalists were thnetopsychist and thnetopsychism itself was the predominant expression of Christian mortalism. And by then, Burns would surely not have been able to conclude that "most of them were poor and ignorant".[1] In fact, judged by the writings of those who openly and vigorously defended it, Christian mortalism had, certainly by the mid-eighteenth-century, attracted the attention of well-trained academics, philosophers and highly-placed ecclesiastics, whose careful and generally well-stated convictions became an indispensable part of that long tradition which continues to articulate an alternative Christian hope.

It thus becomes evident, on etymological grounds alone, that psycho-pannychism is not an authentic expression of Christian mortalism thoroughly understood, any more than a living person who is merely asleep can be said to be dead. The two concepts are mutually exclusive. Thnetopsychists, of course, argued that the biblical grounds for their position ratified, even generated, the inherent meaning of the terminology which came to describe their views and those of their psychopannychistic cousins. This study sets out to demonstrate, therefore, not only the extent and nature of the Christian mortalist impetus in post-Reformation English thought, but more precisely to argue, among other things, that psychopannychism cannot be regarded as a true expression of thorough-going mortalism. That distinction belongs alone to the thnetopsychist construction, and is perhaps the reason for its eventual ascendancy and the eclipse of psychopannychism's tentative disagreement with the traditional view.

Not that these distinctions were always clearly understood at the time. Quite the contrary, in fact. Either by ignorance or design psychopannychism and thnetopsychism were frequently confused, although in fairness it must be said that perhaps it was not always thought necessary to make the distinction. In 1655 Thomas Hall, a zealous Presbyterian defender of immortalist orthodoxy, denounced the author of the recent *Mans Mortalitie*, Richard Overton, as a "pamphleteering mortalist", a "psychopannychist",[2] when Overton, as we shall see, clearly held thnetopsychist views. When in 1659 the erudite Henry More set out to confute the "Psychopannychites"[*sic*] of his day, we are not quite sure who, besides Thomas Hobbes, also a thnetopsychist, he has in mind.[3]

1. *Ibid.*
2. Thomas Hall, *Vindiciae Literarum* (1655), 66.
3. Henry More, *The Immortality of the Soul* (1659), sigs. a7r, 8v, b1r.

In his *Explanation of The Grand Mystery of Godliness*, published the following year, More continued his attack on the "Psychopannychites", arguing that the "souls of the deceased do not sleep, but. . . understand and perceive what condition they are in after death".[1] Yet there were few, if any, thorough-going psychopannychists remaining in England by 1660, at least none we know by name or who have left documentary evidence of their beliefs.

The later seventeenth- and eighteenth-century mortalists themselves, by now almost entirely thnetopsychist, whose convictions we are about to examine in some detail in the following pages, were more concerned with substance than terminology. They would to a man have endorsed the conclusion of one of the more prominent later mortalists, William Temple. "Man is not by nature immortal", Temple maintained, "but capable of immortality". The "prevailing doctrine of the New Testament" is that "God alone is immortal . . . and that He offers immortality to man not universally but conditionally". Hence the authentic Christian teaching about eternal life "is a doctrine not of immortality, but of Resurrection". [2] By the time Temple arrived on the scene, the possibility of achieving immortality and the conditions upon which it could be attained had been the chief concerns of English mortalists for at least the preceding four centuries.

If any further justification is needed for rehearsing again the theological convictions of past generations, it may be found in the writings of the seventeenth- and eighteenth-century Christian mortalists themselves. They protested vigorously at the continuing inclusion of what they saw as an anti-Christian element in the Christian declaration, and the passive Protestant acceptance of a doctrine which in their eyes came palpably from pagan sources via Rome. It must be remembered that even by the mid-eighteenth century the gulf between Protestantism and Catholicism was still very wide, irreconcilable in fact, in the minds of most Englishmen. One suspects that the seventeenth- and eighteenth-century mortalists would have been astounded that after two or three hundred years of enlightenment and progress in virtually every realm of human intellectual endeavour, the greater part of Christendom at the beginning of the twenty-first century would still cling to elements of belief that to them were demonstrably incompatible with the essential Christian revelation. Of course, we do not see things from a seventeenth- or eighteenth-century perspective any longer, and justifiably find reasons for not doing so. Nonetheless, the theological and anthropological insights of these earlier students of human being and destiny may speak, in one way or another, to those who still struggle with the recurring questions of existence and the future,

1. Henry More, *An Explanation of The Grand Mystery of Godliness* (1660), 15, 30. More had in 1642 published *Antipsuchopannychia, or A Confutation of the Sleep of the Soul after Death*, in which similar sentiments had been expressed in verse.
2. William Temple, 'The Idea of Immortality in Relation to Religion and Ethics', in *The Congregational Quarterly*, X (1932), 17; *Nature, Man and God* (1934), xxx, 461-63.

particularly those who find the thought of previous generations a relevant context for the pursuit of similar questions in our own time.

It remains only to add a few words regarding procedure. Further biographical details on most of the English mortalists will be found in the *Oxford Dictionary of National Biography* or the *Dictionary of National Biography* and in the *Biographical Dictionary of British Radicals*. The footnotes, therefore, normally make no reference to any source of such information. Much the same can be said of Continental mortalists, for whom biographical data can usually be found in G.H. Williams' *The Radical Reformation*. Spelling and punctuation have usually been modernised in quotations from original sources, except in titles cited in the text or in footnotes, where the original spelling and punctuation have normally been retained, and on other occasions when retention of the original adds emphasis or is of particular interest. Hebrew and Greek words have been transliterated and appear in italics, whether or not they so appeared in the original text. The works of Luther, Calvin and other Continental authors have been cited from selected English translations rather than from original language editions. New-style dates are used throughout unless otherwise noted, and all books cited were published in London unless otherwise indicated. Biblical quotations are from the Authorised Version. It was finally that version, held in such esteem by so many generations of English Christians, more than any other, which prompted English post-Reformation mortalists in the seventeenth and eighteenth centuries in particular to question the prevailing doctrine of the soul's immortality and which provided them with that alternative hope which is the subject of this study.[1]

1. We are indebted to Alister McGrath for reminding us that the English Reformers themselves drew on Tyndale's New Testament and the Geneva Bible, among other sixteenth-century translations, and that these earlier versions, particularly Tyndale's New Testament, substantially shaped the Authorised version itself, Alister McGrath, *In The Beginning, The Story of the King James Bible* (2001), *passim.*

Chapter One
Continental Antecedents

The extent to which developing post-medieval doctrine in England was influenced by contemporary European thought remains an important factor in any analysis of the English scene. It is clear that much Reformation and post-Reformation English theology derived from the independent thinking of strong English minds open to the catalytic and powerful texts of Scripture recently made available in the original languages and in the vernacular, and interpreted against the prevailing moods and conditions. On the other hand, the presence in England of individuals and congregations fleeing from repression on the Continent, and an awareness there of Continental ideas cannot be overlooked. The two-way flow of both English and Continental believers across the Channel from the earliest days of the Reformation inevitably enhanced the accessibility and credibility of ideas current on the Continent. A.G. Dickens noted "substantial examples of transition from Lollardy to Lutheranism" in London during the early 1500s, and more recently Alister McGrath has reminded us of the influence of Luther on Tyndale's New Testament.[1] Many of the major English mortalists who will appear in this study had European contacts of one kind or another which, in terms of the exchange of ideas, were mutually beneficial. The least that can be said is that English beliefs, including mortalism, in the Reformation and post-Reformation era, developed with an understanding of what was happening in Europe.

In 1597 John Payne, an English refugee in Haarlem, warned against the mortalist beliefs of Dutch Anabaptists,[2] and in 1646 Friedrich Spanheim alerted his English readers to the deviant views of German Anabaptists who taught that the souls of the dead "sleep with their bodies until the last day . . . deprived of all knowledge, both intellectual and sensitive".[3] In 1653 John Biddle translated into English Joachim Stegmann's *Brevis Disquisitio* (1633) which, among other concerns, queried "whether the dead do properly live", asserting that the traditional affirmative answer constituted "the grounds of the greatest

---

1. A.G. Dickens, *The English Reformation* (1964), 33; McGrath, *In The Beginning*, 72-3.
2. [John Payne], *Royall Exchange* (Haarlem, 1597), 19, 22.
3. Friedrich Spanheim, *Englands Warning by Germanies Woe* (1646), 36.

errors among the Papists".[1] In reality, however, it was not only Anabaptist or
Continental Socinianism that may have helped English mortalism on its way.
The psychopannychism of the German reformers Luther and Carlstadt gave
Continental mortalism an early degree of respectability which its later and less
respectable associations with Anabaptists and other radicals did not wholly remove.
It is to Luther's and Carlstadt's rejection of long-standing medieval doctrines
which had undergirded so many of the abuses germinal to the Reformation,
that we will turn first. But before that, it will be helpful to note developments
concerning the soul's immortality in the years preceding the Reformation.

Consolidation of the Traditional Doctrine
It is easily forgotten that the doctrine of the immortality of the soul appeared
relatively late in the development of traditional Catholic theology.[2] Two events
in particular may be said to have precipitated a more definitive formulation of
the medieval belief in the soul's immortality and hence the later, but consequent,
appearance of an alternative mortalist eschatology. These were outcomes of the
Council of Florence, 1438-45, and the Fifth Lateran Council, 1512-17, on the
developing doctrines of purgatory and the immortality of the soul. Even before
that, however, there had been hints of uncertainty over the nature of the soul and
its condition after death from within the higher echelons of the Church itself,
which may have reflected things to come as well as past doubts and ambiguities.

    In 1312 the Council of Vienne, reacting to continued philosophical
assertions in some academic circles of the soul's mortality, denounced as
heretical and "inimical to the truth of the Catholic faith" certain ideas
which appeared to question the superiority of the soul over the body and the
possibility of its independent existence.[3] John XXII, the first of the Avignon
popes, for some years held the view that the departed souls of the righteous
dead do not see God until after the last judgment.[4] He is said to have written
a work on this theme prior to his election to the papal throne in 1316. After
becoming Pope he continued to advance these ideas in sermons as late as 1332,[5]
arousing considerable opposition, particularly from the theology faculty at the
university of Paris, to the point that he was actually accused of heresy. Under
pressure from his theological advisers to conform, he eventually withdrew his
divergent views in favour of the more orthodox Catholic position, declaring

1. John Biddle (tr.), *Brevis Disquisitio; or, A Brief Enquiry Touching a Better Way Then Is
    commonly made use of, to refute Papists, and reduce Protestants to certainty and Unity
    in Religion* (1653), 26. See also *CFF,* II, 177.
2. An acclaimed recent study of death and dying notes that the concept of an immortal
    soul, long cultivated in clerical circles, began to spread "from the eleventh to the
    seventeenth century, until it gained almost universal acceptance", Philippe Aries,
    The Hour of Our Death (1981), 606.
3. Tavard, *Calvin's Theology,* 22-3.
4. *ODCC,* s.v. John XXII, states that he maintained this opinion until his deathbed.
5. Tavard, *Calvin's Theology,* 18.

that his earlier beliefs had been merely a personal opinion.[1] Clearly this was not the mortalism of the Reformation era, but it is difficult to agree entirely with Burns here that the earlier position of John XXII "does not even approach psychopannychism"[2] since it shared one of psychopannychism's major tenets, denial of heavenly glory until after the last judgement.

In 1439 the Council of Florence clarified and declared canonical a belief which had already existed for some time, the doctrine of purgatory, with its essential presupposition that the souls of the dead are conscious and "capable of pain or joy even prior to the resurrection of their bodies",[3] and its corollary that prayers for the dead are valuable and necessary. Few doctrines of the medieval church provoked such widespread opposition from the early Reformers and those who followed them than this idea of an intermediate state between death and a future life where those who had died would undergo purification and punishment prior to the resurrection and the last judgement. The abuses deriving from belief in purgatory were to become one of the major concerns of Luther's Ninety-Five Theses, with his open attack on the sale of indulgences and the "audacious" claim that souls could be released from purgatory thereby. Luther would ultimately conclude that the underlying doctrine of the soul's substantiality and immortality was "a monstrous opinion" emanating from Rome's "dunghill of decretals".[4]

Meanwhile the consolidation of purgatory as a major tenet of the Western Church by the Council of Florence had provided the impetus for a renewed focus on the question of human existence with particular emphasis on the nature of the soul. Interest in such philosophical and theological matters was naturally strong in the universities, where in Italy the discussion came to centre on Aristotelian and Platonic views. At the University of Padua in 1509 it was propounded that Aristotle had taught the mortality of the soul.[5] Pietro Pomponazzi, successively professor at Padua, Ferrara and Bologna, eventually articulated his interpretation of the Aristotelian view in his *On the Immortality of the Soul* (1516) and *Apologia* (1517), maintaining that it was possible to conclude from reason not only that the soul was individual and transient, but also that it was mortal. In so doing, Pomponazzi also asserted that his philosophical conclusions, mere "deductions of human reason", were transcended by the divine revelation of a resurrection to come and needed to cause no offence.[6] Girolamo Cardano of Milan shared Pomponazzi's doubts

1. *NCE*, (2nd edn, 2003), VII, 932, where it is claimed that John XXII's views "threatened the theological foundation of the papacy".
2. *CM*, 152.
3. *NCE*, V, 770; *RR*, 65.
4. *CFF*, II, 73; R.H. Bainton, *Here I Stand, A Life of Martin Luther* (New York, 1950), 54; E.G. Rupp and B. Drewery, *Martin Luther* (1970), 19-25.
5. *RR*, 65. See also Tavard, *Calvin's Theology*, 28-30.
6. *ODCC*,. s.v. Pietro Pomponazzi; *RR*, 66. A more detailed account of Pomponazzi's theology of the soul can be found in Don Cameron Allen, *Doubt's Boundless Sea*

about the soul, if not his reluctance to cause offence. Cardano's *De Animi Immortalitate* (1545) began by considering "whether human souls are eternal and divine or whether they perish with the body", and proposed fifty-four reasons for concluding that the soul was not immortal.[1]

Any hopes that Pomponazzi may have had of avoiding conflict were clearly naive. The ecclesiastical hierarchy had, in fact, already reacted against the new ideas which had been emanating from Padua for some years. In 1513 the Fifth Lateran Council dealt with the problem caused by the proposition that the soul was mortal, denouncing it as a "very pernicious error" and re-asserting that each individually created soul is "truly, and of itself. . . immortal" and capable of existence after death prior to the resurrection. Williams notes that "this importation of *natural* theology into Catholic dogma" was in actual fact "much closer to Platonic philosophy than to the Bible"[2], and then comments more fully on the pronouncement of the Fifth Lateran Council:

> The natural immortality of the soul had become so integral a part of the massive penitential and liturgical structure of Catholic moral theology that the philosophical threat to it moved Leo X, in the first year of his pontificate, to condemn in 1513, at the eighth session of the Fifth Lateran Council, the philosophical proofs and disproofs of immortality in the universities . . . and academic circles. . . . Leo in council asserted that the soul is naturally immortal and, as the substantial form of the body, is susceptible both of the pains of hell and purgatory, and the bliss of paradise.[3]

Those who were soon to deny the soul's immortality, both on the Continent and in England, could be in no doubt about the importance of this doctrine to the entire structure of Roman theology or, perhaps, of the consequences which such denial might incur.

Luther and Carlstadt

Luther's views on the state of the soul after death, arising in large part from his respect for biblical authority over that of the church, began to appear in his response to Leo X's Bull of 1520, 'Exsurge Domine', which re-affirmed papal endorsement of the now established doctrine. In his defense of the propositions he had earlier put forward and which Leo's Bull had condemned, Luther argued that the church's official doctrine of the soul as a spiritual, but

(Baltimore, 1964), 29-45. Allen proposes that it was Pomponazzi who "revived the Athenian disease of doubt".

1. Allen, *Doubt's Boundless Sea*, 56. On Cardano, see Allen, 45-58.
2. *RR*, 66. The much revised entry on 'soul' in the third edition of *ODCC* claims that "there is practically no specific teaching on the subject in the Bible", stating that in the post-Nicene era "a modified Platonic view" of the soul gained acceptance.
3. *RR*, 66-7. The 'Apostolici regiminis', the document by which the Council's official judgment was promulgated, re-asserted the immortality of the soul as necessary dogma. See also *NCE*, I, 595.

substantial, substance and the "form" of the human body, was only a papal opinion.[1] While this was clearly not yet an outright expression of the mortalism he was shortly to declare, it nevertheless demonstrated his profound unease with the prevailing doctrine. This fundamental divergence over the soul and its condition after death would, with the exception of Carlstadt, set him apart from the other major Continental Reformers. Indeed, Luther and Carlstadt alone of all the early Reformers seem to have entertained the doctrine of soul sleep, while Calvin, Bullinger and Zwingli were all advocates of the traditional view and strongly opposed any alternative. Luther's essential mortalism has been questioned, but the evidence seems indisputable that, with occasional lapses towards an inherited medieval view, he held a psychopannychist position for most of his life following his break with Rome.[2]

Certainly this was the understanding of the later Anglican mortalist, Francis Blackburne, who added to his historical survey of mortalism, first published in 1765,[3] an appendix, *An Inquiry into the sentiments of Martin Luther concerning the state of the Soul between Death and the Resurrection*. Blackburne maintained that Luther had been incorrectly accused of thnetopsychism by Cardinal du Perron, but also noted a letter from Luther to Amsdorf in 1522, commenting that in it Luther appeared "much inclined to believe that the souls of the just sleep to the day of judgement, without knowing where they are".[4] This earliest known indication of mortalism in Luther's thought appears to confirm a psychopannychist position as opposed to the thnetopsychism which du Perron had mistakenly seen and which manifested itself shortly thereafter in the thinking of other Continental mortalists. Blackburne was convinced that Luther remained a psychopannychist to his dying day, using the doctrine to refute medieval teachings of purgatory and the invocation of saints in his definitive struggle with the papacy.[5]

Luther must be allowed to speak for himself, however. When he does so, two things in particular are readily apparent : the strength of his convinced and sustained psychopannychism, and the distinction between it and the thnetopsychism which was soon to appear elsewhere on the Continent and

1. *Ibid.*, 197.
2. *CFF*, II, 76. Williams maintains that Luther's occasional ambivalence had a significant outcome: "Little by little within Lutheranism the doctrine of the sleep of the soul was replaced by the idea of a natural immortality", *RR*, 197.
3. Francis Blackburne, *A Short Historical View of the Controversy Concerning An Intermediate State and The Separate Existence of the Soul Between Death and the General Resurrection* (1765). An expanded second edition appeared in 1772 with the same title minus the word *Short*. Unless otherwise stated the 1772 edition is cited in this study. The appendix remained the same in both editions.
4. Francis Blackburne, *An Historical View of the Controversy Concerning an Intermediate State and the Separate Existence of the Soul Between Death and the General Resurrection* (2nd edn, 1772), 344, 348. Blackburne's own views are considered in chapter six.
5. *Ibid.*, 14, 15.

which would find articulate advocates in radical circles, notably among the
Italian Evangelical Rationalists, and which would later flower across the
Channel as the mature expression of English mortalist thought. Although it
has largely been ignored since, Luther's psychopannychism was recognised and
challenged in its own day. In England, Sir Thomas More responded to it in
his well-known *Dialogue* with Tyndale in 1529,[1] thereby providing Tyndale
with the opportunity of defending Luther and at the same time airing his own
conclusions. Here, however, we must note first the views of Luther's himself.
Tyndale's opinions and the later and more widespread thnetopsychism of the
radical Continental reformers will be considered shortly.

Despite moments of hesitation and occasional ambiguities, even contradictions,
Luther's psychopannychism cannot for a moment be seriously doubted. It is
expressed too frequently and too emphatically. Indeed, it is hard to find anywhere
a more concerned or enthusiastic spokesman for psychopannychism, either on
the Continent or in England, throughout the Reformation and immediate
post-Reformation periods. All the essentials of mortalism as interpreted in
psychopannychism can be found in Luther's writings, and most of them occur
repeatedly: the separate existence of the soul, its unconscious sleep after death,
its exclusion from heavenly bliss until the resurrection, and the vital importance
of the resurrection of the body and the re-unification of body and soul at the
last day as the way to immortality and eternal life. The meeting point between
Luther's psychopannychism and the more developed thnetopsychism is their
shared emphasis on death as an unconscious sleep[2] and the necessity of the
resurrection. In 1526 in his lectures on Ecclesiastes Luther noted that the dead
are "completely asleep" and do not "feel anything at all". "They lie there not
counting days or years; but when they are raised, it will seem to them that they
have only slept for a moment".[3] Commenting on Ecclesiastes 9:5, Luther said
that he knew of no more powerful passage in Scripture showing that the dead
are asleep and unconscious. Verse 10 was another text proving "that the dead do
not feel anything", since they are "completely asleep".[4] In his commentary on I
Corinthians 15 he argues that what was prior to Christ's resurrection "true and
eternal death", is now no longer death. "It has become merely a sleep". And for
Christ "it is but a night before He rouses us from sleep".[5] Again, the saints who
died in faith "died in such a manner that after they had been called away from the
troubles and hardships of this life, they entered their chamber, slept there, and

---

1. Generally known as *The Dialogue Concerning Tyndale* , although an introductory
   note to the 1529 edition begins with the words "A Dialogue concernynge heresyes
   and matters of religion".
2. Psychopannychism's literal sleep of the soul as opposed to thnetopsychism's figurative
   use of the term has been noted previously, p. 20. It is an important distinction.
3. 'Notes on Ecclesiastes', in *LW*, 15 (1972), 150.
4. *Ibid.,* 147.
5. 'Commentary on I Corinthians 15', *LW*, 28 (1973), 109-10.

rested in peace".[1] For Luther, death is always a sleep, a time of rest and waiting.

The soul, however, is a separate entity which leaves the body at death. Luther says, " After death the soul enters its chamber and is at peace; and while it sleeps, it is not aware of its sleep".[2] In the lectures on Psalms, he states "The crossing of Jordan is the departure of the soul from the body".[3] Of the Old Testament patriarchs, notably Abraham, Isaac and Jacob, Luther says that each was "gathered to his people", to rest, to sleep, to await "resurrection and the future life".[4] The same is true of all who thus sleep: "There is no doubt that those who have been gathered to their people are resting. . . . There is a place for the elect where they all rest. . . . The human soul sleeps with all senses buried, and our bed is like a sepulchre . . . they rest in peace".[5] Luther holds that we cannot not know the exact nature of the intermediate state, but is sure that the disembodied soul is "freed from the workhouse of the body".[6] Moreover, "it is sufficient for us to know that the saints in the Old Testament who died in faith in the Christ who was to come and the godly in the New Testament who died in faith in the Christ who has been revealed" are safe in the hands of God, "gathered to their people".[7] But "we do not know what that place is, or what kind of place it is".[8] So for Luther both body and soul rest after death, the body in the grave and the soul, still alive but asleep, in some appointed but undefined place, to await the last day.

Despite the moments of doubt, Luther's psychopannychism appears to have been well settled in the years leading up to his death in 1546. In his massive commentary on Genesis, published in 1544, he states more fully, yet still with a degree of mystery:

> Thus after death the soul enters its chamber and is at peace; and while it sleeps it is not aware of its sleep. Nevertheless, God preserves the waking soul. Thus God is able to awaken Elijah, Moses, etc., and so to control them that they live. But how? We do not know. The resemblance to physical sleep – namely that God declares that there is sleep, rest, and peace – is enough. He who sleeps a natural sleep has no knowledge of the things that are happening in his neighbour's house. Nevertheless, he is alive, even though, contrary to the nature of life, he feels nothing in his sleep.[9]

Yet we know that the sleeping dead will live again and, at least to an extent, how it will happen:

And so the Christians who lie in the ground are no longer called dead, but

1. 'Lectures on Genesis, Chapters 21-25', *LW*, 4(1964), 312-13.
2. *Ibid.*, 313.
3. 'First Lectures on the Psalms 1-75', *LW*, 10 (1974), 327.
4. 'Lectures on Genesis 21-25', *LW*, 4, 309-10.
5. 'Lectures on Genesis, Chapters 45-50', *LW*, 8(1966), 317-18.
6. 'Lectures on Genesis 21-25', *LW*, 4, 329.
7. 'Lectures on Genesis 45-50', *LW*, 8, 317.
8. *Ibid.*
9. 'Lectures on Genesis 21-25,' *LW*, 4, 313.

sleepers, people who will surely also arise again. For when we say that people are asleep, we refer to those who are lying down but will wake up and rise again, not those who are lying down bereft of all hope of rising again. Of the latter we do not say that they are sleeping but that they are inanimate corpses. Therefore by that very word "asleep" Scripture indicates the future resurrection.[1]

> For since we call it [death] a sleep, we know that we shall not remain in it, but be again awakened and live, and that the time during which we sleep, shall seem no longer than if we had just fallen asleep. Hence, we shall censure ourselves that we were surprised or alarmed at such a sleep in the hour of death, and suddenly come alive out of the grave and from decomposition, and entirely well, fresh, with a pure, clear, glorified life, meet our Lord and Saviour Jesus Christ in the clouds. . . .[2]

The resurrection at the last day will terminate the sleep of death and bring to reality eternal life and, through the re-unification of soul and body, the fulness of immortality for those who believe. In fact, Luther goes as far as to say of the resurrection that it is "[T]he chief article of Christian doctrine".[3] So Francis Blackburne was undoubtedly correct in saying that Luther's "sleeping man was conscious of nothing", and in concluding that Luther held to "total suspension of thought and consciousness during the interval between death and the resurrection".[4]

Luther found a ready ally for his psychopannychism in Andreas Carlstadt,[5] his unpredictable sometime co-labourer in the German Reformation. The psychopannychism of both Luther and Carlstadt was closely bound up with a strong biblical eschatology, indicating perhaps that a more consistent interpretation of the biblical text as a whole confirmed belief in the sleep of the soul. This was undoubtedly true of Luther. In Carlstadt's case, however, there was possibly more. His psychopannychism may have been generated, in part at least, while a student at Sienna, 1516-17, through contact with the Paduan challenge to the doctrine of immortality, and may therefore have been tinged with the philosophical overtones which characterised Padua's revised Aristotelianism and which, as we have seen, incurred the indignation of the Fifth Lateran Council.[6] Also, Carlstadt's relationship with the radicals of the

---

1. 'Commentary on I Corinthians 15', *LW*, 28, 110.
2. Luther, 'Sermon, the Twenty-fourth Sunday after Trinity', cited in H.T. Kerr (ed.), *A Compend of Luther's Theology* (Philadelphia, 1943), 242.
3. 'Commentary on I Corinthians 15', *LW*, 28, 94. More than one hundred and twenty-five references to death as a sleep and the unconscious state of the dead are said to be found in Luther's writings. The count is based on an analysis in J.G. Walch (ed), *Martin Luther's Sammtlichte Schriften* (1904).
4. Blackburne, *Historical View*, 355, 359.
5. Carlstadt is unaccountably missing from Froom's *Conditionalist Faith*.
6. *RR* (1st edn, 1962), 104.

Reformation was stronger than Luther's, and here again, specifically in the case of the Evangelical Rationalists,[1] for whom the immortality of the soul was inconsonant with reason, mortalism was a common denominator.

Like Luther, however, Carlstadt found that psychopannychism was an effective weapon with which to attack purgatory and the system of indulgences that had developed around it, together with the pivotal doctrine of the Mass. Carlstadt's psychopannychism was first articulated in the context of his radical reinterpretation of the Mass as commemorative rather than sacramental, based on a more literal biblical foundation.[2] It is also probable that the depiction of purgatory as spiritually purgative in the present rather than as punitive in the future, as advocated in a contemporary publication,[3] helped to clarify Carlstadt's convictions regarding the sleep of the soul. In any event, by 1523 Carlstadt had published in favour of psychopannychism, although it is only fair to say that he does not appear in general to have given it as much emphasis as did Luther. It should be said that Carlstadt's understanding of soul sleep, at least at this point, appears to have been just that (psychosomnolence), rather than the more radical thnetopsychism of some of his contemporaries.[4] Advocates of psychopannychism in Germany at the same period include Gerhard Westerburg in Wittenberg and Frankfurt, and the more radical Augustine Bader, c.1530.[5] Westerberg was a colleague of Carlstadt and may have derived his mortalist eschatology from Carlstadt's 1523 publication. Both were exiled from Saxony in 1524, and in 1526 Westerberg was condemned for his teaching on the sleep of the soul.[6] With Westerberg, of course, we have already moved into the ranks of the radicals.

The Continental Radicals

Before we turn to Calvin and his crucial participation in the mortalist debate, it is necessary to trace in more detail the position of the radicals of the Continental Reformation. Opposed vehemently by Calvin,[7] their well-attested opposition to the doctrine of innate immortality may ultimately have contributed more to the continuity of mortalism as a legitimate Christian hope, both on the Continent and

1. See later, p. 36.
2. *ME*, I (1955), 519-20; *RR*, 110-20, 196.
3. Wessel Gansfort, *Farrago Rerum Theologicarum* (Wittenburg,1522).
4. *RR*, 197.
5. *Ibid.*, 196-8, 298.
6. *ME*, IV(1959), 930-1; *RR*, 198.
7. Notably in his *Psychopannychia* (Geneva,1545), which was first published in Strasbourg in 1542 with the title *De statu animarum post mortem liber, quo asseritur Vivere apud Christum non dormire animos sanctos, qui in fide Christi decedunt: Assertio* but written in 1534, Willem Balke, *Calvin and the Anabaptist Radicals* (tr. William Heynen, Grand Rapids, MI, 1981), 26. Heynen's translation reads "Dissertation about the state of souls after death, proving that the saints who died in faith in Christ now live with Christ and are not asleep as far as their souls are concerned".

in England, than did either Luther or Carlstadt. Williams, in his comprehensive analysis of the radical Reformation, maintains that mortalism in its various forms was a crucial element in the theology of many radicals, as important to their identity as anti-Trinitarianism or a revised soteriology. He distinguishes between three types of radicals: Anabaptists, Spiritualists, and Evangelical Rationalists,[1] believing that "some" of the Spiritualists, "many" of the Anabaptists, and "almost all" the Evangelical Rationalists believed in "the sleep or death of the soul prior to the resurrection".[2] This, as we have previously noted, Williams rather loosely terms "psychopannychism", and care is sometimes needed in determining whether at a given point he means psychopannychism or thnetopsychism. Mortalism, in either of its two more recognisable forms, psychopannychism more precisely defined as psychosomnolence, or thnetopsychism, was "a recurrent feature of the Radical Reformation".[3] Tavard argues that by the time Calvin drafted the *Psychopannychia* in 1534 he had been aware for some time of the existence of "false" doctrines about the soul that had "gained considerable ground among some advocates of the reform movement",[4] specifically among the radicals of the Continental Reformation.

The Anabaptist psychopannychists were represented in Austria in the mid-1520s by three disciples of John (Hans) Hut, or Huth: Leonhard Schiemer, John(Hans) Schlaffer and Ambrose Spittelmaier. Hut believed in the imminence of the second coming and preached on the prophecies of Daniel and the Book of Revelation, anticipating the imminent end of the world, the resurrection, judgement and the kingdom of Christ.[5] Schiemer, Schlaffer and Spittelmaier, likewise "confident in the imminence of Christ's second advent", maintained a belief "in the sleep of the soul pending the resurrection and the last judgement".[6] Another follower of Hut, Augustine Bader of Augsburg, also held to soul sleep in the context of the general resurrection at the last day.[7] In Switzerland the Anabaptist leader Michael Sattler was burned in 1527, convicted of numerous charges of heresy, including denying the efficacy of the intercession of the Virgin Mary and the saints since, like all the faithful they were asleep, awaiting the judgement. It would certainly have been of great concern to the Catholic establishment to be told of Mary that "she must with us await the judgment".[8]

1. The Spiritualists emphasised the inner, contemplative life as essential to authentic Christian faith. Williams defines the Evangelical Rationalists as "a fusion of Italian humanism or critical rationalism with selected ingredients of. . . . Anabaptism and visionary Spiritualism", *RR*, 836.
2. *Ibid.,* xxxi, 70.
3. *Ibid.,* 69.
4. Tavard, *Calvin's Theology,* 41.
5. *ME*, II (1956), 846-48.
6. *RR*, 266-7, 279-80.
7. *Ibid.,* 298.
8. *ME*, IV, 431; A.M. Mergal and G.H. Williams (eds.), *Spiritual and Anabaptist Writers* (Philadelphia,1957), 140.

Psychopannychism was known to leading spokesmen of the Reformation, and equally reprehensible to them. Both Zwingli and his successor at Zurich, Bullinger, attacked the doctrine of soul sleep, Bullinger publishing against it as early as 1526.[1] A later English translation of a work by Bullinger testified to the existence of Swiss Anabaptist psychopannychism:

> They say that the souls, after the death of the body (if they do depart in faith), do sleep in the bosom of Abraham till the day of judgment, and that then they enter into everlasting life.[2]

Among the Spiritualist radicals who advocated psychopannychism Carlstadt has already been noted. The sixteenth-century Libertines of the Netherlands, some of whom, Anthony Pocquet among them, were psychopannychists, should also be considered in this connection.[3] Pocquet, a former priest and doctor in canon law, had worked out an elaborate scheme of history in which the world passed through seven stages, the last being the paradisic age. Within the seven phases of history Pocquet developed a mystical, spiritualised interpretation of the redemptive work of Christ, culminating in the resurrection of the righteous. Believers who had died in anticipation of the resurrection were asleep in the grave, to be "awakened to the life of the redeemed at the end of the seventh age".[4] Pocquet, it seems, also promulgated psychopannychism in France and Navarre, sympathetic, perhaps, to the "French evangelical Paduans", and became one of the main targets of Calvin's *Psychopannychia* published soon after.[5] In his chapter "Sectarianism and Spiritualism in Poland", and elsewhere, Williams discusses Socinus's thnetopsychism, explaining that "the second basic principle of his theology" was the natural mortality of man, and drawing attention to a soteriological scheme culminating in "resurrection in a spiritual body at the Second Advent of Christ".[6] Whether or not Socinus was truly a Polish Spiritualist,[7] his mortalism deserves attention for at least two reasons. It was decisively thnetopsychist in character, and it laid a foundation for the later Unitarian

1. Balke, *Calvin*, 32.
2. H. Bullinger, *An Holsome Antidotus . . . agaynst the pestylent heresye and secte of the Anabaptistes* (tr. J. Veron, [1548]), sig. N vi *r*.
3. Pocquet is not included in Froom's *Conditionalist Faith*. Of all the radical mortalists mentioned in this section, only Camillo Renato is treated adequately by Froom. Laelius and Faustus Socinus are mentioned briefly, although Froom recognises the importance of Socinian mortalism in general, *CFF*, II, 86.
4. *RR*, 538.
5. In a letter to Margaret of Navarre in 1545, Calvin warned the queen of the dangerous influence of Pocquet and his associate, Quintin Thieffry, estimating that they had 10,000 followers; cited in Balke, *Calvin*, 22.
6. *Ibid.*, 980, 1162.
7. Williams elsewhere defines him as an Evangelical Rationalist, but notes also that ultimately the Polish churches adopted many features of his Christology and soteriology, *RR*, 1253, 1162.

mortalists in Poland and Transylvania. We shall return to Socinus shortly.

The Evangelical Rationalists, essentially Italian in origin though by the latter half of the sixteenth century spread across eastern Europe, took mortalism convincingly to what Williams calls its "extreme" position of thnetopsychism.[1] The Evangelical Rationalists themselves, with their insistence that reason must prevail in the interpretation of Scripture, and for that matter the eighteenth-century English thnetopsychists, might have called it the logical and consistent formulation of mortalist theology. The Evangelical Rationalists were well represented by Camillo Renato, their most articulate, sixteenth-century spokes-man. Wilbur describes Renato as "a man of keen and fertile mind", well-educated and "persuasive and adroit in discussion". It was widely believed in his day that Italian Anabaptism in its entirety could be traced back to him.[2]

Renato had worked through the problems of human nature and mortality to reach a thnetopsyschist position.[3] One of the four main accusations brought against him at his trial in Ferrara in 1540 was his teaching that the souls of "both the righteous and the wicked expire at the death of the body and have no abiding place until the resurrection and the last judgment".[4] Renato's ideas had unsettled many erstwhile more moderate Protestants in Northern Italy, the Republic of Rhaetia and bordering parts of Switzerland. The Anabaptist Council of Venice, 1550, called to settle disputed points of doctrine among the radicals of Northern Italy, Rhaetia and the affected Swiss cantons, all but unanimously agreed on a ten-point statement of belief which stated "that the souls of the wicked die with their bodies; that for the unrighteous there is no hell except the grave, and that after the death of the elect their souls sleep till the day of judgment".[5] That this represented something of a retreat from Renato's fully-developed thnetopsychism to accommodate the psychopannychistic position should not be allowed to minimise the endorsement of radical Italian mortalist doctrine by the delegates of some thirty conventicles.

The influence of Italian Evangelical Rationalism was felt further afield, particularly in eastern Europe. In Poland and Lithuania the mortalist cause was advanced by Laelius Socinus, who left among his papers a work concerning the resurrection, *De resurrectione corporum*, which, "following Camillo Renato . . . attempted to replace the V Lateran teaching of the natural immortality of the soul" with what he believed to be a more biblical, mortalist alternative.[6] Socinus

1. *Ibid.,* 1149.
2. E.M. Wilbur, *A History of Unitarianism: Socinianism and its Antecedents* (Cambridge, Mass., 1945), 103-4.
3. *Ibid.,* 105. On Renato, see also G.H. Williams, 'Camillo Renato (c.1500-?1575)' in J.A. Tedeschi (ed.), *Italian Reformation Studies in Honour of Laelius Socinus* (Florence, 1965), 105-183.
4. *RR*, 841-2.
5. *Ibid.,* 872.
6. Wilbur, *History of Unitarianism*, 247. Williams calls Renato *praeceptor, dux,* and *informator* of Laelius, *Italian Reformation Studies*, 108. Laelius visited England,

was followed by Gregory Paul who, again following Renato, taught that the soul, like the body, is mortal.[1] This sounds like thnetopsychism once more. There is no possible ambiguity, however, with the energetic Simon Budny, the anti-Trinitarian leader in Lithuania and Little Poland, who in 1576 openly advocated a form of thnetopsychism, declaring that the soul was nothing more than the life of the body and had no independent existence.[2] Already in 1572 a group of students had returned to Transylvania from the university of Padua, with similar views to those of Gregory Paul and Camillo Renato, notably "psychopannychism with a lively expectation of being resurrected" as loyal followers of Christ.[3] Despite the pronouncements of the Fifth Lateran Council, Paduan doubt over the immortality of the soul and the reasonable alternative proposed by the Italian Evangelical Rationalists seem to have taken root well beyond the borders of Northern Italy and the Venetian Republic.

We may now return to Faustus Socinus, 1539-1604, whose own theology was influenced both by his uncle, Laelius, and by Camillo Renato. Laelius Socinus, who we shall meet again in an English setting, had also studied at Padua and had himself been influenced by Renato, in particular by Renato's robust thnetopsychism,[4] which he later used to good effect in discomfiting Calvin over the future state of the righteous. Faustus himself came to hold the Paduan view of man's natural mortality and the death of the soul with the body, a conviction which was central to his influential work *De Jesu Christo servatore*, published in 1578.[5] In the context of this important work, Williams comments on the significance of the whole theological system worked out by Socinus:

> In his Christology, thnetopsychism, and conception of sanctification, Socinus brings together with memorable clarity and baffling simplicity a doctrine of the atonement and justification which (more than any other work thus far discussed) shows how sectors of the Radical Reformation, in various thrusts and tentative endeavours, differed profoundly from the Magisterial Reformation.[6]

We must not allow the close relationship of Socinus' thnetopsychism to his soteriology to escape us here. While not necessarily agreeing with the soteriology

1547/8, at Cranmer's invitation, E.M. Wilbur, *A History of Unitarianism in Transylvania, England and America* (1952), 170; *ODCC*, s.v. Socinus.
1. Williams, in *Italian Reformation Studies*, 105.
2. *RR*, 1149.
3. *Ibid.*, 1122.
4. Williams' references to Renato's mortalism as "psychopannychism", e.g., *RR*, 880, are best explained by his willingness to use the term to describe both psychosomnolence and thnetopsychism. In fact, there can be no doubt about Renato's thnetopsychist position, which Williams himself acknowledges elsewhere, e.g., pp. 841-2. See also Wilbur, *History of Unitarianism*, 105.
5. *RR*, 983-4.
6. *Ibid.*, 989.

itself, it was a relationship that later thnetopsychists, including Trinitarians, would defend with equal conviction. It is also worth pointing out again that although the spokesmen of the Radical Reformation differed profoundly in many respects from their counterparts in the mainstream Reformation, there were those on both sides who found in mortalism, in whichever form they expressed it, a statement of authentic eschatological hope.

As for Faustus Socinus himself, his thnetopsychist doctrine of man's essential mortality, already embodied in the theology of the early Polish Racovians from about 1570, was to become an important element in the later, re-shaped Unitarian system better known as Socinianism. Williams concludes that almost every aspect of Socinus' theology "would soon be taken over by the Minor Church",[1] notably his "hermeneutical and epistemological principles (and) his doctrine of natural mortality" with its thorough-going mortalist emphasis on the resurrection of the righteous.[2] But with Polish Socinianism fully articulated we have reached the seventeenth century and a point beyond the scope of this brief survey of Reformation and immediate post-Reformation Continental mortalist thought. We must now briefly retrace our steps.

Calvin, Servetus and the *Psychopannychia*

Christian mortalism in both its forms was widely known and promulgated across the European continent for much of the sixteenth century. But it should not be thought that the Continental radicals practised or preached their faith, mortalist or otherwise, unimpeded. Spurned and stigmatised for the most part by the leaders of the mainstream Reformation, hunted down frequently by the Inquisition and turned over to the secular authority to be dealt with as deemed expedient, and sometimes betrayed without warning from within, the radicals and their beliefs survived at considerable cost.[3] With respect to mortalist theology in particular, few demonstrated their hostility more consistently than the French reformer John Calvin, both in his treatment of the radical Spaniard, Michael Servetus, and through his own first major theological work, *Psychopannychia*. It is with Calvin, and his contemporary Henry Bullinger, as we shall later observe, that we find clear indications that there may have been a link between the mortalism of the Continental radicals and English mortalism in the sixteenth century.

The episode that led to Servetus's execution in 1553 is notorious and has been the subject of much comment. Servetus's psychopannychism, however, appears to be less well-known. Of three quite different lives of Calvin selected at

---

1. The Minor Reformed Church was the official title of the Polish anti-Trinitarian, anti-paedobaptist radicals of the sixteenth century.
2. *RR*, 1174.
3. E.g., the betrayal by the former priest turned Anabaptist Peter Manelfi of many who had subscribed to the conclusions of the Synod of Venice, and the subsequent activities of the Inquisition, *RR*, 871-3

random,[1] all refer to Servetus's life and teachings in some detail but none mention his psychopannychistic views as one of the several heresies of which he was accused. Even Tavard, who traces the development of Calvin's *Psychopannychia*, seems unaware of the connection. Williams associates Servetus with Camillo Renato as "early representatives"of Continental radical psychopannychism "and the apocalyptic eschatology" in which it was generated. He points out that a meeting arranged between Calvin and Servetus in 1534, for which the latter did not turn up, was to have taken place shortly before the first draft of the *Psychopannychia*.[2] More to the point, perhaps, is the assertion that one of the four main charges brought against Servetus's "matured theological system" was that of psychopannychism, and that at the trial itself Calvin questioned Servetus about his psychopannychistic beliefs.[3] Together with Laelius Socinus, Gregory Paul, John Hut and Camillo Renato, Servetus had advocated his mortalism in the context of an apocalyptic eschatology which anticipated an imminent consummation of history, with the last judgment and the resurrection of the righteous dead at hand. It was this total biblical witness to the future that gave Servetus and those who thought like him their deep eschatological convictions and mortalism its strength and its appeal in sixteenth-century Europe.

Calvin, of course, was not of the same mind at all. He saw mortalism in any form as heresy, and a threat to the order he sought to bring to the Reformation and to the reformed church which he was in the process of shaping and which he fervently hoped would endure into the future. He called mortalists, particularly psychopannychists, "Babblers" and "Hypnologists", and mortalists in general soul-killers, "*psuchoktonoi*, assassins of the soul".[4] Calvin clung to the traditional, prevailing view of immortality, believing in the soul's separate existence and its continuing consciousness after death. The term 'psychopannychia' means literally 'the watching wakefulness' of the soul after death, Calvin's own defined position. The title of his now famous work against psychopannychism, therefore, has come to represent the doctrine he opposed rather than the position he advocated, namely both "the doctrine of the death of the soul (thnetopsychism) and the unconscious sleep of the soul (psychosomnolence) pending the resurrection".[5] As we have already noted, the first draft of the *Psychopannychia* is believed to have been written as early as 1534, with a subsequent draft in 1536, before the first printed edition in 1542, and the first edition under the title of *Psychopannychia* in 1545.[6] It is

1. J. Mackinnon, *Calvin and the Reformation* (1936); E. Stickelberger, *Calvin: A Life* (London and Richmond, VA, 1961); F. Wendel, *Calvin* (1965).
2. *RR*, 70, 903.
3. *Ibid.*, 929, citing Calvin, *Opera quae supersunt omnia* (58 vols.,1863-1900), vol. 8, cols. 739-40.
4. Balke, *Calvin,* 29; Tavard, *Calvin's Theology*, 41. Tavard seems to be unaware of Balke's earlier comments on Calvin and the *Psychopannychia*, Balke, *Calvin,* 25-34.
5. *RR*, 902.
6. Wendel believed that the 1534 version may have been published, *Calvin,* 43. Cf.

immediately apparent that Calvin was concerned about the development of mortalist views over a period of several years early in his career and early in the history of the Reformation as a whole.

Moreover he clearly understood, by the time his thoughts on the matter were finally committed to print, that there were two mortalist camps advocating different positions. One group, the psychopannychists, believed that the soul existed as a separate entity but that it slept during death and thus lost consciousness temporarily. The other group, the thnetophychists, held that the soul was not an entity in itself separate from the body, and that it existed only as long as the body was alive, but that it could and, in the case of the righteous, would exist again following the resurrection. Calvin wrote with commendable clarity and fairness:

> Our controversy, then, relates to the human soul. Some, while admitting
> it to have a real existence, imagine that it sleeps in a state of insensibility
> from death to the judgment day, when it will awake from its sleep; while
> others will sooner admit anything than its real existence, maintaining
> that it is merely a vital power which is derived from arterial spirit on the
> action of the lungs, and being unable to exist without the body, perishes
> along with the body, and vanishes away and becomes evanescent till the
> period when the whole man shall be raised again.[1]

These were the views which Calvin vigorously set out to combat in the *Psychopannychia*. With some reservation, perhaps, concerning the attempted scientific explanation of thnetopsychism, they fairly represent developing mortalist thought in Europe throughout the period.

Williams suggests that the original draft of the *Psychopannychia* may have been directed against Servetus and his mortalist fellow-believers in Paris c.1534.[2] In 1537, much to Calvin's chagrin, psychopannychism was openly advocated in Geneva by two Anabaptist teachers from the Netherlands, Herman of Gerbehaye and Andrew Benoit of Engelen. Calvin's concern apparently arose from the fact that the people of Geneva were "responsive to their preaching". In the following year, while at Strasbourg, and perhaps not for the first time, he became aware of French psychopannychists preaching the sleep of the soul, including that of the Virgin Mary.[3] We have already noted that at about this same time, Anthony Pocquet was teaching psychopannychism in France and Navarre. It was all the tip

RR, 900. Froom also states that the 1534 edition was published, but incorrectly gives the later title, CFF, II, 113. Balke, Tavard and Lane maintain that the first known printed edition was that of 1542, Balke, *Calvin*, 26-7; Tavard, *Calvin's Theology*, 1; A.N.S. Lane, *John Calvin: Student of the Church Fathers* (Edinburgh, 1999), 70.

1. Calvin, 'Psychopannychia', in H. Beveridge (tr.), *Calvin's Tracts*, 3 (Edinburgh, 1851), 419. Cf. Tavard, *Calvin's Theology*, 54-5.
2. RR, 903. The circumstances surrounding the writing of the *Psychopannychia* are covered in some detail by Williams, *RR*, 899-904
3. *Ibid.*, 916. Calvin may also have been aware of the earlier psychopannychism of Otto Brunfels in Strasbourg, c.1530, *ibid.*, 309.

of a dangerous iceberg. "Horrified by the extent of the Anabaptist and Spiritualist movements", with their psychopannychist and thnetopsychist emphases, and seeing in them a serious threat to the stability of the Reformation, Calvin was at last persuaded to publish *Psychopannychia* which appeared, under its earlier title, in Strasbourg in 1542.[1] It was, it might be judged, rather too late.

One further fact concerning the *Psychopannychia* must be noted, particularly in relation to Calvin's pending influence in England. It was originally written, if not before Calvin's final conversion to the Reformed faith, then certainly at a time of transition, turmoil and personal stress.[2] Tavard, in fact, argues persuasively that the point of Calvin's actual conversion may have been after the first draft of *Psychopannychia* had been composed.[3] Whatever the truth may be, it is certain that Calvin's reaction to the growing Continental mortalist threat faithfully reflected the traditional medieval view of the soul, a pre-Reformation eschatology which "does not exhibit a reforming orientation".[4] Balke correctly states that in the *Psychopannychia* "there is no evidence that Calvin was at variance with the Roman Catholic Church".[5] In Tavard's opinion, Calvin, the humanist, "entertained a thoroughly Platonic conception of the soul" which he did not surrender "when he became a biblical scholar".[6] Indeed, a critical evaluation of the *Psychopannychia* reveals that Calvin "has retained Plato's thesis that the soul is a stranger to the body that imprisons it during the present life".[7] It was this view of the soul and its destiny that found its way into Calvin's influential *Institutes*,[8] the first draft of which was being written at the same time that Calvin was revising the *Psychopannychia* for publication and while the questions of mortalism and the soul were still major issues in his mind.[9] There were profound and lasting implications here for both Continental and English Protestantism in their formative years.

The young Calvin's lingering attachment to certain aspects of medieval theology and patristic authority is further evident in his treatment of the relevant biblical texts which, within the scholastic tradition, is undergirded by frequent appeals to the interpretations of these texts by the Greek and Latin fathers. In addition to Tertullian and Augustine, there are recurring references to Irenaeus, Origen, Cyprian, Chrysostom and Jerome, *inter alios*, those who, in Calvin's

---

1. *Ibid.,* 918. Both the Reformers Bucer and Capito had urged Calvin not to publish until the time was more propitious, Balke, *Calvin,* 27.
2. Tavard, *Calvin's Theology,* 10, 39.
3. *Ibid.,* 10, 41.
4. *Ibid.,* 113.
5. Balke, *Calvin,* 34.
6. Tavard, *Calvin's Theology,* 53.
7. *Ibid.,* 77.
8. See Calvin, *Institutes of the Christian Religion,* Bk. I, ch. XV and Bk. II, ch. XXV, where the influence of Plato is evident, e.g. Bk. I, ch. XV.
9. Tavard, *Calvin's Theology,* 7, 9.

mind, "have reverently and discretely handled the mysteries of God".[1] Other considerations aside, if this was the case it is not surprising that the *Psychopannychia* failed to impress those whom it sought to counter, or that it did little to stem the rising mortalist tide across Continental Europe. Such unconcealed respect for the opinions of the fathers would surely have undermined Calvin's impact on more radical minds attracted to the pure word of God and whose own hermeneutic required a "total disregard of the Augustinian and . . . mystical traditions".[2] Arguing that Calvin's "anti-Roman stance" was adopted after he had first written against mortalism and soul sleep, Tavard concludes that while the *Psychopannychia* betrayed Calvin's hostility to the radical wing of the Reformation, it was not in itself a reforming document. "The position it defended was identical with Catholic teaching, and it did not contain one word that was critical of the medieval church or the papacy".[3] Clearly there are significant implications here for English mortalism and the repeated attempts of its opponents in England to suppress it, as well as for the wider eschatology which would later dominate the English-speaking Protestant world. Indeed, we may find in all this a hint of the solution to a question that has remained largely unanswered for four hundred years or more – why mainstream Protestantism, both in England and on the Continent, which in its formative years so emphatically repudiated what it considered to be the doctrinal legacy of the medieval church, retained what was arguably the central plank in the entire dogmatic and liturgical structure of late medieval Catholicism, belief in the immortal soul.[4]

It is enough for now to observe that the confrontation with Servetus and the sequence of events that ultimately led Calvin to publish the *Psychopannychia* are indications of the growing strength of mortalist views on the Continent in the first half of the sixteenth century, and of their wide appeal to many European Christians who had been unsettled by the new Reformation theology. That mortalism steadily gained ground and attention from leading Continental radicals was not, of course, due to Calvin's *Psychopannychia*, but rather in spite of it. It is ironic that mortalist radicals appealed for their authority to precisely the same court that Calvin, and the English Reformers who followed him, all invoked – God's Word in Scripture. The very least that can be said of the widespread dissemination of mortalism across Europe by the middle of the sixteenth century in relation to the development of mortalist opinion in England, is that it confirmed what English tongues and pens were already beginning to articulate.

1. John Calvin, *An excellent treatise of the Immortalytie of the Soule* (tr. Thomas Stocker, 1581), *passim* and 63. See further, ch. 2, pp. 66-68. Lane emphasises Calvin's "great respect for the teaching of the fathers" from which "he did not lightly depart", although his "refusal to accord them authority on a par with Scripture" should not be overlooked. Lane also appears to endorse the older view that the *Psychopannychia* was Calvin's first post-conversion work, Lane, *John Calvin*, 35, 38, 28, 31.

2. Tavard, *Calvin's Theology*, 112.

3. *Ibid.*, 149.

4. See also ch. 2, pp. 67-68.

Chapter Two
English Origins and Developments to 1600

While mortalist doctrines appeared throughout much of Europe in the sixteenth century, in England during the same period they were not as widespread and were less well-articulated. Not until the seventeenth century did English readers of the Bible find opportunity to express their views as vigorously and comprehensively as their European counterparts had done a century or so earlier. Even so, it is clear that a nascent mortalism was known in England and feared as potentially dangerous by the ecclesiastical establishment for much of the sixteenth century, and probably from an earlier period than that. Much of the evidence comes from attempts to suppress these early expressions of developing English mortalism and from sources hostile to it, and care must be taken not to read too much into material that is at times ambiguous. The few known early English mortalists whom we shall shortly encounter are more explicit, but their doctrine was, in general, not as fully developed as it later became. Interestingly enough English mortalism, like its European antecedents, was given its first recorded expression by recognised spokesmen of the Reformation, William Tyndale and John Frith, and before them, though more tentatively, by Wycliffe and his Lollard followers.

That the doctrine of soul sleep had taken root in some English minds as a viable eschatological hope well before the end of the sixteenth century seems indisputable. Perhaps the inscription on a Cotswold tombstone illustrates the fact as clearly as anything known to have been committed to writing at the time. Richard Rainoldes died at Burford in Oxfordshire in 1582. He was one of three bailiffs who had welcomed Elizabeth I to Burford some years earlier, and it may be presumed that he was a man of standing in the community and a respectable Anglican communicant. Inscribed on his tomb in the parish church of St. John the Baptist are these simple and moving words to his wife, "I go to slepe before you, and wee shal wake togeather". There is no hint here of an immortal soul that escapes the body's rest in the grave and enters immediately into the joys of heaven. Richard Rainoldes expected to receive his just reward and enter into eternal life together with his wife at the last day. We can be justified in thinking that Richard was not the only Christian of his day to believe that, and also that there would have been many up and down the land who quietly entertained similar hopes, men and women who had no fear of death because they had confidence in the resurrection.[1] Tyndale, who some fifty years previously had preached reformed doctrine in his nearby native Gloucestershire, had already argued that the resurrection rather than natural immortality was the basis of authentic hope, claiming that the New Testament taught that the "saints should rise again, and not that their souls were in heaven, which doctrine was not yet in the world".[2]

John Wycliffe and Lollard Doubts

But we must begin a century or more earlier with Wycliffe, whose early antagonism to the entrenched doctrines of purgatory and the invocation of saints would lead ultimately to a harvest which he could not possibly have foreseen. Wycliffe it must be acknowledged was, like Luther, at times ambiguous about death and the afterlife.[3] Yet he already foreshadowed many of the concerns and arguments which later mortalists would develop in much greater detail and which they would regard as crucial to their position. A.G. Dickens notes that during the latter years of his life Wycliffe (1378-1384) "had become a manifest revolutionary and heresiarch", and reminds us that he rejected the Roman doctrine of transubstantiation "as a historical novelty and as philosophically unsound".[4] Something akin to that appears also to have been true of his view of contemporary teaching regarding the soul. He rejected current views of the soul's origin taught by the Church as derived from the medieval schoolmen, and opposed the doctrine of purgatory as "so many pious lies . . . only spoke threateningly".[5] Froom is more specific regarding Wycliffe's wider eschatology:

> Though he still believed in the separate existence of the soul, he taught that the state between death and the resurrection is that of sleep. Moreover, he held that the judgment of rewards would not take place until after the resurrection. Furthermore, he believed that the "greatest part" of the reward of the righteous would be "immortalitie or undedlynesse" received at the resurrection.[6]

This seems generally to reflect accurately Wycliffe's position, although it is not entirely correct to say that Wycliffe held that the intermediate state between

1. Peter Marshall cites a similar instance from the same period. In his will of 1585 Thomas Andrews of Bury St Edmunds requested burial with his ancestors "to declare my hope and beleve that they and I shall ryse together in the last day throughe Jesus Christ our onely saviour and Redeemer to lyfe everlasting", P. Marshall, *Beliefs and the Dead in Reformation England* (Oxford, 2002), 210.
2. William Tyndale, 'An Answer unto Sir Thomas More's Dialogue', in *WER*, II, 123.
3. H.B. Workman notes also that his views on purgatory were "by no means consistent", *John Wyclif: A Study of the English Mediaeval Church* (1966), 18.
4. Dickens, *English Reformation*, 22.
5. T. Arnold (ed.), *Select English Works of John Wyclif*, I, (1869), 369; see also Froom, *CFF*, II, 58.
6. *CFF*, II, 59.

death and resurrection is a sleep for all who die. In *The Church and Her Members* Wycliffe says that Christ's church consists of three "parts": the angels who are in heaven; the saints "in purgatorie"; and those now living on earth who yet will be saved.[1] Purgatory, however, is not what it is generally held to be, an "out-patient department of hell", to borrow Eamon Duffy's imaginative phrase.[2] It is a place of rest. For Wycliffe, souls "sleep" in purgatory. The saints already there are "clepid slepyng" (called sleeping), or are "slepynge in purgatorie".[3] Presumably there is very little difference for the sleeping soul itself which at death "goeth from the body",[4] be it in purgatory, in Abraham's bosom, in the grave, or wherever separated souls may rest between death and their re-unification with the body at the last day. To that extent it seems that Wycliffe has moved towards a psychopannychist position. Furthermore, it is superfluous to pray for the departed saints in purgatory because they cannot benefit from such prayers.[5]

However, Wycliffe holds that many of the departed are already in heaven or hell. For example, some saints as well as angels are "in heaven",[6] although praying to so-called saints is worthless as many of them are already in hell.[7] This, it must be conceded, does not sound like mortalism of any kind. Yet we cannot arbitrarily dismiss the re-iterated concept of sleep, or the fact that "the greatest part" of the reward of the righteous would be held over until the resurrection when "immortalitie or undedlynesse" will be received. And what are we to make of the following? "God promiseth to no man either reward or punishment, but under a tacit or express condition".[8] Is there perhaps a hint of conditionalism here? Froom is undoubtedly correct in asserting that Wycliffe's views of purgatory, the invocation of saints, and the concept of death as a sleep were, to a degree, "revolutionary for his day".[9] Yet, as Workman points out, Wycliffe also speaks "in

1. Arnold (ed.), *Select English Works*, III (1871), 53, 339.
2. E. Duffy, *The Stripping of the Altars: Traditional Religion in England c.1400-c.1580* (New Haven and London, 1992), 344.
3. Arnold, *Select English Works*, III, 339; I, 101; see also III, 53, 116. Workman comments: "He held that . . . the soul after its separation from the body must be cleansed . . . and cannot attain at once to full blessedness. . . . (But) he refused to search for the place, duration, or manner of purgation. Of one thing he was convinced: indulgences, trentals, masses and the whole system of prayers for the dead were deceptions of the devil, invented by the father of lies to deceive believers", *John Wyclif*, 18-9.
4. *Ibid.*, II, 215.
5. *Ibid.*, III, 339, 466.
6. *Ibid.*, I, 321; III, 316.
7. *Ibid.*, III, 466.
8. Cited in Mills, *Earlier Life-Truth Exponents*, 8.
9. *CFF*, II, 59. Just how revolutionary Wycliffe's view of purgatory really was can be seen by comparing it to the prevailing views of his day. If we may take Eamon Duffy as a reliable guide, purgatory, rather than hell, had by then become "the focus of Christian fear". All except saints were "bound to spend some time in purgatory", where "visitors saw souls in every posture of physical torment – suspended by meat-hooks driven through jaws, tongue, or sexual organs, frozen into ice, boiling in vats of liquid metal

glowing terms" of the Virgin Mary's "help and her assumption". We "worship Jesus
and Mary with all our might," Wycliffe confesses.[1] We cannot ignore Wycliffe's
ambiguities and apparent inconsistencies, neither can we overlook elements of
mortalist theology, nor that many of his convictions about human destiny would
find fuller articulation in the more developed views of later mortalist writers.

Much the same can be said of Lollard and neo-Lollard beliefs which frequently
found expression in fifteenth- and early sixteenth-century England. Lollardy,
which has been described as typically a "mixture of religious idealism, scriptural
fundamentalism, and anti-clericalism",[2] inevitably challenged the prevailing
doctrine of purgatory and the value of prayers for the dead. Already by 1395
the Lollard *Twelve Conclusions* condemned the latter.[3] Dickens states that denial
of purgatory was a recurring feature of Lollard belief in the ecclesiastical records
of Lollards interrogated for heresy in the early sixteenth century. That Lollardy
survived until then and contributed in "significant degree" to the growth of
Protestantism in England "is a fact based upon massive and incontrovertible
evidence".[4] It would have been remarkable indeed, then, if at some point in the
development of Lollard beliefs, the traditional doctrine of the soul's immortality
had not been challenged. Christopher Hill, in fact, is convinced that the doctrine
of soul sleep was held by Lollards in the fifteenth century,[5] and we may add, by
derivation by early English Anabaptists and the later Lollards in the sixteenth
century. The records suggest that all this was true.

In 1430 Thomas Moon of Ludney in the diocese of Norwich was reported as
believing "that masses and prayers for the dead are but vain, for the souls of the
dead are either in heaven or hell, and there is none other place of purgatory but this
world".[6] Patrick Hamilton in Scotland and William Wingrove of Hitchenchurch
were both accused of holding "that there is no purgatory", and some in the
diocese of Lincoln were reported as "saying that those who die pass straight
either to heaven or hell".[7] Such denial of purgatory is well short of soul sleep or
mortalism, of course. But others had more advanced views. John Tewkesbury,
eventually burned at Smithfield c.1531, affirmed under interrogation "that there
is no purgatory after this life, but that Christ our Saviour is a sufficient purgation

or fire". Usurers were "boiled in molten gold, the gluttonous fed with or fed on by
toads and serpents . . . the proud bound to great iron wheels, covered with burning
hooks", Duffy, *The Stripping of the Altars*, 341, 338-40. Duffy further asserts that
purgatory was "*the* defining doctrine of late medieval Catholicism", 8. In this context,
Wycliffe's view of purgatory as "sleep" was unquestionably revolutionary.
1. Workman, *John Wyclif*, II, 16; Arnold (ed.) *Select English Works*, III, 113.
2. Claire Cross, *Church and People 1450-1660* (1979), 41.
3. Dickens, *English Reformation*, 24.
4. *Ibid.*, 37.
5. Christopher Hill, *The World Turned Upside Down* (1975), 174.
6. S.R. Cattley (ed.), *The Acts and Monuments of John Foxe* (1837), III, 597. See the
   discussion in Dickens, *English Reformation*, 26-7, on the validity of Foxe's evidence.
7. Cattley (ed.), *Acts and Monuments*, IV, 559, 584, 243.

for us", and "that the souls of the faithful, departing this life, rest with Christ".[1]
In 1532, James Bainham of Gloucestershire was questioned about "whether he
thought that any souls departed were yet in heaven, or no". He replied cautiously
that he did not know, "I wot not whether the souls of the apostles or any others
be in heaven or no", but the question reveals what his interrogators had in mind.[2]
In 1541 John Forsett, vicar of St. Edmunds, Salisbury, was discovered by his
bishop, John Capon, to have preached "that the souls of the departed slept until
the general resurrection".[3] In 1546 George Wishart, the Scottish reformer, who
had recently visited Germany and Switzerland, was tried with, *inter alia,* outright
mortalism, "Thou, false heretic, hast preached openly, saying, that the soul of
man shall sleep till the latter day of judgment, and shall not obtain life immortal
until that day".[4] Although Wishart denied the charges, it suggests again, as Burns
notes, that the authorities "saw soul sleeping as a threat well before the triumphant
Reformers condemned the doctrine in the Scottish Confession of 1560".[5]

It was in this early sixteenth-century context of revived Wycliffite and Lollard
dissatisfaction with purgatory, prayers for the dead, the nature of death and
eternal rewards, that the first clear articulations of English mortalism began
to appear. Whether or not William Hugh had Frith or Tyndale in mind in
his rather excessive outburst against psychopannychism in 1546 is not clear.
By then both English reformers had been put to death for heretical opinions
which included mortalism. Hugh's strictures nevertheless confirm the existence
of mortalism, at least in its psychopannychistic form, as anathema to orthodoxy
mid-way through the sixteenth century:

> Truly the error of those is great who persuade themselves that the soul,
> separate from the body, shall sleep unto the last day; and this error is old,
> and was confuted by Origen, and others of his time. Neither was it ever
> since received into the church, unto such time as a pestilent kind of men,
> whose madness is execrable, brought it of late days into the world again.
> But as all others of their opinions are perverse, abhorrent from the truth,
> and devilish, so is this. . . . Therefore, I say, believe not these false deceivers,
> who endeavour not only to persuade the sleep of souls, but also to make
> vain the resurrection of the dead, and so to abolish an article of our faith,
> and to make our religion vain.[6]

The assertion that soul sleepers deny the resurrection is, as Burns comments,
"absurd", and possibly part of a "clumsy attempt to slander the psychopannychists

1. *Ibid.,* IV, 693.
2. *Ibid.,* IV, 703.
3. J. F. Davis, *Heresy and Reformation in the South-East of England, 1520-59* (1983), 28.
4. Cattley (ed.), *Acts and Monuments*, V, 634.
5. *CM*, 112.
6. William Hugh, *The Troubled Man's Medicine* (1546), 36,38 in *The British Reformers from Wickliff to Jewell and Fox*, III (1831).

by wildly extrapolating from their position one that utterly denies a life to come".[1] If this is true, then Hugh had missed the point altogether. Mortalists desired others to understand their doctrine precisely because, in their view, it raised the hope of eternal life on a much more substantial foundation.

William Tyndale, John Frith and William Tracy

We may now turn to the more explicit affirmations of sixteenth-century English mortalism found in the writings of the English reformers, particularly William Tyndale and John Frith. Such affirmations are frequently found *in tandem* with the increasingly outspoken and sustained attacks of the early English Reformers on the medieval doctrine of purgatory. Marshall specifies Tyndale, Frith and Latimer as being prominent in the "deconstruction" of that pervasive medieval doctrine.[2] All three, to a greater or lesser degree, attacked purgatory and advocated a psychopannychistic doctrine of the soul and its condition after death, although Tyndale and Frith seem to have been the most outspoken.

In 1531 Tyndale responded to Sir Thomas More's *Dialogue* (1529),[3] in which the learned and influential More, an ardent defender of the religious *status quo* had, among other things, attacked Luther's psychopannychism and Tyndale's own views of the soul and human destiny.[4] Tyndale's reply, *An Answere unto sir Thomas More's Dialogue*, defended Luther's teaching as being closer to the original scriptural position than More's traditional immortality of the soul.[5] In Tyndale's account, More derides those who accept the Lutheran doctrine of soul sleep, since it leads to lax living. "What shall he care how long he live in sin that believeth Luther, that he shall after this life feel neither good nor evil, in body nor soul, until the day of doom?", More asks. Tyndale replies, "Christ and his apostles taught no other; but warned to look for Christ's coming again every hour".[6] For Tyndale, New Testament hope focussed on the coming of Christ at

1. *CM*, 113. Burns claims too much from this passage, however, asserting that Hugh was unaware of Anabaptist thnetopsychism or annihilationism. The "death of the soul" goes beyond psychopannychism.
2. Marshall, *Beliefs and the Dead*, 53 and ff.
3. Thomas More, *A dyalogue of syr Thomas More knyghte* (1529). The full title refers to the "pestilent sect of Luther and Tyndale".
4. *Ibid.,* sig. r ii *r*.
5. Luther's wider influence on Tyndale should not be overlooked. Tyndale had worked on his translation of the New Testament in Cologne and Worms and may also have visited Wittenberg. He was regarded by More as a "sycophantic follower of Luther" and his New Testament, which resembled Luther's in several respects, was viewed in England as "a partisan Lutheran work", McGrath, *In The Beginning*, 70-72, 83.
6. Tyndale, "Answer to More", in *WER*, II, 196. David Daniell cites this passage from the "Answer to More" but does not comment on Tyndale's belief in soul sleep, or indeed, that of Luther, Daniell, *William Tyndale*, 271-2. Tyndale's psychopannychism is, in fact, of considerable theological and soteriological significance, particularly in the context of his attempt to re-establish New Testament doctrine against that of medieval Catholicism.

the last day, not on a believer's inherently immortal soul. Tyndale accuses More of undermining the biblical teaching by affirming the existence of purgatory and the soul's immortality. "And ye [More] putting them [the souls of the dead] in heaven, hell and purgatory, destroy the arguments wherewith Christ and Paul prove the resurrection",[1] Tyndale says. Again, when More asserts that the righteous saints are already in heavenly glory with Christ, Tyndale objects, "he stealeth away Christ's argument wherewith he proveth the resurrection, that Abraham and all saints should rise again, and not that their souls were in heaven, *which doctrine was not yet in the world*".[2] And again, More's doctrine of the soul's immortality and immediate ascent to heaven at death "taketh away the resurrection quite, and maketh Christ's argument of none effect".[3]

This, without doubt, is Tyndale's chief concern. The doctrine of the soul's natural immortality undermines faith in the resurrection. It even destroys the necessity of resurrection, personal or general, at the last day. "True faith putteth [upholds] the resurrection, which we be warned to look for every hour", Tyndale declares. Furthermore he asks, If souls are already in heaven, "then what cause is there of the resurrection?"[4] Tyndale appeals to I Thessalonians 4 and I Corinthians 15 and with heavy irony accuses More of proposing a way to heaven that is superior to that which is revealed in Scripture:

> Nay, Paul, thou art unlearned, go to Master More and learn a new way. We be not most miserable, though we rise not again, for our souls go to heaven as soon as we be dead, and are there in as great joy as Christ that is risen again. And I marvel that Paul had not comforted the Thessalonians with that doctrine, if he had wist it, that the souls of their dead had been in joy, as he did with resurrection, that their dead should rise again. If the souls be in heaven in as great glory as the angels, after your doctrine, shew me what cause should be of the resurrection?"[5]

For Tyndale, Christians are called to believe that the resurrection at the last day, posited on Christ's own resurrection, is the focus of true hope, and that the concept of the continuing existence of the soul after death destroys the necessity of resurrection altogether. Burns's comment is appropriate, "He was certain that God had clearly announced that the resurrection of the body was the beginning of the whole salvation of Christians, not just an additional reward for souls already in joy".[6]

Tyndale was also concerned about the origin of belief in the immortality of

---

1. Tyndale, "Answer to More", in *WER*, II, 188.
2. *Ibid.,* 123, emphasis supplied.
3. *Ibid.*
4. *Ibid.,* 188-9.
5. *Ibid.,* 123.
6. *CM*, 101-2. Given, it may be assumed, that the redemptive act of Christ on the cross preceded both His own resurrection and that of believers.

the soul. This, as we shall see, is a recurring issue in the mortalist literature. The fact that this belief had its roots in pagan philosophy compromised the purity, and hence the credibility and authority, of the divine revelation in Scripture. It also implicitly questions the basis of Roman dogma as a whole, and thus becomes an issue central to the thrust of the Reformation. It is perhaps for this reason that Tyndale, the early English reformer, is at pains to defend Luther and argue on his own account the necessity of Scripture as the sole authority for authentic Christian faith and practice. The idea that the soul is inherently immortal is, he says, a pagan concept. "Heathen philosophers, denying [the resurrection], did put that souls did ever live",[1] Tyndale asserts. And this essentially pagan idea is now the basis of Roman doctrine. "The pope joineth the spiritual doctrine of Christ and the fleshly doctrine of philosophers together, things so contrary that they cannot agree", and since he is unwilling to concede anything concerning the soul's immortality, "therefore he corrupteth the Scripture to stablish it".[2] It is a serious charge at any time, but never more so than in the early days of the English Reformation, and it did not fall entirely on deaf ears.

The mortalist views which Tyndale had so forcefully set out in his *Answer to More* were shortly confirmed in the introduction to his revised New Testament of 1534. The context of this revision is informative in itself. George Joye, a fellow reformer had, without Tyndale's knowledge or permission, undertaken a revision of Tyndale's 1526 New Testament. One of the major issues in the ensuing exchange between Tyndale and Joye was that of the soul and its state after death and Joye's fervid desire that the New Testament should not be translated or interpreted to support the idea of soul sleep. He had "with breathtaking folly" made several significant changes at relevant places in Tyndale's original English text, some twenty in all, changing the word 'resurrection' to read 'life after this life', or an equivalent alternative phrase,[3] "as one", in Tyndale's words, "that abhorred the name of the resurrection".[4] Tyndale complained that Joye appeared to have an obsession, a "marvellous imagination", about the use of the word 'resurrection', "that it should be taken for the state of souls after their departing from their bodies".[5] Tyndale feared that many might ignore or misunderstand the biblical emphasis on the resurrection of the body as a result of Joye's unauthorised and unscrupulous manipulation of the recently published English New Testament.

Tyndale, therefore, re-affirms his position and what he considers is the biblical teaching on man's future, arising from his careful study of the text in the original and its essential message in the vernacular. On the souls of the departed he says:

I am not persuaded that they be already in the full glory that Christ is in,

1. Tyndale, 'Answer to More', in *WER*, II, 188.
2. *Ibid*, 188-9.
3. Daniell, *Tyndale*, 324.
4. Willyam Tindale [*sic*], *The New Testament diligently corrected and compared with the Greek* (Antwerp, 1534), sig. xxiii, *r,v.*
5. *Ibid.*, sig. xx, *r,v.*

or the elect angels of God are in. Neither is it any article of my faith: for if it were so I see not but then the preaching of the resurrection of the flesh were a thing in vain".[1]

On the contrary, true Christian hope is grounded in the resurrection of the dead as the culmination of a totally biblical eschatology:

> And we shall all, both good and bad rise both flesh and body and appear together before the judgment seat of Christ to receive every man according to his deeds. And that the bodies of all that believe and continue in the true faith of Christ shall be endued with like immortality and glory as is the body of Christ."[2]

This largely concurs with what we have observed in Luther and, as far as we know, was Tyndale's final word on the matter before his untimely death in 1536. As was suggested in the Introduction, it is surely incongruous to deny or ignore what is clearly an article of some importance in Tyndale's overall theological position.

John Frith, Tyndale's assistant in translating the New Testament and fellow martyr, shared similar convictions. In about 1531 Frith wrote his *Disputation of Purgatory* countering the traditional views of More and of John Fisher, Bishop of Rochester, another strong advocate of the medieval *status quo*. Marshall calls Frith's *Disputation* "a formative text for the first generation of English evangelicals", noting that the book was found frequently in the possession of defendants at heresy trials in the 1530s and early 1540s.[3] One of Frith's major contentions is that purgatory is an extra-biblical accretion to the faith. "We neither see it nor hear it, neither have we any mention made of it in Scripture", Frith declares, adding that the doctrine of purgatory was not accepted as an "article of the faith" until after the time of Augustine.[4] Of Christ's promise to the thief on the cross, Frith asks, "Where was purgatory then?"[5] Regarding More's claim that the fires of purgatory were hotter than all known fires, Frith cynically agrees:

> It alone hath melted more gold and silver . . . out of poor men's purses than all the goldsmiths' fires in England . . . it melteth castles, hard stones, lands and tenements innumerable. For all your sects of religion, Monks, Friars, Canons and Nuns, with other priests . . . by this fire have obtained their whole riches and pleasures, even the sweat of England".[6]

1. *Ibid.*, sig. xxv, *v*. Burns seems unaware of Tyndale's revised New Testament when he suggests that Tyndale's last word on the matter is found in the 'Answer to More', *CM*, 100. To say that he is "uncertain about the precise state of the soul between death and resurrection" does not necessarily mean that his psychopannychism is in doubt.
2. Tindale, *New Testament* (1534), sig. xxv, *r*.
3. Marshall, *Beliefs and the Dead*, 51.
4. John Frith, 'A Disputation of Purgatory', in *WER*, III, 104, 147.
5. *Ibid.*, 124.
6. *Ibid.*, 183.

He concludes, "And so we must grant him [More] that this fire is very hot".[1] With respect to the state of the departed dead, Frith goes a step further than Tyndale, asserting that the idea that the souls of the dead are either in heaven or hell is unbiblical. This teaching "plainly destroyeth the resurrection", taking away the arguments "wherewith Christ and Paul do prove that we shall rise".[2] To Frith, as to Tyndale, it is the resurrection that ultimately holds the key to immortality and eternal life.

Frith also took issue with the eschatological views of the Bishop of Rochester who at his trial had used the parable of the rich man and Lazarus to support the doctrines of the soul's immortality and the torments of hell. Frith, who in the *Disputation of Purgatory* had already denied the existence of hell as traditionally understood, arguing that the Hebrew word *sheol* signified merely the grave, "a pit that is digged"[3] and not a place of eternal torment for the damned, had responded to Fisher with incautious boldness. "I am sure my Lord is not so ignorant as to say that a parable proveth anything", he asserted, adding later, "He [Fisher] shall never be able to prove by the Scripture" that the souls of the dead were either in heaven or in hell.[4] The final rewards of both the righteous and the unrighteous would be dispensed at the last day, "in the day of judgment ".[5] "He that departeth in the faith resteth in peace and waiteth for the last day, when God shall give unto his faithful . . . the crown of his glory".[6] Of the worthies of old recorded in Hebrews 11 Frith says they "shall not be made perfect without us".[7] It seems reasonably clear that Frith went to his execution in the certainty of resurrection hope, rather than in the belief that his disembodied soul would soon be in glory.

A contemporary of Tyndale and Frith, William Tracy of Toddington in Gloucestershire, an educated layman, at one time high sheriff of the county, incurred the wrath of the pre-Reformation ecclesiastical establishment on account of his Protestant, biblical faith. Shortly before he died in 1530 Tracy had committed his faith to writing in his last testament.[8] This document, which reflected a Lutheran soteriology and a mortalist eschatology perhaps also derived from Luther, was evidently copied and widely circulated,[9] giving the

1. *Ibid.*
2. *Ibid.*, 192.
3. *Ibid.*, 151.
4. *Ibid.*, 191.
5. *Ibid.*, 192.
6. *Ibid.*
7. *Ibid.*, 193. Cf. Heb. 11:40.
8. Recorded and commented on by both Tyndale and Frith, *WER*, III, 1-16, 245-53.
9. Marshall notes that Tracy's testament was printed in Antwerp in 1535 together with works by Tyndale and Frith, but his claim that the document was the "founding charter of English Protestantism" seems rather excessive, Marshall, *Beliefs and the Dead*, 51, 223. Tracy's testament, "an unequivocal statement of Lutheran belief", was published later in England in 1550, Duffy, *Stripping of the Altars*, 511.

diocesan authorities some cause for concern. Tracy's confession of faith is that of a thoughtful mind, thoroughly familiar with the assurances of Scripture posited on the resurrection of Christ and the general resurrection at the last day:

> I commit me unto God, and to his mercy, trusting . . . that by his grace and the merits of Jesus Christ, and by virtue of his passion, and of his resurrection, I have and shall have remission of my sins and resurrection of body and soul, according as it is written, Job xix, I believe that my Redeemer liveth, and that in the last day I shall rise out of the earth, and in my flesh shall see my Saviour. This is my hope laid by in my bosom.[1]

In this hope Tracy was laid to rest, but on the orders of the chancellor of Worcester his body was exhumed, he was declared a heretic, and his remains burned in 1535. The charges laid against him posthumously were that he held a Lutheran view of salvation, and mortalism.

Burns believes that Tracy's words are open to a psychopannychist or a thnetopsychist interpretation,[2] but they could be construed as not being mortalist at all, though this is unlikely. Frith commented on the case, which had aroused considerable interest,[3] and concedes that some of Tracy's contemporaries charged him with holding a thnetopsychist position, "that he should recount the soul to be mortal".[4] Frith, however, thought otherwise, believing that this was not an honest interpretation, "more subtilely [sic]" than "truly or charitably" gathered from Tracy's own words for the sake of expediency.[5] Frith holds that Tracy's confidence in the resurrection , rather than any belief in immediate glory at death, gave him hope of eternal life. He says of Tracy's statement:

> He trusteth, through Christ, to have resurrection of body and soul . . . for thus doth Paul argue, if Christ be risen, then shall we also rise, and if Christ be not risen, then shall not we rise; but Christ is risen . . . therefore shall we also rise . . . and be immortal, both body and soul, I Cor. 15. And therefore he [Tracy] doth both righteously and godly deduce his resurrection by Christ's, by whom the Father hath given us all things, or else we should not be.[6]

It seems clear enough that Frith understood Tracy to believe that immortality would finally be bestowed at the resurrection. Since Christ has risen, "We shall

1. 'The Testament of William Tracy', *WER*, III, 2-3.
2. *CM*, 103.
3. Craig and Litzenberger state that Tracy's will, which include his last testament, was widely disseminated across England from 1531 onwards, mentioning specifically the counties of Suffolk, Yorkshire, Gloucestershire and Sussex; John Craig and Caroline Litzenberger, 'Wills as Religious Propaganda: The Testament of William Tracy', *JEH*, 44 (1993), 423.
4. 'John Frith's Judgment upon Master William Tracy's Testament', *WER*, III, 247.
5. *Ibid.*
6. *Ibid.*

rise . . . and be immortal, both body and soul". The distinction between body
and soul does not permit a thnetopsychist construction, although it is easy
enough to see how some of his critics could have manipulated the words to make
them so appear. Frith is undoubtedly correct in challenging this interpretation
and justified in concluding that Tracy's mortalism was psychopannychistic. The
line that puts that conclusion beyond any reasonable doubt is as follows: "The
soul, which in the mean season [i.e. after death] seemeth to lie secret", will at
the resurrection "through Christ. . .take again her naturall body".[1] Whether
or not Tracy's mortalism was derived from either Luther or Tyndale remains
unclear. Neither of them, of course, held thnetopsychist views. Coming from
Cotswold country, it is also possible that Tracy's views reflected a long-standing
and lingering Lollard conviction. While the roots of Tracy's mortalism remain
tantalisingly obscure, in essence it is clear enough. It repudiated the official
teaching of the medieval and contemporary English church, and gave him an
equally certain hope of future life.

As far as can be ascertained, Tyndale and Frith are the only two English
writers known to have openly endorsed psychopannychism in the sixteenth
century. Tracy also deserves to be included even though his views were those of
a layman and were only published posthumously.[2] Compared to the number
of mortalists who appeared during the Continental Reformation and soon
thereafter, it is quite remarkable that only three or four names have survived
in England. And three were dead by 1536,[3] before the Protestant faith had
officially replaced Catholicism as the established religion of the land. It is
impossible to measure the influence of their mortalist views, combined or
taken individually. Undoubtedly, Tyndale's would have been the greater. The
Dictionary of National Biography described him as "one of the most remarkable
of the Reformation leaders". Certainly his gift of the New Testament in the
vernacular to his fellow-countrymen was an act of incalculable significance. His
defence of the resurrection against inherent immortality in the introduction
to his revised New Testament of 1534 would not have passed unnoticed. Yet
the extent to which his mortalism prevailed to change the thinking of others
remains uncertain. That mortalism was known in England during the sixteenth
century after Tyndale, Frith and Tracy is indisputable, even if in the main it can
be detected from secondary sources and the measures taken to counteract it.

It also seems beyond dispute that Tracy's will and testament served as a
model for several other Protestant testaments following its circulation in

1. *Ibid.*, 248.
2. *The Testament of Master Wylliam Tracie esquier expounded both by William Tyndale
   and Jhon [sic] Frith* (Antwerp, 1535), cited in Craig and Litzenberger, 421. While
   examining Tracy's testament in some detail, Craig and Litzenberger do not discuss
   his mortalism.
3. Tracy died of natural causes in 1530. Frith was burned at Smithfield in 1533, and
   Tyndale was strangled at the stake and then burned in Holland in 1536.

printed form from 1535 onwards. According to Craig and Litzenberger, one of the first to include verbatim in his own will large portions of Tracy's testament was William Shepherd of Mendlesham in Suffolk.[1] Others followed, including Edward Hoppy of Halifax, Michael Colbrand of Wortling [Worthing?] in East Sussex and Joan Davis and Joan Tymmes, both from Gloucestershire. All specifically included in their own testaments the wording from Tracy's testament which Frith believed was evidence of psychopannychism and which other contemporaries construed to be thnetopsychist.[2] The question remains open as to whether these and other early Protestant wills were drawn up, like Tracy's and so heavily and intentionally dependent on its wording, to protest against the medieval view of the soul and the afterlife, or whether they merely intended to testify to belief in the importance of the resurrection.

Mention must also be made of Hugh Latimer, bishop of Worcester and later one of the Oxford martyrs, whose theological views may also have been shaped in part by Tyndale. Latimer, like Tyndale and Tracy, had been accused of Lutheranism, after declining to preach against Luther's doctrines at the request of his bishop in 1525. A hint of things to come surfaced again in 1532 when Latimer, still not entirely free from suspicion, was "forced to acknowledge" under examination that the souls of saints, apostles and martyrs were already in heaven.[3] The requirement of this demand to conform is, again, enlightening. By 1536 the climate had changed somewhat, and in June Latimer preached to Convocation, which in that year heard complaints against the spread of "erroneous opinions"[4] and which approved Henry VIII's short-lived Ten Articles of Religion. Whether or not Latimer hoped to influence proceedings may never be known,[5] but he concluded the sermon with a call to prayer, "not forgetting those that being departed out of this transitory life, and now sleep in the sleep of peace, and rest from their labours in quietness and in peaceable sleep . . . patiently looking for that that they clearly shall see when God shall be so pleased ".[6]

In a later sermon preached before Edward VI in 1549 Latimer, who had now been engaged to justify the execution of Sir Thomas Seymour, let it be known that it was reported that Seymour had been heard to say that he "believed not the immortality of the soul".[7] At the very least it indicated that the idea may have gained some currency in high places, if not in his own mind. In another sermon Latimer referred to the New Testament account of the raising of Jairus' daughter, noting Christ's words of comfort to Jairus, "She is not

1. Craig and Litzenberger, *JEH*, 44, 426.
2. *Ibid.*, 426-28.
3. Davis, *Heresy and Reformation*, 67.
4. G.E. Corrie (ed.), *Sermons by Hugh Latimer* (Cambridge, 1844), 33.
5. Latimer resigned the see of Worcester in 1539 in protest at the imposition of Henry VIII's Six Articles of Religion intended to restrain the spread of Reformation doctrines.
6. Corrie (ed.), *Sermons*, 40.
7. *Ibid.*, 165.

dead, but she sleepeth", and asking pointedly, "Where was the soul after it went out of this young maid?"[1] Latimer's own reply, at the very least, indicates a leaning to the psychopannychistic view, "It was not in heaven, nor in hell". Nor was it likely to be in purgatory, "a vain, foolish argument".[2] If not in heaven, hell or purgatory, then where? The answer lay in Christ's words, "She sleepeth".[3] Latimer concluded the sermon by emphasising the resurrection and hope in Christ as the only source of life. It would be entirely understandable if Latimer's enemies concluded from all this that he had indeed drunk at the fountain favoured by Tyndale and Luther.

Although Calvin's influence eventually came to predominate as the English Reformation developed, Luther's ideas remained influential. An English translation of Luther's commentary on Ecclesiastes was published in 1573, and although again it is difficult to assess precisely its influence on the development of English mortalism, it may be significant that of all Luther's many works the psychopannychistic *An Exposition of Salomons Booke, Called Ecclesiastes or the Preacher* (1573) appeared in English at this juncture.[4] The least that can be said is that it would have confirmed the idea of soul sleep for any who might have needed such confirmation, and beyond that it may well have planted such seeds in other enquiring minds searching for the truth believed to be available direct from Scripture. That very Scripture, initially available in Tyndale's New Testament and thereafter in other translations heavily dependent on it, continued to project a Lutheran influence for much of the sixteenth century.[5] Alister McGrath reminds us of the "immense" and lasting influence of Tyndale's New Testament,[6] a translation whose mortalist texts George Joye had failed to eradicate.

Documents of the English Reformation
The First Prayer Book of Edward VI, published in 1549 and largely the work of Thomas Cranmer, has been called "an ingenious essay in ambiguity" because it was intentionally worded to allow those who wanted to retain the

1. *Ibid.,* 546, 550.
2. *Ibid.,* 550.
3. Marshall presents convincing evidence that for many early English Protestant believers death was seen as a sleep in which there was no consciousness or awareness of continuing life on earth, and notes the "centrality of the Last Judgement and the resurrection of the body in the theology of Elizabethan and early Stuart Protestantism", Marshall, *Beliefs and the Dead,* 213, 221-23, 220. It was, indeed, only a very short theological step from Latimer's unconscious sleep of the dead to the more fully-developed psychopannychism already evident in Tyndale and Frith. Latimer, it appears, may already have taken it.
4. It is one of only two sixteenth-century English translations of Luther's works held in the British Library.
5. On the Lutheran influence on Tyndale's New Testament and later English translations, see McGrath, *In the Beginning,* 70-73, 78-9, 89 and David Daniell, Preface, vi-viii, in *The New Testament, 1526,* ed. W. R. Cooper (2000).
6. McGrath, *In the Beginning,* 78.

old beliefs and rituals and those who wanted further reform to put their own constructions upon it.[1] It seems unlikely that Cranmer deliberately set out to accommodate the mortalist views of death and the soul which, as we have seen, were already circulating in England and which he would almost certainly have known about, yet this was undoubtedly the effect of this first Edwardian Prayer Book. Before considering this document, we may recall again the essentials of the psychopannychistic view, many of which can be detected at various points in the wording of the 1549 Prayer Book. Psychopannychism does not only regard death as a sleep, biblical though the metaphor is. Such terminology already had a long history, was commonplace in sixteenth-century England and was, moreover, conveniently ambiguous.[2] Psychopannychists believed in the separation of the soul from the body at death and held that the soul did not go immediately to heavenly bliss but that it rested in an unconscious state in a place provided by God to await the resurrection of the body at the last day, when full immortality and eternal life would be granted to the righteous. It seems quite clear that at several points the 1549 Prayer Book allowed, even if it did not encourage, such interpretations.

The Collect for the first Sunday in Advent in the new Prayer Book indicated that "life immortal" would follow Christ's return, the resurrection and the judgement at the last day:

> Almighty God, give us grace that we may cast away the works of darkness, and put upon us the armour of light, now in the time of this mortal life, (in the which thy Son Jesus Christ came to visit us in great humility:) that in the last day, when he shall come again in his glorious majesty, to judge both the quick and the dead, we may rise to the life immortal, through him, who liveth and reigneth with thee and the Holy Ghost, now and ever. Amen.[3]

The prayer to be offered at the Communion service included a reference to the dead now resting in "sleep" in anticipation of the resurrection at the last day:

1. T.M. Parker, *The English Reformation to 1558* (1950), 130; Dickens, *English Reform-ation*, 219. See also M. Davies, *Cranmer's Godly Order: The Destruction of Catholicism Through Liturgical Change* (New York, 1976), 99ff.
2. Philippe Aries reminds us that belief that the dead are asleep "is ancient and constant". It is "the most popular and the most constant image of the beyond", Philippe Aries, *Death*, 23-4. Tyndale and Shakespeare together ensured that the idea would endure in the English language, Tyndale through such passages in his 1526 New Testament as Matt. 9:24, John 11:11, 12 and I Thess. 4:13-17, and Shakespeare through lines such as "Our little life is rounded with a sleep", *The Tempest*, IV, i and "For in that sleep of death what dreams may come When we have shuffled off this mortal coil", *Hamlet*, III, i. Mortalism sought to remove the ambiguity inherent in the idea by explaining more precisely the nature of man's last sleep.
3. *The First Prayer-Book . . . of King Edward VI* [1549], ed. J. Parker (Oxford and London, 1883), 15.

We commend unto thy mercy, O Lord, all other thy servants, which are departed hence from us, with the sign of faith, and now do rest in the sleep of peace: Grant unto them, we beseech thee, thy mercy, and everlasting peace, and that, at the day of the general resurrection, we and all they which be of the mystical body of thy Son, may altogether be set on his right hand, and hear that his most joyful voice: Come unto me, O ye that be blessed of my Father, and possess the kingdom, which is prepared for you from the beginning of the world.[1]

To think against this that faithful believers who "now rest in the sleep of peace" awaiting the "day of general resurrection" are in fact already in heaven at Christ's right hand would seem to contradict the meaning and intent of the prayer, if not to make it superfluous. Furthermore, the "kingdom", i.e. the eternal inheritance of the faithful in which immortality and eternal life would be enjoyed for ever, would become a reality only after the general resurrection at the last day.

The burial service also provides room for a psychopannychistic interpretation which would surely have been approved by Tyndale, Frith and Latimer and all other mortalist sympathisers within the emerging Church of England. The wording of the committal again points to the last day as the time when the promises of eternal life will finally eventuate:

I commend thy soul to God the Father Almighty, and thy body to the ground, earth to earth, ashes to ashes, dust to dust, in sure and certain hope of resurrection to eternal life, through our Lord Jesus Christ, who shall change our vile body, that it may be like to his glorious body, according to the mighty working whereby he is able to subdue all things to himself.[2]

The prayer which was to follow included similar sentiments regarding the souls of the departed now resting in what may easily be regarded as an intermediate state of waiting repose:

Almighty God, we give thee hearty thanks for this thy servant, whom thou hast delivered from the miseries of this wretched world, from the body of death and all temptation; and, as we trust, hast brought his soul, which he committed into thy holy hands, into sure consolation and rest: Grant, we beseech thee, that at the day of judgment his soul and all the souls of thy elect, departed out of this life, may with us, and we with them, fully receive thy promises, and be made perfit [sic] altogether, through the glorious resurrection of thy Son Jesus Christ our Lord."[3]

There is no hint in any of the foregoing of active life or consciousness after death. The soul is always described as being at rest, asleep. In fact, the burial

1. *Ibid.*, 79.
2. *Ibid.*, 147.
3. *Ibid.*, 148.

service was to include the reading, amongst other passages of Scripture, of Psalm 146 and portions of I Corinthians 15, both crucial to the mortalist case. Psalm 146 v. 4 was, in mortalist eyes at least, a description of the death of the righteous man whose hope is in God rather than in his own humanity (vss. 3 and 5): "His breath goeth forth, he returneth to his earth; in that very day his thoughts perish". It is easy enough to see that, whether intentional or not, mortalists who with others who wanted a more thorough reformation in the newly emerging Church of England would have been encouraged by such language and by the choice of such texts.[1]

If, perhaps, the 1549 Prayer Book allowed mortalism, the Forty-Two Articles of Religion of 1553, although short-lived and never enforced, emphatically did not. The intent of this first formal doctrinal statement of the Church of England was clear from the beginning, "for preserving and maintaining peace and unity of doctrine in the Church",[2] according to Archbishop William Wake. The published preamble to the Articles was even more specific, "for the avoiding of controversie in opinions, and the establishment of a godlie concord".[3] Cranmer, who again was largely responsible for drawing up the Articles, and those who assisted him were obviously seeing things with increasing clarity as the Reformation developed and were now aware of certain trends that needed correction if the doctrinal unity of the church was to be preserved. They may even have concluded that what had been published only three years earlier for the edification and guidance of the faithful had given more latitude than had been intended. Burns comes to the point when he says, "Many of these articles were directed against the Anabaptists, and Archbishop Thomas Cranmer and his fellows apparently thought soul sleeping had made gains enough to merit an article condemning both psychopannychism and thnetopsychism".[4] In actual fact, both Articles 39 and 40 address related eschatological issues, although Article 40 pertains specifically to the mortalist alternatives:

1. And this even though the "studied ambiguity" (Dickens, *English Reformation*, 219) of the 1549 Prayer Book as a whole was reflected in the final prayer at the burial service, which referred to the souls of the elect being in "joy and felicity", *ibid.*, 154. The burial service in the Second Edwardian Prayer-Book (1552), although much shorter, conveys essentially the same sentiments regarding death. The substitution of the word 'rest' for 'sleep' in the Collect in the 1552 version is not a substantial change. Harrison states that in the longer term the 1549 Prayer Book was more influential than the later version, a view confirmed more recently by Horie, D. Harrison (ed.), *The First and Second Prayer Books of Edward VI* (London and Toronto, 1977), xv; H. Horie, 'The Lutheran Influence on the Elizabethan Settlement, 1558-1563', *HJ*, 34(1991), 523.
2. William Wake, *The State of the Church and Clergy of England* (1703), 599. Wake was Archbishop of Canterbury from 1716 to 1737.
3. 'Articles agreed on by the Bishoppes, and other learned menne in the Synode at London. . .', in E. Cardwell, *Synodalia* (1842), II, 18.
4. *CM*, 116.

39. The resurrection of the dead is not yeat brought to passe.

The resurrection of the dead is not as yet brought to passe, as though it only belonged to the soulle, whiche by the grace of Christe is raised from the death of sinne, but it is to be loked for at the laste daie; for then (as Scripture doeth moste manifestlie testifie) to all that bee dead their awne bodies, flesh and bone shal be restored, that the whole man maie (according to his workes) have other rewarde or punishment, as he hath lived vertuouslie, or wickedlie.

40. The soulles of them that depart this life doe neither die with the bodies, nor slepe idlie.

Thei which saie that the soulles of suche as departe hens doe sleepe, being without al sence, fealing, or perceiving, until the daie of judgement, or affirme that the soulles die with the bodies, and at the last daie shal be raised up with the same, do utterlie dissent from the right beliefe declared to us in holie Scripture.[1]

It is, to say the least, worth noting that an official doctrinal formulation should go out of its way to specify deviant teachings which departed from the traditional and currently approved position, although the Scottish Confession of 1560 and the Second Helvetic Confession of 1566 were to take a similar line. Hardwick rightly comments that the Forty-Two Articles were drawn up with "an eye to the existing necessities of the time".[2]

It is apparent, then, that one of the many "necessities" driving the form-ulation of the document was mortalism, in both its psychopannychistic and thnetopsychist forms. While no figure can be put on the number of mortalists, then or at any other time, it could not have been inconsiderable. With reference to the geographical and theological background to the Forty-Two Articles, it is known that Anabaptist teachings flourished during the Edwardian era, particularly in Kent and Essex. Hardwick notes a contemporary letter from John Hooper, Bishop of Gloucester and Worcester, to Bullinger which affirmed that some "deny that man is endued with a soul different from that of a beast, and subject to decay".[3] Williams maintains that Kent and Sussex were "hotbeds of Anabaptist activity" and points out that just a few years earlier, in 1547, Ridley and Latimer, later to be burned themselves, had been assigned to deal with Anabaptism in Kent.[4] Dickens remarks that the heresies found in Kent at the time were "widespread and complicated", that the county provided no fewer than fifty-eight martyrs during the reign of Mary and that Anabaptist congregations began to appear in Kent even during the Marian persecution.[5] A later undated tract, *The Vail Turned Aside*, claimed that "most of the Baptists in

1. Cardwell, *Synodalia*, I, 32.
2. C. Hardwick, *A History of the Articles of Religion* (1851), 90.
3. *Ibid.*, 95.
4. *RR*, 1199.
5. Dickens, *English Reformation*, 261, 330.

Kent and Sussex" believed "that the soul sleeps with the body in the grave".[1]

It is reasonable to assume that such beliefs had not just appeared overnight, and it begins to look as though the authorities were justified in fearing that mortalism, among other 'Anabaptist' beliefs, might get out of hand. If these accounts are to be taken as they stand, a development from the psychopannychism of Tyndale and Frith to the thnetopsychism apparently encountered by Hooper was already taking place by the middle of the sixteenth century, at least in some parts of the country. Psychopannychism and thnetopsychism may co-exist but ultimately they are not compatible, and while psychopannychism may have remained the preferred option for some, thnetopsychism would undoubtedly have appealed to more radical students of the biblical text as it had on the Continent a generation or so earlier. Be that as it may, mortalist views of one kind or another seem to have found a foothold in Kent, Sussex and Essex since the earliest days of the English Reformation.

The omission of Article 40, together with Articles 39, 41 and 42, from the Thirty-Nine Articles of 1563, and from subsequent Anglican doctrinal formulae, is an interesting development. Given that the Thirty-Nine Articles were a further and more considered attempt to define the theological position of the Church of England in relation to the doctrinal controversies of the period, including specifically Anabaptist teachings,[2] how is the omission of Article 40, which inveighed against both psychopannychism and thnetopsychism, to be interpreted? There is a long-standing view that it represents a change in attitude to mortalist doctrine. Bearing in mind that by the mid-sixteenth century mortalism had long been regarded as heresy, Nathaniel Henry suggested more than fifty years ago that the omission of Articles 39 and 40 raised the question whether mortalism by 1563 "was heresy at all in England, except to extremely legalistic Calvinists".[3] Henry further argued that it was only under Edward VI and Mary, and later during the Interregnum, that "the sleepy-heads" were considered dangerous, and that from the time of the Thirty-Nine Articles onward mortalism was in England considered "a thing indifferent".[4]

Similar conclusions had been reached some two hundred years earlier by the Anglican scholars Francis Blackburne and Peter Peckard, whose own contributions to the mortalist debate in the eighteenth century we shall review in due course.[5]

---

1. Whiting, *English Puritanism* (1931), 89-90. Whitley attributes the tract to Christopher Cooper of Ashford who was not a Baptist and dates it 1701, *BB,* I, 137. It has not been possible to locate a copy of this rare tract. In the light of the Baptist confessions of faith discussed in chapters 3 and 4 of this study it is possible that the seventeenth- and early eighteenth-century mortalism of the Kent and Sussex Baptists reflected earlier Anabaptist belief in the South-East.
2. *ODCC,* s.v. 'Thirty-Nine Articles'.
3. Nathaniel H. Henry, 'Milton and Hobbes: Mortalism and the Intermediate State', *SP,* 48 (1951), 239.
4. *Ibid.*
5. See chap. 6.

In *No Proof in the Scriptures of an Intermediate State . . . Between Death and the Resurrection* (1756), Blackburne argued that by dropping Article 40 the Church of England indicated that it had changed its position regarding mortalist teachings. It was "a certain sign" that the Church had had second thoughts on the matter, and by 1563 "no longer thought the doctrine 'did wholly differ from the right faith and orthodox belief delivered in the Scriptures'."[1] Peckard interpreted the omission, not as a concession within the Elizabethan *via media* to Catholic immortalism but rather as a concession to Protestant mortalism. Peckard argued that the early leaders of the English Reformation, still to some extent "blinded by the errors of Popery", had supported the doctrine of the immortal soul by the wording of the Forty-Two Articles. Under Elizabeth's more considered policy of religious compromise, however, all references to the disputed matter of the soul, notably belief in an intermediate state, were omitted he said, stating "Everything positive in relation to this point was left out of these [Thirty-Nine] Articles", and adding that the Fortieth Article condemning mortalism had "at the same time shared the same fate".[2] Schaff similarly held that the Thirty-Nine Articles did not continue the attack on mortalism because "certain Anabaptist doctrines" had by 1563 "disappeared or lost their importance".[3] That mortalism had not disappeared seems clearly indicated by the Calvinistic Scottish Confession of 1560 which in Article XVII, 'Of the Immortality of the Soul', stated plainly that the "Elect departed are in peace and rest from their labours, not that they sleep and come to a certain oblivion, as some Phantastickes do affirm", adding for good measure that neither the faithful nor the reprobate dead are asleep "that they feel not joy or torment".[4]

It seems hardly necessary to restate that the Thirty-Nine Articles reflected the necessities and the mood of the day just as the Forty-Two Articles had done a decade or so earlier, or that in so doing they exhibited less hostility to the mortalist position. In view of the Lutheran influence noted earlier in connection with Tyndale, Frith and Tracy, that same influence on the development of the Thirty-Nine Articles may be worth noting again.[5] So also may be the fact that much of the subsequent opposition to mortalism came predominantly from those who advocated a strongly Calvinistic theology.

1. Francis Blackburne, *No Proof in the Scriptures of an Intermediate State of Happiness or Misery Between Death and the Resurrection* (1756), 37.
2. Peter Peckard, *Observations on the Doctrine of an Intermediate State between Death and the Resurrection* (1756), 42.
3. P. Schaff, *The Creeds of Christendom* (6th edn, 1931), I, 619.
4. *Ibid.*, III, 459-60.
5. Schaff documents the influence of two key Lutheran Confessions on the formulation of the Thirty-Nine Articles, the Augsburg Confession of 1530 and the Wurttemberg Confession of 1552, *The Creeds of Christendom*, I, 622-29. See also *ODCC* s.v. 'Thirty-Nine Articles' and Horie, *HJ*, 34, 530-1. Horie also notes that Elizabeth I preferred the 1549 Prayer Book to the later 1552 revision.

Continental Influences

The fate of the Dutch martyrs Hendrik Terwoort and Jan Pieters in London illustrates the existing or developing contemporary link between Continental and English mortalism. Terwoort and Pieters were members of a Flemish Anabaptist congregation arrested and interrogated for heresy in April and May, 1575. Some members of the group recanted, a few escaped, several had their sentences commuted, many were transported back to the Netherlands, one died in prison, but Terwoort and Pieters remained steadfast to the end. They died at the stake in Smithfield on 22 July, despite representations on their behalf by Sir Thomas Bodley and John Foxe.[1] Article XII of their confession reads:

> We believe in the resurrection of the dead, as it is written, Isaiah xxvi. 19, John xi. 25, Dan. xii. 2, John v. 25, in the first epistle to the Corinthians, xv. 22, I Thess. iv. 16. That we shall rise from the dead in our own bodies, Job xix. 25, Isaiah xxvi. 19, I Cor. xv., when the Lord shall come in the clouds with his angels, then shall each one be judged according to his works, Matt. xxv. 34, Rom. ii. 6.[2]

Given the prevailing political climate and the noticeable absence of any reference to the soul's immortality, it is quite possible that psychopannychism may be concealed here. Nor is the similarity between this and contemporary Anabaptist and early English Baptist confessions hard to recognise. Williams records this episode in the context of Jacob Acontius's "intentionally imprecise" but "influential" Anabaptist articles of faith and toleration published in Basle in 1565, but composed against the background of Acontius's membership of the prominent Strangers church in London, and the Elizabethan decree that all Anabaptists must conform to the Anglican establishment.[3] The second and fourth articles of Acontius's declaration state:

> (2) That man is subject to the wrath of and judgement of God. And that the dead will come to life again, the just to everlasting happiness, but the wicked to everlasting torments.
> (4) That if we believe in the Son of God, we shall obtain life through his name.[4]

A mortalist wishing to conceal the true extent of his convictions would have been happy enough with that. The psychopannychist Anthony Pocquet, whom we have already encountered, first appears in connection with the Dutch Spiritualists in the French-speaking region of the Netherlands, probably in the

1. A full account can be found in *RR*, 1205-7.
2. T.J. von Braght, *Het Bloedig Tooneel of Martelaers Speigel der Doops-Gesinde of Weereloofe Christenen* (Amsterdam,1685), 704, cited in *CFF*, II, 131.
3. *RR*, 1204.
4. Jacob Acontius, *Stratagems of Satan,* tr. C.D. O'Malley, California State Library, Occasional Papers, English Series, 5, pt. II (San Francisco,1940), 201.

1530s.[1] His doctrine of the sleep of the soul was one of many new teachings which appealed to early Continental Anabaptists, and which undoubtedly would have been known to, if not espoused by, Dutch Anabaptists fleeing to England from the intense persecution of the 1560s. Given the strength of Dutch Anabaptism at that time, and the strength of their convictions, it would be surprising indeed if mortalism, implicit or explicit, had not found its way across the Channel to find a new home, and perhaps expression, in the London conventicles.

The Continental connection is, however, more evident in the anti-mortalist literature of the period. Henry Bullinger had been the first to attack mortalism on the Continent with his *Von dem unvershamten Frevel*, a wide-ranging refutation of Continental Anabaptism, published in 1531. While not solely directed against soul sleep, it devoted considerable space to rebutting this doctrine which Bullinger so strongly opposed. Williams notes the "esteem which Bullinger enjoyed in England", and draws attention to the fact that within a very short period between 1548 and 1551 three translations of Bullinger's work, or large sections of it, appeared in English.[2] In 1548 John Veron translated the complete work as *An Holsome Antidotus or counter-poysen, agaynst the pestylent heresye and secte of the Anabaptistes*, in which an entire chapter attempted to refute the concept of soul sleep. In 1551 two partial translations of Bullinger's work were published in Worcester, *A most necessary and frutefull Dialogue, betwene ye seditious Libertin or rebel Anabaptist, and the true obedient Christian . . .* , and *A most sure and strong defence of the baptisme of children, against ye pestiferous secte of the Anabaptystes*. According to Bullinger, Anabaptists were "fully persuaded" that after death the souls of the righteous sleep "in the bosom of Abraham tyl the day of iudgement".[3] This appears to be psychopannychism, but does not sufficiently analyse the Continental situation as a whole. Bullinger's use of the term Anabaptist was in keeping with the times. It was little more than a derogatory term of theological contempt, a useful catch-all, frequently used indiscriminately against those thought to hold deviant views. That they frequently included mortalists of one kind or another is beyond doubt.

In 1549 an anonymous English translation was published of a work by Calvin, *A Short Instruction for to arme all good Christian people agaynst the pestiferous errours of the common secte of Anabaptistes*. It contained an abbreviated version of the arguments against soul sleepers outlined in Calvin's recent *Psychopannychia*, incorrectly suggesting that those who held other "Anabaptist" doctrines were *ipso facto* mortalists, but making a distinction between psychopannychists and thnetopsychists, the latter claiming that "the soul is not a substance, or a creature having an essential being; but that it is only the virtue that man hath to breathe,

1. *RR*, 538.
2. *Ibid.*, 313.
3. Henry Bullinger, *An Holsome Antidotus or counter-poysen, agaynst the pestylent heresye and secte of the Anabaptistes* (tr. John Veron, [1548]), fol. N vi r, ff.

to move, and to do other actions of life".[1] We may conclude that the translator of Calvin's *Short Instruction* felt that all this had some relevance to the contemporary English scene. Fully one third of this work was devoted to the refutation of the "shameful" belief in the sleep of the soul, in either its psychopannychistic or thnetopsychist form, asserting that mortalist beliefs were "commonly" held among English Anabaptists.[2] Williams claims that all the above-mentioned pieces were issued at the instigation of the ecclesiastical authorities because "the spread of radical ideas at the outset of Edward's reign was so great".[3]

Bullinger appears to have been almost as influential in England as Calvin, if not in some respects more so, at least at this particular time. In 1577 his *Fiftie godlie and learned Sermons* was first published in English, translated from the Latin edition of 1552, with a second edition in 1584. In 1586 Convocation ordered that Bullinger's sermons be studied by young clergymen in training and that examinations of their notes be held each Michaelmas.[4] The English translation was subsequently adopted as a textbook in the dioceses of Lincoln and Canterbury. It is readily apparent that the doctrines of soul sleep were a cause of great concern to Bullinger. An entire sermon is devoted to a defence of the soul's immortality, against those who believed otherwise. Presumably Bullinger's translators shared the same apprehension that, intentionally or otherwise, this doctrine cast doubt on the certainty of eternal life. Bullinger's virulent opposition is quite evident in the English translation:

> If as yet there be any light-headed men to whom the immortality of the soul seemeth doubtful, or which utterly deny the same, these truly are unworthy to have the name of men; for they are plagues of the commonwealth, and very beasts, worthy to be hissed and driven out of the company of men. For he lacketh a bridle to restrain him, and hath cast away all honesty and shame, and is prepared in all points to commit any mischief, whosoever believeth that the soul of man is mortal.[5]

There may even be more than a hint of thnetopsychism here. In any case, it was an intemperate misrepresentation of mortalists and their motives. More to the point, perhaps, is that its translator may have seen it as a timely response to mortalism's growing appeal to English minds.

There can be little doubt that this was the case when Calvin's *Psychopannychia* was published in full in England in 1581, under the title *An excellent treatise*

1. John Calvin, *A short instruction for to arme all good Christian people agaynst the pestiferous errours of the common secte of Anabaptistes* [1549], sigs.,G[vii]*v*-G[viii]*r*.
2. *Ibid.*, sig. L ii *r, v.*
3. *RR*, 1197.
4. *BB*, I, 3.
5. Henry Bullinger, *Fiftie godlie and learned Sermons. . . containing the chiefe and principall points of Christian Religion* (tr. H. I., 2nd. edn,1584), 767.

of the Immortalytie of the Soule.[1] Thomas Stocker, the translator, believed that mortalism was now widespread in England, and made it clear that its popular appeal was the main reason for his effort to draw renewed attention to Calvin's counter-arguments. Just a year previously, in 1580, Elizabeth I had issued the "Proclamation against the Sectaries of the Family of Love", many of whom were believed to be mortalist. Burns has shown that the mortalism of the English Familists was mostly annihilationist, and argues that Stocker's translation of Calvin coincided with the attempt of Elizabeth's agents to suppress the sect.[2] By then, of course, English mortalism was more diverse and widespread than any links it had with Familism might have suggested. Calvin had originally written the *Psychopannychia* because at that time "there were many . . . greatously [*sic*] infected with this monstrous opinion, That the soules of men dyed together with the[ir] bodies".[3] The thnetopsychist overtones here should be read in conjunction with the book's title, which specified the "erronious opinions"of those who held the soul "to lye asleape" until the last day. It is difficult to know at times whether those who wrote against mortalism did not understand the distinction between psychopannychism and thnetopsychism, even if they did not use this later terminology, or if they simply did not care. In this case, it appears that the distinction was clearly understood. Calvin, as we have already seen, recognised the difference between psychopannychism and thnetopsychism and the fact that already before the middle of the sixteenth century both views had appeared on the Continent.[4] The same can be said of England some forty or fifty years later. Stocker's translation of Calvin's original title seems clearly enough to indicate psychopannychism, yet he goes on to speak of a "foul and hellish error" having "possessed and poisoned at this day the hearts and minds of a great number here at home, within this land ".[5] The error was "that the souls of men dyed together with the[ir] bodies". [6] This seems as clearly to indicate thnetopsychism, and it was this error, now claiming the attention of a growing number of English believers, that provided Stocker with the justification for his translation of Calvin's important work, and the opportunity to say a few words himself. It is a testimony that should not be overlooked.

It seems, then, if we accept Stocker's analysis, that by 1581, in addition to psychopannychism, a thnetopsychist construction of the mortalist 'heresy' was

1. The full title of Thomas Stocker's translation reads, *An excellent treatise of the Immortalytie of the Soule, by which is proved that the soules, after their departure out of the bodies, are awake and doe lyve, contrary to that erronious opinion of certen, ignorant persons who thinke them to lye asleape untill the day of Iudgement.*
2. *CM*, 45 ff, especially 61- 4.
3. Calvin, *An excellent treatise of the Immortalytie of the Soule* (tr. Thomas Stocker), Ep. Ded., sig. Aii*v*.
4. See ch. 1, p. 40.
5. Calvin, *An excellent treatise*, Ep. Ded., sig. Aii*v*.
6. *Ibid.*

gaining ground which required refutation just as Calvin himself had attempted to refute Continental mortalism with the original *Psychopannychia*. Calvin, via Stocker, says of the psychopannychist position: "(Some) think that after a man is dead, that the soul sleepeth until the day of judgment, at which time it shall awake out of sleep, without either memory, understanding, and feeling whatsoever".[1] He then adds that there are others, who say of the soul that it is

> only a power of life which is led by the moving of the pulses, or of lungs and lights, and because it cannot be without a body, therefore they fain that it dyeth and perisheth together with the body until such time as the whole man be raised up again.[2]

This is undoubtedly thnetopsychism, revealing itself in Elizabethan England, alongside the earlier but less radical psychopannychism, both variations of the mortalist departure from orthodoxy now claiming the attention of an increasing number of earnest and concerned believers disaffected with the arrested reformation of doctrine in the national church. In the absence of more conclusive documentary evidence from the sixteenth-century English mortalists themselves, we are indebted to these translations of Calvin and Bullinger, providing as they do important glimpses into the existence of English mortalism in the later decades of the sixteenth century.

The effect of the translated *Psychopannychia* in arresting mortalism in England is hard to determine. It arrived late, and its impact may only have been marginal. Calvin himself, of course, was a highly respected and influential figure in England throughout the second half of the sixteenth century. His letters to Edward VI and Cranmer in 1551 and 1552 urging further reformation in the English church are evidence of this,[3] as are his introduction to an English translation of the New Testament published in Geneva in 1557 and the translation into English in 1561 of the definitive 1559 edition of the *Institutes*. The remarkable popularity of the Geneva Bible in England from 1560 onwards is further testimony to the influence of Genevan theology. A.G. Dickens noted "the Calvinist flavour of Elizabethan Anglicanism"[4] and William Haller emphasises Puritanism's indebtedness to Calvin in doctrine and in life. English Calvinism, he adds, led to "a way of life that eventually far transcended all ecclesiastical and even all religious bounds".[5] Alister McGrath goes further, stating that Calvin is "profoundly worthy" of serious study "by anyone concerned with the shaping of the modern world in

1. *Ibid.*, fols. 1*v*, 2*r*.
2. *Ibid.*, fol. 2*r*. Stocker's translation here and in the preceding note seems to be rather less precise than the later translation of Beveridge cited on p. 40, n. 1.
3. For an English translation of the letters see H.C. Porter, *Puritanism in Tudor England* (1970), 64-72 and H. Robinson (ed.), *Original Letters Relative to the English Reformation*, II (Cambridge, 1847), 707-15.
4. Dickens, *English Reformation*, 228.
5. William Haller, *The Rise of Puritanism* (New York, 1957), 84-5.

general and western culture in particular".[1] Calvin's immense influence on the
English church and English religious thought cannot for a moment be seriously
questioned. The returning Marian exiles, many of whom had taken refuge in
Strasbourg, Basle, Zurich and Frankfurt, as well as in Geneva itself,[2] ensured that
Calvin's influence shaped the early development of English theology, particularly
the theology of contemporary Puritanism and later Nonconformity.

In this context there can be little doubt that Calvin's eschatology and his
preference for the medieval view of the soul and its destiny were mediated
via Puritan preaching and literature and the English translations of his own
works to the contemporary English scene and thereby as a permanent legacy
to English-speaking Protestantism as a whole.[3] It was this traditional view of
the soul, evident and deep-rooted from the beginning in the nascent English
national church and soon to be taken up by Puritanism and after that by
Nonconformity, that the sixteenth-century mortalists, known and unknown,
sought to challenge. That they did so with a modicum of success, albeit against
the odds, seems clear enough from the evidence that has survived.

1. Alister McGrath, *A Life of John Calvin: A Study in the Shaping of Western Culture*
   (1990), xv. See also the collection of essays edited by W. Stanford Reid, *John
   Calvin: His Influence in the Western World* (Grand Rapids, MI, 1982).
2. It has been estimated that at one time or another there were more than 200 members
   of the English church in Geneva which was founded in 1555. Even this is not
   an accurate gauge of the Genevan influence. As Dickens wryly observed, "To be
   influenced, one was not compelled to visit Geneva any more that a good Marxist
   must necessarily visit Moscow or the British Museum", *English Reformation*, 288.
3. More than two hundred years later Joseph Priestley noted that Calvin had been
   "violently opposed" to soul sleep, a fact which "seems to have given a different turn
   to the sentiments of the reformed in general", Joseph Priestley, *Disquisitions Relating
   to Matter and Spirit* (1777), 231.

Chapter Three
The Seventeenth-Century Scene to 1660

The seventeenth century began inauspiciously for English mortalism in general, and for Edward Wightman of Burton-on-Trent in particular. In the previous chapter we saw that the known sixteenth-century mortalists, Tyndale, Frith and Tracy, had died by 1536. With the exception of Wightman, and for a time Sir Thomas Browne, and Clement Writer and the elusive William Bowling,[1] no other mortalists are known by name until Richard Overton, whose *Mans Mortalitie*,[2] published in 1644, was the first full English exposition of mortalist theology. It is theoretically conceivable that from the middle of the sixteenth century mortalism virtually disappeared from English religious thought for more than a century until it reappeared again with Overton and those who followed him, Samuel Richardson and George Hammon from Kent, and Thomas Hobbes and John Milton.[3] In this case, Wightman would have been a notable exception. It is more likely, however, that mortalism survived in the minds of successive generations of English Christians who, like Wightman, sought a more thoroughly biblical faith than they believed could be found in the established church. The absence of any formal apology for mortalism before 1644 cannot be taken as evidence that it had died in the years between Tyndale and Overton. In any case, the evidence in the preceding chapter argues against this conclusion, certainly with respect to the latter half of the sixteenth century. Wightman's beliefs, which if they were as reported, should not be regarded as representative of other English mortalists of the period. In the final analysis, Wightman himself may have been more of a liability than an asset to the mortalist case *per se*.

Edward Wightman
Edward Wightman died at the stake in Lichfield in 1612, convicted in all on sixteen counts of "wicked", "execrable" heresy and "unheard of opinions . . . belched by the instinct of Satan",[4] and deemed worthy of the most severe

1. Browne, Bowling and Writer are dealt with later; see pp. 74ff, 86 respectively.
2. On Overton and *Mans Mortalitie*, see ch. 4, pp. 98ff. On the date of the first edition of *MM*, see p. 98, n. 1.
3. On Richardson and Hammon, see pp. 85, 109 respectively. The views of Hobbes and Milton are also examined in ch. 4.
4. *A True Relation of the Commissions and Warrants for the Condemnation and Burning of*

punishment. His views in general were said to reflect tenets of at least eight heresies condemned in the early centuries of Christian history, as well as some of more recent Anabaptist origin.[1] Wightman first came to the attention of the authorities in the diocese of Coventry and Lichfield in 1609, from which time his fate was more or less sealed. After spending more than six months in prison awaiting trial, he was eventually examined, first in April 1611 for "blasphemous heresies", based largely on a manuscript of his own composition which he is said to have presented personally to James I a month earlier.[2] The examination proceeded slowly and intermittently until November, when the trial proper commenced in the presence of Richard Neile, Bishop of Coventry and Lichfield. Neile reported that William Laud, later Archbishop of Canterbury, had assisted him "in all the proceedings against Wightman from beginning to end".[3]

If the records are to be taken at face value, many of Wightman's opinions were extreme, even by seventeenth-century standards. The basis of his beliefs was insistence on a literal, scriptural foundation for his faith, and a deep conviction "that Christianity is not wholly professed and preached in the Church of England, but only in part".[4] Wightman's Christology was Arian and, predictably perhaps, his views of the Trinity and the Holy Ghost, Socinian. Less predictable, perhaps, were his claims that he was the prophet spoken of in Deuteronomy 18, the suffering servant of Isaiah 53 and the Comforter promised in the Gospel of John. He also claimed that Malachi's prophecy of the coming Elijah was "likewise meant of his person".[5] It has to be conceded that such extravagant claims would have sounded very much like blasphemy to seventeenth-century ears, and it is hardly surprising that he was eventually condemned for heresy "stubbornly and partinaciously" [sic] held, and for "detestable blasphemy".[6] Burrage was probably correct in thinking that Wightman was a Seeker rather than an Anabaptist, despite the fact that he held "that the baptizing of infants is an abominable custom" and that only "converts of sufficient age of understanding" should be baptised.[7] The Baptist historian Thomas Crosby, claiming him as a Baptist, believed that no sane

---

Bartholomew Legatt and Thomas Withman [sic] . . . (1651), 7, 12. Wightman's name is given correctly in a sub-title on p. 7. Despite Froom's assertion to the contrary, there is no evidence that Legatt (or Legate) shared Wightman's mortalist views, *CFF*, II, 34-7. For details of Wightman's trial and execution, see also T.B. Howell (ed.), *A Complete Collection of State Trials* (1816), II, 730-7, and Champlin Burrage, *The Early English Dissenters in the Light of Recent Research* (Cambridge, 1912), I, 216-20.

1. The Ebionites, Cerinthus, Valentinus, Arius, Macedonius, Simon Magus, Manes and Photinus, *A True Relation*, 7, although none of these is associated with mortalism. Accounts of each of the foregoing and their teachings can be found in *ODCC*.
2. *CSPD, 1639-40*, 83-4; Burrage, *Early English Dissenters*, I, 217; *A True Relation*, 9.
3. Burrage, *Early English Dissenters*, I, 217; *CSPD, 1639-40*, 84.
4. *A True Relation*, 8.
5. *Ibid.*, 7, 8.
6. *Ibid.*, 12.
7. Burrage, *Early English Dissenters*, I, 65-6; *A True Relation*, 8.

man could possibly have held such a motley array of divergent opinions, stating that many of the heresies imputed to him were "foolish and inconsistent".[1]

Be that as it may, two of the charges which eventually brought Wightman to the stake related specifically to mortalism, and at one crucial point seem to reflect the thnetopsychist view we have previously encountered in Continental mortalism and hints of which can already be detected in English thought of the period. Certainly the least that can be concluded from the carefully-worded deposition is a psychopannychism that denies any access to heaven for the soul at death. However, this does not explain adequately that the soul is "mortall" in its sleep, and we probably have to recognise an element of thnetopsychism here:

> 11. That the Soul doth sleep in the sleep of the first death, as well as the body, and is mortall as touching the sleep of the first death, as the body is: And that the Soul of our Saviour Jesus Christ did sleep in that sleep of death as well as his body.
> 12. That the souls of the elect Saints departed, are not Members possessed of the triumphant Church in Heaven.[2]

The reference to the soul of Christ is interesting, and in the context of the document as a whole may merely be a re-affirmation of His full humanity, rather than evidence that Wightman shared the Christological beliefs of the English Anabaptist community at Haarlem, as Burns seems to think.[3] While such a connection may have been quite possible, the mortalist beliefs of the Haarlem people cannot be construed to accommodate thnetopsychism as can Wightman's position. The Dutch Anabaptists, according to Payne, held "that the soules do sleepe in [the] grave with the bodies until the resurrection".[4] This is simply soul sleep, without any hint of mortality, as in Wightman. That being so, we may conclude that Wightman's position represents a move towards the thnetopsychism which had already begun to manifest itself in English mortalism and which eventually came to predominate.

Whatever the precise nature of Wightman's mortalism may have been, the amalgam of errors for which he was condemned warrant more than the passing notice accorded him by Burns.[5] It is true that he appears as a "fanatic", with an egocentric opinion of his importance as a chosen mouthpiece for God and for truth,[6] and that the record of his mortalism is virtually the only documentary evidence of English mortalism for the best part of a century, though it was a mortalism compromised by association with a catalogue of strange doctrines.[7]

1. Thomas Crosby, *The History of the English Baptists,* I (1738), 108.
2. *A True Relation*, 8; Howell(ed.), *State Trials*, II, 735.
3. *CM*, 123.
4. [Payne], *Royall Exchange*, 22.
5. *CM*, 123.
6. *Ibid.; A True Relation*, 8.
7. Two anonymous tracts would shortly emphasise mortalism's heterodoxy by classifying it with other deviant doctrines, e.g., *A Catalogue of the severall Sects and Opinions in*

Wightman was also the last person to be burned in England for religious belief.[1] His hesitation at the stake[2] was no more culpable than that of Cranmer before him, and his willingness ultimately to die a reminder of the strength of his own vision and the weakness of the vision of those who ordered him to be burnt. It is one of the many ironies of religious history that this "diseased sheep of the flock of the Lord", put down by the "holy Mother Church" of England lest he "infect by contagion"others of the flock,[3] might have enjoyed a different ending had he lived a century later. As things were a writ was issued on 9 March to the Sheriff of Lichfield for Edward Wightman to be publicly burned as a heretic.[4] He was brought to the stake that same day.

From Wightman to Overton

We have already alluded to Richard Overton's *Mans Mortalitie,* which first appeared in 1644.[5] It was a work of considerable significance in the development of mortalist thought in England, despite its evident stylistic and literary limitations. It was the first of many expositions and treatises to appear over the next one hundred and fifty years advocating mortalism as a legitimate Christian alternative to traditional views of the soul and the life to come. As the restrictions on the press and freedom of individual belief began to ease through the 1640s, so mortalism began to appear more clearly in the beliefs and writings of many of the so-called sectaries. They were, to begin with, mostly Baptist and their contribution to the consolidation and clarification of mortalism requires due consideration. Before that, however, and between Edward Wightman's short-lived espousal of mortalism and Richard Overton's seminal *Mans Mortalitie,* there were other indications of continuing disaffection with the received view of the soul's immortality and its contingent doctrines, and of the struggle to articulate a satisfactory doctrine of the nature of man which could be claimed to accord more fully with the biblical revelation.

In 1605 the Cambridge Puritan Hugh Broughton, a noted Hebrew scholar, had published a work in which he attempted to explain that article of the Apostles' Creed which referred to Christ's descent into hell. The matter had apparently

---

England and other Nations (1646) which drew attention to the "false and dangerous tenents" [*sic*] of Jesuits, Adamites, Seekers, Familists, Hetheringtonians and Anti-Trinitarians, *inter alia,* as well as those of the "Soule-Sleeper", and *A Relation of Severall Heresies* (1646) which also sought to expose the "dangerous opinions" of some twenty heretical doctrines of the time including, again, "Soule-sleepers". See later, pp. 81ff for the views of more well-known contemporary heresiographers.

1. *DNB,* s.v. Edward Wightman; Burrage, *Early English Dissenters,* I, 217.
2. *CSPD, 1639-40,* 85.
3. *A True Relation,* 12.
4. *CSPD, 1611-1618,* 123. For a contemporary account of Wightman's trial, see MS. Ash. 1521 in the Bodleian Library.
5. First published Jan. 1643 (o.s.), reprinted 1644. A revised edition, *Man Wholly Mortal,* was published in 1655 and re-issued in 1675; see *CM,* 154. See also, ch. 4, n. 2.

troubled him for some time, so much so that he declared that whoever defended Christ's "descent into hell", at least as commonly understood, "hath the mark of papistry"[1] and that the popular interpretation imputed heresy to the creed itself. It was strong language for an issue that many would not have regarded as crucial. For Broughton, the problem revolved around the biblical teaching of death, and in particular the meaning of the original Hebrew and Greek words *sheol* and *hades*, usually translated as 'hell' in English versions of the Bible, and understood as signifying a place of punishment to which the ungodly were consigned at death to live in torment. Broughton maintained that the original words did not support such a view, and that hell was not a place of punishment or torment, but rather should be understood as referring to the state of the dead, the final resting place of the departed.[2] It might apply to either the righteous or the ungodly, referring to their abode between death and the resurrection, i.e. the grave. Thus Job wished to rest in *sheol* until his change occurred at the last day.[3] Christ, therefore, could not have descended into a specific place of punishment or torment which did not exist. The problem was clear enough even if Broughton's solution was not entirely so. It would be understandable if thoughts such as these, offered by a learned Rabbinical scholar, had helped Edward Wightman to conclude that Christ's soul as well as His body slept in the sleep of the first death.[4] It would have made any descent into hell quite impossible.

Another convinced adherent of moderate Puritan opinion, the poet George Wither, gave mortalism even more substantial support with his translation in 1636 of an ancient work by the fourth-century Christian philosopher, Nemesius of Emesa.[5] Nemesius had been a neo-Platonist, but in attempting to construct a doctrine of the soul which agreed with the biblical revelation had almost re-written traditional Platonic dualism to the point that the soul, if indeed it did exist as a separate entity, could not function without the body. Wither's translation of Nemesius makes the latter sound at times, at least to later generations, more Hebrew than Platonic:

> Plato seems to affirm that man consists not of a double essence, that is to say, jointly of a Soul and a Body, but rather, that he is a soul, using as it were instrumentally, such a body. . . . When the soul be divided from the body, it is immediately as much without motion as a workman's tools when he hath cast them aside.[6]

1. Hugh Broughton, *An Explication of the Article . . . of Our Lorde's Soule Going from His Body to Paradise* (1605), 40. This work was boldly dedicated to the queen.
2. *Ibid., passim.*
3. *Ibid.*, 10.
4. *A True Relation*, 8.
5. George Wither (tr.), *The Nature of Man. A learned and usefull Tract written in Greek by Nemesius,. . .one of the most ancient Fathers of the Church* (1636). Nemesius' work was valued in the Middle Ages, particularly by Thomas Aquinas, *ODCC*, s.v. Nemesius of Emesa.
6. *Ibid.*, 4-6.

There is something of an ambiguity here, for the workman's tool is clearly a separate entity in his hand, whereas the soul is not one of two entities comprising man, but an intrinsic part of the whole. Man in his totality "is a soul". Nemesius, and presumably Wither also, maintains that both body and soul are interdependent. The body without the soul is not a living creature at all, and vice versa:

> When the soul cometh into the body it perfects the living creature. So then, in a perfect living creature, neither can the soul be at any time without the body, neither the body without the soul: for the soul is not the body itself; but it is the soul of the body: and therefore it is in the body . . . for it hath not an existence by itself.[1]

This is still dualism, of course, but not the dualism of an independent immaterial, immortal soul.

While later mortalists would substitute 'breath' for 'soul', the general direction is clear enough. "Indeed, it is nothing else but life which doth principally form the soul".[2] This is coming close to the "breath of life" of Genesis 2 :7, which brings the soul into existence but yet is not the soul itself.[3] Nemesius concludes that man is created mortal, but with "potential ability to become immortal".[4] At least two elements crucial to mortalist argument are evident in Nemesius as presented for seventeenth-century consideration: man's potential for immortality, and the proposition that the soul is not an entity that can function apart from the body. Presumably Wither was aware of the theological implications of all this when he translated Nemesius' work, calling it "a useful tract", but covering himself with the claim that the Hebrew view of man was that he was "neither altogether mortal, neither wholly immortal, but, as it were, in a state between".[5]

Perhaps the most well-known mortalist in the years between Wightman and Overton was Thomas Browne, physician, and author of the celebrated *Religio Medici*. The *Religio* was first published in 1642,[6] and went through thirty-three editions in English between then and the end of the nineteenth century. It was probably written in the mid-1630s while Browne was still a relatively young man. He referred later to his "greener studies" which had been "polluted" with two or three errors, the "first" and most notable of which being "that the souls of men perished with their bodies, but should yet be raised again at the last

1. *Ibid.,* 132-3.
2. *Ibid.,* 135.
3. "And the Lord God formed man of the dust of the ground, and breathed into his nostrils the breath of life; and man became a living soul", Gen. 2:7.
4. Wither (tr.), *Nature of Man,* 26.
5. *Ibid.,* 24.
6. The 1642 edition was not authorised by Browne, who had originally written the *Religio* without thought of publication.

day".[1] This is clearly thnetopsychism, and although Browne later retreated from it in favour of something less well-defined, "a mystery, without a rigid definition",[2] his earlier views are not likely to have passed unnoticed, either in England or on the Continent, where the *Religio Medici* was soon translated into Latin, Dutch, French and German. In it Browne compares death to sleep, and speaks positively of the security which the last sleep gives to the trusting believer:

> Sleepe is a death, O make me try,
> By sleeping what it is to die;
> And as gently lay my head
> On my grave, as now my bed.
> Now ere I rest, great God let me
> Awake againe at last with thee.
> And thus assur'd, behold I lie
> Securely, or to wake or die.
> These are my drowsie dayes, in vaine
> I do now wake to sleepe againe.
> O come that houre, when I shall never
> Sleepe againe, but wake for ever!

This is the dormitive I take to bedward, I need no other *Laudanum* than this to make me sleepe; after which I close mine eyes in security, content to take my leave of the Sunne, and sleepe unto the resurrection.[3]

Even from his revised stance, Browne looks forward to the resurrection.

> I believe that our estranged and divided ashes shall unite again, that our separated dust after so many pilgrimages . . . shall at the voice of God . . . join again to make up their primary and predestinate forms.[4]

Browne compares the work of re-creation which will follow the resurrection with the original creation of man. At creation, Browne says, all the various species now known to man lay "in one masse 'till the powerful voice of God separated this united multitude into its several species".[5] So it will be at the last day. These "corrupted reliques", the bodies of the dead, transformed by decomposition and "after so many pilgrimages" into minerals, plants, animals, and elements, "scattered in the wilderness of formes" and having seemingly "forgot their proper habits", God will again "by a powerful voice

1. Thomas Browne, *Religio Medici* (1643), 11-12. This was the first edition authorised by Browne himself, but lacks the *Annotations* and Sir Kenelm Digby's *Observations* which appeared with later editions. C.A. Patrides believed that Digby was also a mortalist, C.A. Patrides, *Milton and the Christian Tradition* (Oxford, 1966), 265.
2. *Ibid.,* 19.
3. *Ibid.,* 175.
4. *Ibid.,* 108.
5. *Ibid.,* 109.

. . . command back into their proper shapes and call them out by their single individuals".[1] There is thus no need for concern about the continuity of individuality, even as there is no need for concern about the certainty of resurrection life itself. While the form of mortalism may no longer have appealed to the maturing Browne, the appeal of its substance remained clear enough.

Not everyone was convinced that Browne's break with mortalism was as clean as he claimed it had been. A contemporary, Alexander Ross, maintained that Browne was still tinged with mortalist thought ten years or more after the *Religio Medici* had first appeared, chiding him, "Your vessell retains yet the sent [*sic*] of that liquor with which at first it was seasoned".[2] It was an accusation that was difficult to substantiate, and in any case is largely immaterial. Regardless of how long he had clung to thnetopsychism or to what extent he later abandoned it, Browne was, as one critic of seventeenth-century thought has observed, indisputably a forerunner of Overton and Hobbes.[3] Their works, with others to follow, were soon to raise the mortalist/thnetopsychist temple on a much more substantial and enduring foundation. Browne himself is one of a very few in either seventeenth- or eighteenth-century England whose journey ultimately took him away from a clearly formulated mortalism towards the more traditional but less reasoned belief in the soul's separate existence and innate immortality.

Browne's departure from the mortalist fold probably passed unnoticed at the time. In retrospect it was cause enough for some concern. If he is to be understood correctly, the subjugation of reason to a vague faith that appeared little more than subjective feeling, was a major factor in his reversion to a traditional eschatology. "I am now content to understand a mystery", he wrote later, "without rigid definition. . . . Where I cannot satisfy my reason, I love to humour my fancy".[4] For convinced mortalists and honest enquirers alike, such words were not well chosen. It was precisely this attitude, the subordination of reason in favour of speculation, that so alarmed those who were convinced that reason was essential to the correct interpretation of the biblical revelation. Overton was to have something to say about reason and rationality, and John Locke would defend mortalism in the context of *The Reasonableness of Christianity*. Browne, it would appear, had taken several steps back in opting for fancy above reason.

Although the atypical mortalism of the Independent John Brayne appeared after Overton's *Mans Mortalitie* and therefore strictly speaking falls outside the period between Wightman and Overton, it may not be entirely inappropriate to include him here. Brayne first surfaced, in Anglican garb, as curate of

1. *Ibid.,* 108-9.
2. Alexander Ross, *Medicus Medicatus* (1645), 11.
3. G. Williamson, *Seventeenth Century Contexts* (Chicago,1961), 148.
4. Browne, *Religio Medici,*19.

Hemel Hempstead in 1640 and then as rector of Newland St. Lawrence in Essex[1] before reappearing in the West Country as the Independent minister at Highweek in Devon and Lymington (Limington) in Somerset in 1647 and 1648 respectively.[2] By then, or shortly thereafter, his sympathies had aligned with the theological left, perhaps even as a Seeker.[3] In 1654 Brayne published *The Unknown Being of the Spirit, Soul, and Body Anatomized*, in which he took issue with many "falsely translated" and "corruptly interpreted"[4] texts relating to the nature of man.

Brayne contended that the darkness which prevailed concerning man over the "true nature of his being", both in life and after death, was "very great",[5] and attempted to shed some light on the matter although, it must be conceded, not entirely with success. He recognised the existence of both psychopannychism and thnetopsychism at the mid-point of the seventeenth century, claiming that either view was compatible with authentic Christian doctrine. "There is no destruction of the faith whether we understand one or the other", he declared.[6] Brayne himself held that at creation God had breathed into Adam the "breath of lives"(not "of life", as "corrupt" translations read), thereby giving life to the spirit, the soul, and the body, the breath acting as "a ligament by which spirit, soul and body are kept together".[7] The soul, which is not immortal, is thus an entity created by the in-breathing of God, but returns at death not to God, but to the grave.[8] Brayne repudiated the doctrine of hell, believing that after death the souls of the righteous sleep in the grave awaiting the resurrection, but that unbelievers are totally dead, although "hell torments" follow the last judgment.[9] It seems clear enough that as the thoughts of Wither, Browne and Brayne were circulated and digested, and as the 1640s gave way to the 1650s, English mortalism was beginning to break through the mists that previously had so often obscured it.

1. A.G. Matthews(ed.), *Walker Revised* (Oxford, 1948), 204, s.v. John Taylor; 166, s.v. Edward Turner.
2. W.A. Shaw, *History of the English Church . . . 1640-1660* (1900), II, 448, 418.
3. *BDBR*, I, 91. Nigel Smith has no doubt that Brayne was a Seeker by the time he published *The Unknown Being* in 1654, N. Smith, *Perfection Proclaimed* (Oxford, 1989), 272.
4. John Brayne, *The Unknown Being of the Spirit, Soul, and Body Anatomized. Wherein very many Scriptures falsely translated, and corruptly interpreted, are clearly explained* (1654).
5. *Ibid.*,1.
6. *Ibid.*, 50. The Westminster Confession of Faith, in affirming the traditional doctrine of the soul's immortality in 1647, also recognised the existence of both psychopannychism and thnetopsychism: "The bodies of men after death return to dust and corruption, but their souls (which neither die nor sleep), having an immortal subsistence, immediately return to God who gave them", Article XXXII.
7. Brayne, *The Unknown Being*, 3, 4.
8. *Ibid.*, 13.
9. *Ibid.*, 34, 38.

Early Socinian Advocates

The Socinianism with which Edward Wightman's mortalism had been linked in 1611 was not wholly atypical; a similar association appeared in early Continental mortalism, particularly in eastern Europe through the influence of Laelius and Faustus Socinus. Laelius visited England in the formative years of the English Reformation and was entertained by some of its leaders *c.*1547-8.[1] Sixteenth-century English Anabaptists were frequently seen as tinged with anti-Trinitarianism. But it is John Biddle who is usually held to have been the first to formally advocate Socinian thought in England with his publication of *XII Arguments* against the deity of the Holy Spirit in 1647 and his *Brevis Disqisitio* in 1653, a work which, as we shall shortly see, argued in favour of a mortalist eschatology. Yet Biddle was not the first to propose Socinian mortalism in seventeenth-century England. That had already been done in 1646, and from a quite unexpected direction.

Thomas Lushington, a graduate of Lincoln College, Oxford and later a high churchman of the Laudian school and chaplain to Richard Corbet, bishop of Oxford, had at one time tutored at Pembroke College where the young Thomas Browne had been one of his pupils. Lushington had received a DD degree in 1632, and in 1646 anonymously published a commentary on the epistle to the Hebrews, entitled *The Expiation of a Sinner*. Its unambiguous mortalism is perhaps one reason for its anonymity, although strong Socinian overtones may have been another. Lushington articulates as clearly as anyone the mortalist concept of death as a sleep:

> For when we are dead, and thereby void of all sense of time, the last moment of our life departing, and the first moment of our life returning (for return it shall at the last judgment) will seem one and the same to us at our rising again to life. They who lie in a deep sleep are not sensible of the time that passeth, though the time be very long; and death is a deeper sleep than any sleep of those that sleep alive.[2]

Lushington explained that the Scriptures sometimes speak as if we "were presently after our death translated to the Lord, and so to the joys of heaven", but this was only because they disregarded "the time intercurrent" between death and Christ's coming at the end.[3] In actual fact, the rewards of the righteous are not dispensed until the last day, "by hope of the future resurrection".[4] Of the 'soul' in Hebrews 10:39 Lushington says it signifies "only our life or our spirit, which is the principal part of us, being preserved for us and restored unto us".[5] Eternal life will be "bestowed upon us at the

1. *ODCC,* s.v. Socinus.
2. [Thomas Lushington], *The Expiation of a Sinner* (1646), 228.
3. *Ibid.*
4. *Ibid.,* 239, 283.
5. *Ibid.,* 241.

end of the world", at the "consummation of this present age".[1]

Lushington's work was fiercely attacked by Edmund Porter in *God Incarnate* (1655). Porter condemned it as "a most blasphemous book", both on account of its alleged Socinianism and its mortalism, which "laid the axe to the root and foundation" of the Christian faith.[2] He pointed out that Lushington's work was not original, but in fact the translation of a work by Johannes Crellius (or Krell), Professor of Greek and minister at Rakov in Poland, "the most distinguished scholar among the Socinians", in the words of a later critic.[3] Porter maintained that Lushington had deliberately concealed both his own name and that of the original author, and entitled a chapter of his own work "The Immortality of Men's Souls", setting out to show "against this commentator" that "men's souls die not with their bodies".[4] Porter charged Lushington, "You believe that our souls die with our bodies", looking to the resurrection "by which you reinforce your doctrine of the soul's mortality".[5] Given the clarity of Lushington's mortalism it would have been a difficult charge for him to refute, even if he had wished to do so. In the event, Lushington's commentary on Hebrews was republished in 1655 with the initials 'T. L.' on the title page, but it was a classic instance of shutting the stable door too late. Lushington never recovered from the taint of Socinianism. His thnetopsychist mortalism has escaped attention hitherto, but clearly it cannot be doubted.

No doubt at all attaches to either the Socinianism or the mortalism of John Biddle (or Bidle), an ex-Baptist and the "father of English Unitarianism".[6] It is perhaps unsurprising to discover that he was a mortalist, strongly opposed to the doctrine of the soul's immortality as were many of his Socinian predecessors on the Continent and many of his English Baptist contemporaries. An able scholar and a graduate of Magdalen College, Oxford, Biddle had first been accused of anti-trinitarian heresy in 1644 and thereafter was frequently to suffer imprisonment for his views during the 1640s and 1650s, until he eventually died in gaol in 1662. Froom cites Biddle's *A Twofold Catechism* of 1654 as

1. *Ibid.*, 286.
2. Edmund Porter, *Theos Anthropophros, or God Incarnate. Shewing that Jesus Christ is the Onely, and the Most High God* (1655), Ep. Ded., sig. A 4 r, dated March 1647.
3. *Ibid.*, sig. A 7 r; Wilbur, *History of Unitarianism*, 426. McLachlan, following Porter, saw this as the first translation of a Socinian work into English, H.J. McLachlan, *Socinianism in Seventeenth-Century England* (Oxford, 1951), 108. On Lushington, whom McLachlan claimed as a Socinian, see *Socinianism*, pp. 108-117, although he does not recognise Lushington's mortalism or that of any other Socinian. McLachlan confirms that Lushington had been tutor to Sir Thomas Browne. On Crellius and his influence in England, see A. Gordon, *Cheshire Classis Minutes 1691-1745* (1919), 138, 166 and Keeble and Nuttall, *Correspondence of Richard Baxter*, I, 102.
4. Porter, *God Incarnate*, 23.
5. *Ibid.*
6. *BDBR*, I, 63. See also McLachlan, *Socinianism*, 161-217, but again with no mention of Biddle's mortalism.

evidence of his conditionalism,[1] but apart from a rebuttal of the doctrines of hell and eternal punishment, it is hard to find mortalism in any form in this work. Burns rightly finds it in the *Brevis Disquisitio*, published a year earlier in 1653, but does not explore it at any length.[2] Thomas Lushington aside, Burns is also correct in pointing out that Socinianism did not figure significantly in the development of English mortalism "until the Unitarian Joseph Priestley advocated thnetopsychism in the second half of the eighteenth century".[3] The correctness of this conclusion does not compensate, however, for Burns' failure to recognise the significance of the *Brevis Disquisitio* as an important contribution to the mortalist debate and the fullness of Biddle's own mortalist convictions as reflected there. Biddle's writings are said to have attracted considerable attention in their day.[4]

The *Brevis Disquisitio* was in fact a translation of the German Socinian Joachim Stegmann's earlier work of the same title published in Latin in 1633, and denounced by a committee of the House of Lords in 1641 as a "dangerous book".[5] As in the case of Lushington, Biddle's work gives no indication that it was a translation or that he was not the author. Be that as it may, the *Brevis Disquisitio* explored the question "whether the dead do properly live", a proposition which the author asserted was the ground "of the greatest errors among the Papists".[6] The English title of Biddle's translation showed his Protestant sympathies and his desire that mainstream Protestantism would rid itself of all remaining "notorious errors" that were a legacy of medieval papal doctrine: *A Brief Enquiry Touching a Better Way . . . to refute Papists and reduce Protestants to Certainty and Unity in Religion.*[7] Biddle, with Stegmann, believed that Protestantism had, to its detriment and confusion, only selectively discarded non-biblical doctrines which had originated in Roman dogma.[8]

Nowhere was this more evident than in the matter of death and the existence of the soul. "They suppose that the souls of men in that very moment wherein they are parted from their bodies by death are carried either to heaven, and do there feel heavenly joy, . . . or to hell, and are there tormented and excruciated [*sic*] with unquenchable fire".[9] But heavenly joy and hellish torment "cannot happen to anything which is not alive", the *Brevis* stated. Therefore "they [all immortalists] believe in effect that the dead live".[10] This is not only contrary to

1. *CFF*, II, 146-8.
2. *CM*, 142.
3. *Ibid.*
4. *DNB*, s.v. John Biddle.
5. *CM*, 142. On Stegmann and the *Brevis Disquisitio* see McLachlan, *Socinianism*, pp. 92-95, although again there is no mention of mortalism.
6. Biddle (tr.), *Brevis Disquisitio*, 26.
7. *Ibid.*, 2; title-page.
8. *Ibid.*, 3, 4.
9. *Ibid.*, 26.
10. *Ibid.*, 26-7.

Scripture correctly interpreted, but is also the basis of the Roman doctrines of purgatory, the invocation of saints and Mariolatry.[1] The fundamental issue is the nature of man which, rightly understood, is a harmonious interdependent union of soul and body, the one ineffective and dysfunctional without the other. "Is not living, dying, feeling, hearing, acting, proper to the whole man, or the compound of soul and body? Is not the body the instrument of the soul, without which it cannot perform her functions . . . ?"[2] Consequently "souls separated from bodies are neither dead nor live, and . . . enjoy no pleasure and feel no pain". And again, "Scripture saith that the dead are not, that the spirit returneth to him that gave it, and the spirits of the godly . . . are in the hand of God, but at the Resurrection they shall be joined with their bodies".[3] Any other view would be a denial of the teachings of Christ and Paul which "would be altogether fallacious if before the Resurrection they [the souls of the dead] felt heavenly joy".[4] This seems to be straightforward psychopannychism as distinct from Lushington's thnetopsychism, an interesting indication that perhaps both versions of lingering Continental mortalism were mediated to the English scene via nascent Socinianism in the mid-seventeenth century.

The Evidence of Opponents
Before we come specifically to the mid-century Baptist mortalists and to the earlier seventeenth-century Baptist leaning to mortalism, it may be helpful to note the views of contemporary heresiographers. They regarded mortalism as a seductive heresy to be avoided at all costs. While the caveat that their testimony may not always be reliable is justified, the fact that so many of them warn consistently of the dangers of mortalism cannot be overlooked. Mortalism, it might be said, was a fact of life and in facing it its antagonists demonstrated that it had not simply mushroomed overnight and that now it needed to be dealt with. To a man, the more prominent heresiographers of the time were Presbyterian and regarded mortalism as one of many serious deviations from doctrinal orthodoxy which could be properly contained only by the establishment of a national church, Presbyterian of course, and the weight of doctrinal uniformity. As time has demonstrated their protests were too late. The winds of heterodoxy had been blowing for too long and the seeds of mortalism which had taken firm root were already beginning to bear fruit.

Thus in 1645 Alexander Ross complained about Thomas Browne's youthful mortalist opinions, refusing to see "anything Christian in the Christian mortalist positon"[5] and extravagantly concluding that the souls of mortalists themselves were "fitter to dwell with Nebuchadnezzar's in a beasts body, then

1. *Ibid.*, 27.
2. *Ibid.*, 28-9.
3. *Ibid.*, 29.
4. *Ibid.*, 27.
5. Ross, *Medicus Medicatus*, 11; *CM*, 157.

[*sic*] in their own. . . . ."[1] Shortly thereafter, and with a little more discretion and objectivity, Ross listed the doctrines held by the English Independent Church in Holland, suggesting that their errors had already crossed the Channel and were influencing Independent thought at home. "They teach that the soul is mortal, that just men's souls go not into heaven till the last day, . . . also that the souls of the wicked go not before the last judgment into hell."[2] A contemporary, Ephraim Pagitt, recalled the antiquity of the mortalist error in his *Heresiography*, listing soul sleep as "an old and despicable heresy, raised in Arabia, about the time of Origen".[3] Robert Baillie, the Scottish commissioner to the Westminster Assembly and later principal of Glasgow University, also cited mortalism in 1645 as one of the more notable "errors of the time".[4] The ordinance which Parliament approved in May 1648, "for the preventing of the growth and spreading of Heresie and blasphemy" was obviously not without cause. Among many proscribed beliefs it specified mortalism. "That the soul of any man after death goeth neither to heaven or hell, but to purgatory, or that the soul of man dyeth or sleepeth when the body is dead",[5] were views that required punishment. Another Presbyterian, Thomas Hall, master of the grammar school at Kings Norton since 1629 and later curate there, published *The Pulpit Guarded*, a pastoral epistle warning against the danger of "sects and schisms"which might follow in the wake of false Anabaptist teaching, particularly "that the soul sleeps when it parts from the body, and goes neither to heaven or hell till the day of judgment; and that the souls of men are but terrestrial vapours like the life of beasts, perishing with the body".[6]

1. Alexander Ross, *The Philosophicall Touch-stone.. .*(1645), 127

2. Alexander Ross, *Pansebeia, or, A View of all Religions in the World* (2nd. edn,1655), 70. The 1ˢᵗ edn(1653) had listed "Soul sleepers, who . . . hold that the soul dieth or sleepeth with the body", 411-12.

3. Ephraim Pagitt, *Heresiography, or, A description of the Hereticks and Sectaries of these Latter Times* (3ʳᵈ edn,1649), 148. Mosheim, citing Eusebius, *Ecclesiastical History*, I, vi, 37, designated third-century mortalists as "Arabians", indicating that their mortalism was thnetopsychist, J. L. von Mosheim, *Institutes of Ecclesiastical History* (ed. H. Soames, 1841), I, 270. Humphrey Hody, the seventeenth-century historian, claimed that psychopannychism also flourished in the third century, *The Resurrection of the (Same) Body Asserted* (1694), 211-12.

4. Robert Baillie, *A Dissuasive from the Errours of the Time* (1645), 81-2.

5. "An Ordinance of the Lords and Commons Assembled in Parliament for Punishing Blasphemies and Heresies" (1648), in [John Biddle], *The Spirit of Persecution Again Broken Loose* (1655), 14,18. See also C. H. Firth and R. S. Rait (eds.), *Acts and Ordinances of the Interregnum, 1642-1660,* I (1911), 1133-6.

6. [Thomas Hall], *The Pulpit Guarded with XX Arguments Proving the Unlawfulness, Sinfulness and Danger of Suffering Private Persons to take upon them Publicke Preaching* (1651), fol. c2 r. Apparently two editions of *The Pulpit Guarded* were published in 1651, this and one with *XVII Arguments* in the title. The Bodleian Library copy of the edition quoted here is emended with the author's own notes, suggesting that a third edition might have been intended.

By far the most important of the mid-century heresiographers as a source of information about contemporary mortalism is Thomas Edwards, author of the now well-known *Gangraena*, in which he catalogued the many "Errors, Heresies, Blasphemies and pernicious Practices"of the times. The *Gangraena* first appeared in 1646, just a year after Ross, Pagitt and Baillie had all inveighed against the mortalist threat. Edwards, another ardent Presbyterian, had been known at Cambridge as "young Luther" on account of his reforming zeal.[1] That zeal manifested itself in the diligence with which he painstakingly sought out, listed and described the many heresies which alarmingly threatened the body of Christ with disease and death.[2] Judged by the evidence available from other contemporary sources, Edwards's account, although intemperate at times, seems in substance accurate enough, certainly with regard to mortalism, the errors of which, in one form or another, are clearly enunciated:

> 21. That the soul dies with the body, and all things shall have an end, but God only shall remain for ever.
> 83. That the soul of man is mortal as the soul of a beast, and dies with the body.
> 84. That the souls of the faithfull after death, do sleep til the day of judgement, and are not in a capacity of acting any thing for God, but 'tis with them as 'tis with a man that is in some pleasing dreame.
> 85. That the bodies of the faithful shall not rise again at the resurrection (namely the same that died) but their soules shall have other bodies made fit for them, either by creation or faction from some pre-existing matter, and though the bodies be new, yet the men are the same, because the same souls remain still.
> 88. That none of the soules of the Saints go to Heaven where Christ is, but Heaven is empty of the Saints till the resurrection of the dead.
> 173. No man is yet in hell, neither shall any be there until the judgement, for God doth not hang first, and judge after.[3]

Burns comments that it was in Edwards's interest "to multiply the errors of the sects by making fine distinctions where none were called for".[4] That may have

1. *DNB*, s.v. Thomas Edwards.
2. Jonathan Scott believes that the mid-seventeenth-century religious scene in which sectarianism and heterodoxy blossomed was for the conservative Edwards "the death of reformation", Jonathan Scott, *England's troubles* (Cambridge, 2000), 229, 237. (Cf. p. 84, n. 1.)
3. Thomas Edwards, *The First and Second Part of Gangraena: or, A Catalogue and Discovery of many of the Errors, Heresies, Blasphemies and pernicious Practices of the Sectaries of this time, vented and acted in England in these four last years* (3rd. edn, 1646), 17, 22-3, 31. Error no. 21 probably refers to annihilationism. Error no. 83 is more likely to refer to thnetopsychism, despite its lack of reference to a future resurrection, see *CM*, 74.
4. *CM*, 73.

been true in general. As far as mortalism was concerned, Edwards's analysis seems objective enough.[1]

Edwards also cites two letters from one of his correspondents, a Thomas Sidebotham, who admitted that his doubts about the immortality of the soul arose from the lack of proof available in the Scriptures, which to him appeared to affirm the mortality of man. "In them I cannot find that man or any part of man is immortal, but that he is wholly mortal", Sidebotham claimed, man thus ceasing "to have any lively being betwixt Death and the Resurrection".[2] It was, as we have already observed, one of the most frequently repeated mortalist arguments. Edwards further records a public debate that took place in London in 1646 regarding the mortality/immortality question, with Richard Overton acting as moderator over the proposition "That God made man, and every part of man of the dust of the earth, and therefore man, and every part of man must return to the dust again".[3] The chief protagonists were "Lam and Battee", who Burns identifies, probably correctly, as Thomas Lamb and John Batty, both General Baptists, with Batty a member of Lamb's congregation, and from which he deduces that mortalism was a matter of some importance, and some potential divisiveness, among General Baptists in the 1640s.[4] No-one who is familiar with the literature and the times can doubt that Edwards, while always antagonistic and sometimes excessive, is essentially fair with his representation of mortalism as it came to him through the eyes and ears of his informants. We shall shortly call on him again as the story of mid-seventeenth-century mortalism unfolds, largely, but not entirely, among the ranks of General Baptists.

Baptists and Baptist Confessions of Faith

The predisposition to Anabaptist beliefs on the part of many early Protestants in Kent and Sussex in the sixteenth century and the concurrent appearance there of mortalist convictions laid the foundation for the later and more open

1. Scott notes the "historical importance" of *Gangraena* in the context of Christopher Hill's defence of its essential accuracy, Scott, *England's troubles*, 238. Cf. Hill, *The World Turned Upside Down* (1975), *passim*, where he cites Edwards frequently without apparent reservation.
2. Thomas Edwards, *The third Part of Gangraena, or A new and higher Discovery of the Errors, Heresies, Blasphemies, and insolent Proceedings of the Sectaries of these Times* (1646), 66-7.
3. Edwards, *The Second Part of Gangraena*, 15.
4. *Ibid.*, 14-15; *CM*, 131. Edwards mentions another member of Thomas Lamb's church, a Mrs. Attaway, who was said to believe in the soul's mortality, linking it to a radical millenarian eschatology which justified her in deserting her family and running away with a fellow-believer, William Jenney, who also left wife and family, in the hope that they would never die but live eternally with Christ and the redeemed saints in the New Jerusalem, soon to be established on earth, *Gangraena*, I, 115; II, 9; III, 26-7.

advocacy of thorough-going mortalist theology. We must now examine some
of the more definitive evidence relating to seventeenth-century mortalist belief
among Baptists most, but not all of whom, were General Baptists and many
of whom were from Kent or had Kentish connections. This does not deny the
existence of mortalism among Baptists elsewhere, of course, but it does verify
the significance of the South-East of the country as a stronghold of opposition
to the traditional doctrine of the soul's immortality. During the middle decades
of the seventeenth century several prominent Baptists from counties in the
South-East adopted mortalism as a more biblical alternative to the traditional
eschatology, many of them publishing their new understandings in the context
of vigorous and sometimes divisive debate.

Samuel Richardson is best known for his strong stance against the doctrine
of hell, published in 1658 under the title *Of the Torments of Hell*, an important
work in the continuing attack on eternal torment, which was reprinted several
times through the seventeenth and eighteenth centuries.[1] Whitley points out
that Richardson held many public offices during the Interregnum and that
he was a member of the first Particular Baptist church at Walthamstow under
the leadership of John Spilsbury in the early 1640s.[2] It was about then that
he began to write and publish. Whitley lists twelve works under his name
between 1643 and 1658. Underwood called him "one of the shrewdest and
most influential Baptist leaders in the capital".[3] His mortalist views began to
appear tentatively in his first known work, *The Life of Faith*, published in 1643,
where he indicates that immortality is dependent on the resurrection, "Then .
. . we shall have full and sweet rest . . . and everlasting life. Then shall I never
die or end, but am eternal for (the) duration [sic] . . .".[4] In *The Saints Desire*
(1647), dedicated to Oliver Cromwell and Sir Thomas Fairfax, Richardson
declares that the word 'soul' in Scripture means "the whole man".[5] The later
Torments of Hell is wholly compatible with a fully-developed mortalist theology.
Appealing to the eminent sixteenth-century Cambridge Puritan theologian,
William Fulke, among others, Richardson challenges the creedal affirmation of
Christ's descent into hell and argues again that the Hebrew and Greek words
sheol and *hades* refer only to the grave.[6] While none of Richardson's works,
including the *Torments of Hell*, are full expositions of mortalist thought as such,
the concept of the wholeness of man is crucial to his mortalist understanding
of human existence now and in the future.

At about the same time as Richardson's early works were being published,

1. [Samuel Richardson], *Of the Torments of Hell* (1658); reprinted in 1660, 1707,
   1720, and 1754; *BB*, I, 70.
2. *BB*, I, 226; W.T. Whitley, *The Baptists of London* [1928], 103.
3. A.C. Underwood, *A History of the English Baptists* (1947), 78.
4. Samuel Richardson, *The Life of Faith* (1643),12-13.
5. Samuel Richardson, *The Saints Desire* (1647), 3.
6. [Richardson], *Torments*, 5. Fulke was a Cambridge contemporary of Hugh Broughton,
   who had similarly explained the meaning of *sheol* and *hades*, see above, p. 72-73 .

William Bowling of Cranbrook in Kent appears for the first time through Thomas Edwards's *Gangraena*. Burns feels that Bowling's opinions are not clear enough to identify him as a Baptist, although his reported views on hell were similar to Richardson's and his Christology and eschatology would have found favour with many Baptists of the time.[1] Cranbrook was later to become a centre of General Baptist activity, and Patrick Collinson points out that Protestantism had been established there on an "old Lollard tradition" and that disenchantment with established religion in the form of frequent conventicles had marked Cranbrook's early Protestant experience.[2] The least that can be said is that Bowling would have sympathised with Baptists even if he did not readily identify with them, which he might well have done in any case, since the evidence is inconclusive. Edwards's informant reported that Bowling believed that God alone was immortal, the souls of "devils and all other men" being mortal "as well as their bodies".[3] Ecclesiastes 12:7, a frequently-quoted text, was not to be understood "as if the soul after death was really separated from the body" because "the souls of men rest in the grave with their bodies till the Resurrection, and then Christ raises up both together".[4] The doctrine of hell was unacceptable because it would be inconsistent and contrary to reason for God "to punish the souls of the wicked in Hell while their bodies lay at rest in their graves".[5] Evidently Bowling believed with other mortalists that the soul, the whole man, came into existence through the creative in-breathing of God. The alternative view that the breath of God *was* the soul presented a major difficulty for immortalists in that, as part of God it would like Him be immortal, and so in the case of the reprobate would be "eternally tormented in Hell".[6] The arguments were not always as lucid or as compelling as they might have been, particularly when reported by adversaries, but mortalists felt that the same could be said of those arguments which were used to support the immortality of the soul.

Another contemporary of Richardson and Bowling was the radical Clement Writer (or Wrighter), believed to be from Worcestershire, but with connections in London and the home counties. According to Edwards, Writer had originally been a Presbyterian, then a Separatist, and later turned to "Anabaptism and Arminianism".[7] Such a meandering spiritual journey was not uncommon in the turbulent years of the Commonwealth and Interregnum. Edwards adds that Writer later adopted mortalism, "holding the Soul Mortal: . . . After that he fell to be a Seeker, and is now an anti-scripturist, a questionist and

1. *CM*, 134; Edwards, *Gangraena*, III, 35-6.
2. Patrick Collinson, *The Elizabethan Puritan Movement* (1967), 96, 140, 380.
3. Edwards, *Gangraena*, III, 36.
4. *Ibid.*, 37.
5. *Ibid.*
6. *Ibid.*, 36.
7. *Ibid.*, part I, 27 (the second so numbered).

sceptic, and I fear an atheist".[1] This was in 1646, but Edwards's tendency to excess appears to have got the better of him in this instance, for Writer's own testimony contradicts these severe judgments, even though Richard Baxter also thought that Writer was an "infidel"and an "apostate".[2] It is more likely that he was initially a General Baptist,[3] and that subsequently he explored Leveller and Seeker views, perhaps finding some compatibility with the latter[4] and parting company with the General Baptists. While he undoubtedly had questions about the Bible, its origin and the way it was frequently interpreted by those formally trained for ministry at university, this is not enough to charge him with atheism and infidelity, particularly since he appeals to Scripture as opposed to philosophy to support his mortalist convictions. Writer quotes with approval his contemporary John Brayne, who chides those who "run to philosophy . . . to prove the soul immortal against the Scripture".[5]

Most of Writer's published works appeared in the 1650s, although Edwards had noted his mortalism ten or twelve years earlier. Edwards claimed, in fact, that Writer had provided significant input to Richard Overton's *Mans Mortalitie* which, we recall, had been published in 1644.[6] Whether or not that was the case is difficult to determine. What is beyond doubt is Writer's own mortalism, even though it did not come clearly into the light for another decade. Writer took issue with "learned ministers" in the mainstream Reformation tradition since they had, in his view, capitulated to medieval Catholic theology in the matter of the soul and its condition after death. Writer claimed that Augustine, Tertullian and Jerome had all taught "that the soul and body are both one, and are not to be distinguished", and that Jerome maintained in his day that "the greatest part of the West" were "of the same opinion".[7]

From his reading of the Bible, Writer came to believe that the present life was probationary and preparatory, a time in which believers in Christ could look to the future in hope of the life to come, which Christ would bring to reality at His second coming:

1. *Ibid.*
2. Keeble and Nuttall, *Correspondence of Richard Baxter,* I, 193, 338. Baxter's *The Unreasonableness of Infidelity* (1655) originated from his correspondence with Writer.
3. Perhaps of Thomas Lamb's church, although the usually thorough Whitley does not mention him or any of his works, see *BB,* I.
4. Cf. *BDBR,* 3 (1984), 345. Edwards claimed that he was a leading figure in the church led by Blunt and "Emmes"[sic], "one of the first and prime churches of Anabaptists now in these latter times", *Gangraena,* III, 112. Blunt may be Richard Blunt, who in 1642 led a group of Particular Baptists, B.R. White, *The English Baptists of the Seventeenth Century* (1983), 59-60. Emmes remains unidentified. On Writer, see also *ODNB*.
5. Clement Writer, *Fides Divina* (1657), 108.
6. Edwards, *Gangraena,* I, 27 (the second so numbered).
7. [Clement Writer], *The Jus Divinum of Presbyterie* (2nd.edn,1655), 36.

> This whole life is the time for the Saints and righteous to suffer in,
> for, and in hope of reward and rest in that Kingdom with Christ at his
> coming, 2 Thess. 1:4-9. But these men (distorters of Scripture) would fain
> be reaping before harvest, and before the time of sowing is ended, and be
> reigning in that kingdom before the blessed patriarchs and apostles who
> yet sleep in the dust and who were to be prime heirs and inheritors with
> Christ of that kingdom.[1]

The idea of a triumphant church in heaven prior to the last judgment, so
widely held in contemporary orthodox circles, was unbiblical and erroneous,
"for the making good whereof they teach us that the souls of the righteous
ascend immediately into heaven to God, there to partake of present bliss and
glory".[2] The case of the thief on the cross was proof of this assertion, since
in the traditional view "the soul of the penitent thief went immediately into
Paradise". It was bad exegesis in Writer's view, and he adds with a touch of
irony, "whither no doubt the souls of many penitent theeves [sic] have gone
since".[3] It is quite evident from all the foregoing that Writer's concerns were
not with the Bible itself, but with its interpretation, and to say that he was an
"antiscripturist"[4] is quite as unjustified as labelling him an "atheist" or doubting
his preference for a mortalist eschatology.

Other contemporaries of Writer, Richardson and Bowling included Matthew
Caffyn of Southwater near Horsham in Sussex and George Hammon of
Cranbrook and Biddenden in Kent,[5] both General Baptists. By the mid 1650s
the General Baptists from Buckinghamshire, Hertfordshire and adjoining
counties were looking askance at those from Kent and Sussex who, they
believed, were flirting again with heresies coming in from the Continent, now
under their zealous young leader, Matthew Caffyn.[6] Caffyn's mortalism, one of
several perceived doctrinal deviations, had been worked out and made known
by 1655, when he was still only twenty-seven. Whitley noted Caffyn's longevity,
"a life abnormally prolonged", and his enduring influence on the General
Baptist churches in Kent and Sussex well into the eighteenth century.[7] The
1701 pamphlet *The Vail Turned Aside* accused Caffyn of spreading Socinianism
throughout Kent, Sussex and London.[8] While the charge was somewhat

1. Writer, *Fides Divina*, 99.
2. [Clement Writer], *An Apologetical Narration, or a Just and Necessary Vindication of Clement Writer* (n.d.), 12. This work was written in the context of Writer's clash with Baxter.
3. *Ibid.*
4. *DNB*, s.v. Clement Writer.
5. Hammon's views will be considered in the next chapter.
6. A.H.J. Baines, *The Signatories of the Orthodox Confession of 1679* (1960), 5-11, although Baines does not mention Caffyn's mortalism. See also White, *English Baptists,* 21-2.
7. W.T. Whitley, *A History of British Baptists* (1923), 172.
8. *ODNB*, s.v. Matthew Caffyn.

exaggerated, there can be little doubt that Caffyn's unorthodox Christology as well as his mortalism were the cause of much concern and some division within General Baptist ranks later in the seventeenth century.[1]

In his earlier years Caffyn had clashed with the Quaker, Thomas Lawson, who had accused him of believing that "no man hath eternal life now in him . . . but a promise of it" to come, that no man, not even "the chief of saints" is yet in the kingdom, but has it "by promise", and that Adam, subsequent to eating of the forbidden fruit, "was in a dying condition, growing nearer the time in the which he should be put in an hole in the earth".[2] This was a fair comment, it seems, on Caffyn's position. In his published reply to Lawson, Caffyn emphasised that the future rewards of the righteous would be dispensed at the second coming of Christ and the general resurrection, as opposed to the Quaker view of an already 'realised' eschatology.[3] The Quaker teaching that "Christ is already come the second time", "within the believer", was a denial of the resurrection at the end of time.[4] Caffyn proceeds to outline the biblical sequence of last-day events, Christ's coming, the resurrection of the dead, the last judgment and eternal rewards, as the true pathway to eternal life.[5] "Christ Jesus, who is our life . . . shall appear, THEN shall we appear with Him in glory . . . , Col. iii: 4". The saints inheritance is "RESERVED in heaven" for them, I Pet. 1:4. "Henceforth (saith Paul) there is LAID UP for me a crown of righteousness, II Tim. iv: 8".[6] Biblical eschatology consistently emphasises that future rewards are given at the last day, rather than immediately after death, and Caffyn complains that the "apprehension of present possession of eternal life . . . destroys the truth" of future rewards.[7]

Against this background we may now consider Baptist confessions of faith which appeared between 1644 and 1660. Both Particular and General Baptists published confessions when they felt it was safe or necessary to do so. Compared to other confessions of the time, the Westminster Confession, for example, or even later Baptist confessions, which either specifically assert the immortality of the soul and its transition to heaven at death, or specifically deny mortalist tenets, these earlier Baptist confessions are as revealing in what they do not say as in what they affirm. If silence can be said to be eloquent, it may well be so here. There is no reference in any Baptist confession before 1677 to

1. *Ibid.*; R. Brown, *The English Baptists of the Eighteenth Century* (1986), 21-2; *BB*, I, 219.
2. Thomas Lawson, *An Untaught Teacher Witnessed Against* (1655), 9. The "untaught teacher" was Caffyn, and Lawson's title may have been a jibe referring to Caffyn's claim to have been sent down from Oxford on account of his Nonconformity.
3. See my *A Great Expectation*, ch. 6, pp. 195-210, for a summary of contemporary Quaker eschatology.
4. Matthew Caffyn, *The Deceived and Deceiving Quakers Discovered* (1656), 29-30.
5. *Ibid.*, 29-41.
6. *Ibid.*, 42; emphases in the original.
7. *Ibid.*, 43.

the separate existence or immortality of the soul or to the immediate felicity of the righteous after death. On the contrary, all eschatological references to the future life of the redeemed are contained within a biblical eschatological framework of Christ's second coming, the resurrection of the just and the last judgment.

The first known Baptist confession of faith appeared in 1644, signed by fifteen representatives of seven Particular Baptist congregations in and around London. It reflected an earlier Separatist Calvinistic confession and was largely motivated by the need to distance Baptist theology from certain allegations of doctrinal unorthodoxy.[1] It referred to the natural human condition as being subject to death, eternal life as deriving from a knowledge of Christ, and the work of the Holy Spirit in nourishing "faith, repentance, love, joy, hope and all heavenly light in the soul unto immortality. . . ."[2] Clearly immortality was not an inherent possession but was nevertheless attainable. So the saints will "be raised by the power of Christ, in the day of resurrection, to reign with Christ".[3] The first General Baptist confession was that of thirty congregations in 1651, mostly in Lincolnshire and Leicestershire, motivated again by "pressing controversies of the day", and therefore probably not quite as broad and balanced as it otherwise might have been.[4] It contained seventy-five articles, not one of which referred specifically to eschatological events and touching only peripherally on the soul and its destiny. "God created or made Adam a living soul, in his own likeness".[5] For those who were interested, or were sufficiently theologically aware, it may just have been enough to indicate a mortalist view of the nature of man.

Other confessions, both of Particular and General Baptists, soon appeared which were more eschatologically specific. The brief 1655 General Baptist confession of the Midland Association looked forward to "the time appointed of the Lord" when "the dead bodies of all men, just and unjust, shall rise again out of their graves (to) receive according to what they have done in their bodies, be it good or evil".[6] There is no thought here of rewards prior to the resurrection, although the terminology might be considered less than definitive.

1. White, *English Baptists*, 8, 58.
2. *The Confession of Faith of those Churches which are commonly (though falsly) called Anabaptists* (1644), Articles IV, VI and XIX. This, and the other Confessions referred to, are conveniently brought together in their original form in W. L. Lumpkin, *Baptist Confessions of Faith* (1959).
3. *Ibid.*, Article XL.
4. White, *English Baptists*, 44.
5. *The Faith and Practise of Thirty Congregations, Gathered According to the Primitive Pattern* (1651), Article 11. A crown of glory "in the life to come" is promised in Article 43.
6. *The Midland Association Confession* (1655), Article 16, more correctly referred to by its formal title, *Sixteen Articles of Faith and Order unanimously asserted to by the Messengers met at Warwick, the 3rd Day of the 3rd Month, 1655.*

In the next year the Particular Baptists of Somerset issued a lengthy confession of faith which in four articles spelt out in great detail the hopes which its signatories, and those they represented, held for the future. Again, there is no hint of heavenly glory for disembodied souls at death and the rewards of both the righteous and the damned are still held to be in the future:

> XXXIX. That it is our assured expectation, grounded upon the promises, that the Lord Jesus Christ shall the second time appear without sin unto salvation, unto his people, to raise and change the vile bodies of all his saints, to fashion them like unto his glorious body, and so to reign with him, and judge over all nations on the earth in power and glory.
>
> XL. That there is a day appointed when the Lord shall raise the unjust as well as the righteous, and judge them all in righteousness . . . every man in his own order . . . taking vengeance on them that know not God and obey not the gospel of our Lord Jesus Christ, whose punishment will be everlasting destruction from the presence of the Lord.
>
> XLI. That there is a place into which the Lord will gather all his elect, to enjoy him for ever, usually in Scripture called heaven. . . .
>
> XLII. That there is a place into which the Lord will cast the devil, his angels and wicked men, to be tormented for ever . . . usually in Scripture called hell. . . .[1]

The conference which produced this confession in 1656 was presided over by Thomas Collier, whose passive millenarianism would readily have endorsed such expectations.[2]

In 1660 the General Baptists produced a "brief" confession, which Dr. B.R. White claims was the "most widely used General Baptist statement of faith" for the next generation. It was endorsed by forty-one signatories, half of whom were from London and Kent,[3] including Matthew Caffyn and George Hammon. Like the 1656 Particular Baptist confession, it emphasised that the future life and glory of the saints depended on Christ and His resurrection from the dead, again making no reference to the soul's innate immortality or survival after death. Having stated in Article 1 that by the Fall man "came into a miserable and mortal estate", Articles 20-22 set out the gospel hope:

> XX. That there shall be (through Christ who was dead, but is alive again from the dead) a Resurrection of all men from the graves of the Earth, Isa. 26:19. both the just and the unjust, Acts 24.15. that is, the fleshly bodies of men, sown into the graves of the earth, corruptible [sic], dishonourable, weak, natural . . . shall be raised again, incorruptable [sic], in glory, in power, spiritual, and so considered, the bodies of the Saints

1. *A Confession of Faith of several congregations of Christ in the county of Somerset, and some churches in the counties near against* (1656), Articles XXXIX, XL, XLI, XLII.
2. B.S. Capp, *The Fifth Monarchy Men* (1972), 79, 90.
3. White, *English Baptists*, 54, 95.

(united again to their spirits) which here suffer for Christ, shall inherit the Kingdom, reigning together with Christ, I Cor. 15. 21, 22, 42, 43, 44, 49.

XXI. That there shall be after the Resurrection from the graves of the Earth, An eternal judgement, at the appearing of Christ, and his Kingdom, 2 Tim. 4.1. Heb. 9. 27. at which time of judgement which is unalterable, and irrevocable, every man shall receive according to the things done in his body, 2 Cor. 5. 10.

XXII. That the same Lord Jesus who shewed himself alive after his passion, by many infallible proofs, Acts 1.3. which was taken up from the Disciples, and carried up into Heaven, Luke 24.51. Shall so come in like manner as he was seen go into heaven, Acts 1.9.10.11. And when Christ who is our life shall appear, we shall also appear with him in glory, Col. 3.4. . . . when Christ shall appear, then shall be their (the saints) day . . . then shall they receive a Crown of life, which no man shall take from them. . . . "[1]

White is probably correct in pointing out that this confession did not represent General Baptists as a whole, but its own inherent claim to have been "owned and approved by more than 20,000"[2] is some indication of General Baptist strength and perhaps of a preference for that type of eschatology already endorsed by Matthew Caffyn and George Hammon. It also gives some substance to Mosheim's earlier generalisation that General Baptists believed "that the soul, between death and the resurrection at the last day, has neither pleasure nor pain, but is in a state of insensibility".[3]

1660 is well past the mid-point of the seventeenth century and the relative freedom of the 1640s and 1650s, but it is worth recalling that the 1660 General Baptist confession represented views that had been maturing, at least in some parts of the country, for several decades or longer. The exclusion of the soul's immortality as an article of belief cannot be dismissed as a careless oversight, particularly in a document that was to be presented to Charles II at the Restoration, and for which the signatories stated that they were willing to suffer persecution, loss of goods, and even life itself. We may be sure that the Confession had been worked and re-worked to ensure accuracy and consensus in all points. The soul's immortality was omitted because it was not deemed crucial, even biblical, and perhaps because the alternative was more acceptable to the majority of those whom the confession represented.

1. *A Brief Confession or Declaration of Faith* (1660), Articles XX, XXI, XXII. The use of the word "spirits" rather than "souls" in Article XX may not have been coincidental. It is unlikely that Caffyn or Hammon would have subscribed to a document that contradicted views which they both held.

2. White, *English Baptists*, 95; *A Brief Confession,* subscript.

3. Mosheim, *Ecclesiastical History*, III, 578.

The startling change in the eschatology of the 1679 so-called *Orthodox Creed: or A Protestant Confession of Faith*[1] is also worth noting. This confession, also of General Baptist origin, was drawn up in Buckinghamshire partly to counter the perceived doctrinal errors of the Caffynites in Kent and Sussex.[2] On the state of the dead the contrast between it and preceding Baptist confessions could not have been starker. Article 49, "Of the State of Man after Death, and of the Resurrection of the Dead", set out the traditional medieval view of the soul and the afterlife as clearly as any traditionalist could have desired, taking care to challenge quite specifically mortalist views:

> The bodies of men after death return to dust, and see corruption; but their souls, or spirits, which neither die nor sleep, having an immortal subsistence, immediately return to God who gave them; the souls of the righteous being then made perfect in holiness, are received into Paradise, where they are with Christ, and behold the face of God in light and glory, waiting for the full redemption of their bodies; and the souls of the wicked are cast into Hell, where they remain in torment and utter darkness, reserved to the judgment of the great day. And besides these two places for souls separated from their bodies, the holy Scripture mentions none.[3]

While much subsequent history, as well as the contemporary debate, has centred around the Christological issues involved in the formulation of this document, the mortalist element must not be forgotten, since it was clearly of significance to those who framed and endorsed it. The 1679 *Orthodox Creed* enjoyed only limited acceptance and Caffyn, still influential, shortly thereafter convinced the General Baptist General Assembly not to adopt it.[4] Later Baptist confessions would reflect the traditional views of the soul and death,[5] but mortalism had by then made its mark and with thanks to the seventeenth-century Baptists, in the main from Kent and Sussex, who had helped to make it possible, it would never again disappear from English religious thought.

1. It was, in fact, the confession of a relatively small number of General Baptist congregations in Buckinghamshire and Hertfordshire, supported by a few in Bedfordshire and Oxfordshire. Its rather pretentious title was in part intended to distance Baptist communities from any potential accusation of involvement in the Popish Plot of 1678 by asserting identity with the truths of the historic Christian Creeds of Nicaea and Chalcedon.
2. Baines, *Orthodox Confession*, 5; White, *English Baptists,* 21-2.
3. *An Orthodox Creed: or, A Protestant Confession of Faith* (1679), Article 49, 74-5.
4. *ODNB*, s.v. Matthew Caffyn.
5. On the relationship and similarity between the 1679 General Baptist Confession ("Creed") and the slightly earlier Particular Baptist *A Confession of Faith, Put forth by the Elders and Brethren of many Congregations of Christians (Baptized upon Profession of their Faith) in London and the Country* of 1677, see p. 110, n. 2.

Seventeenth-Century Anglican Probings

Most of the evidence for the existence of mortalism in the first half of the seventeenth century discussed in this chapter has come from the theological left wing, from Baptists and those who had seceded from the Baptist movement in preference for an even more radical theology. Few voices, if any, from the establishment have been heard in favour of the mortalism which Tyndale and Frith had propounded in the early days of the English Reformation. Ultimately, as we shall see, this apparent Anglican reluctance to entertain mortalist theology would be quite reversed, even though it would take another hundred years or so for that to happen. Yet even now, mid-way through the seventeenth century, there were hints of things to come. Thomas Lushington has already been noted in a Socinian context. He was, in fact, just as notable from an Anglican standpoint, being one of a very few known seventeenth-century Anglicans to venture into mortalist territory.

The respected Caroline divine and Oxford scholar, Edward Reynolds, later Bishop of Norwich, appears to have been another.[1] Reynolds explored the nature of man from a philosophical perspective, beginning his *Treatise of the Passions and Faculties of the Soul of Man* (1640) by arguing that the soul, "the reasonable part of man", is not independent in an "absolute" sense, but depends on its conjunction with the body in order to function.[2] The relationship of soul and body is similar to that of water being channelled through pipes.[3] For Reynolds, the soul is best understood as the mind. In a manner reminiscent of the sixteenth-century Paduan scholars and the Italian Evangelical Rationalists, Reynolds is openly Aristotelian in his defence of the soul's strong dependance on the body, but with the lapsarian annotation that the Fall wrought in man "a general corruption" which "did, amongst the rest, infatuate the mind and smother the soul with ignorance".[4] There are, in fact, two observable defects in the soul of man, natural imperfection and inequality, the former frequently accentuated by sickness or bodily weakness. "There is no more significant and lively expression of a vigorous or heavy soul, than a happy or ill-ordered body",[5] Reynolds says. It was the recognition of what much later would be known as the psychosomatic nature of man.

The soul, however, is not merely equatable with reason or the functions of the mind, nor is it in the final analysis totally dependent on the body. Through

---

1. In 1643 he was appointed to the Westminster Assembly as a Presbyterian, *ODCC*, s.v. Edward Reynolds, although he was regarded by More and Cross as a representative Anglican, P.E. More and F.L. Cross, *Anglicanism* (1962), 805. He received the see of Norwich in 1661.
2. Edward Reynolds, *A Treatise of the Passions and Faculties of the Soul of Man* (1640), 3, 4. The *Treatise* is now regarded as an important work in the study of early psychology, as well as an early statement on the essential relationship between mind and body.
3. *Ibid.*, 7.
4. *Ibid.*, 5.
5. *Ibid.*, 7.

faith and other "pious and religious operations" the soul may be "carried beyond the sphere of sense and transported unto more raised operations".[1] The functions and abilities of the soul, moreover, are mutable and subject to modification by education, custom and circumstance.[2] However, the soul ultimately is separable from the body and therefore not corrupt or mortal in the same way as the body, although the resurrection of the body is essential for the soul's eternal existence, being a "partaker" of the soul's glory and essential to it.[3] Reynolds also notes again the soul's limitations, "Our souls are not here noble enough to conceive what our bodies shall be there."[4] It is not entirely clear whether all this should be construed as psychopannychism or something less, or whether it is best understood as a moderate Anglican attempt to find a *via media* between the more extreme mortalist alternatives and the traditional view which appears to have been equally unsatisfactory. Certainly it does not sound like classic immortalism.

There is much less ambiguity in the anthropological and eschatological views of another prominent contemporary Anglican, Jeremy Taylor. Taylor, like his contemporary and fellow-bishop, Edward Reynolds, is cited by More and Cross in their discerning and enlightening analysis of the thought and practice of the Church of England in the seventeenth century as a representative spokesman of Anglican devotion and doctrine.[5] Prior to his appointment as bishop of Down and Connor in 1661 Taylor had been a respected Cambridge scholar, later widely known for his literary attainments and noted as a casuistical preacher. He was successively chaplain to William Laud and Charles I. We would not expect to find mortalism or any hint of it here. Yet Taylor's doctrine of man, his views on death and his emphasis on the resurrection as the way to eternal life would all have sat well on the lips of any recognised mortalist spokesman of the seventeenth or eighteenth centuries. Indeed, Fisch thought that Taylor shared "nearly all Milton's heresies", specifically his materialism and his mortalism.[6]

Taylor thinks more in terms of the whole man than of the individual soul. While the soul is to be thought of as a separate entity, it is incomplete and ineffective without the body. The man is the whole person and not merely, or even principally, the soul, which is "an incomplete substance" yet "a part

1. *Ibid.,* 8.
2. *Ibid.,* 10.
3. *Ibid.,* 408, 420, 428.
4. *Ibid.,* 429.
5. More and Cross, *Anglicanism,* 808. The inclusion of Reynolds and Taylor as representative Anglicans should remind us of the tolerance within the Anglican communion, even at this comparatively early stage, of divergent views on matters of considerable importance. Taylor, whose mortalism is really quite transparent, is one of the more frequently-quoted writers by More and Cross on other aspects of Anglican faith and practice.
6. Harold Fisch, *Jerusalem and Albion* (New York, 1964), 178, 152. See later, pp. 114ff for an analysis of Milton's own views.

of the whole man".[1] Further, "whatever is spoken of the soul considers it as an essential part of man, relating to his whole constitution, not as it is of itself an intellectual and separate substance". So in death "man is not". He is "dead".[2] The resurrection brings restitution, reconstitution of that which originally existed. It is "the restitution of our life, the renovation of the whole man".[3] Thus man does not live after death prior to the resurrection, even though the soul is a separate entity, because it cannot function apart from the body. It is the resurrection that brings man to life again. "All our hopes, all our felicities, depend upon the resurrection; without it we should never be persons [again], men or women."[4] And therefore of death and the separation of soul and body, "Then the state of separation could be nothing but a phantasme, trees ever in blossom, never bearing fruit, corn forever in the blade, eggs always in the shell".[5] For Taylor the resurrection provides an alternative hope every bit as certain and credible as that drawn by most of his contemporaries from the soul's immortality. Yet he believed that the souls of the faithful leave the body at death, and are "laid up" in the hands of God "till the day of recompense" to "rest in hope".[6] In another passage also reminiscent of Luther, Taylor speaks of the sleep of death "in which state we are unconcerned in all the changes of the world; and if our mothers or our nurses die, or if a wild boar destroy our vineyards, or our king be sick, we regard it not, but during that state are as disinterest [sic] as if our eyes were closed with the clay that weeps in the bowels of the earth".[7]

On the basis of such sentiments it would be entirely permissible to conclude that Taylor was a confirmed psychopannychist who has hitherto escaped notice. Certainly he reminds us that at the mid-point of the seventeenth century enquiring minds both within and without Anglicanism continued to be dissatisfied with traditional views of death and the soul, and that often only a very fine line was drawn between orthodoxy and heterodoxy as far as human nature and destiny were concerned.[8]

1. Taylor, *The Great Exemplar*, 564.
2. *Ibid.*, 565.
3. *Ibid.*
4. *Ibid.*
5. *Ibid.*
6. Jeremy Taylor, *The Rule and Exercise of Holy Dying* (1651), 221-2.
7. *Ibid.*, 4.
8. See ch. 4, p. 1, n. 2, for another Cambridge scholar, Isaac Barrow, also claimed by More and Cross as a representative Anglican.

Chapter Four
The Major Seventeenth-Century Advocates

Despite the appeal of mortalism to various English believers since the earliest days of the Reformation, there was no attempt at a systematic exposition of mortalist theology until Richard Overton's now well-known *Mans Mortalitie* appeared in 1644. We must, therefore, retrace our steps to examine more closely *Mans Mortalitie*, the first argued defence of English mortalism and a seminal work by any criteria, and then the writings of those who soon followed Overton: Thomas Hobbes the political and metaphysical philosopher, George Hammon the influential Baptist leader, John Milton the republican poet, and the empiricist philosopher and theologian, John Locke.[1] All were convinced mortalists, and on account of the extent of their writings or their own prominence, they may be regarded as the major mortalist spokesmen of the seventeenth century.[2] With the exception of Hammon, and perhaps Overton, the influence of these more prominent mortalist writers extended well into the eighteenth century, and even beyond. Their focussed and often detailed expositions defined mortalism more clearly and carried it forward for the consideration of future generations, thereby establishing a continuum in mortalist thought extending from Tyndale and Frith in the 1530s to Joseph Priestley in the 1780s and 1790s. With names like Hobbes, Milton, and Locke in its favour, mortalism could never again be dismissed as the aberrant

1. Locke has recently been redefined as a rational theologian whose "primary concern was Scripture and its interpretation", even a "Protestant philosopher" for whom there were "two sources of theology, nature and revelation", Nuovo, *John Locke,* xx, xxi. See also p. xxx, and on Locke's theology as a whole V. Nuovo, "Locke's Theology, 1694-1704" in M.A. Stewart (ed.), *English Philosophy in the Age of Locke* (Oxford, 2000).
2. Froom includes the Cambridge mathematician and classicist Isaac Barrow as a conditionalist. While Barrow's sustained opposition to the doctrine of eternal torment would have found favour with mortalists, it is doubtful that he entertained mortalism *per se*. For Barrow, *sheol* is the grave, death is "real destruction of life" and hell a doctrine that "hath made some persons desperately doubt the truth of the whole body of that religion whereof this is supposed to be a fundamental article" and "a great scandal to human reason", Isaac Barrow, *Two Dissertations, ad cal* with *Sermons and Fragments attributed to Isaac Barrow,* ed. J.P. Lee (1834), 203-4, 211; *The Works of the Learned Isaac Barrow,* II (1683), 399.

meandering of uninformed minds. With their assistance, it became a more credible alternative for those in the future as well as the present who might question the validity of the traditional eschatology.

Richard Overton and *Mans Mortalitie*

We have already alluded to Overton's *Mans Mortalitie* as a seminal work in the development and definition of mortalist thought. It was, in reality, more than that. It not only sowed the seeds which would later come to full fruition in the works of others perhaps better qualified and more respected than the radical sectary Overton, but was itself in all likelihood the fruit of seeds sown in earlier years when conditions had prevented their mature development. There is no doubt, of course, about the significance of *Mans Mortalitie* in its own time, or of its continuing influence in the seventeenth century, with several reprints or revisions before 1675.[1] Froom is quite correct when he says that the mortalist convictions expressed so forcefully in *Mans Mortalitie* "were not the passing whim of an enthusiast" but "the settled conviction of a careful student".[2] The eighteenth-century mortalist historian, Francis Blackburne, thought that *Mans Mortalitie* itself was somewhat "uncouth", but its author "a master of his subject".[3]

Overton himself is something of an enigma. Edwards says that he was a member of a Baptist church by 1646 and a "desperate Sectary",[4] and Whitley

1. Whitley mentions five versions, including a copy of a 1644 edition appended to an anonymous refutation published at Oxford in 1645, but omits the 1675 edition of the revision *Man Wholly Mortal* which first appeared in 1655, see *BB*, I, 16, 61. Wing, *STC,* gives a first edition of *Mans Mortalitie* in 1643, published in Amsterdam, and a 1674 edition of *Man Wholly Mortal* in addition to the 1655 and 1675 editions. Froom and Burns both state that a first edition of *Mans Mortalitie* appeared in 1643. It is more likely that 1643 is an old-style date, and that the first edition was published in 1644, new-style, with a re-print that same year. Williamson noted that on the title-page of the BL copy Thomason had deleted Amsterdam and written in its place "London", adding that it was "not uncommon"at the time for books published in London to be labelled Amsterdam "as a matter of caution", G. Williamson, 'Milton and the Mortalist Heresy', *SP,* 32 (1935), 556. Burns, *CM,* 155, is satisfied that the debate over the identity of R.O., the author cited on the title-page of all versions, has been settled in favour of Richard Overton, citing Perez Zagorin, 'The Authorship of Mans Mortalitie', *The Library,* 5th. Ser., V (1950-51), 179-82; Joseph Frank, *The Levellers* (Cambridge, Mass., 1955), 263-65; and D. M. Wolfe, "Unsigned Pamphlets of Richard Overton,1641-1649", *Huntington Library Quarterly,* XXI (1957-58), 167-201.
2. *CFF,* II, 167. Burns describes him as "a gifted and articulate propagandist", *CM,* 155.
3. Blackburne, *A Short Historical View of the Controversy Concerning an Intermediate State and The Separate Existence of the Soul Between Death and the General Resurrection* (1765), 49.
4. Edwards, *Gangraena,* III, 148.

claims him as a Baptist author throughout the 1640s and 1650s.[1] Burns believes he was a General Baptist and sees no reason to believe that he ever left the fellowship of General Baptists.[2] Others, however, contend that he was a Leveller, even a leader in the Leveller movement in the late 1640s.[3] These two views are not necessarily inherently contradictory. What is beyond doubt is the extent of his writings, largely of a political nature, particularly during the 1640s. He is conservatively described as a "pamphleteer" in the *Dictionary of National Biography*. Whitley lists twenty-one works under his name between 1642 and 1655, only two of which, *Mans Mortalitie* of 1644 and its revision in 1655, are theological in content. The remainder are all political or socio-political tracts, attacking the government or advising it, arguing the causes of prisoners or the people, or the Leveller party. Given the nature of the times and his own clear preference for a biblical faith, it is a little surprising that his theological output was restricted essentially to one work. Perhaps there is some justification for Edwards's contention that others had a hand even in that.[4]

Mans Mortalitie was first published in Amsterdam by John Canne, the Independent theologian and minister of the exiled English Independents in Amsterdam, who may also have sympathised with mortalist views.[5] It was subsequently republished in London in 1655 as *Man Wholly Mortal*. The 1655 version was essentially a revision of the earlier version, "corrected and enlarged", and re-organised but with few additions of argument or substance. Apart from the title itself, the title-page is almost identical in both editions, and sets out the author's intentions with a few well-chosen phrases:

> A Treatise Wherein 'tis proved, both Theologically and Philosophically, that whole Man (as a rationall Creature) is a Compound wholly mortall, contrary to that common distinction of Soule and Body: And that the present going of the Soule into Heaven or Hell is a meer Fiction: And that at the Resurrection is the beginning of our immortality, and then Actuall Condemnation, and Salvation, and not before.[6]

1. *BB*, I, 12-39, 61.
2. *CM*, 124.
3. E.g., Hill, *The World Turned Upside Down*, 37-8, 64-5; cf. *BB*, I, 34, 38-9.
4. Edwards, *Gangraena*, I, 27 (the second so numbered), where Edwards states that Clement Writer was reported to have had "a great hand" in the writing of *Mans Mortalitie*.
5. The first edition of *Mans Mortalitie* may in fact have been printed in London, Amsterdam being given as the place of publication as a ruse to confuse the authorities, McLachlan, *Socinianism*, 191. Canne's millenarianism is noted by Capp, *Fifth Monarchy Men*, 244.
6. *MM*, title-page. Whitley does not question the authorship of the 1655 revision, *BB*, I, 61. The title page of the 1655 *Man Wholly Mortal* substitutes the phrase "That as whole man sinned, so whole man died" for "that whole Man (as a rationall Creature) is a Compound wholly mortal".

This, together with the text itself, argues strongly against the conclusion that *Mans Mortalitie* was "one of the first frankly materialistic works of the century".[1] This assertion can only be allowed by imposing a strictly philosophical, metaphysical definition of materialism on what Overton himself claims is theologically and philosophically based. His work, as the title illustrates, was in fact more theological than philosophical and therefore, it would seem, more than materialistic since it presents man as a spiritual being with the possibility of an eternal future.

In attacking "the Hell-hatch'd doctrine of th'immortall soule"[2] Overton was not attempting to undermine religion or belief, or hope in the future, but rather what he considered to be a perversion of them all. Adam had been a real man living in a real world, as were his descendants, all of whom had been taken captive by alien ideas. The truth about man and human existence must be re-stated and defended. The "errour-leading doctrine"[3] of the soul's natural immortality must be shown for what it was, a distortion of the truth as originally revealed and recorded in Scripture, and a foundation for other false doctrinal assertions emanating from Rome, namely hell and purgatory. According to Scripture, "all hope of future life and being is in the Resurrection".[4] With reference to Christ's second coming, Overton says that believers will receive their "Crown of Righteousness. . .at that day". Consequently "none ever entred [*sic*] into Heaven since the Creation".[5] This does not sound much like philosophical materialism, nor can it be. Overton was a man of his time, a time when even the political process was circumscribed by religious belief and when it would shortly give way to an experiment in practical politics that would fall just short of a theocracy. *Mans Mortalitie* challenged the theological *status quo* in a way that Overton and others at the time challenged the political establishment. It was all part and parcel of a great urge to be free, free from the constraints of monarchy, papacy, prelacy and picked parliaments, and to be free man must understand himself, his origin and his destiny. Overton's main concerns, then, are the constitution of man as originally created, the nature of his existence in life and his condition in death, his future if that future is not guaranteed by natural immortality, natural procreation in relation to mortality and immortality, and the place of reason in arriving at a true understanding of the nature of the soul and human existence. All is to be understood and brought into balance in the light of the biblical text interpreted according to reason and internal consistency.

The Genesis account of human origins is crucial to a correct understanding of human nature and destiny. Although Adam was created immortal, he

1. Fisch, *Jerusalem and Albion*, 191.
2. This colourful phrase comes from one of Overton's supporters, *MM*, sig. A2 *v.*
3. *Ibid.*
4. *Ibid.*, 7.
5. *Ibid.*, 6.

became mortal by the Fall, and hence mortality, the capability and inevitability of dying, "is derivated to all Adam's posterity".[1] His original immortality did not exist because an immortal soul inhabited his mortal body, but on account of the fact that he existed as a complete entity endowed with life, but under threat of death if disobedient. His immortality was thus conditional. In the creative process, God imparted the breath of life to the lifeless body He had made, and man "became a living soul". "That which was formed or made of the earth, became a living soul, or creature, by breathing . . . the breath of life . . . That lifeless lumpe became a living soul", Overton says. And he adds an important rider, "that which was breathed before it was breathed, was not a living soul".[2] It was merely breath which, when infused into the body, caused a living soul, a man, to exist. Man is therefore a unity, "a creature whose several parts and members are endowed with . . . faculties, each subservient to other, to make him a living, rational creature".[3] He is "a compound" of breath and body, a unity, a totality, "wholly mortal", as a consequence of natural generation as well as original creation.

Death, then, is naturally that condition which is the opposite of life. It results from separation of breath from the body. When that happens death occurs, the person dies. He ceases to exist. The 'soul' is no more because the living person is no more. Death "returns man to what he was before he was, that is, not to be".[4] After death "man is voyd of actuall Being", "he absolutely IS NOT".[5] Man is not like a tree, which after being cut down may sprout again, but "totally fadeth and perisheth".[6] There is nothing within him that is inherently immortal or which survives the moment of death. "Anatomize man, take a view of all his lineaments and dimensions, of all his members and faculties, and consider their state severally, and all are transitory, even all that goeth to the subject man is corruptible",[7] Overton maintains. Biblical texts which assert man's mortality and explain his condition in death, include Job 14:1, 2; Psalm 103:15, 16; 146: 4; Ecclesiastes 3:19; 9: 4-6; John 3:13; I Timothy 6:14, 16; James 4:14.[8] The repeated and consistent emphasis within these and other biblical passages cannot be overlooked or their teaching denied.

Overton is particularly concerned that reason be allowed its rightful place in arriving at a true understanding of man, the soul, death and the future. He believes that the subordination of reason in the interpretation of Scripture and the formulation of doctrine has contributed to the "ridiculous invention

1. *Ibid.,* 1, 2.
2. R[ichard] O[verton], *Man Wholly Mortal* (1655), 29, 30.
3. *MM,* 10.
4. *Ibid.,* 2.
5. *Ibid.,* 6, 7(emphasis in the original).
6. *Ibid.,* 4.
7. *Ibid.,* 13.
8. *Ibid.,* 4, 6.

of the soul", and "immortality after death".[1] It is self-evident that reason and understanding define man as a distinct and superior order of being. All the human faculties, notably "reason, consideration, science . . . distinguish man from a beast [and] are augmented by learning, education etc., lessened by negligence, idleness, etc., and quite nullified by madness". Man's ability to think cognitively, to reflect, to remember, "the fulness of man's faculties in full order. . . make him a living, rational creature . . . more excellent than the beasts".[2] This is the essence of his humanity. Yet these powers are not of themselves immortal, but occur as the result of man's existence as a unified entity. Reason does not constitute immortality or contribute to it. Rather, it enables man to understand himself and his mortality and grasp its significance.

It is particularly important for Overton that reason prevail in understanding human procreation in relation to the existence of the individual 'soul'. Overton holds that mortality rather than immortality is the logical consequence of the normal procreative process. That which is generated by mortal man in the course of the natural order cannot be immortal. "Mortal Adam must beget mortal children . . . For that which is immortall cannot generatively proceed from that which is mortall".[3] This logical conclusion in the wake of man's nature correctly understood, renders untenable the idea that the soul is infused at or immediately after conception, an idea which Overton regards in any case as fraught with philosophical and theological difficulties.[4] Man's essential wholeness and his ultimate dependence on Christ and the resurrection at the last day for eternal life is a more reasonable explanation of human being and human destiny than the traditional and highly speculative doctrine of the immortal soul.

Thus, man's hope for the future lies not within himself, but with God, and God's promises in Christ. The "going of the soul into heaven or hell" at death "is a mere fiction". It is contrary to reason and to revelation. "The place of glory for the dead saints is not yet, and shall not actually be till the dissolution of heaven and earth",[5] at the last day, with the resurrection of the dead and the last judgment. Resurrection itself is not "the addition of gross matter to life", as it would be if the traditional view were to prevail, but "the restoration of life from death".[6] This includes corporeality and rationality, "and is the beginning of our immortality". This is the biblical alternative, the "hope of future life, grounded upon the Resurrection". The last day seals "the end of our faith" and "the salvation of our souls".[7] Overton's Christocentric conclusion fairly

1. *Ibid.*, 9.
2. *Ibid.*, 9-11.
3. *Ibid.*, 33.
4. *Ibid.*, 33-5.
5. *Ibid.*, 23.
6. *Man Wholly Mortal*, 39.
7. *Ibid.*, 53.

represents the thnetopsychism he advocated with such conviction, and which would eventually be the dominant form of English mortalism:

> Thus, having found Mans Foundation to be wholly in the dust, from thence taken and thither to returne: Let this then be the use of all: That man hath not wherewith at all to boast. . . but is provoked wholly out of himself, to cast himself wholly on Jesus Christ with whom in God our lives are hid, that when he who is our life shall appear, he might also with him appear in glory, to whom be the honour of our immortality for ever, and for ever".[1]

Overton may have been an untutored pamphleteer from the swelling ranks of the radical left and his *Mans Mortalitie* unpolished and, in some eyes, "uncouth". He had nonetheless grasped the essentials of thnetopsychist mortalism well enough and his work remains as the first coherent expression of that mortalism in the English language.

Thomas Hobbes and the *Leviathan*

The notable change in recent years in the interpretation of Hobbes is due largely to a recognition, long overdue, of the significance of the religious content of *Leviathan* (1651). Letwin reminds us that more than half of the *Leviathan* is related to Christian doctrine and that "the rest is full of God and Scripture".[2] Commenting specifically on earlier interpretations of *Leviathan*, Geach speaks of the "obstacles" which he claims have hitherto hindered a correct understanding of Hobbes, commenting candidly that they consisted "mainly of calumny and ignorance",[3] and noting in his re-interpretation of Hobbes that the latter believed, among other things, that "men are mortal animals", and that "when a man dies, he rots and all his thoughts perish".[4] It

1. *MM*, 43.
2. S.R. Letwin, 'Hobbes and Christianity' in P. King (ed.), *Thomas Hobbes, Critical Assessments* (London and New York, 2000), IV, 150; originally published in *Daedalus*, vol. 105 (Winter, 1974). See also S.R. Sutherland, 'God and Religion in *Leviathan*', in King (ed.), *Hobbes, Critical Assessments*, IV, 107-114; D. Johnston, 'Hobbes's Mortalism', *HPT*, X(1989); R. Tuck, 'The Civil Religion of Thomas Hobbes', N. Phillipson and Q. Skinner (eds.), *Political Discourse in Early Modern Britain* (Cambridge, 1993).
3. P. Geach, 'The Religion of Thomas Hobbes', in King (ed.), *Hobbes, Critical Assessments*, IV, 280; originally published in *Religious Studies*, Vol. XVII, Dec. 1981. Geach believes that the treatment meted out to Hobbes by earlier critics amounts to "character assassination, something of an English tradition", particularly in Oxford, where his books were burnt, 281.
4. *Ibid.*, 282. Johnston argues that Hobbes's denial of the soul's incorporeality and immortality was "one of the most salient and controversial features" of the *Leviathan*, *HPT*, X, 647. In the context of the mortalism of Hobbes and Milton, Thomas proposes that in mortalist thought man's pre-eminence over animals "was something which only became evident at the Resurrection", Keith Thomas, *Man*

is, as we shall see shortly, a fair enough condensation of the eschatology which Hobbes himself sets out in considerably more detail, particularly in ch. 38 of *Leviathan,* 'Of the Signification in Scripture of Eternal Life, Hell, Salvation, The World to Come, and Redemption'. That Hobbes was not an atheist, or a materialist in the strictest sense, is clear enough from even a cursory reading of *Leviathan*.[1] As Martinich points out, Hobbes, "as a Christian", considered both Old and New Testaments "to contain the revelation of God to human beings".[2] Hobbes did not disbelieve the Bible but the interpretation imposed on it by those not adequately qualified to do so, and the random and often quite illogical application of principles derived from such study.[3] Letwin states quite categorically that Hobbes was a Christian and a Protestant,[4] conclusions which Geach endorses but with the important qualification that Hobbes's Christianity was "extremely heretical" by the standards of both contemporary Protestant and Catholic belief.[5] It seems highly likely, in fact, that Hobbes leant rather heavily towards a Socinian theology which, among other things, proposed that "men are material and mortal beings; immortal souls are a heathenish myth; (and) men's only hope of a future life is God's promise of resurrection, of which Christ's resurrection is our surety".[6]

Martinich is also positive about Hobbes's essentially Christian stance, stating that he was "a sincere member of the Church of England" with a "preference for

---

and the Natural World (1983), 123. Not all mortalists, including even Hobbes and Milton, while concurring with the significance of the resurrection, might have agreed with such a radical assessment.

1. Joseph Priestley would later identify himself with this criticism of Hobbes, "Like Mr. Hobbes, I may for generations live under the imputation of absolute atheism", *Disquisitions Relating to Matter and Spirit*(1777), xvi.
2. A.P. Martinich, *A Hobbes Dictionary* (Cambridge, Mass. and Oxford, 1995), 47.
3. One of the essentials of Hobbes's political theory was that the stability of society was threatened by the unchecked freedom of sects in preaching and practising their newly-discovered beliefs. The possibility of potential social disintegration had already come about by the time *Leviathan* was published in 1651 and may even have contributed to its composition. Cf. Hill, *The Century of Revolution, 1603 -1714,* 173-5.
4. Letwin, in King (ed.), *Hobbes, Critical Assessments,* 158. The earlier examination of Hobbes's theology by Nathaniel Henry should not be overlooked. Henry pointed out that Hobbes was "no atheist", remarking that "on the subject of the intermediate state, he is scholarly [and] exegetical, rather than dogmatic", Henry, 'Milton and Hobbes: Mortalism and the Intermediate State', *SP,* 48(1951), 241. With the advantage of later studies, Henry might not have concluded that Hobbes's position on the soul, death and the intermediate state was "orthodox Calvinistic", 241.
5. Geach, in King, *Hobbes, Critical Assessments,* 281.
6. *Ibid.,* 286. Geach (p. 284) draws from three sources in addition to *Leviathan* itself in arriving at the conclusion that Hobbes "professed a variety of Socinianism": the Racovian catechism, the theological writings of Joseph Priestley, and *Christendom Astray* by the Christadelphian, Robert Roberts. Cf. Tuck in Phillipson and Skinner (eds.), *Political Discourse,* 131.

the liturgy prescribed by the Book of Common Prayer".[1] Martinich is equally emphatic regarding Hobbes's eschatological beliefs, saying quite unambiguously that he "was a mortalist" who "correctly argues that the doctrine of the immortality of the soul is not biblical".[2] Martinich suggests four reasons why Hobbes denied the doctrine of the immortal soul, among them that it supported the Roman Catholic doctrine of purgatory and the doctrine of everlasting punishment in hell, both of which Hobbes himself rejected as false.[3] Commenting on Hobbes's treatment of the matter in *Leviathan,* Martinich states that the doctrine of the soul's immortality "is said to be one of the doctrines of the Kingdom of Darkness", a doctrine, moreover, which "diminishes the salvific work of Jesus".[4] Geach concurs, pointing out that Hobbes held that the formula 'Jesus is the Christ, the Son of God' was "the essential Christian creed", arguing "charitably" that anyone "who holds this doctrine fast has enough faith for salvation even if the great and terrible day burns up the rotten structure of superstition he has reared upon this foundation".[5]

It is from one standpoint at least not surprising that Hobbes has been misunderstood and that he has become the subject of divergent opinion, or that his mortalist eschatology has until recently been overlooked. In his own day he was misread, even misrepresented. One of his more outspoken contemporary critics, John Bramhall, later Archbishop of Armagh, attacked the *Leviathan* with immoderate gusto, asserting that "Hobbian principles" had the potential to destroy the essence of Christian religion in virtually every particular:

> the existence, the simplicity, the ubiquity, the eternity, and infiniteness of God, the doctrine of the blessed Trinity, the Hypostatical union, the kingly sacerdotal and prophetical offices of Christ; the being and operation of the Holy Ghost, heaven, hell, angels, devils, the immortality of the soul, the catholic and national churches; the holy Scriptures, holy orders, the holy sacraments, the whole frame of religion and the worship of God; the laws of nature, the reality of goodness, justice, piety, honesty, conscience, and all that is sacred.[6]

Bramhall acidly concluded that Hobbes's disciples, if they could believe such a catalogue of errors, may as well "feed with ostriches".[7] In actual fact few, if any, of them did so believe.

1. Martinich, *Hobbes,* 16, 2-3.
2. *Ibid.,* 257. There is a useful discussion of Hobbes's use of the word 'soul' and his opposition to the doctrine of natural immortality at pp. 275-77.
3. *Ibid.,* 276.
4. *Ibid.,* 257. See pp. 158-162 for discussion of Hobbes's interesting and important concept of the Kingdom of Darkness, which owes its temporal existence largely to misinterpretations of Scripture.
5. Geach, in King (ed.), *Hobbes, Critical Assessments,* 284-5.
6. John Bramhall, *The Catching of Leviathan* (1658), 501-2.
7. *Ibid.*

One of Hobbes's more unexpected supporters was the liberal Roman
Catholic Thomas White, whose *De Medio Animarum Statu* (1653), translated
into English in 1659 as *The Middle State of Souls,* questioned the prevailing
Catholic doctrine of purgatory and was shortly added to the *Index* of proscribed
books, together with all his other works. Francis Blackburne later recorded that
both Hobbes and White had been censured in parliament in 1666 for "atheism,
blasphemy and profaneness" for calling into question the natural immortality
of the soul.[1] It is doubtful if White did question the soul's immortality, but
his assertions that man is "truly one entity", it therefore being impossible to
separate soul from body, that the resurrection at the last day is the basis of
Christian hope, and that souls are not admitted to the highest joys of heaven
before the judgment and the last conflagration, besides sounding Hobbesian,[2]
would have been anathema to a post-Restoration parliament as well as to the
ecclesiastical establishment.

Although Bramhall was accurate enough concerning hell and the immortality
of the soul, he had clearly been carried away in his wider criticism of Hobbes.
The *Leviathan* did not propose all that Bramhall contended it did. It did not
attack faith in, or the possibility of, eternal life, but rather the presuppositions
that led to erroneous conclusions regarding man's future. Hobbes later replied
to Bramhall claiming that his criticisms were arbitrarily selective and that he
had taken passages out of context in arriving at his reconstruction of Hobbes's
views of the future state.[3] Hobbes defended the position he had taken in
Leviathan. "My doctrine is this", he stated:

> First, that the elect in Christ from the day of Judgment forward, by virtue
> of Christ's passion and victory over death, shall enjoy eternal life, that is,
> they shall be immortal.
>
>   Secondly, that there is no living soul separated in place from the
> body, more than there is a living body separated from the soul.
>
>   Thirdly, that the reprobate shall be revived to Judgment, and shall
> die a second death in Torments, which death shall be everlasting.[4]

This is straightforward thnetopsychist theology, based on a careful and
reasoned study of the biblical text as a whole. Man's immortality commences at
the last day and derives from Christ. Man is created a unity, hence a living soul
cannot exist apart from the body. Wicked men will ultimately be destroyed
rather than suffer eternal torment. In addition to demonstrating that Hobbes
was a mortalist, the foregoing re-inforces the more fundamental point of his
allegiance to Scripture. It is extremely difficult to see how Hobbes can be passed

1. Blackburne, *Historical View*, 132-3.
2. Thomas White, *Of the Middle State of Souls* (1659), 98, 37-8, 260.
3. Thomas Hobbes, *An Answer to a Book Published by Dr. Bramhall called The Catching
   of the Leviathan* (1682), Ep. Ded., sigs. A*r*, *v*.
4. *Ibid.,* 87-8.

off simply as a materialist[1] with the atheistic connotations that term carries, or how his religious convictions can be ignored or minimised in the cavalier fashion that they so frequently have been by nineteenth- and twentieth-century critics. Burns is much nearer the mark in pointing out that one half of the *Leviathan* is given to demonstrating that all Hobbes's central ideas are clearly taught in Scripture, and when he concludes with some generosity:

> One may view Hobbes's biblicism as an elaborate sham, or as a concession to the prejudices of the age, or as the aberration of a man so conditioned by the dominant Christian culture that he could not himself see the absurdity of using Scripture to support his essentially irreligious philosophy, but the fact remains that when Hobbes argued from Scripture, he argued like a Protestant, maintaining that Scripture itself and not reason was his supreme authority.[2]

Hobbes's subsequent reply to Bramhall is sufficient evidence of that, and a refutation of the always doubtful proposition that his philosophy was essentially irreligious.

Hobbes was also opposed by Alexander Ross, whose *Leviathan drawn out with a Hook* (1653) was only marginally less intemperate than John Bramhall's later assault. Ross believed that the *Leviathan* was "like that beast in the Revelation which opened his mouth into [*sic*] blasphemy against God".[3] Hobbes himself was an "Arabian" in "making the soul to rest with the body till the resurrection", a "Luciferian" in "making the soul of man corporeal", and an "Originist" [*sic*] "by putting a period to hell torments".[4] For those familiar with the history of the Christian church it was a clever attack, even though Ross seems unsure about the precise nature of Hobbes's mortalism. Was he a psychopannychist in allowing the soul to rest with the body after death? Or was he a thnetopsychist in holding that the soul only existed in relation to the body? The Arabian allusion was intended to clarify the point. Certain heretics in Arabia in the third century had held thnetopsychist views, and Ross explains, "The Psychopannychits [*sic*] of this age come somewhat near these Arabians, for though they hold not the death or dissolution of the soul, yet they hold it sleeps with the body in the grave".[5] This describes contemporary psychopannychism accurately enough but does not tell us whether Hobbes himself was psychopannychist or thnetopsychist. It may have suited Ross's purposes to let the issue remain clouded and merely to say that Hobbes was a mortalist and charge him with ancient heresy "which may prove of dangerous

1. See later p. 114, n. 4 for comment on the concept of materialism.
2. *CM*, 184.
3. Alexander Ross, *Leviathan Drawn out with a Hook: Or Animadversions Upon Mr. Hobbs his Leviathan* (1653), To the Reader, sigs. ai *v*, aii *r*.
4. *Ibid.*, sigs. aiv *r,v.*
5. *Ibid.*, 49.

consequence to green heads and immature judgements".[1]

The *Leviathan* itself, of course, clarifies the matter, since it is the primary source from which we can derive Hobbes's mortalist beliefs. Commenting on the original creation of man, Hobbes says that in Genesis 2:7 the breath of life which the Creator breathed into the lifeless body of Adam "signifies no more but that God gave him life . . . . not that any ghost, or incorporeal substance entered into and possessed his body".[2] This is the crucial point in the thnetopsychist position. The living person is the soul. It makes the idea of a separate, independent soul unbiblical, inconsistent and impossible. "That the soul of man is in its own nature eternal, and a living creature independent of the body, or that any mere man is immortal otherwise than by the resurrection in the last day (except Enos and Elijah) is a doctrine not apparent in Scripture",[3] Hobbes contends. At the risk of appearing unnecessarily repetitive, we should note again Hobbes's appeal to Scripture. Referring to the book of Job, Hobbes adds, "The whole 14 chapter of Job . . . is a complaint of this mortality of nature; and yet no contradiction of the immortality of the resurrection. . . . Immortal life beginneth not in man till the resurrection".[4] He adds later, "The soul in Scripture signifieth always either the life or the living creature, and the body and soul jointly, the body alive".[5]

For Hobbes, the doctrine of the soul's immortality is a legacy of Greek demonology rather than original Christian thought, and one of its many erroneous and pernicious consequences is the doctrine of eternal torment.[6] Hobbes is in full agreement here with psychopannychists and thnetopsychists before and after him, as well as other biblical scholars, some of whom we have already encountered, who could not find in Scripture the doctrine of hell as popularly conceived. He points out that the real meaning of hell is the grave, "where all men remain till the resurrection", signified in the Greek by the word *hades*, literally "a place where men cannot see . . . as well the grave as any other deeper place".[7] Everlasting fire means eternal destruction rather than eternal torment, Hobbes explains on the basis of his own study of the relevant texts. Sodom and Gomorrah are examples of hell fire and signify, not "a place of torment", but are "to be taken indefinitely, for destruction".[8] The unredeemed wicked will thus eventually be annihilated. Man may become immortal, however, and live forever, but not as the result of any inherent immortal attributes. God alone is immortal according to I Timothy 6:16, from which it follows "that the soul of man is not of its own

1. *Ibid.,* Preface, i.
2. Thomas Hobbes, *Leviathan* (1651), 209.
3. *Ibid.,* 241.
4. *Ibid.*
5. *Ibid.,* 339.
6. *Ibid.,* 340.
7. *Ibid.,* 242.
8. *Ibid.,* 243.

nature immortal, but of grace, that is to say, by the gift of God", through Jesus Christ.[1] On the basis of I Corinthians 15:54 Hobbes states, "There was no immortality of anything mortal till death was overcome, and that was at the Resurrection".[2] So "all the immortality of the soul that shall be after the resurrection is by Christ, and not by the nature of the soul".[3] It would be difficult to find a more coherent and emphatic defence of thnetopsychism than is given here by Hobbes.

By common consent Hobbes belongs to that select band of thinkers who have significantly influenced the development of Western thought. His work still commands, and deserves, respect. He also belongs to that much smaller group of seventeenth-century thinkers who believed they could see the fallacy and the peril of belief in the immortal soul and who were bold enough to propose a considered alternative. Hobbes's theology, as indeed some of his other ideas, was not popular with many of his contemporaries, and has largely been ignored since. Yet Burns's conclusion bears some consideration:

> We may not like his absolutist politics, we may deplore his extreme Erastianism, we may judge his anti-clericalism immoderate and the theology he derives from Scripture perverse, but we must nevertheless be slow to declare insincere Hobbes's professed Christian faith, and his avowal that the word of God as revealed in Holy Scripture gives us truths that are beyond the reach of reason. . . . We may, of course, at the risk of falling into dogmatism, decide what the "true line" of Christian belief was in the period, but if such a definition excludes on the grounds of mortalism the troublesome Hobbes from the company of Christians, there is danger that it will also, with more offense to our sensibilities, exclude the poet of *Paradise Lost*.[4]

That Hobbes and Milton were of one mind concerning the nature of the soul and human destiny strengthens the argument that the thnetopsychist view of man as it developed in England during the seventeenth and eighteenth centuries deserves more attention than it has hitherto received, and the conclusion that Hobbes himself was more a believer than an atheist.

George Hammon

Relatively little is known of the General Baptist George Hammon and clearly he does not have the stature of Hobbes, or Milton, or even Overton. Yet as a long-standing and influential Baptist leader of his time, "a very eminent and remarkable man"[5] according to the early Baptist historian, Thomas Crosby, his

1. Hobbes, *Answer to Bramhall*, 88.
2. *Ibid.*, 89.
3. *Ibid.*, 92.
4. *CM*, 184-5.
5. Crosby, *English Baptists*, III, 103.

mortalism, which has hitherto escaped attention,[1] was argued as convincingly as that of any of his more illustrious contemporaries. It could even be said that Hammon's influence in his own time was greater than that of Milton since his mortalist writings were known in his own day whereas those of Milton were not. As a leader among the General Baptists in Kent throughout the 1650s and the 1660s and a signatory to the important 1660 General Baptist Confession of Faith, Hammon's doctrinal stance would not have been unknown to many of the 20,000 followers the Confession claimed to represent. Whitley notes that he was still in fellowship with congregations at Cranbrook and Biddenden in 1669 and 1672 respectively,[2] and it is reasonable to assume that his association with these groups continued until his death c.1680. By that time official Baptist opinion had moved away from mortalism in favour of the immortality of the soul,[3] and may explain why Hammon did not publish in favour of mortalism after his *Truth and Innocency, Prevailing against Error and Insolency* had appeared in 1660. Hammon's thnetopsychism found expression in this and in two other works published between 1655 and 1660, and he himself refers to an earlier work, presumably lost, in which he had first broached mortalist opinions.[4] In 1661, while in Maidstone gaol, he is recorded as joint author, together with six others, all General Baptists, of *Sions Groans for her Distressed*, an appeal to Charles II and his parliament for liberty and equality in religious matters, "grounded upon Scripture, reason, and authority".[5] It

1. Hammon is not mentioned by Mills, Froom, or Burns.
2. *BB*, I, 219.
3. By the late1670s both General and Particular Baptist confessions of faith endorsed the immortality of the soul. Article XXXI of the Particular Baptist *A Confession of Faith* (1677), "the most influential of all the Calvinistic Baptist confessions of faith"(Brown, *English Baptists*, 8), reprinted in 1688, and article XLIX of the General Baptist *An Orthodox Creed* of 1679 both refer to the "State of Man after Death, and the Resurrection of the Dead" and state "the bodies of men after death return to dust and see corruption; but their souls, which neither die nor sleep, having an immortal substance, immediately return to God who gave them . . .". In fact, at this and other points the two confessions are identical. Both documents state that at creation man was created with an immortal soul. The Particular Baptist Confession of 1677 was based on the Westminster Confession and the Savoy Confession of 1658, both reflecting a highly Calvinistic theology. Whether or not Thomas Monck and his associates who framed and advocated the 1679 General Baptist Confession were aware of this background and that they were leading their erstwhile Arminian and free-will congregations into Calvinistic pastures is an interesting question. It is impossible to believe that they did not know of the similarity between the two confessions. The emphatic repudiation of both psychopannychism and thnetopsychism in confessions representing both wings of the contemporary Baptist churches which had not long previously tended in the opposite direction deserves further exploration.
4. George Hammon, *A Discovery of the Latitude of the loss of the Earthly Paradise by Original Sin* (1655), 33.
5. See *BB*, I, 83.

was not a theological tract, but these were the essential presuppositions which undergirded the development of General Baptist theology. They were also fundamental to Hammon's mortalism.

His first known defence of mortalist doctrine appeared in a work entitled, *A Discovery of the Latitude of the Loss of the Earthly Paradise by Original Sin* in 1655, written to counter the teachings of the established clergy in general and of Matthias Rutton of Baughton in particular, who had "darkened the doctrine of the gospel" by traditions received from the Fathers.[1] Hammon had in mind here the doctrines of hell and eternal torment. "It is not God's way to afflict the punishment of hell before He hath tried souls at the general judgment",[2] he stated. He was also opposed to the doctrine of the soul's immortality, for "all that is man dyeth and is mortal".[3] "God breathed into Adam the breath of life, and so he became a living soul".[4] It should be obvious, then, that before that his 'soul' did not exist. Moreover, "many times in Scripture the mortal part of man is called the soul".[5] And in the grave there is no recollection of time, so "Adam's death . . . unto the time of his resurrection will be to him but a moment of time".[6] Hell is a fiction, and the frequently – quoted parable of the rich man and Lazarus is irrelevant, since a parable "proves nothing".[7] Shortly thereafter, in *Syons Redemption, and Original Sin Vindicated,* Hammon spoke again of the unconscious sleep of the righteous, "all the time of their sleep, although they lie many years in the dust, it will be but as it were a moment".[8]

Hammon's most extensive defence of the thnetopsychist view of man appeared in 1660 in his *Truth and Innocency, Prevailing against Error and Insolency,* a work written in response to the Puritan rector of Sutton Vallence in Kent, Hezekiah Holland, who had published an exposition of the book of Revelation in which he had argued that the Millennium was already past.[9] In an age which produced many interpretations of apocalyptic prophecy and in which millennial expectation ran high, this was not a popular view. Hammon, himself a convinced millenarian, could not allow Holland's anti-millenarianism to go unchallenged. In fact, he had already shown his own millenarian colours in *Syons Redemption Discovered* (1655), identifying the papacy as the Antichrist and the Pope as the Man of Sin, and anticipating a literal thousand-year reign of Christ on earth with the saints

1. Hammon, *A Discovery,* Ep. Ded., sig. A2 r. Baughton is probably Boughton under Blean, Kent.
2. *Ibid.,* 28.
3. *Ibid.,* 33-4.
4. *Ibid.,* 48.
5. *Ibid.*
6. *Ibid.,* 33.
7. *Ibid.,* 30.
8. George Hammon, *Syons Redemption, and Original Sin Vindicated* (1658), 86.
9. Hezekiah Holland, *An Exposition or Epitome of the Most Choice Commentaries Upon the Revelation of Saint John* (1650),154. Holland dated the millennium from AD 73 to 1073.

in the New Jerusalem, after which "the Lord will restore the whole creation into its primitive excellency".[1] Hammon is thus one of the few known mortalists who advocate thnetopsychism in the context of a radical millenarianism. Given the tendency of the Baptist community in general to a millenarian eschatology and a belief that they were living in the last days, it would not be surprising if there were others. Millenarianism normally required a resurrection of the righteous at the beginning of the millennium and a resurrection of the wicked at its end. Hammon himself had argued precisely this in *Syons Redemption, and Original Sin Vindicated* (1658), an earlier exchange with Hezekiah Holland, in which he had again proposed the sleep of the soul.[2] Soul sleep requires resurrection and Hammon's millenarianism was fertile soil for the growth of mortalist ideas.[3]

To Hammon, as to Overton, man is "wholly mortal". The word 'soul' has a wide range of meanings in Scripture, "sometimes to be understood (as) one thing, and sometimes as another". The Greek word *psuche* "doth signify several things", including mind, will, soul, breath, life, wind, heart, delight, pleasure, affection, wrath, etc. In principle, "the whole individual man is taken for the soul".[4] On Genesis 2:7, a crucial text for thnetopsychists, Hammon maintains that it was not the breath that became a living soul, but the man into whom the breath had been infused. So when the breath leaves the body at death, the living soul ceases to exist. Hammon explains his understanding of man's creation thus:

> it was not a living soul inferred into him, but by being breathed upon, the man that was made of the dust of the earth BECAME a living soul (mark the word BECAME a living soul). Now it was not the breath that became a living soul, but it was the man which became a living soul: and if the breath be not that which is called the living soul, what is man when his breath returns to God that gave it? Surely it is a dead lump".[5]

Since at death the soul ceases to exist, the condition of man in death is one of total unconsciousness. "The time between his death and resurrection will be no more to him than the time was to him before he was born".[6]

Hammon reinforces his thnetopsychism by reminding his readers of the origin and subsequent development of the doctrine of the immortal soul. It had originated, he points out, with "heathen philosophers, which did suppose that moral vertue [*sic*] should be rewarded hereafter".[7] Presumably this is a

1. George Hammon, *Syons Redemption Discovered* (1655), *ad cal.* with *A Discovery of the Latitude of the Loss of the Earthly Paradise by Original Sin,* 154 and *passim.*
2. Hammon, *Syons Redemption,* 85-6.
3. The majority of seventeenth-century millenarians, however, preferred the traditional eschatology of the soul.
4. George Hammon, 'A Discourse Touching the Mortality of the Soul', *ad cal.* with *Truth and Innocency, Prevailing against Error and Insolency* [1660], 35.
5. *Ibid.,* 38. (Emphasis in the original.)
6. *Ibid.,* 44.
7. *Ibid.,* 49.

reference to pre-Christian Greek philosophers of the Platonic, Aristotelian and neo-Platonic schools. But since they did not know that there was to be a resurrection of the body at the last day, "they have imagined such a thing as a soul to live and receive a reward". This view later infiltrated Christian thought and the Church of Rome "readily received" it, whence "the church of England have received it by tradition".[1] It was the simplification of a process which others had already set out in greater detail, and like all Hammon's works the 'Discourse' concerning the 'Mortality of the Soul' was probably intended principally for readers within his own community. Ever wary of the potential threat from Rome, as were all Nonconformists of the day, Hammon even allows for the possibility that attempts had been made to corrupt the text of Scripture, "I am ready to believe that the church of Rome have also abused our Greek copies in many particulars, to bear a face toward their opinion".[2] However unlikely this may have been, it underlines the fear which many Nonconformists shared at the Restoration, and the deep-seated belief that Rome would go to any lengths to regain lost ground and re-establish her traditional doctrinal authority.

Once again, the resurrection at the last day is to be the focus of devout expectation, "the foundation of the godly man's faith and hope".[3] The ultimate resurrection of man is grounded in the resurrection of Christ. The one gives rise to the other in the divine order of salvation events. Man's resurrection is assured by that of Christ, even as the mortality of man makes the resurrection a necessity. All is logical and consistent, revealed and reliable, and Hammon summarises the thnetopsychist faith which for him was the true teaching of Scripture:

> When God takes away mans breath, he dyeth, and so dust returns to dust, and the Spirit (viz. breath) to him that gave it; and that breath that returns to God, as it made the man that was made of earth to become a living soul, capable to enjoy what God gave him; even so in the resurrection, when that dust is raised by God (and every bone and member in its proper place) then shall God give forth the same breath of life again into every man; and so they shall be thereby capable to receive according to what they have done in the body, whether it be good or whether it be evil . . .".[4]

This was Hammon's last word on the subject, but it was clearly not enough to prevent the radical shift in official Baptist opinion which was soon to follow. We may be reasonably sure, however, that the thnetopsychism which for so long had found receptive minds among the General Baptists of Kent

1. *Ibid.*
2. *Ibid.*
3. George Hammon, 'The Resurrection of the Body Proved', *ad cal.* with *Truth and Innocency, Prevailing against Error and Insolency* [1660], 51.
4. *Ibid.*, 50.

and neighbouring counties, and among the earlier Anabaptists of the area, did not disappear altogether. There would have been many for whom the old teachings were the right way, and in which they found re-assurance and hope. If thnetopsychism did linger on in some congregations and in some Kentish minds it would have been due, in large measure, to George Hammon's emphatic declarations of the 1650s and early 1660s, and the lingering influence of his writings among General Baptist believers.

Milton's *Paradise Lost* and the *De Doctrina Christiana*

Milton, like Hobbes, has been variously interpreted and his mortalism in particular has been the subject of much divergent comment, even speculation.[1] Masson believed that Milton came to mortalist conclusions relatively late, probably between 1649 and 1660, and suggested that he may have been indebted to Hobbes for his thnetopsychism.[2] Saurat, on the other hand, proposed that Milton's mortalism derived from his "new friends" among the sectaries, including Overton and perhaps Clement Writer, and that he contributed to Overton's 1655 *Man Wholly Mortal*.[3] Fisch speaks of Milton's "materialism" in conjunction with his "mortalism" linking it to that of Overton and leaving the impression that Milton was indebted to Overton for both.[4] There is no convincing evidence for any of these propositions. Burns, after Haller, argues that Milton was not personally acquainted with any of the "sectaries" of his age, including Overton, although he is ready to allow that, to some extent, Milton may have been indebted to Overton's *Mans Mortalitie* and he notes that "Milton and Overton are in substantial agreement".[5] What cannot be gainsaid is the mortalism itself, "the Hebraic concept of the organic relation between body and soul" in which the soul "is more properly life, that which animates the physical body itself" and which "is not detachable from it, nor thought to subsist without it".[6]

1. D.M. Wolfe's analysis of the Puritan and sectarian background to Milton's thought does not mention the contemporary mortalism which Milton himself endorsed, *Complete Prose Works of John Milton* (ed. D.M. Wolfe, New Haven, CN and London), I (1953), 2.
2. D. Masson, *The Life of John Milton*, III (1873), 839.
3. Saurat, *Milton, Man and Thinker*, 269. Williamson believed that Saurat's view of Milton was in many respects flawed, Williamson, 'Milton and the Mortalist Heresy', *SP*, 32, 553.
4. Fisch, *Jerusalem and Albion*, 150-2. 'Materialism' is used again here, as it is by other critics of seventeenth- and eighteenth-century mortalism, strictly in the philosophic sense rather than the later sense of that which is the opposite of spiritual. The 'material' view of man excludes the existence of an immaterial component called 'soul' or 'spirit'. It is important to a correct understanding of Christian mortalism to remember that its advocates, frequently charged with materialism, were not unspiritual on that account.
5. *CM*, 1.
6. Fisch, *Jerusalem and Albion*, 149.

Milton's mortalism appears principally in the *De Doctrina Christiana,* or *A Treatise on Christian Doctrine,* his great theological work which today would be regarded as systematic theology, written in Latin probably in the late 1650s, but unpublished in his own day and undiscovered until 1825.[1] The question thus arises concerning the extent of the influence which Milton's mortalism enjoyed in the seventeenth century. The answer is, probably very little. One reason for the non-appearance of the *Treatise on Christian Doctrine* in his own day may have been the confession of millenarianism, albeit in a mild form, which it also contained. While Milton may not have been personally connected with contemporary sects and sectaries, he nevertheless shared many of their theological preferences,[2] including a millenarian belief in the soon-coming kingdom of Christ upon earth. He may have judged it prudent to avoid too close an affinity with what could have been interpreted as radical eschatology[3] when the freedom and openness of the Interregnum were waning and the possibility of restored monarchy and episcopacy was beginning to appear. Be that as it may, the *Treatise on Christian Doctrine* was not widely known during Milton's lifetime, if at all, and the influence of his mortalism may have been greater in succeeding generations than it was in his own. This, of course, only marginally minimises the significance of Milton's own thnetopsychism argued, as it was, thoroughly, coherently and in the context of a well-structured theology.[4]

The high-minded Milton, one suspects, would have been slow to

1. While the debate over the authorship of the *De Doctrina Christiana* is beyond the scope of this study, which assumes the traditional authorship, it may be noted that the arguments in favour of Milton's authorship in the prefatory note to the work in the Columbia edition of Milton's prose works are still compelling. William B. Hunter, Jr., in the article on mortalism in *A Milton Encyclopedia,* similarly argues that Milton propounds mortalist doctrine "explicitly" in the *De Doctrina Christiana,* William B. Hunter, Jr., (ed.), *A Milton Encyclopedia,* 5(1983), 155.
2. Burns holds that Milton espoused several General Baptist doctrines, *CM,* 170.
3. Sumner concluded, on the evidence in the *Treatise on Christian Doctrine,* that Milton avoided "the extravagant and fanatical opinions" of the Fifth Monarchy Men and other extreme millenarians, C.R. Sumner, (tr.), Milton, 'A Treatise on Christian Doctrine', in *The Prose Works of John Milton,* IV (1853), 484. For an incoming Royalist government it would have been convenient to ignore such distinctions. Sumner associates Milton's millenarianism with that of Mede. This view of Milton's theology is still needed to balance later interpretations, such as that of Nathaniel Henry who regarded the *De Doctrina Christiana* as "the fullest expression of the theology of the radical sects of the Reformation", 'Milton and Hobbes', *SP,* 48, 247.
4. While perhaps an overstatement, Henry's assessment of the significance of the theology of the *De Doctrina Christiana* is not without merit. It [*DDC*] "may be considered to correspond to the work of Calvin for the Presbyterians, Luther for the Lutherans, and Aquinas for the church of Rome", 'Milton and Hobbes', *SP,* 48, 247.

acknowledge any indebtedness to others for his convictions. He claims to
have owed his theological views to no-one, but to have derived them from
Scripture alone.[1] Certainly Scripture is his final authority, as the *Treatise on
Christian Doctrine* demonstrates with its abundant biblical references, even
though he acknowledges reason as a complement of revelation and a necessary
component in the interpretation of the biblical text. Thus, to the "testimonies
from Scripture" or "the testimony of revelation", "may be added . . . arguments
from reason" in "confirmation" or "support"of biblical doctrine. [2] Doctrine,
of course, is in itself a fundamental concept, since it provides the substance of
Christian faith, defining that which is to be believed over against the exercise
of personal faith, or the act of believing. Milton's doctrines of man, the soul
and eternal life are contained in chapters VII, XXII and XXXIII of the *Treatise
on Christian Doctrine*, "Of the Creation", "Of the Death of the Body" and "Of
Perfect Glorification" respectively.

There are also indications of mortalism in some of the later poetry, including
the following from *ParadiseLost:*

> . . . He form'd thee, Adam, thee O Man.
> Dust of the ground, and in thy nostrils breath'd
> The breath of Life; in his own Image he
> Created thee, in the Image of God
> Express, and thou becam'st a living Soul.[3]

And again, if more tentatively:

> . . . Yet one doubt
> Pursues me still, lest all I cannot die,
> Lest that pure breath of Life, the Spirit of Man
> Which God inspir'd, cannot together perish
> With this corporeal Clod: then in the Grave,
> Or in some other dismal place, who knows
> But I shall die a living Death? O thought
> Horrid, if true! yet why? It was but breath
> Of Life that sinn'd; what dies but what had life
> And sin? the body properly hath neither.
> All of me then shall die: let this appease
> The doubt, since humane reach no further knows.[4]

In the light of the more definitive statements of the earlier *Treatise on Christian
Doctrine* these allusions to man's original creation and eventual dissolution
appear unambiguously mortalist. Sewell argued that Milton's mortalism was

1. Milton, 'Treatise on Christian Doctrine', in *Prose Works* , IV, Dedicatory Epistle, 2.
2. *Ibid.,* 191, 480.
3. Milton, *Paradise Lost*, II, 523 ff.
4. *Ibid.*, X, 782 ff.

a "corollary of the psychology outlined in *Paradise Lost*", concluding that "Milton thinks of man as an integral whole".[1] Even so, it is the *Treatise on Christian Doctrine* itself which enables us to declare him a thorough-going thnetopsychist.[2]

As with all the mortalist apologists we have encountered to date, Milton finds it necessary in his attempt to understand and articulate the human condition to begin with the biblical doctrine of creation, for unless we understand correctly what man is and how he is composed, it will not be possible to understand what happens at death and beyond. Referring to the creative process recorded in Genesis 1 and substantiated in other "various passages of the Psalms and Prophets", Milton says, "it was not the body alone that was then made, but the soul of man also".[3] In other words, the soul did not exist prior to, or apart from, the body, "which precludes us from attributing pre-existence to the soul which was then formed, a groundless notion sometimes entertained, but refuted by Gen. 2:7."[4]

The word 'soul' means essentially a living creature and may refer, as it sometimes does in Scripture, to an animal.[5] When used of man, however, it means a living person, "the whole man . . . a living soul".[6] The word 'spirit' simply means breath, nor has "any other meaning in the sacred writings, but that breath of life which we inspire . . .".[7] At creation this breath was breathed into the body which had been made from the dust of the ground and a living person came into being. Milton thus describes the man who came into existence as a result of the divine creative act:

> Man having been created after this manner, it is said, as a consequence, that man became a living soul; whence it may be inferred (unless we had rather take the heathen writers for our teachers respecting the nature of the soul) that man is a living being, intrinsically and properly one and individual, not compound or separable, not, according to the common opinion, made up and framed of two distinct and different natures, as of soul and body – but that the whole man is soul, and the soul man, that is to say, a body, or substance individual, animated, sensitive, and rational; and that the breath of life was neither a part of the divine essence, nor the soul itself, but as it

1. A. Sewell, *A Study in Milton's Christian Doctrine* (1967), noting that "Milton's psychology would allow no division between the 'soul' and the body . . .[they] are not two, but one and indivisible".
2. A.L. Rowse is one of the very few Milton scholars from any period who correctly designates Milton's mortalism as thnetopsychism, A.L. Rowse, *Milton the Puritan* (1977), 199.
3. Milton, 'Christian Doctrine', in *Prose Works*, IV, 187.
4. *Ibid.*
5. *Ibid.*, 189.
6. *Ibid.*, 188.
7. *Ibid.*

were an inspiration of some divine virtue fitted for the exercise of life and
reason, and infused into the organic body; for man himself, the whole
man, when finally created, is called in express terms a living soul.[1]

Milton shares with Overton a traducian view of subsequent human generation,
for thereafter each human being becomes "a living soul" (Gen. 2:7) by natural
procreation, rather than by divine intervention, "the human soul is not created
daily by the immediate act of God, but propagated from father to son in a
natural order".[2] Eve was made from a rib taken from Adam's side "without the
necessity of infusing the breath of life a second time", and thus "Adam himself
begat a son in his own likeness after his image".[3]

Again, death is the reversal of life. "The death of the body is the loss or
extinction of life", the common definition, supposing it to result from the
separation of soul and body being "inadmissable".[4] Milton asks, "What part of
man is it that dies?" "Is it the whole man, or the body alone, that is deprived
of vitality" at death? He proposes to answer the question from "numberless
passages of Scripture" and regardless of the opinion of those "who think that
truth is to be sought in the schools of philosophy rather than in the sacred
writings".[5] His answer is straightforward thnetopsychism, "the whole man
dies". Referring to repeated statements of David in Psalms 6:5; 88:11-13;
115:17; 146:2, etc., which affirm that those who are dead do not praise God,
Milton says, "Certainly if he had believed that his soul would survive, and
be received immediately into heaven, he would have abstained from all such
remonstrances, as one who was shortly to take his flight where he might praise
God unceasingly".[6] And of Paul's anticipated crown of righteousness, Milton
argues, "If a crown were *laid up* for the apostle, it follows that it was not to be
received immediately after death" but "at the same time it was to be conferred
on the rest of the saints, that is not till the appearance of Christ in glory".[7]
Milton deals succinctly with several biblical passages often quoted in support
of the immortal soul and its immediate passage to heaven at death and argues
that they do not, when correctly interpreted, contradict the overall biblical
assertion that death is a sleep from which the dead will be awakened at the
resurrection.[8]

For Milton, as for Tyndale and those who followed him in the English

1. *Ibid.*
2. *Ibid.*, 189.
3. *Ibid.*, 191.
4. *Ibid.*, 270.
5. *Ibid.*
6. *Ibid.*, 271-2.
7. *Ibid.*, 273.
8. *Ibid.*, 276ff. The passages Milton deals with are, in order, Psalm 49:15;
   Ecclesiastes12:7; Matthew 10:28; Philippians1:23; I Peter 3:19; Revelation 6:9;
   Luke 23:43; Luke 23: 46; II Corinthians 5:1-20.

mortalist tradition, man's hope of a future life is dependent on the resurrection at the last day. Citing Job's Old Testament hope, Milton points out that belief in the resurrection of the dead "existed even before the time of the gospel", and that it was "confirmed under the gospel by the testimony of Christ".[1] In the New Testament the term resurrection includes "the resuscitation of the dead", and "a sudden change" of the living, thus ensuring that all the righteous will be recipients of eternal life.[2] In Milton's eschatological framework the resurrection is preceded by Christ's second coming, and followed by the last judgment and "coincident" with it, the millennial reign of Christ on earth, and finally the destruction of all evil, including evil angels, wicked and unbelieving men, and the devil himself.[3] In contrast to the opinion of most mortalists, as well as other biblical scholars, Milton rather surprisingly does not believe that hell is the grave, but a "place of punishment . . . beyond the limits of this universe", where the wicked will receive their due and just rewards, "the intensity and duration of these punishments variously intimated". Their end is "eternal death"which consists in part, surprisingly perhaps, of "eternal torment". But this is "beyond the limits" of the earth and its environs as originally created, where the righteous will enjoy "eternal life".[4] Milton's thnetopsychism finally results in considered justification of the character and will of God, with the "universe", to use Milton's own term,[5] returned to its pristine estate, the ultimate realisation of the divine purpose.

John Locke and the Reasonableness of Christian Mortalism

With Locke we come to the last of the major seventeenth-century proponents of Christian mortalism, and the first to have exerted a more far-reaching influence than any of his predecessors. Locke's mature religious writings, despite some early ambiguity,[6] can best be understood from a thnetopsychist view of man and his future. Nuovo affirms Locke's mortalism and argues convincingly that if we are to understand Locke correctly, all his writings must be read in the context of the "deep and pervasive influence" of his religious thought.[7] Wainwright points out that Locke's interest in the scriptural basis of Christian doctrine began

1. *Ibid.,* 480.
2. *Ibid.,* 481.
3. *Ibid.,* 482-4.
4. *Ibid.,* 489-90.
5. Although Milton uses the word more narrowly than in modern usage, e.g., 'Christian Doctrine', in *Prose Works,* IV, 187, 268, 490. See also ch. 7, p. 191ff.
6. Wainwright remarks cautiously that Locke's view of the intermediate state is not always easy to determine, but notes that his language "is usually consistent with mortalism" and his "repeated insistence" on human mortality and the necessity of resurrection, A. W. Wainwright (ed.), *Locke, Paraphrase and Notes,* I, 51-4.
7. Nouvo, *John Locke,* xvi, xxxiii. Theological works constituted the largest single category of books in Locke's own library, J. Harrison and P. Laslett, *The Library of John Locke* (Oxford, 1971), 18.

early, c. 1660-61, and that with the passing of years he appears to have spent "an increasing amount of time on biblical studies".[1] Alan Sell has shown in *John Locke and the Eighteenth-Century Divines*, that Locke's view of personal identity and the nature of man flowed forward causing concern, even consternation, for much of the eighteenth century. Noting that the "vast majority" of Locke's contemporaries accepted without question the long-standing dualistic view of the body's materiality and the soul's immateriality, Sell states that Locke's "epistemological scepticism concerning our ability to know that a person is an immaterial substance" provoked intense debate.[2] This doubt, together with the conviction that the soul's supposed immateriality "was not crucial to resurrection and eternal life",[3] would have been more than enough to rouse the indignation of those who championed the traditional position. Those who took him to task for views which, in their opinion, attacked the very heart of Christian belief, included the erudite Richard Bentley, Master of Trinity College, Cambridge, Thomas Burnet, Edward Stillingfleet, Joseph Butler, and those stalwart eighteenth-century defenders of an evangelical faith, Isaac Watts, Philip Doddridge and John Wesley.[4] These names alone illustrate the extent of Locke's influence throughout the eighteenth century, as theologian as well as philosopher, and the dismay shared by many at his perceived radical views of human being. In fairness, it must be said that Locke had his supporters as well as his critics, among them Edmund Law, Bishop of Carlisle, whose own convinced mortalism will be considered in the next chapter.[5]

For all that, Locke belongs essentially to the late seventeenth century, "one of the finest Genius's of the age he lived in",[6] to borrow the words of a later disciple and, perhaps more significantly, "not merely as a progenitor of the Enlightenment, but as one of the last of the Reformers".[7] Locke did not, of course, come to his task entirely unaware of similar concerns in contemporary thought. Charles Blount, the deist, whose later work was contemporaneous

1. *Locke, Paraphrase and Notes* (Wainwright, ed.), II, 2, 3. Wainwright contends that Locke's major concern in studying Scripture was to understand "the way to Salvation" and proposes that the last of four stages by which God offers to deliver mankind from "the condition of mortality" in which it now languishes as a consequence of Adam's transgression is resurrection from the dead. Then all who have sincerely believed in Christ, by whose own death and resurrection "all humanity was restored to life", will receive eternal life, *Paraphrase and Notes*, I, 39, 40.
2. Alan Sell, *John Locke and the Eighteenth-Century Divines* (Cardiff, 1997), 242.
3. *Ibid.,* 240.
4. *Ibid.,* 242ff.
5. Locke's supporters included John Tillotson, Archbishop of Canterbury, described by Nuovo as his friend and theological adviser, *John Locke,* 266. Tillotson shared at least Locke's aversion to the doctrine of eternal torment, see later, p. 124, n. 7.
6. Vincent Perronet, *A Vindication of Mr. Locke, from the Charge of giving Encouragement to Scepticism and Infidelity* (1736), Preface.
7. Nuovo, *John Locke,* lvii.

with that of Locke, may be cited as one example. Blount had earlier in *Anima Mundi* (1679) attempted a history of belief in the soul's immortality in which he portrayed both dualism and a monism which held to the death of the soul, a position which he seems at times to favour. Even so, it is not entirely clear that his death of the soul is not more akin to annihilationism than thnetopsychism. However, in *The Oracles of Reason* (1693) Blount's reference to certain Old Testament texts usually quoted in a thnetopsychist context[1] is followed by the comment that they have all been "misapplied, through weakness of misunderstanding" to support the idea of the soul's death. It is "irrational and useless" to believe the soul to be mortal.[2] This seems merely to reinforce an essential immortalism expressed earlier in the *Anima Mundi*.[3] Champion acknowledges that in Blount's work "it is often difficult to discern the author's own beliefs" amidst "the deliberate morass of different and conflicting positions".[4] It is a fair comment and may represent the genuine difficulties encountered by those who in the seventeenth century attempted to come to grips with the philosophical and theological dimensions of man and his soul, even from an historical perspective. Blount's work was known to Locke[5] whose own mind was turning to a consideration of the soul, its nature and its destiny, although he would soon reach different and considerably more well-defined conclusions.

Locke's leaning to a mortalist view of man can be traced back at least to 1683, although it did not begin to appear definitively until the revised edition of his *Essay concerning Humane Understanding* in 1694[6], and in his 'Adversaria Theologica 94' at about the same time.[7] In the latter, Locke commented briefly on the use of *psuche* in various New Testament texts and at length on the meaning of 1 Corinthians 15:40-55, which he argues seems to denote plainly "the different state of a man before & after the resurrection".[8] Paul, he says, "speaks of the whole man as dying & the whole man as raised", and so asks, 'What was this man before the resurrection, and what is he afterwards?' Paul's answer, Locke says, is that the same person who was corruptible and mortal prior to the resurrection is incorruptible and immortal after. Locke then comments:

1. Eccles. 3:19; 3: 20, 21; 7:12; 9:5.
2. Charles Blount, *The Oracles of Reason* (1693), 119, 127.
3. Charles Blount, *Anima Mundi* (1679), 92-3.
4. J.A.I. Champion, *The Pillars of Priestcraft Shaken* (Cambridge, 1992), 148.
5. A copy of the *Anima Mundi* was among the books in Locke's library, Harrison and Laslett, *Library of John Locke*, 88.
6. See Sell, *John Locke*, 240, and Locke's *Essay*. The original title has ". . . *Humane Understanding* . . .".
7. On the date and content of the 'Adversaria', an unpublished notebook of theological reflections, see Nuovo, xxix, xxx. It may be helpful to remember that Locke did not edit the 'Adversaria' for publication.
8. Locke, 'Adversaria Theologica 94', in Nuovo, *John Locke*, 28-9.

'tis plain that tis the same that is corruptible which puts on incorruption, v. 53. So that immortality is not at all owing nor built on immateriality as in its own nature incorruptible. The Apostle knew not that argument which is so much insisted on but quite the contrary, and says this corruptible must be changed & put on incorruption & this mortal must put on immortality. Which corruptible & mortal is not meant of the body in contra distinction to the soul but of the whole man, as is plain by the preceding part of this chapter, particularly vss. 18, 19, 22, 35-37. That which is sewn [sic] is the whole seed, [and] that which dies is the whole seed.[1]

Locke then deals with an objection sometimes raised from a passage in II Corinthians, saying that Paul's later comment should be taken in the context of I Corinthians 15:

If any one think that from St.Paul's way of speaking II Cor. 5:1, 2, 3, 4 he may conclude that there is in us an immaterial immutable substance distinct from the body I desire him to compare I Cor. 15:35,36,37,38 & then see whether by that argument he must not as well conclude that in a grain of wheat there is an immaterial substance which is called the grain of wheat as well as in the other place tis an immaterial substance which is called we, Jn. 5:28,29. And it is further remarkable that in the whole new testament there is no such thing as any mention of the resurrection of the body how ever it crept into our creed, but every where the resurrection is spoke of as the whole man.[2]

Nuovo summarises this passage in the 'Adversaria' by saying that for Locke "it is not just the body that is resurrected but the whole man who, before this, was altogether mortal".[3]

The mature expression of Locke's thnetopsychism is found in the substantial theological treatise *The Reasonableness of Christianity, As delivered in the Scriptures,* published first anonymously in 1695, and in his paraphrase and notes on I Corinthians 15, published posthumously in1706.[4] Locke's renowned controversy with Edward Stillingfleet, Bishop of Worcester, during the last decade of the seventeenth century originated with Stillingfleet's unease over Locke's views of human existence, personal identity and the nature of the soul, and culminated in his concern that Locke's ideas substantially undermined the biblical doctrine of the resurrection of the body contending, among other

1. *Ibid.,* 29-30.
2. *Ibid.* The entire note, which is the second and most comprehensive argument offered against the idea of *Anima Humana Immaterialis,* is transcribed by Nouvo.
3. *Ibid.,* xxxiii.
4. See also his *Resurrectio et quae Sequuntur* which Nuovo, after Wainwright, dates c. 1699 (*John Locke,* liv), and which is in effect a brief exposition of the relevant sections of I Corinthians 15 with references to I Thessalonians 4.

things, that Locke "implied that the dead might be raised with different bodies from those which they had during their mortal lives".[1] The debate was never satisfactorily concluded for Stillingfleet died in 1699, although by then Locke had repeatedly emphasised the necessity of the resurrection in *The Reasonableness of Christianity.*[2] Those who believe receive immortality *at* the resurrection and enter into eternal life *after* the resurrection.[3] Locke felt that many of the details concerning the resurrection of the body which others seemed to believe were so important had not been revealed in Scripture, and rested in the assurance of I Corinthians 15 that the righteous would receive life again at the resurrection, content to let others argue about the precise nature of the resurrection body.[4]

Locke's insistence on the resurrection as the gateway to immortality for all believers is reiterated in his comments on I Corinthians 15:42 ff. Noting that the resurrection of the dead here referred to by Paul is in fact the resurrection only of "the just", i.e., the redeemed, Locke states that by virtue of the resurrection believers will "all be changed . . . by putting on incorruptibility and immortality", since "when the dead are raised, they who are alive shall be changed in the twinkling of an eye".[5] Further, with regard to the body, "this corruptible thing must put on incorruption, and this mortal thing must put on immortality".[6] Incorruption and immortality are not natural, pre-resurrection attributes. They are attained only through the resurrection of the dead and the accompanying change in the condition of believers then living. Lest there be any doubt, Locke emphasises that "corruption", i.e. the "flesh and blood" which all men possess by virtue of being human, cannot "inherit incorruption, i.e. immortality". But through the resurrection that which hitherto has been incorruptible "shall put on incorruption" and that which has been mortal "shall put on immortality".[7] In other words, that which believers do not presently possess, immortality, they will possess in the future, when resurrected from the

1. [Edward Stillingfleet], *The Bishop of Worcester's Answer to Mr. Locke's Second Letter* (1698), 32-44; Locke, *Paraphrase and Notes* (Wainwright, ed.) I, 2.
2. [John Locke], *The Reasonableness of Christianity, As delivered in the Scriptures* (1695), 10, 11, 203, 207.
3. *Ibid.,* 203-4, 232.
4. John Locke, 'Paraphrase and Notes on the First Epistle of St. Paul to the Corinthians'(1706) in *A Paraphrase and Notes on the Epistles of St. Paul* (1707), 100. He did concede, however, that the spiritual body would have in it "an essential and natural life", able to "subsist perpetually of itself, without the help of meat or drink"and without "decay or any tendency to dissolution", 101. Thomas Beconsall was not satisfied with Locke at this point, and opposed him in *The Doctrine of a General Resurrection: Wherein the Identity of the Rising Body is asserted, against the Socinians and Scepticks* (Oxford, 1697) arguing for "the resurrection of the same body", 14ff. A copy of Beconsall's book was in Locke's personal library.
5. *Ibid.,* 99.
6. *Ibid.,* 100.
7. *Ibid.*

grave or translated with those living at the coming of Christ. Thus "all men [i.e. the righteous] shall return to life again at the last day".[1]

Sell has concluded, in an otherwise excellent study, that "Locke does not offer a fully-fledged eschatology".[2] Judged by the detailed extent of some contemporary eschatologies that may be true, but Sell seems to overlook the foregoing, as well as the thnetopsychist excursus with which Locke opens *The Reasonableness of Christianity*. The latter is, unfortunately, a serious oversight for Locke's view of man and his ultimate destiny cannot be evaluated adequately without it. Nuovo has understood Locke much more accurately when he points out that I Corinthians 15: 20-1 represents "the central theme" of *The Reasonableness*.[3] Locke begins by arguing that Adam was created with conditional immortality which he lost as a consequence of disobedience and the Fall. "By this fall he lost Paradise . . . i.e., he lost bliss and immortality", Locke says.[4] Commenting on Genesis 2:17, he explains that Adam had been warned that by eating the forbidden fruit he would die, although "in the day he did eat he did not actually die, but was turned out of Paradise from the Tree of Life . . . lest he should take thereof and live for ever". Locke then says, "This shows that the state of Paradise was a state of Immortality . . . which he lost that very day", adding that all this is clear to anyone who "unbiassed reads the Scriptures".[5] Consequently, "loss of immortality is the portion" of all subsequent sons and daughters of Adam, since by Adam's transgression "all men are mortal" and subject to death.[6] It was thus that death impinged on human existence and became part of the human experience. Death is a consequence of man's natural condition of mortality. It is logically and experientially the opposite of immortality. The meaning of death should be plain enough, but it has become distorted. Given that by death some understand "endless torment in hell-fire", Locke says "it seems a strange way of understanding a law, which requires the plainest and directest [*sic*] words, that by death should be meant eternal life in misery".[7] The doctrine of eternal torment is the result of "vain philosophy and foolish metaphysics of some men".[8]

1. [Locke], *Reasonableness of Christianity*, 207.
2. Sell, *John Locke*, 262.
3. Nuovo, *John Locke*, liv.
4. [Locke], *Reasonableness of Christianity*, 3.
5. *Ibid.*
6. *Ibid.*, 13, 4.
7. *Ibid.*, 4, 5. Locke cites Tillotson's sermon on Matt. 25:46, "Of the Eternity of Hell Torments", in support of his assertion that "everlasting punishment does not necessarily signify a life in eternal torments", *Reasonableness of Christianity*, 15. Tillotson's sermon, where he argues that the words 'forever' and 'everlasting' do not in Scripture always signify "an endless duration", referring to the eternal fire of Jude 7 which destroyed Sodom and Gomorrha as "fire that was not extinguished till those cities were utterly destroyed", is included in his *Works* (1741), III.
8. [Locke], *Reasonableness of Christianity*, 8.

The thnetopsychism implicit in *The Reasonableness of Christianity* is apparent in Locke's understanding of death and what happens then to human identity and consciousness, and of how death and its consequences are reversed. "I must confess by death", he says, "I can understand nothing but a ceasing to be, the losing of all actions of life and sense".[1] Adam was to return eventually to dust, "and then have no more life or sense than the dust had out of which he was made".[2] This is the human condition. It is an incontrovertible consequence of Adam's sin. It has passed to the entire race. "Loss of immortality is the portion of all". But it does not mean that man is without hope. It does not, as Locke's critics contended, undermine faith in a future life. Regardless of death, man may aspire to eternal life and immortality. It is provided by Christ, through the gospel, through the resurrection. In a sequence of unambiguous statements, Locke asserts that Christ has conquered death and consequently has made eternal life possible for those who now live under the penalty of sin and the threat of death. There is therefore hope. "From this estate of death, Jesus Christ restores all mankind to life, I Cor. 15.22 ". "The life which Jesus Christ restores to all men is that life which they receive again at the Resurrection". "Men are by the second Adam restored to life again". "Christ will bring them all to life again".[3] Believers who thus rest in their graves asleep "become immortal", "put on immortality", "return to life again", through their faith in the redemptive work of Christ "at the resurrection ".[4] It is difficult to read in all this anything but thnetopsychism, and difficult to understand why Locke's critics could not see that his Christian mortalism eventually brought a believer to the same desired end as did belief in the soul's immortality. It is, moreover, clear that Locke's mortalism is not only anthropologically oriented, as might be expected from his interest in the nature of man and the *Essay concerning Human Understanding*, but that it is also strongly Christological. This quite transparent Christology substantiates Nuovo's assessment of Locke's theology as a whole, that it is grounded in the proposition that the principal benefit that "Christ has gained for mankind is immortality".[5]

There were other difficulties with the traditional eschatology, beyond its incipient attack on biblical Christology, as the mortalists never tired of pointing out. Locke himself, driven by his own philosophical questionings brought to

1. *Ibid.,* 6. Locke's use of the term 'soul' is a consequence of a fully developed thnetopsychist view of man. The 'soul' is the mind, the thinking, rational aspect of the living person, and as such is therefore immaterial.
2. *Ibid.,* 7.
3. *Ibid.,* 10,11.
4. *Ibid.,* 204, 207.
5. Nuovo, *John Locke,* xlix. Nuovo clears Locke of the charge of Socinianism even though he concedes that Locke had read the works of both Laelius and Faustus Socinus, whose own thnetopsychism we noted in ch. 1, see Nuovo, *John Locke,* li, lii, xviii. Locke may also have known of the work of Crellius, *Paraphrase and Notes* (Wainwright, ed.), 467-8.

bear on the assertions and assumptions of ecclesiastical dogma, pointed out one of the more unreasonable and unacceptable consequences deriving from belief in the soul's immortality. In the *Essay concerning Human Understanding* Locke argues from the traditional standpoint:

> Taking, as we ordinarily do, the soul of a man for an immaterial substance, independent from matter, and indifferentiable to it, there can, from the nature of things, be no absurdity at all to suppose that the same soul may, at different times, be united to different bodies, and with them make up, for that time, one man.[1]

We may be sure that none of those who so strenuously opposed Locke, defending the immortality and immateriality of the soul as essential to personal identity, would have wanted to be pushed in that direction. Perhaps in Locke's mind *The Reasonableness of Christianity* was also an attempt to demonstrate the unreasonableness of unrevealed paganism and corrupted versions of Christianity which relied on infiltrated pre-Christian thought to substantiate their most hallowed doctrines. At the very least it requires that Locke's view of man be evaluated from a theological as well as a philosophical perspective.

So, from all the possible starting points available to him, Locke begins his great theological treatise on the reasonableness of the Christian faith with a lengthy and reasoned exposition of the thnetopsychist view of man. From that point he develops his thesis that authentic Christian faith is essentially reasonable, that is to say it is normally consonant with reason, sometimes beyond reason, but never contrary to reason. It seems indisputable that, in Locke's considered view, an understanding of man's constitution and nature is not only of first importance in its own right, but that it is also the necessary foundation for understanding the rest of the Christian revelation.[2] That revelation, when understood with the aid of reason, can be seen as a coherent account of man's past, present and future. It also seems that Locke wanted to say that the idea of the soul's immateriality and immortality was not only unscriptural, but also inherently unreasonable and inimical to biblical revelation and the ultimate realisation of the divine purpose.

1. Locke, *Essay concerning Humane Understanding* (2nd edn, 1694), 190.
2. The relationship of man's nature and guilt to the concept of original sin is an important dimension of Locke's overall theology and is explored in the opening pages of *The Reasonableness of Christianity* and elsewhere in Locke's writings, but is beyond the scope of this study. Nuovo summarises it by saying "The only consequence of Adam's sin that Locke allows may be justly passed on to posterity is death", *John Locke*, liv.

Chapter Five
Early Eighteenth-Century
Debates and Digressions

In the previous chapter it was suggested that John Locke belonged principally to the seventeenth century. His dates, 1632-1704, substantiate the assertion, even though the influence of his writings, most of which were published before 1700, was felt for generations to come. Conversely it may be said that Locke's contemporary, Henry Layton, 1622-1705, belonged more to the eighteenth century than to the seventeenth, precisely because most of his mortalist writings appeared after 1700 and were only published for general circulation in 1706.[1] These distinctions are, of course, merely superficial. The truth is that Locke, the influential philosopher and Layton, the little-known lawyer, both mortalists, belong to both the seventeenth and eighteenth centuries. Human thought and philosophical enquiry rarely pause to acknowledge the calendar or the passing of centuries. The mortalism advocated by Locke and Layton was a development of earlier English mortalist thought and, in Layton's case, a reaction to earlier and contemporary assertions of the soul's immortality, themselves in many instances reactions to mortalist doctrine. The writings of Locke and Layton were also catalysts for further debate, definition and re-definition as the eighteenth century unfolded. We may think of them, together with William Coward and Samuel Bold, as the link between the influential mortalists of the mid-seventeenth century, Overton, Hobbes and Milton, and the equally influential Anglican mortalists of the mid-eighteenth century, Edmund Law, Peter Peckard, and Francis Blackburne.

An indication of mortalism's continuing appeal around the turn of the century may be found in two sermons of George Bull, preached during the 1690s and published posthumously in 1713.[2] Bull, with an Oxford D.D.

---

1. See Appendix I for a bibliography of Layton's works, most of which had been published individually for private circulation before the bound collection of 1706. Locke's personal library contained seven of Layton's works, including an early version of the *Search after Souls*, printed only for private circulation, Harrison and Laslett, *Library of John Locke*, 170-1.
2. The sermon 'That the Soul of Man Subsists after Death' was dated 1710 in the collected works of Bull published in 1827. Both sermons are undated in the 1713 edition. They were also published in 1765 by Leonard Chappelow, again in opposition to the mortalist 'heresy' still raising its head in his day, see ch. 6, p. 150, n. 2.

and later to be bishop of St. Davids, had preached vigorously against both psychopannychism and thnetopsychism, affirming that "the soul of man subsists after death, in a place of abode provided by God for it, till the resurrection".[1] Bull had been particularly concerned to refute the thnetopsychist opinions of "many professed Christians" who denied the continued existence of the soul after death and who maintained that "the soul dies and is extinguished with the body" until the resurrection "of the whole man".[2] It may justifiably be asked, 'Against whom were Bull's strictures directed?' Baptist eschatology had by the 1690s undergone significant change, Milton's *Treatise on Christian Doctrine* was unknown, and Locke's views, if yet published, were unlikely to have greatly influenced the average believer. Just who the "many" were whom Bull sought to counter is not clear. They are not named and have left no evidence, but evidently there were enough of them and their views weighed sufficiently heavily on Bull's mind to require specific attention and, after the writings of Layton, Coward and others had been circulated and digested, to warrant publication. It may be, of course, that the late publication of Bull's sermons was an attempt to stay the influence of the early eighteenth-century mortalists whose own writings were by then already in circulation.

While George Bull's work also suggests a continuity between late seventeenth- and early eighteenth-century mortalism, the consolidation and clarification of the mortalist case in the early eighteenth century was unquestionably indebted to Locke, Layton and Coward. Despite some tentative and short-lived diversions in other directions, George Benson, Joseph Nicol Scott, and the anonymous author of *The Materiality and Mortality of the Soul of Man, and its Sameness with the Body* reinvigorated the mortalist cause in the late 1720s and the 1730s.[3] The combined efforts of these early eighteenth-century mortalists and those who shortly followed them ensured that mortalism in its thnetopsychist form finally came of age as an alternative source of hope for English Christians doubtful about the soul and its future but still convinced of the certainty of the future life promised to believers in divine revelation.

Samuel Bold, Henry Layton and William Coward
The mortalist writings of Samuel Bold (1649-1737), like those of his contemporary Henry Layton, also appeared during the last decade of the seventeenth century and the first decade of the eighteenth century. They anticipated the lively and lengthy debate provoked by Locke, a debate which

1. George Bull, *Some Important Points of Primitive Christianity Maintained and Defended in Several Sermons and Other Discourses*(1713), I, 39.
2. *Ibid.*, 48.
3. *The Materiality and Mortality of the Soul of Man, and its Sameness with the Body, Asserted and Prov'd from the Holy Scriptures of the Old and New Testament* (1729). The contents of this carefully titled work and the views of Benson and Scott are examined later.

was in turn greatly amplified and extended by Layton and Coward. Although remembered for his dissenting sympathies – he had resigned as vicar of Shapwick in Dorset in 1682 after preaching and publishing in defence of dissenters – Bold is best known as a personal friend of Locke and an early defender of Locke's often controversial philosophical and theological views.[1] Although originally a staunch immortalist,[2] Bold's opinions changed through his acquaintance with Locke and the influence of Locke's writings.[3] Bold's *Observations on the Animadversions . . . on a Late Book Entituled, The Reasonableness of Christianity*, a defence of Locke's famous work against the high Calvinist John Edwards,[4] was published in 1698 while Bold was rector of Steeple in the Isle of Purbeck. It was one of the first of many affirmations of Locke's theology and understanding of human being which were to appear over the next half century or so.

In the *Observations* Bold, following Locke, argued that immortality, which mankind had lost through Adam's transgression, was to be restored by Christ. Indeed, Bold found that Locke, through the "sole, attentive and unbiassed reading of the Scriptures", had been obliged to conclude that the various aspects of Christ's intervention in human history, His "coming into the world", could be reduced to one fundamental purpose – to provide immortality for humankind.[5] His sufferings, death and resurrection were all directed to that end. "Satisfaction itself was not the ultimate end of his coming into the world", Bold declared. Christ's death and resurrection were related to "a further end . . . the great end for which Christ came into the world". This was unequivocally the provision of "immortality for mankind". It was "the great end of his undertaking. . . . He hath purchased immortality for mankind", and has done so "absolutely".[6] Christ's provision of immortality is the only way by which mortal man can become immortal. So Bold asks, "What can be pretended for men's being immortal, any other way than by Christ?" "He will raise them

1. Locke's library contained eleven of Bold's works, including all those which Bold published in defence of Locke during his lifetime, Harrison and Laslett, *Library of Locke*, 89.

2. See his *Meditations Concerning Death* (1696).

3. Wainwright points out that Locke intended that Bold should edit the manuscript of his posthumous *Paraphrase and Notes on the Epistles of St. Paul* and that it is "highly likely" that he had read the work and discussed it with Locke before the latter's death in 1704, Wainwright (ed.), *Locke, Paraphrase and Notes*, I, 10.

4. John Edwards, *Some Thoughts Concerning the Several Causes and Occasions of Atheism, Especially in the Present Age* (1695).

5. Samuel Bold, *Observations on the Animadversions . . . on a Late Book Entituled, The Reasonableness of Christianity, As delivered in the Scriptures* (1698), 9, 85-6. Bold had a year previously defended Locke against Edwards's attack on *The Reasonableness of Christianity* and his implied charge of Socinianism in *Socinianism Unmasked* (1697) in *A Short Discourse of the True Knowledge of Christ Jesus . . . .with some Animadversions on Mr Edwards's Reflections on The Reasonableness of Christianity, and on his book Entituled Socinianism Unmask'd* (1697).

6. Bold, *Observations*, 87, 85.

from death", and it will happen at the last day.[1] Even then, eternal life could not be taken for granted, since it would be bestowed "upon certain conditions". Specifically, it is for those "who heartily take Jesus for their Lord, and faithfully obey and follow Him". These obedient followers "shall at the Resurrection be everlastingly blessed".[2] Citing the fourth-century theologian Athanasius, Bold asserted that Christ's redemptive work in its entirety could better be explained from a mortalist standpoint than from the standpoint of traditional medieval soteriology. The "truth of the case" was that the Saviour came to provide that which man did not already possess inherently. Hence the immortality "lost by Adam's transgression" is "restored . . . by Christ, in that he will raise them all from death".[3]

In a work published the following year, 1699, also written in defence of Locke, Bold stated with regard to the nature of man, that two fundamental articles of faith were derived from "divine revelation". Firstly, "That man became mortal by sin", and secondly, "That after the resurrection men will be immortal".[4] In a yet later work, this time in defence of Locke against Daniel Whitby and Samuel Parker both of whom had argued against Locke, contending that death means only death of the body, Bold pointed out that in Scripture as well as in "propriety of speech" death impinges on the whole person. "Death rather happeneth to the man", he says, and not merely to the body [5], adding that the concept that after death "man continues safe and sound" was beyond his comprehension.[6] It is the whole person that dies, as it is the whole person which will be resurrected. As we have seen it was not unfamiliar territory, but it would be fought over with great zeal and considerable erudition as the mortalist debate was argued back and forth for much of the eighteenth century.[7]

Henry Layton was without question the most prolific writer in the history

1. *Ibid.*, 86-7.
2. *Ibid.*, 86. Bold makes a distinction between "immortality" and "eternal bliss", both of which were lost by Adam's transgression. Immortality "is restored to all men by Christ, in that he will raise them all from death". Eternal bliss is for those only who in this present life "heartily take Jesus for their Lord, and faithfully obey and follow Him". Those not called to eternal bliss at the resurrection suffer the punishment of the damned.
3. *Ibid.*
4. Samuel Bold, *Some Considerations on the Principal Objections and Arguments. . . against Mr. Lock's Essay of Humane Understanding* (1699), 25.
5. [Samuel Bold], *A Discourse Concerning the Resurrection of the Same Body* (1705), 19-20.
6. *Ibid.*, 20.
7. The protagonists in the early years of the eighteenth-century debate were evidently not all of the same calibre. In a letter to Locke in 1703 Bold commented tartly on John Broughton's *Psychologia*, saying that it had "not at all enlightened" him, its principal effect being to confirm "that there are a sort of men who affect to write about what they do not understand", Bold to Locke, Aug. 23, 1703, in E.S. De Beer(ed.), *The Correspondence of John Locke*, VIII (Oxford,1989), 8, 49.

of English mortalism.[1] Little is known of Layton except that he was the eldest son of Francis Layton of Rawdon, Yorkshire, and that he studied at Oxford and Grays Inn before being called to the Bar. Yet between 1690 and 1704 he produced at least fourteen separate works in defence of the mortalist position,[2] all in the first instance published privately, anonymously, and without date. They were collected after his death in 1706 and published in two volumes as *A Search after Souls: or, The Immortality of a Humane Soul, Theologically, Philosophically, and Rationally Considered*, by "A Lover of Truth". Virtually all the works in this collection were Layton's responses to current or earlier publications by various individuals who had written on the nature and origin of the soul from a philosophical or theological standpoint, advocating its immateriality and immortality.[3] Layton's strong aversion to this traditional view led him to devote the last fifteen years of his life to refuting the arguments advanced in its favour. To Richard Bentley's proposition that the existence of an immortal soul in man is self-evident, Layton stoutly responded in 1692, "But this I do utterly deny and think the contrary more evident".[4] He argues that there is nothing identifiable as a separate entity within man enabling him to function as a rational being, "not any particular thing in man's composition that thinks, argues, etc.", or which enables him to undertake "all other natural things". It is the man himself, "the whole composition of soul and body by a divine and admirable contexture united", which lives and functions as a human being, "and not that something which he will surmise to be the soul".[5] Bentley, whose learning and scholarship was by now well established, was probably unaware of Layton's criticisms, and in any case might have considered them beneath him.

Layton came to his mortalist convictions late in life. He says that he first began to reflect seriously on the nature of the soul and the afterlife in 1690 after reading the second edition of Richard Baxter's *Dying Thoughts*, which had been published in 1688. Regarding Baxter's affirmation of the soul's ascent to heaven at death to be with Christ, and "the necessity of believing it", Layton

1. Layton is noticed by Blackburne, Mills and Froom, and also by D.M. Canright, *A History of the Doctrine of the Soul* (Battle Creek, MI, 1870), but is not given the attention he deserves by any of these writers. On Layton, see also a letter dated 1709 from the antiquary William Smith, who was Layton's nephew, to Ralph Thoresby, in [J. Hunter] ed., *Letters of Eminent Men Addressed to Ralph Thoresby, F. R. S.*, II(1832), 194.
2. See Appendix I for an analysis and bibliography of Layton's works.
3. Appendix I also includes bibliographical information on the works to which Layton responded between 1690 and 1704.
4. [Henry Layton], *Observations upon a Sermon Intituled, A Confutation of Atheism from the Faculties of the Soul, alias, Matter and Motion cannot think: Preached April 4, 1692. By way of Refutation* [1692],1, in *A Search after Souls: or, The Immortality of a Humane Soul, Theologically, Philosophically, and Rationally Considered* (1706), I.
5. *Ibid.*, 2, 3.

wrote in 1691, "It seemed an over-great morsel to swallow all this together".[1]
He advises Baxter that it would become him better "to enquire after . . . the
attainable truth of things", specifically the soul and its destiny, than "to sit
down contented with his own present conceit".[2] Presumably this was intended
to turn Baxter's thoughts to Scripture and make him realise that his position
might be erroneous. On Ecclesiastes 3:19, a standard text for mortalists and
a tricky one for their opponents, Layton complained that Baxter passed over
it "as lightly as if it were a straw".[3] But Layton's well-intentioned advice was
all too late. Baxter died that year, and it is highly doubtful that he would have
been persuaded in any case.

From then on, Layton embarked upon a tireless campaign of refutation,
taking up theological cudgels to belabour many of those who ventured
to publish in favour of the soul's immortality and separate existence. They
included Walter Charleton, the royal physician, William Sherlock, Dean of
St. Paul's, and William Nicholls, rector of Selsey and Bushey and subsequently
Canon of Chichester, as well as lesser lights including Timothy Manlove,
John Broughton and Thomas Wadsworth, whose *Antipsychothanasia, or, The
Immortality of the Soul Explained and Proved by Scripture and Reason* (1670),
was one of the first pro-immortality works considered by Layton after he
had read Baxter's *Dying Thoughts* in 1690. Layton's search for souls, which
took him through the writings of these and other immortalists, led him to a
thnetopsychist position as unambiguous, well-defined, and consistently argued
as that of any English mortalist before or since. Blackburne later said, after
the most careful investigation, that Layton "made no scruple of opposing the
sentiments of some of the greatest heroes of his own time".[4]

It would be tedious and repetitive to analyse Layton's mortalism in any
great detail, as indeed Layton himself frequently became in dealing at length
with each new publication favouring the soul's immortality and which he felt
required a response. Suffice it to say that no aspect of mortalist theology was
left untouched and few of its opponents' arguments unanswered in the 1500
pages Layton wrote between 1691 and 1704. It was a massive output, even by
the standards of the day. He came to believe early in his enquiry that the idea
of an immortal soul antedated Christianity and that it could be found in many
pre-Christian Greek philosophers, including Pythagoras, Anaxagoras and
Plato, claiming that the majority of the early Greek and Latin church fathers
did not accept it.[5] Moreover, the idea was contrary to revelation – "we find

1. [Henry Layton], *A Search after Souls and Spiritual Operations in Man* [1691], 3; in
   A Search after Souls, I.
2. *Ibid.*, 7.
3. *Ibid.*, 4.
4. Blackburne, *Historical View*, 183.
5. [Henry Layton], *Observations upon Mr. Wadsworth's Book of The Souls Immortality,
   and his Confutation of the Opinion of the Souls Inactivity to the Time of General
   Resurrection* [1690], 8,16; in *A Search after Souls*, I.

not one text in Scripture, that says in express terms, man hath an immaterial, or separately subsisting, or immortal soul"[1]- and contrary to "sound" reason, Layton's two "guides" to the "discovery of truth", to which he professed "an absolute subjection".[2] "Both by reason and revelation we may, and do, attain a more large knowledge of God".[3] Although Scripture is authoritative, Layton's view of the Bible as revelation is reasonable and balanced. He maintains that he is "no idolizer of the Scripture", believing that every saying and sentence therein is divine truth but holding that "whatsoever doctrines or opinions can be proved by a strong current or stream of Scripture texts, ought to be accepted and believed as absolute truths and the very word of God".[4] It was a proposition which led him to assert repeatedly and uncompromisingly that the Bible did not support innate human immortality.

In addition to revelation and reason, Layton argues that observation and experience must be allowed to inform us concerning the nature of man. If it can be demonstrated that the soul, during the lifetime of a man, acts even in some instances of itself and apart from the body, then it might be admissible to believe in its separate existence. But experience and observation consistently demonstrate that this does not happen.[5] Against the argument that a separate soul is necessary for man to function as a rational being, Layton counters that observation and experience indicate the contrary. It is the person, the "whole man", that constitutes a living, acting, rational being, not a distinct, immaterial entity within him. Layton argues that the natural world as a whole functions in accordance with this principle of wholeness. "Plants live, grow, flourish and fructify" of themselves, as dynamic, autonomous organisms. Insects and animals do likewise. So with man. He may "perform all his natural functions by the like means of a material spirit, inspiring and acting the proper organs which God hath made apt for such purposes".[6] The soul is the living person, not an entity that can function apart from the body. It cannot "act without the bodily organs, think without the brain, . . . see without an eye, speak without a tongue, or generate without a proper organ for that purpose".[7]

Layton frequently identifies the soul with the mind, man's rational, thinking

1. [Layton], *Search after Souls and Spiritual Operations*, 196.
2. [Henry Layton], *A Reply to a Letter Dated Sept. 14. 1702*, 70, in *Search after Souls*, II.
3. [Henry Layton], *Observations upon a Short Treatise, Written by Mr. Timothy Manlove: Intituled, The Immortality of the Soul Asserted . . .*(1697?), 77, in *Search after Souls*, I.
4. [Layton], *Reply to a Letter*, 69.
5. [Layton], *Search after Souls and Spiritual Operations*, 170-2.
6. [Layton], *Observations . . . Confutation of Atheism*, 2. By the phrase "material spirit" Layton seems to intend that which later writers would describe as the life force, even life itself. Spirit is not to be understood in the sense in which some other later writers use it loosely as a synonym for soul.
7. *Ibid.*, 3.

faculty, and hence associates it with the brain: "and in no part of the body can the soul act rationally but in the head".[1] In response to John Broughton's assertion that nature confirms the soul's immortality, Layton contends that the opposite is, in fact, the case. Observation of human experience and physiology do not support the existence of an immaterial entity in man, not even in the brain, essential though that organ is to human identity and functionality:

> Experience assures us that the members and organs of the head employ themselves . . . in the agitation of the mind, and in life we cannot perceive any particular motor which acts or works amongst them. And when after we are Dead our Heads are dissected, nothing could ever be found therein, but Brain, Nerves, Veins, Arteries, Muscles, Skins, Films, Nodes, and other Material and necessary Organs, and Instruments, which I think God did use in that person whilst alive for producing Life, Intellect, and Thought in him; and may, and I think doth do so in all Persons who have a Sound and Healthful Life in the World.[2]

While immortalists might have been able to pick holes in that argument, it was much more difficult to dismiss the essential mortalist concept of the whole person. Thus Layton speaks frequently of the "compositum". It is man in his functional completeness, a thinking, rational being that is a soul in the true sense. In defence of mortalism's fundamental doubts about the soul's separate existence and its ability to function rationally as a distinct entity, and to emphasise the inability of its advocates to provide a convincing and "satisfactory" account of the soul and its activities, Layton requires a more convincing argument than any of its proponents had hitherto been able to provide:

> Except they do give a better Account of their Soul, and its power and manner of acting than men can do of the manner of acting in the head and brain, by the animal (material) spirits and other natural parts and powers of the body, it seems they are not to be believed, or admitted to impose upon men their doctrine of a spiritual and self-subsisting soul as a distinct being from that of the body.[3]

In Layton's own terms, the wholistic explanation of man as a "compositum" explains human existence more satisfactorily and more rationally than the prevailing, historically conditioned immortalist view.

On the basis, then, of revelation, reason and observation, Layton's search for the human soul ended in thnetopsychism. "My sort of soul", he says, "is very congruous". It is as set forth in Scripture and confirmed by experience,

---

1. [Henry Layton], *A Second Part of a Treatise Intituled A Search after Souls* [1692?], 107, in *Search after Souls*, I.
2. [Henry Layton], *Observations upon a Treatise Intitled Psychologia : or, An Account of the Nature of the Rational Soul* [1703], 40, in *Search after Souls*, II.
3. [Layton], *A Search after Souls and Spiritual Operations*, 14.

the man's self, his person, his very life, "the soul and the body . . . affected and affixed one to another, for they are both of a piece; are generated, grow, stand, decay, and fall together, rejoice and suffer, share and share alike . . . The soul cannot understand without the brain, and if that be crazed or spoiled, the soul cannot understand".[1] So at death, in the thnetopsychist view we have now seen so frequently in the writings of earlier mortalists, the soul ceases to exist, death itself is called a sleep and man's hope is bound up with Christ and His future. "Men die; thus they rest, and believers sleep in Jesus, till the time of the restitution of all things". At Christ's coming, amongst other things, "Men shall be restored to their former beings and become the same persons that they were before". And "such a rest, is a pious death, and in assured hope of a joyful resurrection".[2] Layton speaks here for all mortalists, psychopannychist as well as thnetopsychist. Beyond the sleep of death, understood literally or metaphorically, the resurrection awaited the faithful believer, and it was this that mattered most. The resurrection added hope and assurance to mortalist belief, giving it substance and credibility, and few expressed it better or with more conviction than Henry Layton, English mortalism's prolific early eighteenth-century apologist.

Before death terminated Layton's search in 1705, the like-minded William Coward had embarked on a similar journey, spurred on by a conviction that belief in the immortal soul was "derogatory" to true Christian faith and the ground of "many absurd" and "superstitious opinions".[3] Coward, a physician who practised in Northampton before moving to London, was a graduate of Wadham College, Oxford, a member of the College of Surgeons from 1695 until his death in 1725, and the author of medical works, religious pamphlets and occasional poetry. His claim to fame, however, lay in a series of works published in quick succession in the 1700s, in which he investigated the immortal soul doctrine from rational, biblical and philosophical standpoints, and which from the start generated lively discussion, and eventually notoriety. His *Grand Essay: or A Vindication of Reason and Religion* (1704) was reviewed by a committee appointed by the House of Commons, who decided that it and his other works contained "offensive doctrine", and ordered them to be burned by the common hangman.[4] The doctrines which caused offence could only have been his mortalism since to that point he had not written on any other topic. His first work, *Second Thoughts Concerning Human Soul, Demonstrating the Notion of Human Soul As believ'd to be a Spiritual Immortal Substance,*

1. [Layton], *Second Part of a Treatise*, 100, 103.
2. *Ibid.*, 153.
3. [William Coward], *Second Thoughts Concerning Human Soul, Demonstrating the Notion of Human Soul As believ'd to be a Spiritual Immortal Substance, united to Human Body, To be a Plain Heathenish Invention, And not Consonant to the Principles of Philosophy, Reason, or Religion* (1702), title-page.
4. *DNB*, s.v. William Coward.

united to Human Body, To be a Plain Heathenish Invention, And not Consonant to the Principles of Philosophy, Reason, or Religion (1702) was published under the pseudonym Estibius Psychalethes, and drew replies from Benjamin Keach, John Turner, John Broughton, and William Nicholls, many of whom quickly attracted the attention of Henry Layton. Coward and Layton were thus drawn into an unpremeditated alliance in the mortalist cause, and the doctrine of the soul's immortality simultaneously came under attack on two flanks.

Coward seems to have been content to allow Layton to respond to most of those who opposed him, but did publish, a year later, *Farther Thoughts Concerning Human Soul, in defence of Second Thoughts* (1703) in part a response to Turner's *Brief Vindication of the Separate Existence and Immortality of the Soul* (1702) which had quickly appeared to rebut Coward's mortalism. *Farther Thoughts* sustained and clarified Coward's position, and raised the level of the debate which by now was beginning to attract considerable attention. The following year, 1704, saw the publication of a second edition of *Second Thoughts*, dedicated to the clergy of the Church of England, which argued that the doctrine of the soul's immortality was "incoherent" and "inconsistent with itself, and the common principles of reason".[1] Coward also took the opportunity here to distinguish his thnetopsychist position from that of psychopannychism, declaring "I do not say the soul sleeps, but man, . . . without life, will lie in the grave, and in a state of insensibility until the day of general resurrection, as in a deep sleep . . .".[2] Earlier Coward had described himself as a "Vitanimist", "one who holds man not compounded of an immaterial substance called soul, and a material substance called body, but do boldly assert . . .that he is compounded only of life and body. . .".[3] The term does not appear to have been perpetuated, although it does place a positive emphasis on the nature of man in life in contrast to the more frequent thnetopsychist emphasis on his condition after death.

In that same year, 1704, Coward published the notorious *Grand Essay* in which he set out, once again, to underline the importance of reason in determining a credible faith, and to demonstrate that belief in the immateriality and immortality of the soul was both unbiblical and unreasonable. He complained that to question the concept of " immaterial substance" was to court the charge of "Hobbism", even though the idea that immaterial substance has existence was inherently self-contradictory and contrary to reason.[4] "I can as soon conceive a black whiteness", Coward said, "as frame such a conception in my mind".[5]

1. [William Coward], *Second Thoughts Concerning Human Soul* (2nd. edn,1704), Ep. Ded., sig.A3 *r.*
2. *Ibid.,* sig.A7 *r.*
3. [William Coward], *Farther Thoughts Concerning Human Soul, in Defence of Second Thoughts* (1703), 25.
4. W[illiam C[oward], *The Grand Essay: or a Vindication of Reason and Religion* (1704), 1.
5. *Ibid.,* 6.

With concerns reminiscent of Locke – the sub-title of *The Grand Essay* reads *A Vindication of Reason and Religion* – Coward argued that the principal focus of rational enquiry, "the main and first act of reason", is the enquiry concerning one's own existence. "How came I here, to be a living substance on earth?" The obvious answer is that each individual is a "consequence" of natural generation coming, as a whole person, "from his parents".[1] To accept the notion that an immaterial substance is at some point infused or adjoined to that which is naturally generated is tantamount to "the abandoning and dereliction of the evidence of our senses".[2]

The official response to *The Grand Essay* and to Coward's previous works, all of which he had published anonymously, did not deter him from proceeding with *The Just Scrutiny* (1705), under the initials 'W.C.' It was his last known mortalist work, and turned out to be a robust defence of his earlier views. It consisted chiefly of responses to letters occasioned by his previous publications, including one from Samuel Clarke, then chaplain to the Bishop of Norwich. Turning to Genesis 2:7, as so many mortalists did, Coward says of Clarke, perhaps with a hint of exasperation, "One would think it almost impossible, out of so plain a text as this, for any man to devise a spiritual or immaterial substance. . .".[3] In Coward's eyes it might also be thought that a man of Clarke's learning would have known that the so-called Christian doctrine of the immortal soul could be traced back to pre-Christian Greek philosophy, to Pythagoras, Socrates and Plato, "by whose writings . . . the doctrines of our holy religion are corrupted and debased".[4] Neither ignorance nor tradition excuses the perpetuation of error. Much the same could be said of irrational speculation for, as Froom points out, Coward, in *Ophthalmiatria* (1706), ridicules the Cartesian notion of an immaterial soul residing in the pineal gland.[5] It was too good an opportunity for an alert physician *cum* mortalist to miss.

Coward undoubtedly touched some sensitive spots with his vigorous attacks on the doctrine of the immortal soul and its origin. Few Anglicans or Nonconformists of the day wished to be reminded that the doctrine was "wholly and originally deriv'd from the heathens", a "Platonic philosophic maze", bequeathed to Protestantism via the lingering influence of the medieval church.[6] And few wanted to concede that it was contrary both to reason and revelation, or that the Bible "never mentions" the "immortality of the soul, or a

1. *Ibid.*, 112.
2. *Ibid.*, 36.
3. W[illiam] C[oward], *The Just Scrutiny: or a Serious Enquiry into the Modern Notions of the Soul* [1705], 48.
4. *Ibid.*, 52.
5. *CFF*, II, 195; William Coward, *Ophthalmiatria* (1706). Layton had also noted the Cartesian proposition in *Observations upon a Treatise intitled, A Discourse concerning the Happiness of Good Men in the next World* [1704], in *Search after Souls*, II, 22.
6. [Coward], *Second Thoughts*, 47, 50-1; *Farther Thoughts*, Ep. Ded., sig. a3 *r*.

soul that never dies", or anything of equivalent meaning.[1] Benjamin Keach, in
the heat of the moment, declared that Coward's *Second Thoughts* was "a most
pernicious piece" that had greatly increased doubt about the soul's immortality.[2]
Fifty years later, Caleb Fleming still thought it necessary to rebut Coward and
his fellow mortalists, claiming that they could be considered the originators "of
the materialists later defence of the soul's mechanism and mortality".[3] Fleming
seems to have been unaware of those earlier mortalists who had preceded Coward
and Layton, although like Keach he clearly recognised the threat to the soul's
immortality in what they themselves had to say. Coward himself, of course, took
a different view of the matter. In defending thnetopsychism and advancing its
claims, he declared, "I have not done the least injury to Christianity".[4] Evan
Lloyd, who came to Coward's defence in 1707, felt the same. Coward's view of
man, he said, strengthened and maintained the "grand fundamental point of the
Christian religion", the general resurrection and the last judgement.[5]

Some Notable Fellow-Travellers

The debate prompted by the writings of Layton and Coward drew to it two of
the most distinguished scholars of the day. We have already encountered Samuel
Clarke, a staunch advocate of the traditional immortalist position, who clashed
with Coward in 1706 and who by then was already becoming established as an
able metaphysician and controversialist. Clarke, however, was more concerned
with the views of Henry Dodwell, a noted patristic scholar, whose *Epistolary
Discourse* (1706) argued in favour of the natural mortality of the soul, thus
incurring Clarke's indignation. Dodwell was widely recognised as one of the most
able and distinguished men of his time, a "most profound scholar" of "immense
learning",[6] who had held the Camden professorship of ancient history at Oxford
before being deprived in 1691 for refusing the oath of allegiance to William
and Mary. Clarke's somewhat uncharitable and condescending response, *A Letter
to Mr. Dodwell* (1706), claimed to answer "all" Dodwell's arguments, stoutly
defending the soul as "created naturally immortal . . . not having in itself. . .
any principle of corruption" and therefore inherently possessing eternal life.[7]
While opposed to thnetopsychism, Dodwell strongly contested the idea of the
soul's natural immortality, declaring it to be a heresy, derived from Plato, which
had infected the church in the fourth century,[8] maintaining that the majority

1. Coward, *Farther Thoughts*, 9.
2. [Benjamin Keach], *The French Impostour Detected* (1702), 92.
3. Caleb Fleming, *A Survey of the Search After Souls* (1758), 94.
4. Coward, *The Just Scrutiny*, 210.
5. Evan Lloyd, *A Muzzle for a Mad Dog* (1707), 6. Lloyd, of Clonlanwyid, defended
   Coward's thnetopsychism against James Leslie.
6. *DNB*, s.v. Henry Dodwell, the Elder.
7. Samuel Clarke, *A Letter to Mr. Dodwell, Wherein all the Arguments in his Epistolary
   Discourse against the Immortality of the Soul are particularly answered* (1706), 6.
8. Henry Dodwell, *An Epistolary Discourse, Proving from the Scriptures and the First*

of Christian believers in the early centuries "disliked" the doctrine of the soul's immortality.[1]

As the full title of the *Epistolary Discourse* shows, Dodwell argued that the soul was "a principle, naturally mortal", and proposed the novel view that immortality was imparted by the Holy Spirit at baptism. Taking the baptism of Christ as a crucial guide, Dodwell contended that the subsequent bestowal of the Spirit on believers at their own baptism was " the only ordinary means appointed by our Saviour for our receiving it [immortality]".[2] Nature alone "is not sufficient to make the soul immortal".[3] Dodwell thus seems to have been a conditionalist of sorts, holding that the soul was indeed a separate entity, capable of becoming immortal, but only by the gift of God. Man was created and therefore remains "a candidate for immortality".[4] Unbaptized souls who have not received "the immortalizing Spirit" remain mortal.[5] Dodwell says comparatively little about the intermediate state of souls thus made immortal, but indicates a position generally analogous to psychopannychism. Souls of the baptised rest after death in the "heaven of the blessed", the "place of happy souls", until the resurrection.[6] This is not their final reward, however, but a "separate state" that "will end, as it must do when the soul and body shall be joined together again, and that eternally", at the last day. Then "the places of separate bodies and separate souls shall have an end also".[7] Thus a potentially immortal soul, actually immortalised through baptism, does not die but rests in a psychopannychistic state until the last day.

Besides incurring the wrath of Samuel Clarke, Dodwell aroused that of Edmund Chishull, a fellow of Corpus Christi College, Oxford, and vicar of Walthamstow, Essex, who accused him of heresy,[8] a charge refuted at length by Dodwell in his *Preliminary Defence of the Epistolary Discourse*(1707). Here Dodwell coins the curious but useful phrase "precarious immortality", applying it to his doctrine of the natural mortality of the human soul, and thereby seeming to confirm his own brand of conditionalism. "This precarious immortality is not an immortality properly so-called in the sense of the sacred writers", Dodwell explained, adding that it also differed from the immortality proposed by contemporary

Fathers, that the Soul is a Principle Naturally Mortal; but Immortalized Actually by the Pleasure of God, to Punishment, or to Reward, by its Union with the Divine Baptismal Spirit (1706), xxvi, lxxii, 4,5,33.
1. *Ibid.,* 100.
2. *Ibid.,* 105.
3. *Ibid.,* 106.
4. *Ibid.,* xxi. Dodwell later explains that man was originally created neither mortal nor immortal, but "capable of either, by the determination of his own freewill", 101.
5. *Ibid.,* lxxvi.
6. *Ibid.,* 261.
7. *Ibid.,* 270.
8. Edmund Chishull, *A Charge of Heresy Maintained Against Mr. Dodwell's late Epistolary Discourse concerning the Mortality of the Soul* (1706).

Platonic philosophers of the biblical era.[1] Dodwell juxtaposes the phrases "actual mortality" and "natural mortality", arguing that the "actual mortality" of the soul does not necessarily follow from its "natural mortality". Human souls may live or die eternally, but only at the pleasure of God since inherently they have "no principle in their nature that can secure their existence".[2]

Dodwell continued to press his case against Clarke and Chishull and for the inherent mortality of the soul in *The Natural Mortality of Humane Souls Clearly Demonstrated from The Holy Scriptures and the concurrent Testimonies of the Primitive Writers* (1708), re-affirming his own unique conditionalist position. The one condition on which the soul could achieve immortality was through the operation of the Holy Spirit. Asserting that "Scripture confines immortality to God", Dodwell argued that without "union with the Divine Breather himself, the Holy Spirit"[3], immortality was unachievable. Even the initial divine in-breathing, "common to all mankind", was insufficient. That in-breathing imparted life, but could not "secure its [the soul's] continuance for one single moment, much less for eternity". Lasting union with the same "divine, uncreated Spirit", "the quickening Spirit, to which the immortality of the soul is ascribed by the Scripture"[4], was essential and irreplaceable. Unmoved by the arguments of not inconsiderable adversaries Dodwell thus persisted in the views he had initially advocated in the *Epistolary Discourse*.

Apparently more concerned with man's inherent mortality and how immortality might be achieved than with either a precise definition of the soul or the state of the soul after death, Dodwell remains unclear in the *Epistolary Discourse* and in subsequent works[5] regarding the distinction between the psychopannychist and thnetopsychist positions.[6] Speaking of man's mortality and the temporary union of the soul with body, essentially a psychopannychist concept, he goes on to speak of the death of the soul, the thnetopsychist view:

1. Henry Dodwell, *A Preliminary Defence of the Epistolary Discourse Concerning the Distinction between Soul and Spirit* (1707), sig. Br. Dodwell used the phrase "precarious immortality" again in *The Natural Mortality of Humane Souls Clearly Demonstrated* (1708), 6, also written in opposition to Edmund Chishull.
2. Dodwell, *Preliminary Defence*, sig. Br.
3. Henry Dodwell, *The Natural Mortality of Humane Souls Clearly Demonstrated from The Holy Scriptures and the concurrent Testimonies of the Primitive Writers* (1708), 25. The "primitive writers" prove to be largely only Justin Martyr, whose dialogue with Trypho Dodwell uses here in support of his own central proposition. The distinction between Justin Martyr's translated text and Dodwell's commentary is not always easy to see.
4. *Ibid.*
5. In addition to works already cited, see also Dodwell's *The Scripture Account of the Eternal Rewards or Punishments of all that hear of the Gospel, without an Immortality necessarily resulting from the Nature of the Souls themselves that are concerned in those Rewards or Punishments* (1708).
6. It is only fair to point out that Dodwell was probably not interested in the distinction.

When the time comes that this conjunction must be dissolved, the soul forsakes the body, and the man does no longer continue in his existence. So when the season comes that the Soul must no longer be, the quickening Spirit is departed from it,[1] and the Soul does no longer continue in its existence but returns again to that [Original nothing] from whence it was taken. . . . And here[2] the Soul is asserted to die as truly and properly, and in the same sense, by the withdrawing the quickening Spirit from it, as the man is said to die by the separation of that same soul from its human body.[3]

Such ambiguities aside, for Dodwell the soul was unarguably an inherently mortal entity. For Clarke precisely the opposite was true. The soul was "created naturally immortal. . .not having in itself any composition or any principles of corruption"and will "naturally or of itself continue for ever".[4] Clarke, the defender of orthodoxy, was concerned, like Chishull, that Dodwell's book would be misunderstood to the lasting detriment of its readers. "Many who see the imprudent title of your discourse", he wrote of the *Epistolary Discourse,* "will conclude that you suppose the soul to perish at the dissolution of the body".[5] This may not have been exactly what Dodwell had intended, but it did underline the soul's inability to attain immortality in and of itself.

The little-known Joseph Pitts came to Dodwell's defence with two works, both published in 1708, *The Holy Spirit the Author of Immortality, or Immortality a Peculiar Grace of the Gospel,* and *Immortality Preternatural to Human Souls: The Gift of Jesus Christ, Collated by the Holy Spirit in Baptism.* In the latter he contended, as had Dodwell, that immortality belonged essentially only to God and became available to believers as a consequence of the gospel and that it was conferred through baptism. Any hope that man might have of immortality was thus grounded in Christ, the Second Adam, who overcame death,

which he manifested by his resurrection, and so demonstrated hereby, that what was in its own nature actually mortal, might become immortal, and give unto man real and substantial hopes of becoming immortal, whereas the original belief of a natural immortality suggested by the devil was a lie, and instill'd into men . . . groundless hopes.[6]

Pitts, like Layton and perhaps from him, uses the term "compositum" to describe the constitution of man, speaking of both body and soul as "essential constituent" parts of a whole that cannot be dichotomised without losing that

1. The distinction between spirit and soul was an important argument throughout the *Epistolary Discourse* and the *Preliminary Defence.*
2. With reference to a passage in Justin Martyr.
3. Dodwell, *Natural Mortality of Humane Souls* , 20-2.
4. Clarke, *Letter to Mr. Dodwell,* 6.
5. *Ibid.,* 4.
6. [Joseph Pitts], *Immortality Preternatural to Human Souls* (1708), Preface, 43.

essence, but speaking also in terms of a soul that appears to have a separate identity.[1] Yet man's natural condition is clear enough: "All created rational beings are peccable, mutable, subject to fate, necessity, death, because they are not immortal".[2] Both Dodwell and Pitts leave unanswered questions. They are neither precisely psychopannychist nor thnetopsychist, and it is easy to see why Clarke found their position "confused". Nonetheless, they preferred the company of mortalists to immortalists, further evidence that for many thoughtful minds of the time the doctrine of the soul's immortality was unsatisfactory.

William Whiston and Thomas Burnet, both to some extent ambivalent on their views of the soul, also belong here. Whiston succeeded Isaac Newton as Lucasian professor of mathematics at Cambridge in 1703,[3] but was deprived of the professorship and banished from the university in 1710 accused, justifiably it seems, of Arianism. He had earlier received Anglican ordination as a deacon, and for a brief period between 1698 and 1703 had been vicar of Lowestoft-with-Kissingland in Suffolk. His theological peregrinations eventually led him into fellowship with General Baptists, but this was not until 1747. Whiston was a prolific writer, publishing on many subjects scientific, historical and religious. He is perhaps best known for *Primitive Christianity Revived* (1711), a title which reveals the drift of his religious thinking, and a translation of the works of Josephus which remains the standard edition. Hints of mortalism appeared in the early *New Theory of the Earth* (1696) which, with Newtonian support, confirmed the Genesis account of creation and in which Whiston tentatively advanced the view that Adam "became a living soul" when his body was infused with "the breath of life". Man, created in the image of God, was thus "capable of some degree" of immortality.[4] But this must be taken with the later sermon

1. *Ibid.*, 6.
2. *Ibid.*, 37, 42.
3. Newton himself seems to have remained silent on the subject, although there are hints that he may have been sympathetic to the mortalist viewpoint. While visiting Locke at Oates in 1703 he read Locke's draft manuscript on the epistles of Paul to the Corinthians, commenting that he was "highly favourable", an opinion it would have been difficult to reach if he had entertained any doubt about Locke's thnetopsychism, there so clearly and repeatedly expressed, Wainwright (ed.), *Locke, Paraphrase and Notes*, II, 5. In his own commentary on the books of Daniel and Revelation Newton attributed the development of the medieval doctrines of prayers for the dead and the invocation of saints to the "separate souls who were supposed to know what we do or say, and to be able to do us good or hurt", adding that it was this "very notion"which undergirded heathen belief in an afterlife and the worship of pagan deities, Isaac Newton, *Observations Upon the Prophecies of Daniel, and the Apocalypse of St. John* (1733), 209. McLachlan points out that Newton's library contained works by the Continental mortalists Socinus and Crell(or Krell), and that Crell was a personal friend of Newton, H. McLachlan, *Sir Isaac Newton, Theological Manuscripts* (Liverpool, 1950), 12, 15.
4. William Whiston, *A New Theory of the Earth. . .Wherein The Creation of the World in*

'Against the Sleep of the Soul'(c.1700), in which he stated that the soul "does not sleep between death and resurrection, being in a condition "either of happiness or misery as soon as ever it is departed out of this world".[1]

As with many of his predecessors and contemporaries, Whiston's interest in the nature and destiny of the soul was strengthened by his deep opposition to the doctrines of hell and eternal torment, concepts which he seems first to have openly questioned in 1709. By then, he says, he had thought for many years that if these concepts were "a real part of Christianity" they would be a more insuperable barrier to faith than all "the objections of unbelievers put together".[2] Whiston later claimed that both Newton and the metaphysician Samuel Clarke had been "of the same sentiments" concerning hell and eternal punishment, Clarke holding that "few or no thinking men were really of different sentiments".[3] Whiston himself declared that the doctrine of hell was "absurd", a reproach to Christianity no less "than the Athanasian Doctrine of the Trinity, the Calvinist Doctrine of Reprobation, or the Popish Doctrine of Transubstantiation".[4] After careful scrutiny of relevant biblical texts and the opinions of many of the early Fathers, Whiston states, "Neither the Devil, nor his angels . . . nor wicked men, are to be cast into Gehenna, or Hell fire" until the last judgment has determined the destiny of the wicked. Only then will all men, "composed of the same soul and same body that sinned . . . united together again" at the resurrection, receive their just rewards.[5] Whiston claims that early Christians "had little notion" of punishing "a separate soul, or a *soul* in another vehicle or body, for what the *man*, composed of a soul and present body, had been guilty of".[6] This may be read as psychopannychism, the doctrine which Whiston had earlier repudiated. It would be unjustified on the strength of this statement alone to claim that Whiston later changed his mind concerning the nature of the soul, although his stout opposition to the doctrines of hell and eternal punishment would have branded his eschatology suspect in the eyes of many traditionalists.[7]

Similar ambivalence can be detected in the writing of Thomas Burnet, whose

Six Days, The Universal Deluge, And the General Conflagration As laid down in the Holy Scriptures, Are shown to be perfectly agreeable to Reason and Philosophy (1696), 161, 229.

1. William Whiston, *Sermons and Essays Upon Several Subjects* (1709), 80.

2. William Whiston, *Historical Memoirs of the Life and Writings of Dr. Samuel Clarke* (3rd.edn, 1748), 75.

3. *Ibid.* Walker is aware of Whiston's opposition to hell and eternal torment, but does not relate it to mortalism, D.P. Walker, *The Decline of Hell*, 96-103.

4. William Whiston, *The Eternity of Hell Torments Considered: or, A Collection of Texts of Scripture, and Testimonies of the three first Centuries relating to them* (1740), 2.

5. *Ibid.*, 3-19, 52-98, 109.

6. *Ibid.*, 109.

7. Froom assumes from Whiston's opposition to the doctrine of hell and eternal torment that he "championed the cause of Conditional Immortality", *CFF*, II, 224.

De Statu Mortuorum et Resurgentium,[1] translated in 1727 with the title *Of The State of the Dead and of Those that are to Rise*, testified strongly to belief in the soul's immortality and its survival after death, while denying it full access to heaven until the resurrection, a belief that is "dissonant with Scripture".[2] Burnet's translator, Matthias Earbery, commended him for his pains "to explode that too commonly received doctrine of our going post from the grave to heaven" because it ran contrary to the doctrine of the resurrection.[3] Careful reading suggests that, in replying to those for whom the soul is "really corporeal" and "equally perishable", Burnet was advocating a rather liberal form of psychopannychism at times shading into a conservative form of traditional immortalism, with death placing few constraints on the soul, "which still acts in the strongest bonds of sleep".[4] Thus, although Scripture says that death is a sleep, the analogy is "not to be taken in too strict and gross a sense", as this would imply that after death the soul remained unconscious and inactive, "void of action and . . . conscious existence".[5] At the same time, however, the soul's activity after death must not be taken in a "universal and absolute sense", neither is the soul "immediately admitted to the beatific vision", since both would render the resurrection "useless and unnecessary".[6] Burnet's modified psychopannychism seems to be confirmed when he contradicts certain "Neotericks" who claim that the after-death consciousness of the soul is taken too far. These new thinkers will have the soul immediately translated to "the highest glories of the beatific vision" or consigned to "the utmost miseries of hell". Both eventualities, Burnet says, are "extremes".[7] While the soul survives death with the ability to think after separation from the body, the ultimate realisation of Christian hope "depends" on the resurrection at the coming of Christ.[8]

Contemporary Nonconformist Voices
The anonymous author of the thnetopsychist *The Materiality or Mortality of the Soul of Man And its Sameness with the Body*(1729)[9] was much less ambiguous.[10] Concerned that the doctrine of the soul's immortality was the

1. First published for private circulation, the first known edition appearing in 1720.
2. Thomas Burnet, *De Statu Mortuorum et Resurgentium* (tr. M. Earbery, *Of the State of the Dead and of Those that are to Rise*,1727), *passim*, 48.
3. *Ibid.*, Preface, sig. A4 r.
4. *Ibid.*, 16, 32.
5. *Ibid.*, 49.
6. *Ibid.*, 119, 55.
7. *Ibid.*, 47.
8. *Ibid.*, 14, 51.
9. The strongly exegetical nature of the work contrasts with the more philosophical *Ontologos . . . An Essay to Prove that the Soul of Man is not, neither can it be, Immortal* (Dublin, 1721), attrib. to William Henrick, which makes little reference to the biblical text.
10. The attribution to Joseph Hallett III, 1691(?)-1744, is doubtful. Hallett affirmed his belief in the soul's immortality in *A Free and Impartial Study of the Holy Scriptures*, also published in 1729, although he admits to doubts over the doctrine's origins, 191, 210. Mills and Froom mistakenly interpret Hallett's stance as mortalist; Mills, *Earlier*

foundation of "gross errors", including necromancy[1] and deification of the dead, the writer stated at the outset, "Nothing in man survives the death of the body" for "from that moment all sensation and consciousness utterly cease".[2] The underlying proposition of this well-argued tract is that in Scripture the word 'soul' refers primarily to the body, that is, to the body as a manifestation of the whole person. This is evident enough in life, but is also true of the body in death, "The soul of man, according to the Scriptures, is a man's self, his body or person, whether alive or dead".[3] As in thnetopsychist theology in general, Adam became a living soul by the union of his body, composed of the dust of the ground, and the breath of life. In this author's view, however, he was a soul before that union occurred, "a dead soul", but a soul nonetheless, "so that before God had breathed into his nostrils the breath or spirit of life he was a soul, or a man without life. Hence a dead man is called in the Scriptures a dead soul".[4] Genesis 14:21; 9:5; 36:6; Exodus 1:5; I Chronicles 5:21; Jeremiah 25:29, etc., are cited in support of the position, with the comment, "these passages plainly show that . . . the word 'soul', when used with respect to man, means the man himself, or his body, as made originally of the dust of the earth".[5] Mortalists in general would have agreed with the first part of the proposition. Some may have been less enthusiastic about the idea that a lifeless body was a soul, at least in the sense in which they had always understood it.

Meanwhile, Locke's influence continued to undergird eighteenth-century mortalism at this period, mediated through the pen of George Benson, a competent Nonconformist scholar and divine who drew on the Pauline epistles to argue the mortalist case. Benson, initially a strict Calvinist, had ministered to a Nonconformist congregation in Abingdon between 1722 and 1729, when a decided shift in his thinking from Calvinism to Arminianism necessitated a break with the Abingdon people. Always loyal to the dissenting tradition he was, by 1742, established as joint pastor with Samuel Bourn[6] of a Presbyterian congregation in Birmingham. By then he was a convinced mortalist, a doctrine he defended for the rest of his life. Benson had always demonstrated considerable

Life-Truth Exponents, 38-9; *CFF*, II, 227-28. In *A Collection of Notes on Some Texts of Scripture* (1729), Hallett affirms that the soul can "think out of the body", I, 215, 6.

1. An early reference to what two centuries later would be known as Spiritualism. The supposed communication with the dead could not have been attempted under any form of mortalism. The practice of necromancy in the seventeenth and eighteenth centuries invites further research, since it is generally held to have been first revived in more recent times in North America in the nineteenth century, e.g., *CFF*, II, 1051ff. No instances were encountered in the research for this study.
2. *The Materiality or Mortality of the Soul of Man*, fol. A2 v, 1.
3. *Ibid.*, 2.
4. *Ibid.*
5. *Ibid.*, 4, 5.
6. On Bourn's own mortalism see later, pp. 166-167.

intellectual acumen, having been able, it was said, to read the New Testament in Greek from the age of eleven. In 1744 he received the Doctor of Divinity degree from Aberdeen. A disciple of Locke, Benson is chiefly known for his paraphrases and notes on the New Testament epistles, which he modelled after Locke's own paraphrases of certain of the Pauline epistles.

In his exposition of I Thessalonians (1732), Benson sought to demonstrate the nature and certainty of Christian hope as opposed to the "wavery expectations" of the "heathen" belief in the soul's immortality.[1] On the basis of I Thessalonians 4:13-18 Benson admonished his Christian readers to focus their hopes of eternal life on the resurrection of the dead, since the Bible consistently laid "the greatest stress "upon that event as the time when all men would receive their just rewards, and since it was inherently and consequentially derived from Christ's own resurrection. Indeed, the death of Christ was important, not only as an atoning act of redemption, but also as a necessary pre-requisite to His resurrection. Christ could only rise from the dead if He had first died. Hence Scripture emphasises the death of Jesus as an historical event of supreme significance. "The apostles were careful to show that our Lord Jesus Christ was actually dead, in order to convince men that his was a real resurrection".[2] Clearly, if Christ had not died, He could not have risen, and if He had not risen there could be no resurrection of believers at the last day. Faith would thus be in vain. As it is, however, the dead in their graves currently enjoy "a short sleep", to be awakened "by the mighty power of God, as one of us can awake a person that is asleep".[3] And that awakening will be to immortality and eternal life.

Ten years later Benson published the *Paraphrase and Notes on the First Epistle of St. Peter*, in which he re-emphasised the crucial connection between Christ's resurrection and the ultimate resurrection of believers. In the context of a consistent biblical theology, Christian hope is rooted in an historical event, the resurrection of Christ. It is, again, a hope of immortality yet to come, provided by the gospel, for men who are born naturally mortal. Commenting on the seminal mortalist text at I Peter 1: 3 Benson suggests that the original Greek phrase, *eis elpida zosan,* translated as "a lively hope" in the Authorised Version, would be better rendered "to the hope of life". Thus translated, it expresses "more clearly the thing intended", that though men "at their natural birth . . . were born to die, yet, by being begotten again by the gospel, they were raised to the hope of an immortal life".[4] Then comes Benson's comment on the crucial relationship between Christ's resurrection and the general resurrection of the righteous dead at the last day. It is, of course, as we have seen in the writings

1. [George Benson], *A Paraphrase and Notes on St Paul's First Epistle to the Thessalonians* (1732), 56.
2. *Ibid.*
3. *Ibid.,* 57.
4. [George Benson], *A Paraphrase and Notes on the First Epistle of St. Peter* (1742), 34.

of other mortalists, a fundamental concept for the authenticity of Christianity and Christian hope:

> Because of the strict connection between Christ's rising again, and the resurrection of all his followers, to a happy immortality, God is represented as begetting them all again together with Christ, to the hope of that blessed immortality to which his son was advanced upon his resurrection from the dead.[1]

Men are not naturally or inherently endowed with immortality. It is to be *hoped* for. It is "the hope of life" to come, "to be bestowed at the revelation of Jesus Christ" in the future.[2]

In concluding this chapter on the earlier eighteenth-century mortalists, we should note a contemporary of George Benson, Joseph Nicol Scott who, like Benson, was a dissenting minister and also a qualified physician.[3] Scott practised medicine at Norwich, and initially assisted his father, Thomas Scott, at Norwich Old Meeting, but was dismissed for Arianism c. 1737. Subsequently he preached at the French Church in Norwich, and in 1743 published *Sermons Preached in Defence of All Religion, Whether Natural or Revealed*. Scott, like William Whiston and many others of his age, mortalist and immortalist alike, strongly opposed the "vulgar opinion" concerning hell and the eternal duration of "future misery" for the unsaved.[4] In terms reminiscent of Whiston, Scott chided those who had put a "wrong construction" on certain passages of Scripture, fearing that "a real disservice" had been done to the "cause of revelation, by having clogged its defence with so great a weight".[5] Many, he feared, would stand "chargeable" for having laid this "stumbling-block" in the path of potential believers who, in the climate of eighteenth-century rationalism, had been turned away from faith by the doctrine of eternal punishment.[6] To affirm that the impenitent would

---

1. *Ibid.*, 35.
2. *Ibid.*, 37-8.
3. The physician and philosopher David Hartley also thought about man's present life and future prospects. His reflections finally culminated in the publication of his celebrated *Observations on Man, his Frame, his Duty, and his Expectations* in 1749. While the *Observations* opens with the categorical assertion "Man consists of two parts, body and mind" (I, i) it becomes apparent that this does not preclude the existence of an independent soul which survives death, although with greatly reduced capacities. Hartley remains ambivalent about the precise state of the soul during the intermediate period, seeming to prefer a modified psychopannychism, with the soul "in a state of inactivity, though perhaps not of insensibility" between death and the resurrection, David Hartley, *Observations on Man, his Frame, his Duty, and his Expectations* (1749), II, 402.
4. Joseph Nicol Scott, *Sermons Preached in Defence of All Religion, Whether Natural or Revealed* (1743), II, Sermon XVII, 329, 348.
5. *Ibid.*, 330.
6. *Ibid.*

continue to live in eternal suffering, Scott maintained, "is not only to affirm that which is not affirmed in Scripture, but which, in reality, contradicts it, and renders the Scripture-account of things inconsistent with itself ".[1]

We must not fall into the trap of allowing opposition to the doctrine of eternal torment to pass as incontrovertible evidence for a mortalist theology. That this was not so in Scott's case seems clear enough. The basic premise of his argument against eternal punishment was that death means negation of life, a "loss or deprivation of life".[2] He maintains that it is incumbent on all who advocate the doctrine of eternal torment to produce the biblical evidence to show that those who are ultimately condemned will be "continued without end alive". Claiming to have examined every biblical reference to the future punishment of the wicked, Scott says he has not found "one single text" which either affirms or implies "eternal and endless misery".[3] To propose eternal existence after death in whatever form or condition was inherently and etymologically an irrational contradiction. It was an argument that mortalists of every age, as well as others who, for whatever reason, have been uncomfortable with the concepts of hell and eternal torment, have found persuasive.

1. *Ibid.*, 343.
2. *Ibid.*, 332. Scott argues here that in the interpretation of Scripture "we ought not to depart from the strict and proper import of words and have recourse to an improper or figurative sense without necessity".
3. *Ibid.*, 335.

Chapter Six
The Ascendancy of Thnetopsychism

It will not have passed unnoticed that of all the mortalists encountered to date from the earliest days of the English Reformation, only a very few were clergymen or ministers. Of the few who were most, as we have observed, were Nonconformists. The most prominent and influential seventeenth-century mortalist apologists – Overton, Hobbes, Milton, Locke – were not from the ranks of the clergy at all. Anglicans, and in particular Anglican clergy, have in the main been conspicuous by their absence. Compared to the total number of beneficed clergy throughout the country during the seventeenth and early eighteenth centuries, the two or three Anglicans who have appeared in the preceding pages constituted only a tiny fraction of the whole. Even if academics with Anglican convictions are included, the number is still minimal. Yet with prominent Reformers and proto-Anglicans like Tyndale, Frith and Latimer in the vanguard of the mortalist camp, we might have expected more from within Anglicanism over a period of one hundred and fifty years.

Another curious feature, specifically characteristic of the early eighteenth-century mortalist literature, is the almost consistent anonymity with which it was presented. The works of Layton and Coward, at least nineteen in all, were nearly all published anonymously or pseudonymously. Fifty years later Caleb Fleming was still confused about the authorship of some of these works. While this anonymity did not detract from argument or substance, it does remain something of a mystery. Perhaps the facts that Layton was unable to find a publisher in London, that the 1706 collection of his works was suppressed, and that Coward's *Grand Essay* had been proscribed by the House of Commons are indications of an over-sensitivity, if not an outright antipathy, to mortalist doctrine at the turn of the century, an antipathy which still lingered as the anonymous *Materiality or Mortality of the Soul of Man* went to press in 1729.

Whatever the reason or reasons might have been, as we come to the mid-point of the eighteenth century, much of this is about to change. The three major mid-century mortalist spokesmen were all Anglicans who boldly nailed their colours to the mast prepared to take on all comers. More Anglicans soon appeared and notable Nonconformist preachers and scholars were added

to the ranks. And with one inexplicable exception,[1] every mortalist work
of this period, and there were many, was published under the name of its
author. The Anglicans all eventually attained distinction in the ecclesiastical
hierarchy. Edmund Law became Bishop of Carlisle; Peter Peckard, Dean of
Peterborough; Francis Blackburne, Archdeacon of Cleveland and a Prebendary
of York; and John Tottie, Archdeacon of Worcester and a Canon of Christ
Church, Oxford. Leonard Chappelow, no friend of mortalists, complained in
1765 that mortalism, an "old heresy" revived again, had "taken root in one of
our famous universities".[2] He was referring to Cambridge, and would have had
in mind, amongst others perhaps, Law, Peckard and Blackburne in particular.
William Whiston and Isaac Barrow were both Cambridge men, and before
them the young Milton had studied at Christ's and Hugh Broughton, whose
antipathy to the doctrine of hell was noted earlier, had been a fellow at both
Christ's and St. John's. Perhaps the seeds of mortalist dissent had been sown at
Cambridge long before Chappelow realised.[3] Law at the time was Master of
Peterhouse, and Blackburne had studied at St. Catharine Hall. Peckard later
became Master of Magdalene College and Vice-chancellor of the university.
All were staunch and articulate thnetopsychists, thus giving rise to the most
significant point to be argued in this chapter, the ascendancy of thnetopsychism
as the dominant expression of Christian mortalism in the eighteenth century.
In fact, all the major mortalist writers of the time were, without exception,
thnetopsychist. Psychopannychism, which had prevailed in earlier times, both
on the Continent and in England, if it is now heard at all is heard only in a
whisper. In what can be seen as the more cohesive and internally consistent
thnetopsychist view of man and his eternal future, Christian mortalism had
finally come to maturity as a credible alternative to the still predominant
doctrine of the soul's immortality.

The Mid-Century Anglican Divines

Edmund Law, 1703-1787, an acknowledged disciple of Locke[4], a latitudinarian,
unsurprisingly perhaps, was an able and recognised biblical scholar who deserves
more attention than he has hitherto received. In addition to his ecclesiastical
preferments, Law also held the chair of Knightsbridge professor of moral

1. [Blackburne], *No Proof in the Scriptures* (1756), published in response to a sermon
   by Peter Goddard against Law which proposed the intermediate state "from
   Scripture".
2. Leonard Chappelow, *Two Sermons Concerning the State of the Soul On its immediate
   Separation from the Body* (Cambridge,1765), vi, xi. The two sermons here republished were those originally preached by George Bull in the 1690s, see p. 127.
3. It is only fair to point out that Oxford produced its share of mortalists, Hobbes,
   Locke and Coward among them.
4. A four-volume edition of Locke's works published in 1777 was edited by Law, "the
   most convinced . . .Lockean divine . . . in the eighteenth-century church", *ODNB*,
   s.v. Edmund Law.

philosophy at Cambridge from 1764. For the degree of Doctor of Divinity in 1749 he had in controversial circumstances defended the thnetopsychist doctrine of soul sleep, and William Paley his biographer, with characteristic perspicuity, asserted that Law's chief claim to recognition was his later articulate and persuasive defence of mortalism:

> The tenet by which his name and writings are principally distinguished, is, that Jesus Christ, at his second coming, will, by an act of his power, restore to life and consciousness the dead of the human species; who by their own nature, and without this interposition, would remain in the state of insensibility to which the death brought upon mankind by the sin of Adam had reduced them.[1]

It was a position which Law uncompromisingly defended and expanded with careful scholarship and at times in great detail from that point on. He became Bishop of Carlisle in 1768, retaining the see until his death nearly twenty years later. Law's most important work, the *Considerations on the State of the World With regard to the Theory of Religion*, was first published in 1745, four years before the presentation of his doctoral thesis. Its influence, and that of its author overall, is difficult to measure, but it could not have been inconsiderable. A second "enlarged" edition appeared in 1749 and a definitive third edition in 1755, with four further editions by the time of his death in 1784. A new edition, including a life of Law by William Paley, was published by Law's son in 1820.

The *Considerations* examines the relationship between civilisation and Christianity, projecting an optimistic view of the future of man and the world based on Law's belief that Christianity would eventually transform human society in its entirety, thus bringing about Christ's kingdom on earth. "Every people, nation and language shall at last embrace the true religion",[2] Law asserted. The gospel, "still visibly or invisibly enlarging over the world . . . will always go on to do so, till the kingdom of Christ be fully come".[3] It is the anticipated "progress of natural religion and science . . . the continual improvement of the world in general" which, under the dominant influence of the ever-expanding gospel, will ensure the final outcome.[4] This outcome is itself necessitated by the divine purpose to restore "the whole posterity of Adam to that immortality which he forfeited". Immortality, God's gift through Christ, is "not in any respect a property of our own nature as derived from Adam", but rather "an additional privilege conferred by God" through Christ

1. William Paley, 'A Life of Edmund Law', xii, in G. H. Law (ed.), *Considerations on the Theory of Religion* (1820).
2. Edmund Law, *Considerations on the State of the World With regard to the Theory of Religion* (2nd edn, 1749), 194.
3. *Ibid.*, 203.
4. *Ibid.*, 245.

and the gospel.[1] The coincident civilisation of the whole world and the final triumph of Christianity concur with the restoration of man's immortality.[2] It would appear that this restoration to Edenic conditions as one of history's eventual outcomes was one of Law's more important considerations.

Later editions of the *Considerations*, particularly the third edition of 1755 and the fourth edition of 1759, considerably expanded Law's mortalist theology, demonstrating that it was obtained from as thorough and painstaking an analysis of the biblical material as any mortalist apology before or since. The third and subsequent editions contained an appendix, *Concerning the Use of the Words Soul or Spirit in Holy Scripture, and the State of Death there described*, a lucid and comprehensive study of the relevant biblical words and passages, from which Law made several observations: 1. That the Hebrew words *nephesh* and *neshamah* and the Greek words *pneuma* and *psuche*, generally translated 'soul' or 'spirit', were also variously translated, in fact "most commonly denote",[3] persons or living people (e.g. Gen. 17:14; Lev. 4:2; Num. 31:28; Matt. 26:38; Acts 2:43; II Pet. 2:14) who can, among other things, eat(e.g. Exod. 12:16), faint (e.g. Psa. 107:5), be hungry (e.g. Psa. 107:9), prosper (Prov. 11:25), and be killed(e.g. Gen. 37:21).[4] 2. Living creatures (e.g. Gen. 1: 20, 24; Deut. 20:16; I Cor. 15:45) .[5] 3. The body, dead or alive (e.g. Num. 5:2; Psa. 105:18).[6] 4. Life, of man or beast (e.g. Gen. 9:5; Exod. 4:19; Prov. 13:3). 5. Breath (e.g. Gen. 2:7; Psa. 150:6).[7] He also noted many instances in both Old and New Testaments where death was referred to as a sleep (e.g. Deut. 31:16; I Kings 11:43; Job 7:21 and 14:11, 12; John 11:11-13; I Cor. 15:6; I Thess. 4: 13).[8] Law concluded from his study of the biblical text that the soul was not a separate, immaterial entity and that death was a "sleep, a negation of all life, thought, or action", a state of "silence, oblivion, destruction, corruption", and that the resurrection of the dead "at the coming of our Lord Jesus Christ" was therefore "the grand object of our faith, hope, and comfort".[9]

The 1755 edition of *Considerations* also included a treatise separately

1. *Ibid.,* 205-6.
2. An important implication of Law's argument is that the corruptions which had contaminated Christianity through the ages, including natural immortality, would all be eliminated as a knowledge of truth increased.
3. Edmund Law, 'An Appendix Concerning the Use of the Words *Soul* or *Spirit* in Holy Scripture, and the State of Death there described', *ad cal* with *Considerations on the Theory of Religion* (3rd edn,Cambridge, 1755), 347. The title of the *Considerations* changed with this edition, although, apart from the additions noted in the text above, the content remained essentially the same.
4. *Ibid.,* 347-51.
5. *Ibid.,* 353.
6. *Ibid.*
7. *Ibid.,* 354-9.
8. *Ibid.,* 367-8.
9. *Ibid.,* 367, 382.

entitled *The Nature and End of Death under the Christian Covenant,* in which Law argued that it was necessary to understand correctly the nature of death in order to understand fully God's redemptive purposes for the human race, "in what sense we are delivered from death by the sufferings and death of Christ".[1] Such an understanding could only be achieved by referring back to the first instance in which the concept of death appears in Scripture and the first awareness of death in human experience. What did Adam and Eve understand by the sentence, "Thou shalt surely die"?, Law asks. He replies, "A total loss"of everything that they then possessed or could hope to possess in the future.[2] This necessarily included loss of life, a cessation of existence, even though at the time that might have been difficult for them to envisage. Law suggests that to understand death in any other way would have been to lessen the intent and the effect of the sentence:

> This surely, and nothing less, must be implied in that most solemn sentence: nor can we well conceive the unhappy subjects of it to have been at that time so very ingenious as to explain it all away by distinguishing upon the different parts of their constitution, and so concluding that by death no more was intended than only living in some different manner, or a continuation of their consciousness and real existence in some other place.[3]

"No", Law exclaims, "that was the philosophy of after ages"[4] Law says emphatically that eternal life is promised through Christ. It is "not an inherent property of our original nature". Christ "opens for us the true and only way to immortality, through the gate of the resurrection".[5] Since through Christ believers have already "gained the victory . . . over death and the grave", Law insists that Christ's resurrection is the basis of authentic hope. "We are as sure of our own resurrection" as we are of His.[6] Thus is hope "full of immortality"and "our departure and dismission from this mortal state becomes our entrance and admission" to the immortal state "in the morning of the resurrection".[7]

1. Edmund Law, 'The Nature and End of Death under the Christian Covenant', *ad cal.* with *Considerations on the Theory of Religion* (3rd edn,1755), 325.
2. *Ibid.,* 325-26.
3. *Ibid.*
4. *Ibid.*
5. *Ibid.,* 328-29. Law cites in this connection the Hebraist and biblical scholar, John Taylor, "a very competent judge of scripture-language". Resurrection, or being made alive again, presupposes "1. That the dead are not made alive till the resurrection, for the resurrection of the dead, and being made alive, are here expressions of the same signification. 2. That, had not a resurrection been provided, we should never after death have been made alive", John Taylor, *The Scripture Doctrine of Original Sin* (1740), 24.
6. Law, *Considerations* (3rd edn,1755), 329-30.
7. *Ibid.,* 342.

Peter Peckard, 1717-1797, came to almost identical conclusions about the nature of man and the gospel hope of immortality, and via a similar journey, a distinguished academic and ecclesiastical career. A graduate of Corpus Christi, Oxford, he had published three ably written works in defence of mortalism by 1760, earning a reputation for heterodoxy on the state of the soul between death and the resurrection which appears to have followed him for the remainder of his life. By 1760 he was both rector of Fletton and vicar of Yaxley. In order to obtain the necessary dispensation to hold both livings simultaneously he had been examined by Thomas Secker, Archbishop of Canterbury, who disapproved of his mortalist views and who required him to sign what was intended to be at least a partial retraction. Edmund Law later quipped that Peckard "had escaped out of the Lollards Tower with the loss of his tail".[1] Peckard subsequently enjoyed a rapid succession of preferments and honours: Master of Magdalene College, Cambridge in 1781; Vice-chancellor of the University in 1784; the Doctor of Divinity degree in 1785; Dean of Peterborough in 1792. There is through all these years no record of him contradicting anything he had written in the 1750s on the nature of the soul or the condition of man in death, and no indication that his mortalism was thereafter considered a liability. It all suggests that any concessions he may have made in earlier years were minimal, even inconsequential.

Peckard's first work, *Observations on the Doctrine of an Intermediate State between Death and the Resurrection* (1756), attacked traditional belief in an intermediate state as an erroneous and groundless hope offered as a sop to those in mourning:

> Every tender mother or disconsolate widow is taught to sooth her grief by reflecting that her infant is immediately changed into a round-faced cherub with curling locks, or her husband into a guardian angel with a large pair of expanded wings.[2]

This false doctrine of an intermediate state detracted from the true doctrine of a future state as the focus of Christian hope, hence the *Observations* argued in favour of a consistent biblical eschatology in which the believer's future was assured. "The doctrine of a future state", provided that it was well-argued and based on sound principles, "is the impregnable fortress of truth",[3] he declared. Peckard thus affirms that Christian faith moves inexorably towards the future. Unfortunately, this orientation to the future had been "greatly weakened" by "metaphysical reasonings" which had undermined biblical eschatology and, more importantly, had detracted from the redemptive work of Christ.[4] In Peckard's view, and arising naturally from his adherence to the principle of *sola scriptura*, the biblical doctrine was clear enough, "Scripture expressly

1. *DNB*, s.v. Peter Peckard.
2. Peckard, *Observations*, 11.
3. *Ibid.*, 3.
4. *Ibid.*

asserteth the mortality of man", he stated, "and the restoration to life from
that mortality by. . . Jesus Christ".[1] This theme ran throughout Peckard's work
from beginning to end, and found frequent and emphatic expression. The
doctrine of the soul's immortality negated the redemptive work of Christ at
its very heart, effectually making it superfluous and unnecessary. It is probably
the most damning charge brought by mortalists against the soul's inherent
immortality, and Peckard saw it clearly enough:

> Jesus Christ came into the world on purpose to redeem men from death
> and to give them life and immortality. It is very certain that he could not
> redeem them from that state in which they were not, nor give them that
> life and immortality which they already possessed. So that by this scheme
> [the natural immortality of the soul] the whole notion of redemption by
> Jesus Christ is absolutely and entirely destroyed.[2]

And again, "By allowing men a natural principle of life, we do in effect hinder
them from coming to Christ that they may have life".[3] It was clearly a plea for
a renewed Christocentric soteriology and eschatology in which the indissoluble
and essential links between the two were no longer ignored.

Peckard followed the *Observations* with *Farther Observations on the Doctrine
of an Intermediate State* (1757). Again, the emphasis was on Christ as opposed
to inherent human nature for eternal life. There is no point whatever in talking
about the possibility of a future life apart from God's revelation in Jesus Christ.
He is the resurrection "and the life". The ultimate purpose, "the great end",
of His incarnation and passion "was to bring life". All who would see eternal
life "must come to Him for it". Conversely, if man possesses immortality by
nature, "then Christ is not the life",[4] Peckard argues. It all sounds very direct,
very evangelical, to modern ears. To Peckard, the Whig divine, it was more a
matter of truth and the elimination of "Platonic philosophy" from Christian
dogma.[5] The implications, if not readily apparent, can be deduced, and are of
momentous consequence for true believers and for the true faith. The doctrine
of the immortal soul undermines the foundations. It strikes at the heart of the
gospel. It denatures the Christian message by robbing it of the one thing that
most clearly gives it its identity. "If this immortality arises from an original and
inherent principle of our nature, then we have it exclusively and independently
of the merits and mediation of Jesus Christ".[6] Others, of course, had said it
before. But Peckard was concerned with the present, perhaps also with the
future. Each new generation must hear the truth of the life that is found only
in Christ, and be warned of the untruth that had so frequently and so readily

1. *Ibid.*, 4.
2. *Ibid.*, 19.
3. *Ibid.*, 39.
4. Peter Peckard, *Farther Observations on the Doctrine of an Intermediate State* (1757), 66.
5. *Ibid.*, 36.
6. *Ibid.*, 67.

been received by an uninformed and gullible people. There were few in the eighteenth century with Peckard's ability to make it known.

Caleb Fleming was one of many contemporaries of Law and Peckard who thought quite differently. We have already come across Fleming, an ardent defender of the doctrinal *status quo*, as an adversary of William Coward. In actual fact, Fleming's *Survey of the Search after Souls* (1758), attacked Law and Peckard as well as Coward, defending the traditional view of the soul's immortality and "immediate" and "perfect felicity" in heaven.[1] In so doing, Fleming allowed his imagination to run rather too freely. He believed that in heaven the soul would not remain in a disembodied state throughout eternity. He proposed, rather, that it would on entry to heaven be provided with "a prepared vehicle, disentangled and forever disengaged from all mortal principles". This "prepared vehicle" would be the soul's "habitation" thereafter, enabling "the man" to enter "immediately" upon a life of consciousness and activity, the "perfect felicity" of the heavenly state. This "new organ" for the soul would be "commodiously and completely fitted for all those exercises and enjoyments" which a redeemed soul might expect the state of heavenly bliss to provide.[2] With only a little more imagination, the possibilities were endless.

Such speculation was the perfect opportunity for Peckard's ready mind and able pen. His *Observations on Mr. Fleming's Survey* (1759) was a considered, logical and, at times, tart demolition of Fleming's flights into fancy. It proposed thnetopsychist mortalism as a more credible alternative, more reasonable and more consistent with the revelation in Scripture. Remarking that "everyone who knows anything of human nature, knows how readily we believe what we wish to be true",[3] Peckard in response rehearsed the main points of the thnetopsychist position: the nature of man in life and death, the nature of the intermediate state, the necessity of Christ's redemptive and mediatorial work, the true source of immortality, the hope and necessity of the resurrection and the origin of the immortality doctrine.[4] Fleming's doctrine, particularly when enhanced with its speculative adornments, dispensed with the resurrection of the body altogether. It was, in Peckard's view, a major distortion of the revealed truth of Scripture, which could not be allowed to pass unchallenged. Pointing the finger at the errant Fleming, Peckard declared that it was "absolutely incumbent" on all who defended the doctrine of the soul's immortality, "particularly those who undertake to teach or explain" it to others, "to show that the doctrine of immortality from a natural principle, and the doctrine of immortality through the mediation of Christ, can be consistent".[5] Fleming had not only failed at

1. Fleming, *A Survey*, 38. Fleming incorrectly attributed the anonymous *Search after Souls* to Coward instead of Layton.
2. *Ibid.*, 38-9.
3. Peter Peckard, *Observations on Mr. Fleming's Survey* (1759), 93.
4. *Ibid.*, 22-32.
5. *Ibid.*, 114.

this crucial point; he had cut away man's need of Christ altogether.

Peckard's own thnetopsychist position was set out again in his response to Fleming and with the reasoned dependence on biblical revelation that we have observed frequently in the work of earlier English mortalists, and the finesse and logic that might be expected of a Cambridge scholar. Since through Adam man is by nature mortal, at death "every man will then become what he was before his conception". He will "return to a state of utter insensibility", and continue in that condition "till the course of this world shall be finished; when all mankind will be awakened together to a second and an immortal state of consciousness though the merits of Jesus Christ, and through him alone".[1] Peckard's allegiance to biblical theology is evident as he compares that which was lost by the first Adam with that which was regained by the second Adam:

> If the first *Adam* had continued in his obedience, he would not have been subject to death; and consequently Jesus Christ, the second *Adam*, would not have redeemed us. Our redemption by the second *Adam* was owing to the transgression of the first; and the nature of this redemption is determined by the nature of the punishment inflicted upon his crime, which involved all his posterity in a state of suffering: Because it is from this punishment, whatsoever it be, that we are redeemed by the second *Adam*. His crime was disobedience to an express command of God, and his punishment for this crime was *death*. *Death,* in the true and proper sense of the word, without any refinement whatsoever. Death is the ceasing to live. The cessation of life necessarily supposes the cessation of all the faculties that make the difference between life and death; such as consciousness, perception, sensibility. The ceasing to live, act, be, the total loss of consciousness, etc. is then the punishment of *Adam's* crime, in which all his posterity are so far concerned, as to suffer the same sentence of death, though not under the idea of punishment, not having *sinned after the similitude of his transgression.*[2]

The reversal of this sentence, the calling us again to being, life, action, the restoring us to sensibility, perception, and consciousness, is the redemption performed by Christ. But neither can this suffering, entailed upon us by *Adam*, be undergone by us, nor can this redemption by the mediation of Christ be performed by him, except the object of both suffering and redemption be, truly and properly speaking, mortal.[3]

Peckard has been lightly treated by historians of English mortalism,[4] even by those who have sought more broadly to convey the religious thought of the age. He was, in retrospect, one of mortalism's ablest and most articulate spokesmen.

1. *Ibid.,* 39, 40.
2. The emphasis in the original appears to be a typographical error.
3. *Ibid.,* 96-7.
4. E.g. Froom, after Mills. Burns does not consider eighteenth-century writers at all.

Peckard's final word on man's essential mortality appeared in 1776 with the publication of his *Subscription: or, Historical Extracts*. The 'historical extracts' were, in fact, accounts of certain periods of church history relating to the corruption of Christian doctrine and the development of creeds and confessional statements intended to preserve the integrity of the faith. The association of mortalist thought with subscription, or more precisely Peckard's aversion to subscription, is more than incidental. It illustrates a further important link with the latitudinarianism of fellow-mortalists Law and Blackburne. Only two years previously Law had entered the current subscription debate which had been generated by a petition to Parliament against subscription to the Thirty-Nine Articles by Blackburne and a group of like-minded liberal Cambridge scholars in 1772.[1] In *Considerations on the Propriety of Requiring Subscription to Articles of Faith* (1774), Law had opposed enforced subscription, holding that it was contrary to Reformation principles, including freedom of conscience and the right of individual belief, and argued instead for a thoroughly Scripture-based faith which resulted from sound exegesis of the biblical text.[2] Clearly the doctrine of the soul's immortality, a corruption emanating from Rome, would thereby be excluded. The petition to repeal subscription eventually failed in a House of Commons debate, but it is ironic that Law and Blackburne, and those who supported them, were opposed because their desire for greater individual freedom in matters of faith was seen as opening the door to deceivers, greater heresy and ultimately to 'Popish emissaries'.[3]

Peckard took the argument further. "Errors" had, in "the process of time become systematical doctrines"[4] now incorporated into the faith and requiring subscription. Earlier teachers of Christian belief had been "too much influenced by the sublime and baseless visions of pagan philosophy, pagan theology, and pagan metaphysics", particularly by "the theology and metaphysics of Plato".[5] Peckard reduced the infiltration of Platonic thought into Christian doctrine to two main issues: the doctrine of the Trinity, which was contrary to the unity of God as set forth in Scripture, and "the natural immortality of man", which subverted the "fundamental" biblical doctrine of "a resurrection from death

1. Although sympathetic in principle, neither Law nor Blackburne signed the petition.
2. [Edmund Law], *Considerations on the Propriety of Requiring Subscription to Articles of Faith* (1774), *passim*.
3. B.W. Young, 'The Soul sleeping System: Politics and Heresy in Eighteenth-Century England', *JEH*, 45 (1994), 67. Young's analysis of the Cambridge group led by Law as "ultra-Protestant" and "promoters of further Reformation within the Church of England" is essentially correct. Young further argues that aversion to Catholic beliefs and practices was a "central element in the revival of mortalism" in the eighteenth century, but seems unaware of the preceding advocates of mortalist belief in the earlier eighteenth-century writers Layton, Coward and Bold, 72 ff.
4. Peter Peckard, *Subscription: or, Historical Extracts* (1776), 14.
5. *Ibid.*, 16.

and a future judgement".[1] Referring to the post-apostolic age and specifically
to the Constantinian era, Peckard observed of these earlier times, "The religion
of Christ made a rapid progress and great numbers were converted even to
their representation of the Christian faith". "Here began the misfortune
and great corruption of the church", Peckard insists, "Not in the numbers
converted to Christianity, but in the numbers perverted after their conversion
to these vain doctrines of fallible men".[2] Heresies multiplied, as did "creeds
also or distinguishing confessions of faith".[3] Nor did things improve in the
Reformation era. Noting the "obstinacy" of Luther over the real or symbolic
presence and other doctrinal disputes between the early Reformers, Peckard
maintains that "narrow-minded and unchristian" insistence on confessional
exclusivity had "well-nigh totally crushed the Reformation in its very infancy".[4]
So things had continued, more or less, to the present time.

Against this background Peckard asks, with reference to subscription, creeds
and confessions, "What can be determined concerning this state of things?"
His answer reflects not only his own convictions, but also those of Law
and Blackburne, and perhaps also of others in contemporary latitudinarian
Cambridge circles who contested subscription, as well as many other mortalists
of his own and earlier generations:

> On this principle, the traditions or opinions of men, whatsoever may
> be their denomination, have no obligation upon me, any farther than
> as they are agreeable to the word of God. Everything that is contained
> in the genuine Scriptures, I firmly believe, and everything that can be
> fairly deduced from them. But, in this case, I have the right, and ought
> to have the power to judge for myself. With great readiness would I
> subscribe to the opinions of Athanasius, of Arius, of Socinus, of Luther,
> of Calvin, or Arminius; to the doctrines of the Church of Rome, of
> Geneva, of England, so far as they may be respectively agreeable to
> the word of God. . . . The only criterion in this matter is the Holy
> Scripture, which I would honestly endeavour to understand as well as
> I could, without attachment to any human traditions, or any system of
> opinions whatsoever.[5]

Subscription to any formal creed of confession of faith was therefore "absolutely
unjustifiable", since it required assent to contaminated doctrine which was no
longer biblically defensible, in particular "all the nonsense of an intermediate
state of existence between death and the resurrection".[6]

1. *Ibid.*, 17-19.
2. *Ibid.*, 21.
3. *Ibid.*, 23.
4. *Ibid.*, 32.
5. *Ibid.*, 135.
6. *Ibid.*, 12, 21.

During the late 1740s and the 1750s Law and Peckard provided between them at least six major works advancing and defending the mortalist position. Francis Blackburne, 1705-1787, their contemporary and ally, added three more, culminating in his *Short Historical View of the Controversy Concerning An Intermediate State and The Separate Existence of the Soul Between Death and the General Restoration* (1765).[1] Blackburne is remembered from this work as the first English historian of mortalist thought, even though his two earlier works dealing with the mortalist issue had been of a more polemical nature,[2] and even though the *Short Historical View* itself began with a lengthy discussion of mortalist theology and its implications. Blackburne was a Cambridge graduate, another disciple of Locke and a friend of Edmund Law. His first foray into the mortality/immortality debate in 1756 was in fact in defence of Law, whose work on the biblical use of the words 'soul' and 'spirit' appended to the 1755 edition of his *Considerations on the Theory of Religion* had been attacked by Peter Goddard, whom Blackburne later dismissed as knowing "little or nothing of the matter".[3] In that context Blackburne argued, as others before him had done, that there was no biblical proof for the conscious existence of the soul after death, and that the righteous would not be rewarded until the last day. They "shall not have eternal life or salvation, shall not put on immortality, be received unto Christ, enter into his joy, behold his glory, or be like him, *till* the resurrection. . .".[4] To make such assertions was to swim against the tide, even in defence of a Cambridge philosopher who was, despite his known mortalism, eventually to become a bishop. Blackburne, however, was his own man, evidently of a bent to think for himself in matters of doctrine and faith, having "early made up his mind never again to subscribe to the Thirty-Nine Articles".[5]

This antipathy to subscription, as well as to creeds and confessions *per se,* undergirded Blackburne's work, including his mortalist theology. It eventually came to public attention in his best-known and controversial book, *The Confessional.* Here Blackburne, "the zealous and consistent Protestant",[6] argued strenuously that subscription and confessions of faith brought stagnation to the church, mitigating against reformation and further discovery of biblical truth. "We are just where the Acts of Uniformity left us", he protested, "and

1. Second edition 1772, as *An Historical View*, etc.
2. [Blackburne], *No Proof in the Scriptures*, and [Blackburne], *Remarks on Dr. Warburton's Account of the Sentiments of the Early Jews Concerning the Soul* (1757). Of Peter Goddard's attempt to counter Edmund Law's *Considerations,* Blackburne commented, "Mr Goddard will find that purgatory, saint-worship, transmigration, and a thousand other fooleries will stick to his system like the leprosy", *No Proof in the Scriptures,* 34.
3. Blackburne, *Historical View,* 334.
4. [Blackburne], *No Proof in the Scriptures,* 1.
5. *DNB,* s.v. Francis Blackburne.
6. F. Blackburne (ed.), 'Some Account of the Author', in *The Works, Theological and Miscellaneous, of Francis Blackburne* , I (1804), lxix.

where, for ought that appears in the temper of the times, the last trumpet will find us".[1] Charging that the Church of England retained "her own unscriptural impositions", Blackburne went on to argue against the religious *status quo* and for continuing reformation of doctrine and further understanding of the biblical message, lamenting "Prejudice and partial affection carry their point every day, against the loudest remonstrances of reason and the clearest light of revelation".[2] Much of this laxness and confusion was due in Blackburne's view to a *laissez-faire* attitude to the church of Rome, "popery", to use Blackburne's own bald terminology, an attitude which characterised the contemporary Anglican establishment. "The zeal of both pastors and people in the Church of England against popery and popish emissaries" had "visibly declined" of late. "We have left her to go about and perform all her functions without offence and without observation".[3] Such lack of vigilance, born of uninformed tolerance and circumscribing confessions, resulted in apathy, confusion and error.

There is some evidence that one of Blackburne's major concerns in attacking subscription, the Thirty-Nine Articles of the Church of England and confessions in general, was the mortalist view of man, or perhaps we should say the lack of it in many contemporary doctrinal formulations. To begin with, *The Confessional* appeared after the publication of all his works dealing with the mortalist question.[4] It is reasonable to assume that the sentiments there expressed were penned in the light of the mortalism so strongly set out in *No Proof in the Scriptures, Remarks on Dr. Warburton's Account* and the *Short Historical View*. Indeed, it is not unreasonable to assume that the continuing strength of Blackburne's mortalist convictions may have been in part at least the motivation for *The Confessional* itself. More specifically, commenting on a number of confessions examined, Blackburne noted that eleven out of sixteen in question took "no notice of the resurrection of the dead", one of "the fundamental articles of the Christian religion".[5] Then, in the context of his opposition to subscription and his belief that the understanding of truth should be progressive, Blackburne notes that the 1563 Articles of Religion omitted two of the previous Articles of 1553, those relating specifically to the future punishment of the wicked and the sleep of the soul after death.[6]

This old controversy, recently revived by Law, Peckard and Blackburne

1. Francis Blackburne, *The Confessional, or, A Full and Free Enquiry into the Right, Utility, Edification, and Success of Establishing Systematical Confessions of Faith and Doctrine in Protestant Churches* (2nd edn,1767), xxxvii. Blackburne excluded himself from further preferment by the outspoken frankness of *The Confessional.*
2. *Ibid.*, xxii, 338-9.
3. *Ibid.*, lxvii, xxxvii.
4. With the exception of the second edition of the *Short Historical View.*
5. *Ibid.*, 14.
6. *Ibid.*, 47. The 1563 revision actually omittted Articles 39-42 of those published in 1553. Blackburne comments on the two relevant to his argument. See also pp. 59ff.

himself would probably never have seen the light of day if "assent to this 40th article [that "The soulles of them that departe this life doe neither die with the bodies [sic], nor slepe idlie"] had still remained a part of our ministerial subscription".[1] It all underlined the need for "the current labours of able and honest pastors" to correct "human inventions" and "misapplications of scripture-expressions", and the desirability of "searching the scriptures in all doubtful cases".[2] Clearly, the final punishment of the wicked and the state of the soul after death were cases in point. And lest the real issue, the importance of understanding correctly the nature of the soul and its true condition after death, might be forgotten or overlooked, Blackburne asserts, " The very vitals of Popery chiefly subsist by this doctrine of an intermediate state. Take away this doctrine, and you lay the grand fabrick of that church in ruins".[3] In the final analysis this was the nub of Blackburne's plea for a more authentic and responsible Protestantism and for complete freedom in religious belief and matters of conscience.

Blackburne had also entered the lists against the learned William Warburton, whose early work, *The Divine Legation of Moses* (2 vols, 1737, 1741), caused much debate for some thirty years. Warburton's work, examining *inter alia* the absence of any doctrine regarding future rewards and punishment "in the Jewish dispensation", was destined, in Blackburne's view, to "sink under a most manifest and mortifying incapacity of demonstration".[4] Blackburne objected to Warburton's use of the word 'jargon' referring to mortalism's belief in the sleep of the soul. Those who talk of the soul's "sleep between death and the resurrection, use a jargon which confounds all languages, as well as reason",[5] Warburton had said. Blackburne rejoined "It may ring in some delicate ears like jargon, and still have all the properties of good sense and sound reason". It was, moreover, "the jargon of the New Testament".[6] More specifically, man ceased to exist at death, whether or not the soul could be said to sleep. The body then returned "to the earth, as it was" and the "spirit" or breath of life, which had "no relation to the immortal soul", returned "to God who gave it."[7] Like others, Blackburne pointed out that the idea of the soul's immortality undermined all the essentials of the Christian faith. If this doctrine could "be deduced from the principles of the Christian religion, then the doctrines of redemption, restoration, resurrection etc., are rendered unnecessary by the

---

1. *Ibid.*, 48.
2. *Ibid.*
3. Blackburne, *No Proof in the Scriptures,*33.
4. William Warburton, *The Divine Legation Of Moses Demonstrated, on the Principles of a Religious Deist, From the Omission of the Doctrine of a Future State of Reward and Punishment in the Jewish Dispensation*, II(1741), 446-468; Blackburne, *Historical View*, 334.
5. Blackburne, *Historical View*, 334.
6. *Ibid.*, 335.
7. [Blackburne], *Remarks on Dr. Warburton's Account*, 19.

principles of Christianity itself".[1] Blackburne perhaps hoped that Warburton would at least reconsider his opinion that soul sleep was merely "jargon" or a "semi-pagan dream"; it is doubtful that he did so. But Blackburne had made his point and it, as well as Warburton's opinions and Fleming's fancies, has survived for posterity to evaluate.

Blackburne's main mortalist work, the *Short Historical View*, is something of an enigma. After a lengthy preface in which he discusses mortalist theology and the likely effect of continuing belief in the soul's immortality on contemporary Protestantism, Blackburne embarks on his historical review of mortalist thought. It is, without doubt, factual, informative, essentially accurate and frequently discerning. Froom calls it "epochal", "a classic" in its field that remains unsurpassed.[2] It is, in fact, meagre in content at several points, minimal in its coverage of certain issues and relevant publications and, one feels at times, selective, particularly in its omission of information that would have been available at the time. For a history of the mortalist debate to the middle of the eighteenth century, it is unexpectedly and disappointingly brief. The *Historical View* nonetheless retains its importance as the first attempt at a cohesive and sequential history of the mortalist viewpoint from the middle of the fifteenth century to its own day, a period of some three hundred years. For much of that time, mortalism had been forced on to the defensive as the previous chapters in this study have demonstrated. Even in Blackburne's time those who ventured to publish in its favour did so at the risk of misunderstanding and calumny. Both Law and Peckard, "patterns" of "moderation, solid reasoning and good sense", Blackburne says, had been subjected to "the vilest calumny" and were the objects of "the most absurd" insinuations.[3] Blackburne's *Short Historical View*, limited though it was, succeeded in communicating the often opprobrious nature of the mortalist controversy, as well as its chief points and the leading characters who had been involved in three centuries of debate. From these standpoints it remains an important contribution to the mortalist literature.

Much of Blackburne's work appears to have been motivated by a conviction that the Reformation had failed to deal adequately with the doctrine of the immortal soul, and a resulting fear that its widespread and deep-rooted hold on contemporary Christendom posed a serious threat to the credibility of Protestantism, even to authentic Christian faith itself. This conviction surfaces in *No Proof in the Scriptures of an Intermediate State* in which Blackburne asserts that allegiance to the Roman doctrine of the soul's immortality continues as a Protestant article of faith for fear of upsetting the people in the pew. "'Tis dangerous they say, to unsettle men's minds, and direct them from the paths wherein they have been accustomed to walk".[4] This reluctance accounts for

1. *Ibid.*, 46.
2. *CFF*, II, 206, 208.
3. Blackburne, *Short Historical View*, xxiv.
4. [Blackburne], *No Proof in the Scriptures*, 36.

Protestantism's refusal to "review their old systems and cast out of them all things that offend", specifically everything that disagrees "with the written word".[1] In the context of his own thorough-going thnetopsychism, Blackburne spells out the fears which make an understanding of the mortalist issue so necessary. While the Reformers

> were studiously lopping the branches of superstition and imposture, they inadvertently left the stock, with a vigorous root in the ground, which their successors, with a surprising inattention to the pernicious consequences of their misapprehension, have been cultivating to a fresh growth, to the great hazard not only of the Protestant religion, but even of Christianity itself, which is at this hour well nigh choaked and obscured under the thick shade of this venomous exotic.[2]

Blackburne points out once more that the doctrine of the soul's immortality is crucial to the Roman doctrinal system as a whole. This fact could not be over-emphasised. Immortalism was critical to Rome's identity, the "chief prop" thereof and "necessary to the support of the better half of popish superstitions".[3] Blackburne finds it "remarkable" that contemporary Protestants, "who have on most occasions refused to be governed by tradition, seem to have submitted to it in this matter with the most implicit deference".[4]

It was undoubtedly a dilemma for Protestant advocates of the immortal soul, many of whom found mortalist doctrine, and soul sleepers themselves, a cause of irritation, even anger. Blackburne felt that he knew the reason for this frequently vented hostility. Mortalism was, he believed, a difficult issue for its opponents to deal with. For those caught in the dilemma and unable or unwilling to capitulate to mortalism's arguments, it was often easier to respond antagonistically than rationally. Mortalism, he thought, struck "at the pride of the philosopher, the enthusiastic visions of the mystic, the lucrative systems of interested churchmen, and the various prejudices and superstitions of their respective disciples". It was, as a consequence, frequently "loaded with all the obloquy and scandal which bigotted and provoked adversaries" could lay upon it.[5] It was uncompromising language, and it revealed the frustration, the indignation perhaps, which mortalists themselves felt when, in their view, the opposition refused to recognise the origin of the soul's immortality or its threat to the integrity of the Protestant faith and the various confessions and creeds which sought to explain and defend it.

By the time Law, Peckard and Blackburne arrived on the mortalist scene not much remained to be said by mortalists that had not been said previously.

1. *Ibid.*
2. Blackburne, *Historical View,* lxv, lxvi.
3. *Short Historical View,* xxxvii, 86.
4. *Historical View,* lxviii.
5. *Ibid.,* lxvi.

There were always new and different ways of saying the same thing, of course, and together they said what they judged had to be repeated for their own generation. They did so ably, with clarity and with conviction. Few had advocated the mortalist cause more persuasively. Certainly no Anglicans had previously championed thnetopsychism so thoroughly or so openly. The days of hesitant anonymity, ambivalence and ambiguity, seen particularly in the early years of the eighteenth century, had largely passed. From the middle of the eighteenth century onwards mortalists would be able to live comfortably, more or less, within the Anglican fold, even if they lived at its edge. And some, as we have just observed, lived much nearer the centre.

Later Eighteenth-Century Advocates

The mid-century Anglicans Law, Peckard and Blackburne, then, had given mortalism a new status. It was now undeniably Christian, respectable, to a degree, as well as reasonable. As the eighteenth century proceeded it is not surprising to find that a host of witnesses now appeared, willing to lay aside the weights which previously had encumbered them. They were Anglican and Nonconformist, clergy and laity, learned scholars and men from other walks of life whose opinions in the usual course of things would normally have been respected. We need only note some of them in passing, and two or three of them in greater detail. John Robinson, a physician, was interested in the issue from both biblical and philosophical perspectives and concluded that "the antient opinion" which asserted the soul's immateriality and immortality as a "thinking substance" was "quite false".[1] Benjamin Dawson, philosopher and philologist and from 1760 conforming rector of Burgh in Suffolk,[2] who had come to the defence of Law and Blackburne in the mortalist controversies of the 1750s and 1760s , soon confirmed his own mortalist stance with several publications, including *An Illustration of Several Texts of Scripture* and *Remarks on . . . the State of the Soul after Death*, both published in 1765.[3] John Alexander, a Presbyterian minister and reputedly one of the most able Greek scholars of the day, critically examined I Corinthians 15 and concluded that it supported mortalist theology.[4] The author of *A Warning Against Popish Doctrines* (1767) re-stated an old mortalist conviction when he said that the idea of man's

1. J[ohn] R[obinson], *Philosophical and Scriptural Inquiries into the Nature and Constitution of Mankind* (1757), title page. The Bodleian Library copy of this rare pamphlet contains only the first or "Philosophic" part.
2. Formerly a Presbyterian minister, also claimed by Unitarians on account of his theological leanings "towards the Priestley school".
3. The latter dedicated to Law out of the author's "esteem for his character and learning", and noting the "present brisk agitation "of the question.
4. John Alexander, *A Paraphrase upon the Fifteenth Chapter of the First Epistle to the Corinthians* (1766), particularly the Preliminary Dissertation, *passim*. Cf. his *Sermon on Ecclesiastes ix.10*.

inherent immortality was a "human invention".[1] John Tottie, a canon of Christ Church, Oxford and Archdeacon of Worcester, preached a sermon before the University of Oxford in 1772 in which he declared that the resurrection of the body was "the primitive faith of God's people from the earliest ages" and that belief in the survival of the soul detracted from it.[2] The Creator "alone . . . is essentially and necessarily eternal", having "life in himself ", and the authority and will to "dispense it and continue it to his creatures"[3], Tottie declared. There were others up and down the land who, as the eighteenth century unfolded, also came readily to mortalism's defence.

Samuel Bourn of Norwich[4] is a case in point. His mortalism derived from a rejection of the doctrine of eternal torment which he opposed on three grounds: it was inconsistent with reason, it compromised the character of God, and it contradicted the plain teaching of Scripture. Bourn, a Presbyterian, had published in 1760 *A Series of Discourses on the Principles and Evidences of Natural Religion and the Christian Revelation*, yet another attempt to reconcile reason and revelation. In 'The Gospel Doctrine of Future Punishment', Discourse XV, Bourn argued that the biblical teachings of death and resurrection make it impossible to believe in the immortality of the soul and hence in a future condition in which the wicked will necessarily be in a state of consciousness in order to be tormented eternally in hell. Bourn held that at death all "sink into a state of inactivity and insensibility". This happens to "every person . . . at the moment of death". The "plain, simple, primary" notion of death is that it is "a cessation of life". It is "a sleep", a state in which all awareness of time and events ceases.[5]

Moreover, the New Testament writers always mean by resurrection "restoration to life". It is that future event "by which the person who dies passes from death to life, from a state of inaction and insensibility, to a state of action and enjoyment".[6] The New Testament does not teach that this transition occurs at death, or "without any reference to what becomes of the body".[7] Bourn holds that the Greek word *anazao* always has the meaning of 'resurrection' or 'rising again' in the New Testament and that it never signifies the possibility of future happiness and glory for the soul without the body prior to the last day. In the New Testament sense, the resurrection is of the whole person and not

---

1. *A Warning Against Popish Doctrines: or Observations on the Rev. Mr. Thomas Broughton's Defence of an Inherent Immortality in Man; Shewing it to be a Doctrine of Human Invention* (1767).
2. John Tottie, *Sermons Preached before the University of Oxford* (1775), 254.
3. *Ibid.,* 115-6.
4. Samuel Bourn III, 1714-1796.
5. Samuel Bourn, *A Series of Discourses on the Principles and Evidences of Natural Religion and the Christian Revelation* (1760), xxxiii, xxxiv.
6. *Ibid.,* xxix.
7. *Ibid.*

only of the body.[1] By consistently taking resurrection in "the plain and general sense"of the New Testament, "we shall preserve the simplicity of the Gospel", finding "its doctrine, as well as its language, most intelligible and rational".[2]

Hence the doctrine of eternal torment, the object of Bourn's attack, is unbiblical, "void of all foundation in the holy Scriptures".[3] Death is the final end of the wicked, not continuing life in torment. It is here that Bourn appeals to reason as well as to Scripture. "To imagine that by the term death is meant an eternal life, tho' in a condition of extreme misery", Bourn says, "seems to [confound] all propriety and meaning of words".[4] When Christ says to the finally impenitent, "Depart from me . . . into everlasting fire prepared for the devil and his angels", His intention is clear, and consistent with the biblical revelation as a whole. "The meaning is a total, irrevocable destruction".[5] Sodom and Gomorrah are biblical examples of that destruction, "so effectively consumed and destroyed that they could never be rebuilt". So Bourn concludes, "The image of fire unquenchable or everlasting is not intended to signify the degree or duration of torment, but the absolute certainly of destruction beyond all possibility of a recovery".[6]

Bourn was questioned about his views by a fellow Presbyterian, Samuel Chandler, whose forty-year ministry at the Old Jewry in London and his protracted war against deism and Roman Catholicism had established him as a well-known figure in religious circles in the capital and beyond. Chandler had been awarded an honorary Doctor of Divinity by Glasgow University in recognition of his contribution to the theological debates of the times. He was apparently concerned that Bourn's position could be interpreted to deny that the wicked would be punished in accordance with their guilt. In a letter to Chandler, Bourn made it clear that his own concern was with the "absurd, cruel, anti-Christian, and diabolical doctrine of infinite or never-ending misery and torment",[7] and not with the fundamental idea of punishment

1. *Ibid.*, xxix-xxxiii.
2. *Ibid.*, xxxiii.
3. 'The Gospel Doctrine of Future Punishment', in *A Series of Discourses,* 376.
4. *Ibid.*, 382.
5. *Ibid.*, 383-4.
6. *Ibid.*, 384.
7. Samuel Bourn, *A Letter Concerning the Christian Doctrine of Future Punishment* (1759), in *Discourses,* I, 440. The *Letter* is not included in all editions of the *Discourses.* Grantham Killingworth, the Norwich millenarian Baptist, also entered the debate with Bourn, apparently more concerned to defend the underlying doctrine of the soul's immortality than hell and eternal torment. In 1761 he published *The Immortality of the Soul Proved from Scripture . . . an Answer to the Rev. Mr. Sam. Bourne's Reasons against it.* Killingworth complained that the "cavils and objections" against the soul's immortality were "legion", and argued that the distinction between soul and body was better grounded in Scripture than the divine/human nature of Christ, *The Immortality of the Soul,* 22, 25.

for the wicked. He was even willing to concede that, on the strength of the New Testament evidence, there might even be degrees of punishment for the ungodly "proportionate to their guilt", but was unwilling to concede that "unquenchable fire", and similar expressions, were intended to convey eternal torment, but only " total destruction, or annihilation, or ceasing to exist".[1] Even death and hell themselves will finally be cast into the lake of fire, a point which Bourn regards as "decisive".[2]

Nor should we overlook the Unitarian George Clark, who likewise refuted the doctrine of eternal torment in the context of a thorough-going mortalist theology because it dishonoured God and misrepresented his character. It was "grossly absurd", a "wicked " doctrine, "incompatible" with the character of God, and it had consistently proved "insufficient" to achieve what many of its advocates had claimed for it, "virtuous actions".[3] Clark felt that a criminal would more likely be "racked and disquieted by fear of the gallows. . . HERE, than through fear of the wrath of God ... hereafter".[4] He complained to the publisher of a sermon by Jonathan Edwards, 'The Eternity of Hell Torments', that it contradicted the Scriptures which "constantly declare that eternal life, incorruption, immortality, non-subjection to death" is the reward of the "penitent and obedient", but that "death, destruction . . . a denial of eternal life, is the irreversible fate of the disobedient".[5] Clark concluded that the final annihilation of the wicked was "so demonstrably the doctrine of Scripture and of reason" that it was remarkable the Christian world had been "so long without possession of this almost self-evident truth".[6]

We have observed more than once that opposition to the teachings of hell and eternal torment did not necessarily flow from a mortalist theology. In Clark's case, however, it evidently did. He speaks in traditional thnetopsychist terms of the "whole" man, "a compound being", not constituted of a body and a soul "of distinct natures and properties".[7] Death he understood, on biblical grounds, "as a sleep, . . . a state of darkness, silence, forgetfulness, inactivity, corruption, insensibility, terms that imply a total absence of every perception".[8] Consequently the rewards held out in Scripture for the faithful and the punishment designated for the unfaithful are not dispensed at death as commonly believed. They are reserved for a future state, when either eternal life or eternal death will be the portion of each human being who has ever lived.

1. Bourn, *A Letter*, in *Discourses*, I, 441.
2. *Ibid.*
3. [George Clark], *A Vindication of the Honor of God: in a Scriptural Refutation of the Doctrines of Eternal Misery and Universal Salvation* (1792), 4,13.
4. *Ibid.*
5. George Clark, *A Vindication of The Honour of God and the Rights of Men* (1789), 11.
6. Clark, *Scriptural Refutation*, 246.
7. *Ibid.*, 60-1.
8. *Ibid.*, 49.

The two future alternatives thus anticipated confirm the essential thneto-psychist truth of human nature and existence. In reviewing the biblical evidence, Clark concluded that the final reward of the righteous was life and immortality, a condition inherently and manifestly different from man's current situation:

> We see that the future state of the obedient is termed life, immortality, eternal life, being ever with the Lord, abiding forever; as that which is unperishable, incorruptible, and passeth not away; as an undying state, a state in which there shall be no more death; as a state in which death or mortality is swallowed up in victory; as a saving, preserving, or keeping of life; as a state in which death shall not be seen for ever; as an eternal house, an eternal inheritance, that fadeth not away.[1]

The future condition of the unrighteous, the disobedient, is to be seen on the other hand as something which stands in stark contrast to the immortal life of the faithful. It is, in fact, the very opposite condition, total and irreversible oblivion, death eternal and absolute, the utter negation of life and everything it is normally understood to signify:

> We also find that the future state of the disobedient is termed death, the second death, destruction, perdition, corruption; as a state in which they shall not have life, in which they shall not see life, in which they shall suffer a loss of life.[2]

There is little room for misunderstanding here. The strength and bare unambiguity of Clark's thnetopsychist language makes it the more remarkable that he has not been noticed previously.

Joseph Priestley

Joseph Priestley, with whom this account of the origins and development of English mortalism concludes, was without doubt one of its most distinguished, if controversial, advocates. Priestley's theological journey through Presbyterianism, Arianism, Socinianism, Unitarianism and Universalism clearly indicates his dissatisfaction with orthodoxy and neo-orthodoxy at several major points. The radical views he came to hold of the person of Christ, the atonement, and the nature of the Bible,[3] should not be allowed to obscure the perspicacity of his mortalism or the clarity with which he expressed it. For one who is supposed to have rejected the inspiration of the Bible[4] his constant appeal to both Old and New Testaments and his perceptive analysis of the text in defence of the mortalist

1. *Ibid.*, 238.
2. *Ibid.*
3. See *ODCC*, s.v. Joseph Priestley.
4. A less rigid assessment of his view of Scripture is conveyed in the more recent *ODNB* entry on Priestley. The title of one of his last works, *Doctrines of Heathen Philosophy Compared to those of Revelation* (1804), seems to substantiate the point.

position is quite remarkable. His reputed conversion in later life to Universalism and a belief in the possibility of moral progress after death cannot detract from the influence of his thnetopsychism on the continuing development of English mortalism during the 1770s and the 1780s and probably beyond that.

Priestley tells us himself that he first entertained doubts about the soul's immortality when preparing an abridgement of David Hartley's *Observations on Man* for publication in 1775,[1] tending at the time to feel that "man does not consist of two principles so essentially different from one another as matter and spirit" but rather "that the whole man is of some uniform composition".[2] Hartley's *Observations,* first published in 1749, had opened with the categorical assertion "Man consists of two parts, body and mind".[3] While both the *DNB* and the *ODNB* describe Priestley as a theologian and scientist, with the passing of time he has come to be remembered more for his scientific endeavours than for his theology, with the exception of a few works which undeniably validate his claim to recognition as a religious thinker of consequence. Two of these works in particular convey his reasoned and vigorous mortalism, *Disquisitions Relating to Matter and Spirit* (1777) and the widely-read *History of the Corruptions of Christianity* (1782) which caused much debate and which was burned by the common hangman in Dort in 1785.[4]

In *Disquisitions Relating to Matter and Spirit*, Priestley approached the ever-challenging problem of human nature from biblical and philosophical standpoints, stating that the very idea of an immaterial soul residing in a material body was contrary to reason and calling the prevailing doctrine of the soul's immortality a "vulgar hypothesis".[5] He also defends himself against charges of atheism levelled against him on account of earlier questions he had raised regarding the soul's supposed immortality, some of which had come from "quarters where more candour and better discernment might have been expected".[6] The possibility that, like Hobbes, he might "for generations lie under the imputation of absolute atheism"[7] does not appear to have dismayed him. Proceeding "from reason and the Scriptures", Priestley declares that it is irrational and unbiblical, hence unacceptable, to conclude "that all the powers of man do not belong to the same

1. Published as *Hartley's Theory of the Human Mind* (1775). Priestley felt that Hartley's original *Observations* had been "clogged with a whole system of moral and religious knowledge" which, although "excellent" was irrelevant to the understanding of the mind itself. He intended to publish the excluded parts of the *Observations* later.
2. Joseph Priestley, *Disquisitions Relating to Matter and Spirit* (1777), Preface, xiii.
3. David Hartley, *Observations on Man, his Frame, and his Expectations* (1749), I, 1.
4. *DNB,* s.v. Joseph Priestley.
5. Priestley, *Disquisitions* , Preface, xiii. The title page states that the *Disquisitions* is followed by *The History of the Philosophical Doctrine concerning the Origin of the Soul, and the Nature of Matter,* with particular reference to the doctrine's influence on the development of Christianity.
6. *Ibid.,* xiv.
7. *Ibid.,* xvi.

substance, when they are observed to have a constant and necessary dependence upon one another".[1] He believes that the soul may be equated with the mind, which only functions in conjunction with the body when it is alive. He says that if the 'soul' can function apart from the body it is reasonable to assume that there would be some evidence of that before death.[2]

Of the biblical evidence Priestley observes "remarkable silence on the ... immateriality of the human soul". He can find nothing in the books of Scripture to support the soul's immortality "except a few passages ill translated or ill understood".[3] The considerable weight of biblical evidence is unmistakably thnetopsychist. It depicts human existence proceeding on the basis of the "whole man" and not from a dualistic hypothesis. Man's essential mortality is affirmed by "the uniform language of both the Old and New Testaments".[4] We have noted earlier mortalist exegesis of Genesis 2:7, a text crucial to mortalism and to mortalism's understanding of man. At the risk of appearing unnecessarily repetitive, we may note in passing Priestley's interpretation of this critical passage. Affirming that "the whole man" was made of the dust of the ground, Priestley observes:

> God made this man, who was lifeless at first, to breathe and live. For it evidently follows from the text, that nothing but the circumstance of breathing made the difference between the unanimated earth, and the living soul. It is not said that when one constituent part of the man was made, another necessary constituent part, of a very different nature, was superadded to it; and that these two, united, constituted the man; but only that the substance which was formed of the dust of the earth became a living soul, that is became alive, by being made to breathe.[5]

After carefully examining the use of the word 'soul' in several texts he concludes, "In all these passages it is most evident that the word 'soul' is synonimous [sic] to man. . ."[6] and then adds, "If in this there be any allusion to an immaterial and immortal part in man, it is wonderfully concealed".[7] Of the New Testament text Priestley argues that if the sacred writers

> really believed the existence of the soul as a principle in the human constitution, naturally distinct from and independent of the body, it cannot but be supposed that they would have made some use of it in their arguments for a future life. But it is remarkable that we find no such arguments in all the New Testament.[8]

1. *Ibid.,* xv, 33.
2. *Ibid.,* 35.
3. *Ibid.,* 114. The mortalist response to those biblical passages most frequently brought against their position is outlined in Appendix II.
4. *Ibid.,* 119.
5. Priestley, *Disquisitions,* 115.
6. *Ibid.,* 116.
7. *Ibid.,* 118.
8. *Ibid.,* 119.

Priestley also refers to the biblical accounts of various individuals brought back to life after having died, "persons having been recalled from death", and comments:"Yet upon none of these occasions is there the least mention made of the immaterial soul which, upon the common hypothesis, must have been in a state of happiness or misery, and must have been recalled from there to its old habitation".[1] It was a point appreciated by mortalists, if not always by others.

The same analytical scrutiny of biblical exegesis is evident in the *History of the Corruptions of Christianity*. Having again rebutted the dualism necessary to the existence of an independent soul, Priestley sets out again the wholistic position, opening the way for his re-affirmation of man's way into the future:

> There is no instance, either in the Old or New Testament, of this soul being supposed to be in one place and the body in another. They are always conceived to go together, so that the perceptive and thinking power could not, in fact, be considered by the sacred writers as any other than a property of a living man; and therefore as what ceased of course when the man was dead, and could not be revived but with the revival of the body.[2]

It is necessary to understand man's constitution in the present life in order to understand his hope of life to come. This final phrase brings us to the heart of Priestley's eschatology. It is the "revival of the body", the resurrection, which is the key to man's future. Even the most cursory reading of the *Disquisitions* shows how frequently Priestley returns to the resurrection at the last day as the only valid source of hope. Although life ceases at the point of death, this is not the end, for the temporary extinction of life at death is not the same as annihilation. When we say that a candle is extinguished "we surely do not mean that it is annihilated, that there is nothing left to light again".[3] This illustrates "precisely" the apostle Paul's "idea of the resurrection of the dead".[4] Priestley maintains that Paul, who wrote "largely on the subject, and to Greeks, by whom the doctrines of Plato were respected",[5] consistently stresses the resurrection as the key to immortality. So man's hope of a future life "depends upon the resurrection of the dead, and has no other foundation whatever".[6]

So Priestley, like other mortalists, affirms resurrection as the only valid hope of future life and immortality. In so doing, he deals with an objection frequently brought against the resurrection hope by its opponents, even by some of its more tentative or thoughtful advocates – the question of personal identity beyond the grave, when the body has putrefied and "the parts that composed it are dispersed" and even "form other bodies which have an equal claim to the same

1. *Ibid.*, 122.
2. Priestley, *History*, I , 401.
3. Priestley, *Disquisitions,* 164.
4. *Ibid.,* 165.
5. *Ibid.,* 130-1.
6. *Ibid.,* 252.

resurrection". For this reason, in the minds of some doubters resurrection is not only "improbable", but "impossible",[1] contrary to normal human experience and the known processes of decay and decomposition. Also, bodily resurrection raises weighty moral and philosophical questions. Can the expectation of future rewards and punishment be just "if the man that rises again be not identically the same as" as the man who lived and died?[2] Does not the continuity of personal identity require "identically the same" person that lived previously?

Believing himself in the continuity of both personal identity and identicalness, Priestley suggests at least a partial answer for those who have genuine doubts about such a possibility. His suggestion lies in the distinction between "the identity of the man", i.e. physical identity, and the "identity of the person", i.e. personality. It is the latter which ought to be the main consideration.

Although this distinction "may appear a paradox", similar distinctions are found in the natural world, and should be allowed to illustrate the truth of the continuity of human identity. The river Thames is a body of water which flows continuously between its banks and along its bed, and although the water itself is "continually and visibly changing", it is nevertheless the same river today as it was a thousand years ago.[3] The same may be said of the Nile, the Euphrates, and the Tiber. They each have an identity as rivers "independently of the water of which they alone consist". Similarly with forests, which consist of many trees growing together in given locations. The forests retain their identity as forests, although "all the trees of which they consist decay" and are replaced by other trees.[4] Neither rivers nor forests are actually composed of the same material today as they were in the past, but nonetheless have retained their identity through considerable change. Applying the analogies, Priestley concludes:

> Admitting, therefore, that the man consists wholly of matter, as much as the river does of water, or the forest of trees, and that this matter should be wholly changed in the interval between death and the resurrection; yet, if after this state we shall know one another again, and converse together as before, we shall be, to all intents and purposes, the same persons. Our personal identity will be sufficiently preserved, and the expectation of it at present will have a proper influence on our conduct.[5]

While this line of argument might not have entirely satisfied the most high-minded thinker, it would probably have quelled many doubts about the retention of personal identity beyond the corruption of the grave.

Continuity has always been an argument that has appealed to theologians and historians of dogma, and Priestley concluded the first volume of his *History of the Corruptions of Christianity* with a brief survey of the history of mortalism

1. *Ibid.*, 156.
2. *Ibid.*
3. *Ibid.*, 157.
4. *Ibid.*, 158.
5. *Ibid.*, 160.

and its opposition to the soul's natural mortality.[1] He stoutly maintains that the first Christians did not believe in an immortal soul. The distinction between soul and body, being "originally a doctrine of Oriental philosophy", had later spread "into the Western part of the world", a process which Priestley traces back through Greek thought to its earliest Egyptian, Chaldean and possibly Persian and Indian origins, arguing that these pre-Christian pagan associations had "exceedingly altered and debased the true Christian system".[2] Thereafter it was a slow but sure decline into apostasy, although some Christian believers in Arabia kept mortalist doctrine alive "as late as the third century". Eventually even they capitulated, seduced by the teachings of Origen.[3] Most of the early fathers, in fact, were Platonists, and "borrowed many of their explanations of scripture doctrines from that system".[4] The medieval church subsequently built the doctrine of purgatory on the foundation of the immortal soul, the doctrine which eventually came to dominate eschatological thought during the Middle Ages. It was, however, opposed by the Waldensians who "never admitted it", later by Luther in Germany, and in England by Wycliffe, although he "could not entirely shake it off".[5] Others did shake off both the doctrines of purgatory and the immortality of the soul, however, and from then on Priestley maintained, "in every period since the Reformation", mortalism, that is to say thnetopsychism, had never wholly disappeared from the English religious scene.[6] From the earliest days of the English Reformation, in fact, it had always attracted "a considerable number of followers", he says.[7] In more recent times mortalism had "gained ground very much", mainly as a consequence of the writings of prominent men, Law and Blackburne in particular. Yet the doctrine of the soul's continuing consciousness in an intermediate state would probably never be eradicated "a long as belief in a separate soul is retained". [8] On this sombre but realistic note Priestley's account closes. If this and the preceding chapters in this study are at all a reliable guide, we must conclude that his summary and assessment were in all essentials correct.

1. Section V of the *History*, vol. I, entitled 'The History of Opinions Concerning the State of the Dead'. Priestley's historical survey was brief because it recognised the availability of Blackburne's recent account from which it largely was drawn.
2. Priestley, *History*, I, 168, 156, 266-8.
3. *Ibid.*, 402, 407.
4. Priestley, *Disquisitions*, 294.
5. Priestley, *History*, I, 423.
6. *Ibid.*, 424.
7. *Ibid.* Priestley frequently cites Mosheim's *Institutes*, which states that there were "great numbers" of General Baptists in England in the seventeenth century and that mortalism was a major tenet among them, J.L. von Mosheim, *Institutes of Ecclesiastical History* (tr. J. Murdock, ed., H. Soames, 1841), III, 577-578. Mosheim's account is insufficiently definitive of the Baptist thnetopsychism known from other sources and can be read more easily as psychopannychism, which generally it was not.
8. *Ibid.*, 424-5.

Chapter Seven
The World to Come – Realised Immortality

One further question remains to be answered if mortalist theology in its totality is to be fully comprehended and, at the end, fully realised. It relates to the ultimate destiny of the redeemed who receive immortality at the resurrection. Given mortalism's emphatic repudiation of the soul's traditional release to heavenly glory at the moment of death, what then would be the final reward of the faithful? Where would believers, resurrected from the dead or transformed from among the living and made immortal at the coming of Christ, enjoy eternity if not in heaven? There were contingent questions also, no less insistent, which arose as human destiny and the final outline of eschatological events were carefully considered. Where would the kingdom of God, referred to so frequently in Scripture and so eagerly anticipated by believers, finally be established? How were the prophetic words of Isaiah, Peter, and John with reference to a new earth to be understood? And, not least of all, how were the words of Jesus himself to be interpreted, "The meek shall inherit the earth?" It is a question, or series of questions, which demanded attention if mortalism's vision of the future was not to end in futile oblivion. In attempting to find the answers mortalist advocates proposed we shall be reminded once again of the driving force behind the entire mortalist quest – its pursuit of the truth concerning human nature and destiny derived from the biblical revelation as thoroughly and objectively interpreted as was thought possible.

The strength of this motivation should not elude us. Without exception, the mortalists we have encountered lived and wrote at a time when truth was deemed absolute and its discovery considered both desirable and attainable. To be in the vanguard of those who sought truth was honourable and responsible. If that quest led to exclusion or calumny, as it did for many mortalists, among others who contended for minority viewpoints, it was a price that was willingly paid. Francis Blackburne, who came relatively late to the defence of the mortalist cause and who could afford the stigma of heterodoxy and theological isolation more than many, protested strenuously about the Calvinistic mind-set which "treated all who questioned the natural immortality of the soul, as impious, heretical, and no better at bottom than atheists".[1] Blackburne may be regarded

1. Blackburne, *Historical View*, 332.

as speaking here for all mortalists. They would have argued passionately that the nature of man in life and in death were crucial issues in the quest for truth, compromised as they believed that quest to be by the prevailing eschatology. Beyond that, the doctrine of the immortal soul undermined truth at the point of its ultimate realisation in human experience, by proposing a way to eternal life which was contrary to that promised in Scripture.

The Saints Eternal Home

Belief in a world to come, a new created earth, was not restricted to those holding mortalist views. Indeed, mortalist insistence on the earth made new as the final home of the redeemed appeared in the context of a much wider anticipation of that new world. Commenting on the widespread sixteenth- and early seventeenth-century belief that those who had lost loved ones would meet them again in heaven immediately after death, Peter Marshall points out that some early English Protestants "preferred to imagine a meeting-again which would take place at the end of time, when the Lord returned in glory and the bodies of the dead rose from their graves to rejoin their souls upon a new earth".[1] While disagreeing with the intermediate state of souls in heavenly bliss, thorough-going mortalists would readily have concurred with the ultimate destination of the redeemed here envisaged. The thought of millions of disembodied spirits inhabiting a nebulous place called heaven either for eternity or during an indeterminate intermediate period was not in the least compatible with mortalist eschatology, or indeed, with biblical eschatology as a whole as mortalists understood it. Taking passages such as Isaiah 65:17-25 and 66: 22, 23, II Peter 3:10-13, Revelation 21:1-5 and Christ's promise in Matthew 5 that the meek would inherit the earth, mortalists asserted that the redeemed, after the resurrection when they had become again "the same persons that they were before", would live in a re-created earth. It was what Henry Layton had in mind when he spoke of "the restitution of all things".[2] It was this belief in a new created earth as the eternal home of the saved that came to prevail in the minds and hearts of many early English Protestants who turned to their Bibles for an understanding of the future.

This belief that at the consummation of history and as the grand finale in the divine purpose, there would be a new earth had been introduced early into English Protestant eschatology. John Napier, the mathematician and inventor of logarithms, whose exposition of the book of Revelation was translated into Dutch and French soon after it first appeared in English in 1593 and which had gone through five English editions by 1645, was among the first to consider seriously the biblical promises of new heavens and a new earth. Basing his

---

1. Marshall, *Beliefs and the Dead*, 219.
2. This is to pass over the complicated question of seventeenth-century millenarianism which has, in any case, received considerable attention over the past half century or so. But see also p. 181, n. 1.

exposition on thirty-six propositions within the historicist school of prophetic interpretation[1], Napier believed that he and his generation were living in the seventh and last age of the world and that after the dissolution of the world there would be a new earth, subsequent to Christ's second coming and the last judgment.[2] Arthur Dent, a graduate of Christ's College, Cambridge, and Puritan rector of South Shoebury, Essex also wrote a commentary on the book of Revelation, first published in 1603. Like Napier, Dent looked for a literal new earth after the last judgement, asserting that the present world must continue for ever, but "greatly altered and changed in condition and quality".[3] God would "restore the world to that excellent and pristinate estate wherein it was before Adam's fall".[4] Dent's book, *The Ruine of Rome,* proved to be even more popular and influential than that of Napier, reaching at least eleven English editions between 1603 and 1662. Napier and Dent were but two of many English Protestant biblical scholars whose minds turned to the books of Daniel and Revelation throughout the seventeenth century and whose works continued to influence the religious thought of the age long after they were dead. David Pareus, professor of theology at Heidelberg, whose *Commentary Upon the Divine Revelation* was influential on the Continent and which was translated into English in 1644, confirmed that belief in a new earth was not restricted to English believers. Commenting on II Peter 3:10 in his explanation of the final chapters of Revelation Pareus observed, "We gather that a new heaven and a new earth is to be looked for historically and properly", anticipating "the supernatural change of the whole universe which shall be at Christ's coming".[5]

Joseph Mede, the noted Cambridge Hebraist and biblical scholar, and probably the most influential of all the early seventeenth-century English prophetic expositors, proposed a similar eschatology. Mede held that the Noachian deluge referred to in II Peter 3 was a type of the final cleansing of the earth. Noting that the phrase "pass away" in v. 10 reflected a Hebraism which indicated a change from one state to another, Mede believed that the final conflagration in which the "elements" would "melt with fervent heat" and "the

1. In contrast to the preterist and futurist schools, historicism held that the prophetic outlines in the books of Daniel and the Revelation covered the entire period of history between the time when they were written and the end of the world. Preterism proposed that these prophecies had all been fulfilled in the early centuries of the Christian era, while futurism projected their fulfilment to the end of the age.
2. John Napier, *A Plaine Discovery of the whole Revelation of Saint John* (Edinburgh, 1593), 5th edn (1645), 164, 228.
3. Arthur Dent, *The Ruine of Rome: or An Exposition upon the whole Revelation* (1603), 284.
4. *Ibid.,* 285, 287.
5. David Pareus, *In Divinam Apocalypsin. S. Apostoli et Evangelistae Johannis Commentarius* (Heidelberg, 1618), tr. E. Arnold, *A Commentary Upon the Divine Revelation of the Apostle and Evangelist John* (Amsterdam, 1644), 550, 554.

earth. . . be burned up", had been pre-figured by the Flood, in that a radical topographical change had then taken place without the total destruction of the earth.[1] The latter-day burning of the earth was to be in preparation for a "restored" earth, Mede said, pointing out that there had long been a school of rabbinical thought which had also maintained the necessity of a "renovation of the world".[2] Thomas Adams, a contemporary of Mede and chaplain to the Lord Chief Justice, Sir Henry Montague, was also drawn to the second epistle of Peter and the idea of renovation. In a massive commentary running to more than fifteen hundred pages, Adams spoke of the "permutation of the world", asserting that the end of the present order was "certain" and "determined", affirming that the anticipated process would be "perfective" rather than "destructive", and claiming by way of confirmation Christ's own promise that the meek would "inherit the earth".[3]

Belief that the earth was destined to be the final home of redeemed believers was rooted in Old Testament prophecy, notably various passages in Isaiah and specifically the prophetic outline in Daniel ch. 2, set out in the form of a great image which was generally believed to represent the major kingdoms of the world from Daniel's own time until the consummation of world history. This particular prophecy was well known and considered seminal in the seventeenth century. Mede called it "The A.B.C. of prophecy", a "prophetical chronology of times", extending from the beginning of Israel's captivity in Babylon "until the mystery of God should be finished".[4] The image consisted of four main parts, each composed of a different metal. The head of gold was understood to represent the kingdom of Babylon, the chest and arms of silver the Medo-Persian empire, the belly and thighs of brass depicted Greece, and the legs of iron represented the Roman empire. The feet and toes, made partly of iron and clay, symbolised the ten nations which finally emerged from the conquered Roman empire after its demise in A.D. 476, and which had ultimately become ten kingdoms in Europe. A stone, made without human hands and widely held to represent the kingdom of Christ,[5] smote the image on the feet, thus depicting that the final conquest and disintegration of all earthly kingdoms and the establishment of the kingdom of God would occur in the times of the divided nations of Europe which had arisen after the collapse of Rome. Mede thus held that Daniel's prophecy reached down to Christ's second coming

1. II Pet. 3:10; Joseph Mede, 'A Paraphrase and Exposition of the Prophecie of St. Peter, concerning the Day of Christ's Second Coming'(1642), in *The Works of the Pious and Profoundly Learned Joseph Mede, B. D.* (J. Worthington, ed., 4th edn,1677), 613-5.
2. *Ibid.,* 610.
3. Thomas Adams, *A Commentary or Exposition upon the Divine Second Epistle Generall, written by the Blessed Apostle St. Peter* (1633), 1358-9.
4. Mede, *Works,* 743, 654.
5. Daniel's own interpretation of the vision specifically related the stone to the Kingdom of God, Dan. 2: 44, 45.

and that the stone represented the kingdom of Christ, established in principle at His first coming and to be completed and visibly realised at His second coming.[1] Another contemporary of Mede, Thomas Parker, whose *Visions and Prophecies of Daniel Expounded* was published in 1646, similarly argued that Daniel's image reached down "unto the last days" and that the stone depicted the kingdom of the saints which was to be established following the fall of the Antichrist.[2] The point, as Parker observed, and as the whole host of prophetic interpreters recognised with him, was that the stone which destroyed the image eventually became a "great mountain, and filled the whole earth".[3] It was a crucial point which mortalists in particular came to insist should not be lost or overlooked. Christ's own promise that the meek would inherit the earth would finally be realised after His coming at the end of time and the resurrection of the dead.

This belief in a new earth as the eternal home of the redeemed came to full expression in a treatise by the Presbyterian vicar of Broadclyst in Devon, John Seager. In 1650 Seager published *A Discoverie of the World to Come* in which he insisted that the new earth predicted in Scripture was not a synonym for heaven as generally and often loosely understood by immortalists, but referred to a future world to be brought into existence by God and to follow the dissolution, but not the destruction, of the present evil world.[4] Seager began by asserting that many Christians were ignorant of the biblical teaching regarding the world to come, believing that there was "no difference betwixt the world to come and the highest heaven".[5] Christ had ascended to heaven after His resurrection, but not into the world to come, "which then had no being".[6] According to I Chronicles 16:30, Ecclesiastes 1:4, Psalm 96:10 and Isaiah 45:18 the earth itself was eternal and could not be "moved" or destroyed.[7] Moreover, it had been created to be inhabited. At its dissolution, therefore, it would be changed "as touching its present and pristine condition, form, and manner of being" but not wiped out of existence.[8] So "the world to come shall begin immediately. . . upon the dissolution of this present world" which will not be completely destroyed in the fires of the last day but "dissolved", reduced to "dust and ashes", and then re-formed.[9] Calling on the same biblical texts previously noted, Seager goes to great lengths to describe the new earth,

1. Mede, *Works,* 104, 656.
2. Thomas Parker, *The Visions and Prophecies of Daniel Expounded*(1646), 2, 5.
3. *Ibid.,* 7,8; Dan. 2:35.
4. John Seager, *A Discoverie of the World to Come According to the Scriptures* (1650), 25-6. Little is known of Seager (or Seagar), and the *Discoverie* is his only known work.
5. *Ibid.,* 2-3.
6. *Ibid.,* 7.
7. *Ibid.,* 38-9.
8. *Ibid.,* 39.
9. *Ibid.,* 54,36,38.

emphasising that according to the textual evidence it can only be understood literally, and stressing that this eschatological consummation of human history is a ground for Christian hope.[1] Seager proposed a three-fold interpretation of the kingdom of Christ: the essential kingdom, the personal-divine kingdom and the personal-human kingdom. The essential kingdom is that kingdom shared by the Trinity, the divine rulership over all. The personal-divine kingdom is the spiritual kingdom established by Christ at His first coming and Christ's subsequent rule in the church. The personal-human kingdom is yet to come when Christ will rule personally, "bodily and visibly", in the earth made new after the dissolution of the present world.[2] Ultimately, therefore, the kingdom of God is the new earth, where Christ and the saints will live and reign eternally.

Seager was keen to ensure that the creation of the new earth should be correctly understood in its proper place in the sequence of final eschatological events. In harmony with his understanding that the earth was eternal and indestructible he was anxious to preserve its continuity in the cataclysmic events of the last day. In fact that day, "the great day of the Lord", a literal day soon to come, would see a rapid sequence of events in which the creation of new heavens and a new earth would be of first priority. In Seager's scheme, the following order would prevail:

1. The dissolution of the present world.
2. The creation of a new earth, "the world to come".
3. The subjugation of all Christ's enemies.
4. The final resignation of the kingdom to the Father.
5. The glorious appearing of Christ.
6. The resurrection of the dead.
7. The last judgment.[3]

So he says, "the world to come shall begin immediately upon the destruction of this present world", enabling fulfilment of the promise in Psalm 72:8 that Christ's dominion should be "from sea to sea, and unto the ends of the earth", and also making possible the eternal reign of the saints in which, "under Christ", they would possess the new earth and reign forever, fulfilling now the promise of Revelation 5:10.[4]

Seager was also concerned to refute the idea that the biblical promises of the world to come were to be understood metaphorically as referring merely to a change in the moral and spiritual condition of the present world, a "Reformation-change", to be brought about by the latter-day world-wide proclamation and acceptance of the gospel. Although this view had attracted "many patrons, advocates and followers of late years", it was nonetheless

1. *Ibid.,* 62-75.
2. *Ibid.,* 132-4.
3. *Ibid.,* 54.
4. *Ibid.,* 64-5.

erroneous, leading amongst other things to millenarianism,[1] an 'error' which was gaining ground rapidly in Seager's day and which he stoutly opposed. Those who have allowed themselves to be so deceived into anticipating "strange forms of religion, (church) government and discipline" leading to a "new Reformed church" in the world, justly deserve "to be censured". To Seager the reasons for descent into such error were obvious, and those who promulgate these ideas deserve to be reprimanded because:

1. They incorrectly interpret, or put a "false gloss" on, those texts which clearly speak of new heavens and a new earth.
2. They use a figurative or allegorical interpretation of Scripture "when the proper and literal sense" is required.
3. They "wrest" other biblical references to suit their own incorrect interpretations.
4. The conclusion reached "by their wrestings" is "grossly erroneous",[2] and therefore misleading.

Those who sought the truth would be better advised to consider the biblical text itself, free from false and misleading gloss, especially the writings of Peter and Paul, or perhaps the godly example of Abraham, who "looked for a city with foundations, whose builder and make is God, Heb. 11:10" and who "hoped for the world to come, wherein this city shall be found".[3]

Thus by the middle of the seventeenth century many immortalists holding the traditional view of the soul and its intermediate, disembodied state in heaven had also come to believe in a more substantial and tangible eternal resting place. Some immortalists, probably a majority, continued to pin their hopes on heaven, but the scenario of a renovated earth, purged from all evil and restored to its pristine, Edenic state was unquestionably an attractive proposition. To those in the mortalist camp who thus understood things it was a more coherent view of the future, more consistent with biblical eschatology as a whole than the traditional immortalist hope of an immaterial soul living for a season in a nebulous heaven and re-united at last with a body, however "spiritual" the body might prove to be. The promised new earth came to be a significant point of concurrence, although not always openly recognised, between those with otherwise quite different and often contentious eschatological hopes.

1. On the millenarianism that was rife in seventeenth-century England see, for example, W.M. Lamont, *Godly Rule*(1969); C. Hill, *Antichrist in Seventeenth-Century England* (1971) and *The World Turned Upside Down* (1972); B.S. Capp, *The Fifth Monarchy Men*(1972); K.R. Firth, *The Apocalyptic Tradition in Reformation Britain, 1530-1645* (Oxford, 1979); J. van den Berg, 'Joseph Mede and the Dutch Millenarian Daniel van Laren', J. K. Cameron, 'The Commentary on the Book of Revelation by James Durham (1622-58)' and Sarah Hutton, 'Henry More and the Apocalypse', all in M. Wilks (ed.), *Prophecy and Eschatology* (Oxford, 1994), in addition to Ball, *A Great Expectation: Eschatological Thought in English Protestantism to 1660* (Leiden, 1975).
2. Seager, *Discoverie*, 72.
3. *Ibid.*, 73.

The Mortalist Vision

We may now return to Hobbes, the first of the English mortalists known to have taken mortalist theology to its logical conclusion by proposing a new earth as the final abode of the redeemed,[1] and whose carefully reasoned analysis of the human condition and the divine response leaves little room for misinterpretation. Chapter 38 of Hobbes's *Leviathan* was, as already noted, entitled 'Of the Signification in Scripture of Eternal Life, Hell, Salvation, the World to Come, and Redemption'. We may be sure that the examination of these various aspects of the future, particularly of the entire *ordo salutis,* in one chapter was not coincidental. The *Leviathan* was published just a year after Seager's *Discoverie of the World to Come* and in a climate in which the works of Napier, Dent, Mede and other prophetic expositors were still avidly consumed and widely influential. Hobbes would almost certainly have known of them. In his own view the first man Adam had been created with conditional immortality and given the earth as his home. As a living person with a material, animate body he was to live out his life in that environment. If Adam had not sinned, "had not broken the commandment of God, he had enjoyed it (immortality) in the Paradise of Eden everlastingly",[2] Hobbes says. Adam and Eve did sin, however, but the consequences of that sin, passed to their posterity, the entire human race, were countered and eradicated by Christ, who recovered for mankind what Adam (and Eve) had lost, namely eternal life. All that follows in the human saga is to be seen as the recovery of man's lost immortality, since Adam and Eve, "if they had not sinned, had lived (i.e. would have lived) on earth eternally".[3]

Hobbes wants us to see that the reality of eternal life in the future is dependent on a material environment such as man's first parents enjoyed and that such an environment is a fulfilment of the divine purpose in the scheme of salvation. He explains:

> Concerning the place wherein men shall enjoy that eternal life which Christ hath obtained for them, the texts before alledged [*sic*] seem to make it on earth. For if as in Adam all die, that is, have forfeited paradise and eternal life on earth, even so in Christ all shall be made alive; then all men shall be made to live on earth, or else the comparison were not proper.[4]

Citing Revelation 21: 2 and 10, in which the prophet John saw the New Jerusalem "coming down from God out of heaven", Hobbes comments, "As if he should say the new Jerusalem, the paradise of God, at the coming of Christ, should come down to God's people from heaven, and not they go up to it from

---

1. Earlier mortalists, notably Overton, were more concerned with the nature of man and his condition in death. Hobbes was, in fact, only the second writer to articulate considered mortalist thought, though this was not his main concern in *Leviathan*.
2. Hobbes, *Leviathan*, 238.
3. *Ibid.,* 239.
4. *Ibid.*

earth". Similarly of Acts 1:11 and the return of Christ which would usher in the new creation, Hobbes notes that the disciples were assured Christ would "so come as you have seen Him go up into heaven" and comments, "Which soundeth as if they (two angels who addressed the disciples, thus generally interpreted) had said, He should come down to govern them . . . eternally here, and not take them up to govern them in heaven". These projections of the eventual reign of God were "conformable to the restauration of the kingdom of God", originally "instituted under Moses . . . a political government of the Jews on earth".[1]

Hobbes continues the argument by asserting that there is no textual evidence for concluding that " faithful" Christians, those "elected in Christ" to eternal life, will spend that eternity in heaven. Giving evidence again of his acceptance of biblical authority and a thorough knowledge of the text, he says that:

> The place wherein men are to live eternally, after the resurrection, is the heavens, meaning by heaven those parts of the world which are the most remote from earth, as where the stars are, or above the stars in another higher heaven called *Coelum Empyreum* (whereof there is no mention in Scripture, nor ground in reason) is not easily to be drawn from any text that I can find.[2]

Hobbes defines the 'kingdom of heaven' as "the kingdom of the king that dwelleth in heaven" whose people of old, Israel, themselves dwelt on earth. The "new kingdom of heaven", made possible by the redemptive work of Christ, will be similarly structured, "because our king shall then be God, whose throne is heaven, without any necessity evident in the Scripture that man shall ascend to his happiness any higher that God's footstool the earth".[3] Further, ensuring that all this is clearly understood to relate to the underlying issue of immortality, Hobbes reminds us that all whose names are written in the Book of Life are "ordained to life eternal at the resurrection" and that the concept of inherent immortality, "that the soul of man is in its own nature eternal, . . . or that any mere man is immortal otherwise that by the resurrection in the last day, is a doctrine not apparent in Scripture".[4] The kingdom of heaven, in which redeemed believers will at last be immortal, will therefore become a reality in the new earth, the world to come.[5]

In this context Hobbes examines the meaning of hell, the lake of fire, Gehenna,

1. *Ibid.* Hobbes's intention here is to stress the earthly location of the kingdom rather than its political nature. He would have been the last to want to give encouragement to Fifth Monarchy aspirations.
2. *Ibid.,* 240.
3. *Ibid.*
4. *Ibid.,* 241.
5. Martinich points out that in Hobbes's thought "the world to come", also referred to in *Leviathan* as the kingdom of God, "goes from the day of judgement to eternity", and like the "old world and the present world" will be on earth, *Hobbes,* 311.

everlasting fire, the punishment of the wicked and the final destruction of evil and the perpetrators of evil, none of which provide evidence that "there shall be an eternal life therein of any individual person, but the contrary, an everlasting death", after which any man so punished "shall die no more".[1] Hobbes then returns to "the joys of life eternal" for the redeemed. Eternal life and salvation are, in fact, "the same thing", both in Scripture and according to reason, and must be related to man's original destiny in the divine purpose:

> To be saved is to be secured, either respectively against special evils, or absolutely against all evil, comprehending want, sickness, and death itself. And because man was created in a condition immortal, not subject to corruption, and consequently to nothing that tendeth to the dissolution of his nature, and fell from that happiness by the sin of Adam, it followeth that to be saved from sin is to be saved from all the evil and calamities sin hath brought upon us.[2]

Salvation, then, is the restoration of man to that happy and sinfree condition which he enjoyed before the fall. This "the faithful are to enjoy, after the day of judgment by the power and favour of Jesus Christ" who, for that very reason, is called man's Saviour. Salvation, correctly understood, finally restores man to "the kingdom of heaven" on earth, all evil, enemies, death, misery and want eternally vanquished. "It seemeth then", Hobbes asserts, "that this salvation should be on earth,

> For by salvation is set forth unto us a glorious reign of our king, by conquest, not a safety by escape; and therefore there where we look for salvation we must look also for triumph, and before triumph for victory, and before victory for battle, which cannot well be supposed shall be in heaven.[3]

Citing Isaiah 33: 20-24 Hobbes again asserts, "By which it is evident that salvation shall be on earth, when God shall reign, at the coming again of Christ".[4]

Hobbes concludes chapter 38 of the *Leviathan* by commenting specifically on the term "the world to come", stating that from all that he has just argued concerning salvation and the kingdom of God it was "not hard" to understand what was meant by "the world to come". He explains that the Bible speaks of three different worlds: the old world, the present world, and the world to come, all signifying the present world in three different epochs or conditions, respectively the old world that existed before the Flood, the world that now is and the new world that is yet to be:

1. Hobbes, *Leviathan*, 245.
2. *Ibid.*
3. *Ibid.*, 246.
4. *Ibid.*

So the first world was from Adam to the general flood. Of the present world our Saviour speaks (John 18:36) . . . Of the world to come St Peter speaks 'Nevertheless we according to his promise look for new heavens and a new earth'. This is that world wherein Christ coming down from heaven in the clouds, with great power and glory, shall send His angels and gather His elect from the four winds and from the uttermost part of the earth, and thenceforth reign over them.[1]

It is this world, the world yet to come at the end of days, at the coming of Christ, as real and tangible as the present world but infinitely more superior, the everlasting kingdom of God on earth, that Christ's redemptive intervention in human history has made possible for man to enjoy throughout eternity.

In the context provided by Hobbes and those who had preceded him the now blind Milton could easily voice the ultimate mortalist hope of a new earth in his enduring *Paradise Lost*, which first appeared in 1667, with several reprints before the second edition in1674. Shortly before this, as has already been noted, Milton had more formally committed his theology to writing in the *De Doctrina Christiana*, speaking there in terms reminiscent of Mede, Napier, Dent and Hobbes of "the renovation of heaven and earth" and of the fact that this renovated earth was "to be possessed by us in perpetuity".[2] The repeated references to new heavens and a new earth in *Paradise Lost* are significant not because they projected some new theology, but because they reminded contemporary readers of that which they already knew as one of the fundamental truths in the divine revelation. There is more, then, than the human race or guilty mankind in focus in Milton's line which claims that the Second Adam "quitted all to save a world from utter loss".[3] Having portrayed the Son's second coming, the resurrection of the saints who "sleep", and the last judgment, he continues:

> The World shall burn, and from her ashes spring
> New Heav'n and Earth, wherein the just shall dwell
> And after all their tribulations long
> See golden days, fruitful of golden deeds,
> With Joy and Love triumphing, and fair Truth.[4]

The Son is the "Destin'd restorer of Mankind" and by Him "new heav'n and earth shall to the ages rise",[5] the earth itself purged by fire at the last day and renewed as the eternal home of the just.

In the final book of *Paradise Lost* Milton dwells at length on the Seed of the woman by whom the restoration of Paradise is assured and achieved. The

1. *Ibid.*, 247-8.
2. Milton, 'Christian Doctrine', in *Prose Works*, IV, 493.
3. Milton, *Paradise Lost*, Bk. III, 307-8.
4. *Ibid.*, 334-38.
5. *Ibid.*, Bk. X, 645-7.

assault on truth through "speculations and traditions"and on those who seek truth amongst such speculation and tradition continues in an ever darker world until the last events finally unfold and the divine purpose hidden in the woman's Seed comes to fruition:

> The Woman's seed, obscurely then foretold,
> Now amplier known thy Saviour and thy Lord,
> Last in the Clouds from Heav'n to be reveal'd
> In glory of the Father, to dissolve
> Satan with his perverted World, then raise
> From the conflagrant mass, purg'd and refined,
> New Heav'ns, new Earth, Ages of endless date
> Founded in righteousness and peace and love,
> To bring forth fruits, Joy and eternal Bliss.[1]

An earlier Milton critic concluded that he, Milton, remained "undecided about whether the apocalypse meant an annihilation or a transformation of the physical earth", and that he chose to remain uncommitted on this "crucial issue".[2] The evidence seems to indicate quite the reverse.[3]

C.A. Patrides takes a textually more justifiable view, even going as far as to say that Milton is "the most distinguished English expositor of the literalistic belief in the conflagration of the universe",[4] the "conflgrant mass, purg'd and refined" resulting in "new Heavn's" and "new Earth". There are too many allusions in *Paradise Lost* alone to this new world order[5] for it to be ambiguous or merely incidental or peripheral to Milton's view of the future. Taken together with the many expressions of the wider mortalist theology in *Paradise Lost* previously noted[6] they remind us that Milton's great epic is one of the enduring articulations of the entire mortalist vision.

Locke also was familiar with the phrase 'the world to come', using it in both *The Reasonableness of Christianity* and the *Paraphrase and Notes on the Epistle of St. Paul to the Ephesians* with reference to the kingdom of God,

1. *Ibid.,* Bk. XII, 535-51.
2. P. Miller, *Errand into the Wilderness* (Cambridge, Mass., 1956), 221. Miller suggested that the elect would discuss the end of the world "endlessly down the vistas of eternity" (p. 218), but did not indicate where the discussion would take place. He failed to see that, despite Milton's "obsolete cosmology" and "anxiety" about "the Copernican universe" (p. 221), Milton anticipated continuity rather than annihilation and that he probably did so from within the Copernican system.
3. Other allusions to a new earth in *Paradise Lost* can be found in Bks. X, 638; XI, 66; XI, 900-1; XII, 463-65.
4. Patrides, *Milton and the Christian Tradition,* 277.
5. Patrides notes that the concept appears "with surprising frequency" in *Paradise Lost; Milton and the Christian Tradition,* 277.
6. See ch. 4, p. 116.

eternal life and the ultimate reward of the righteous. While Locke's use of the term is not always as precise as it was in the writings of Napier, Dent, Seager, Hobbes and others who had used it before him, its import is nonetheless clear enough. Perhaps Locke thought that a hundred years or more of frequent and consistent usage had endowed the term with sufficiently clear meaning not to require further definition, or that the term itself was inherently self-defining. Be that as it may, in the mind of one whose use of theological language was always precise and to the point, the phrase 'the world to come' could mean little else than a future world in which the righteous would enjoy corporeal existence, even though the resurrection body would be different from the body in its present state.[1]

In chapter ten of *The Reasonableness of Christianity* Locke discusses Christ's answer to the questions His disciples had asked concerning the destruction of Jerusalem and the signs of His second coming and the end of the present world. Christ had answered the disciples by warning them of deceivers to come and by reminding them of the fact that the "gospel of the kingdom, i.e. the good news of me, the Messiah, and my kingdom", was to be proclaimed in all the world before the kingdom finally arrived.[2] Locke then explains that the disciples' question about Christ's coming and the end of the world was framed from within contemporary Jewish belief about the world and its future. Referring to the Jewish concept of two worlds, "the present world, and the world to come", Locke says that in Jewish belief the latter, the world to come, was equated with the kingdom of God, and that this world to come, when it finally arrived, "was to put an end to this world". At that time the righteous would be raised from the dead "to enjoy, in that new world, a happy eternity" together with those of the Jewish nation then living.[3]

Locke then explains that the disciples were confused over these two things, "the visible and powerful appearance" of Christ's kingdom, and "the end of the world", and that in Christ's reply to their question He did not explain the difference or the relationship between the two. Locke points out that Christ then went on to speak of His "last coming to judgement . . . to put a final end to this world, and all the dispensation belonging to the posterity of Adam upon earth". Locke implies that Christ intentionally juxtaposed the present and future worlds, or the present and future kingdoms of Christ, and "made His answer obscure and hard to be understood by them".[4] For all that the world to come, either in Jewish or Christian thought, was a reality distinct

---

1. Locke's views on the nature of the resurrection body and his debate with Edward Stillingfleet are discussed by Wainwright, *Locke, Paraphrase and Notes*, I, 51-4, although Wainwright seems to think that Locke was more interested in the intellectual abilities than the physical condition of the resurrected righteous, *ibid.*, 54-5.
2. [Locke], *Reasonableness of Christianity*, 163-4.
3. *Ibid.*, 164-5.
4. *Ibid.*, 165.

from "this present world". Quoting Luke 21: 31 and Matthew 25: 1 and 31
Locke reminds us that Christ spoke much of the kingdom, particularly "the
appearance of his kingdom at the day of judgement".[1]

A more straightforward theological understanding of the world to come
appears in Locke's posthumous *Paraphrase and Notes* on Ephesians ch. 2. Locke
writes here at some length of salvation and the kingdom of God in a manner
which clearly indicates that to him the two concepts are inseparably linked.
One who is saved is "brought back again . . . into the kingdom of God",
"brought out of the kingdom of darkness, in which they were as dead men,
without life, hope, or so much as a thought of salvation, into the kingdom
of God".[2] But such are also saved *for* the kingdom of God. When by faith
in Christ they came to be reconciled to God they were then "in the way of
salvation", and if they "persevered could not miss attaining it, though they
were not yet in actual possession (of it)".[3] All this is crucial to understand.
They were in the kingdom, and yet were not in it. The kingdom had arrived,
but it had not arrived. As soon as men have received the gospel "they are in
the kingdom of God, in a new state of life". God in His great mercy sent
Paul to the Ephesians, as well as to other Gentiles, "to bestow on them the
knowledge of salvation, reconciliation, and restoration into his kingdom".
"Men by baptism are admitted into the kingdom of God".[4] It all happens now,
in this present world. The kingdom is here and calls those who believe into its
redemptive fellowship.

But there is more. Those who have thus been "translated" into the kingdom
of God, having passed from death to life, are now "*in the way* to eternal life".[5]
The journey has begun but it has not yet ended, although such believers are
"sure to attain" the kingdom if they "persevere in that life which the gospel
requires".[6] So present life in the kingdom already revealed is not "actual
possession of eternal life in the kingdom of God in the world to come".[7]
That remains for the future. Salvation might in the interim be forfeited and
lost. Only those who persevere to the end and gain entrance into the future
kingdom will "actually" have an eternal inheritance. It is the old yet ever new

1. *Ibid.*, 166-7.
2. Wainwright (ed.), *Locke, Paraphrase and Notes*, II, 628. Locke's paraphrase of
   Ephesians 2 : 7-8, the passage to which these and the following comments relate,
   reads, "That in the ages to come he might shew the exceeding riches of his grace in
   his kindness towards us through Christ Jesus. For by God's free grace it is that ye
   are through faith in Christ saved and brought into the kingdom of God, and made
   his people. . . " . The word "saved" attracts most of the comment noted here.
3. *Ibid.*
4. *Ibid.*, 629.
5. *Ibid.*, emphasis supplied.
6. Locke is much concerned with the relationship between faith and works throughout
   this whole section, anxious to rebut any hint of antinomianism.
7. *Ibid.*, 630.

tension between the present and the future. Many have been confused here, Locke says. There is a present kingdom, a provision of grace, "faith being all that was required to instate a man in it". But there is also a future kingdom, "the kingdom of God in the world to come", admittance to which depends also on grace but also on perseverance to the end and a righteous life in this present world. Locke explains in characteristic detail:

> These two Considerations of the Kingdom of Heaven some Men have confounded and made one; so that a Man being brought into the first of these, wholly by Grace without Works, Faith being all that was required to instate a Man in it, they have concluded that for the attaining eternal Life, or the Kingdom of God in the World to come, Faith alone, and not good Works, are required, contrary to express Words of Scripture, and the whole Tenour of the Gospel. . . But 'tis by Grace we are made Partakers of both these Kingdoms; 'tis only into the Kingdom of God in this World we are admitted by Faith alone without Works; but for our Admittance into the other, both Faith and Obedience, in a sincere Endeavour to perform those Duties, all those good Works which are incumbent on us, and come in our way to be performed by us, from the time of our believing till our Death.[1]

The import of this last phrase in Locke's wider eschatology must not be overlooked.[2] After death there is resurrection, and it is resurrection of the dead (or translation of the living) which throughout Locke's religious writings is the gateway to eternal life and the kingdom of God in the world to come. This is most evident in his comments on I Corinthians 15 and in the *Resurrectio et Quae Sequuntur* (the Resurrection and what follows), although in the latter Locke is more concerned with proving that the resurrection at the coming of Christ is the resurrection only of the righteous dead than with what happens thereafter. He does say, however, that "the saints shall then have spiritual and immortal bodies",[3] from which we may perhaps conclude that he envisaged some kind of corporeal existence in the world to come. Of Christ's second coming, Locke says again, " Then Christ shall set up his kingdom wherein he shall subdue all rule and all authority and power that opposes him. . . ", after which follows the "full conclusion of God's whole dispensation to Adam and his posterity".[4] It is tantalising to speculate on what Locke wrote, or might have written, in the unfinished *Resurrectio*. Having dealt with the destiny of the wicked at some length, he then proposes to "see what the Scripture discovers

1. *Ibid.*
2. That eschatology is in itself significant. Wainwright quite rightly remarks, "Locke was often preoccupied with the question of the ultimate destiny of the human race", *Locke, Paraphrase and Notes*, I, 51.
3. Locke, *Resurrectio et Quae Sequuntur*, in Nuovo, *Locke*, 232.
4. *Ibid.*, 236-7.

to us of the state of the just after the resurrection".[1] However, the manuscript ends abruptly at this point and we do not get even a glimpse of what follows for the righteous after the resurrection. If we may be allowed to judge by what Locke has said elsewhere, it may well have been something about the world to come.[2]

Further Considerations

One further argument appearing to support the case for a renovated, recreated and reinhabited earth must not be allowed to pass unnoticed. In the form of a nascent cosmology it still found its roots in Scripture for, as Isaiah had said, God had in the beginning created the world "to be inhabited"(Isaiah 45:17, 18). The immediate context of this reaffirmation of the divine purpose is instructive, indeed necessary, if we are to understand the strength of seventeenth- and eighteenth-century belief about the world to come, and the more so in light of the convictions of Hobbes, Milton, Locke and other mortalist believers concerning man's salvation and ultimate destiny in a new earth to come. Isaiah 45 deals with the unique creative and redemptive activity of God, particularly in relationship to His will for the human race. God's purpose in creating the earth to be inhabited (v. 18), is set against the assurances of "everlasting salvation" and a "world without end"(v. 17). That the purposes of the sovereign and redeeming God should not at last eventuate was unthinkable for all Christians, mortalist or immortalist alike, throughout the period covered by this study. The passage is seminal for those who wish to understand, as far as it may be understood, the divine purpose in the original creation of man and his world and the restoration of lost righteousness and immortality.

The attempt to relate the future of the earth to the rest of the observable universe, a relationship held as being within the divine purpose, had first appeared in the work of John Napier who had argued that the earth itself could not be annihilated since its continuing existence in the scheme of things was essential to the "perpetual motions of the spheres, planets and stars".[3] There may be echoes

1. *Ibid.,* 237.
2. The discussion over Locke's supposed reliance on Hobbes, particularly with reference to *The Reasonableness of Christianity,* may not yet be over. J.C. Higgins-Biddle discusses the issue at length in *John Locke: The Reasonableness of Christianity* (Oxford, 1999), lxxiv-cxv, 'The Charge of Hobbism'. The charge had been laid against Locke by earlier critics, including Alexander Gordon, *Heads of Unitarian History* (1895) and J.M. Robertson, *A Short History of Freethought Ancient and Modern*(2 vols.,1914-15) and later by L. Strauss, *Natural Right and History* (Chicago, 1953) and C.B. Macpherson, *The Political Theory of Possessive Individualism* (Oxford, 1962). Higgins-Biddle argues, not entirely convincingly, that Locke did not derive many of his religious ideas from Hobbes. Locke's unfinished treatment of the destinies of the wicked and the righteous in the *Resurrectio* follows a similar outline used by Hobbes in *Leviathan,* where Hobbes says of the "salvation" of the righteous "in the kingdom of heaven", "it seemeth that this salvation should be on earth", *Leviathan, 246.*
3. Napier, *Plaine Discovery,* 250.

here of the early post-medieval cosmology which Copernicus had injected into European thought and which was to appear with increasing frequency, even in English theological works, as the implications of that cosmology began to be understood. A hundred and fifty years after Copernicus, Humphrey Hody, Regius professor of Greek at Oxford, argued for the resurrection of the body and a future corporeal existence of the redeemed in a new earth. In *The Resurrection of the (Same) Body Asserted* (1694), Hody opposed the idea of an ethereal future life in heaven, asserting "our heaven will be nothing but a heaven upon earth" and saying that it was more logical to suppose that in the life to come the redeemed will have "solid and material bodies" since they will live, as in this life, "on some solid and material orb".[1] Mortalists could easily endorse such ideas as the teachings of Scripture appeared to be confirmed by a growing understanding of the surrounding universe and the relationship of the earth to it.

Hody may have been influenced by the recent work of Thomas Burnet, whose impressive four-part *Telluris Theoria Sacra* or *The Sacred Theory of the Earth* had been published in 1684 and which attempted to portray the entire history of the earth as part of a vast and enduring creation. Burnet, one of the second generation of Cambridge Platonists and himself a distinguished scholar,[2] and whose own atypical psychopannychism we have already encountered, sought to understand the future of the earth in the light of the biblical record of its past and the developing cosmology. The first two volumes of *The Sacred Theory* examined the biblical record of the creation and the flood which, in the light of II Peter 3 and other passages relating to the new earth, it was necessary to first understand in order to see the ultimate condition of the earth as it would be after the last eschatological events had run their course. The certainty of a new earth was to Burnet "as plain a doctrine in Christian religion as the conflagration itself".[3] This is a reference to the fires that would purge and refine the earth at the last day, thus making it inhabitable for the redeemed in the same way that the flood had purged and cleansed the Noachian world. Burnet's new earth, whose axis would be restored to its original position in relation to the sun, as it was "before any disorder came into the natural . . . world" as a consequence of the great upheaval caused by the flood,[4] was firmly set in an immense, surrounding, orderly cosmos:

> The fixt stars are not all in one surface as they seem to us, nor at an equal distance from the earth, but are placed in several orbs higher and higher, there being infinite room in the great deep of the heavens, every way, for

1. Hody, *Resurrection*, 206.
2. Burnet's *Telluris Theoria Sacra* and *De Statu Mortuorum* are discussed in Walker's *Decline of Hell*, ch. IX, ostensibly in relation to his rejection of eternal torment.
3. Thomas Burnet, *The Theory of the Earth, Containing an Account of the Original of the Earth, and of all the General Changes which it hath already undergone, or is to undergo Till the Consummation of all Things* (2nd edn, 1691), II, sig.a *r*.
4. *Ibid.*, 31.

innumerable stars and spheres behind one another to fill and beautify the immense spaces of the universe.[1]

In the context of this wider cosmology Burnet speaks of the "Great Instauration" of the world, "a restitution and reviviscency" thereof, its renovation rather than its annihilation, observing that the final state of the earth and its inhabitants would be akin to the "paradisaical world".[2] Both the earth itself and those who will live in it will be restored to their original state. Those who inhabit the new earth "shall not die but be translated to a blessed immortality" and the earth itself will have a "straight and regular situation to the sun and the axis of the ecliptic".[3]

Burnet's final comment on the ultimate state of redeemed believers appeared in the posthumous *De Statu Mortuorum*, where he contemplated the glories of life in the new earth with keen anticipation. Once again the new earth is seen in a wider cosmological context:

> When being exalted above all the planets, we shall view the boundless ocean of the universe and innumerable glories of the worlds, floating along the vast stream of the sky, each filled with its proper inhabitants . . . then we shall contemplate the fixed stars, those eternal celestial fires, those numberless suns of prodigious magnitude, succeeding one another without end through all the immense spaces of the sky, what pleasure, what rapture will not this prospect of the universe raise in us?[4]

Although Burnet may here have allowed his imagination to run away with him, phrases like "boundless ocean of the universe", "numberless suns of prodigious magnitude" and "immense spaces of the sky", besides having a distinctly modern ring to them, suggest a considered view of the universe within the parameters of contemporary knowledge. This basic cosmology, confirmed by the many biblical promises of a new earth, would have met the

---

1. *Ibid.,* 29.
2. *Ibid.,* 31, 133, 138. Burnet's use of "great instauration" is an interesting evolution of the term from its earlier seventeenth-century connotation. Bacon's great 'Instauratio Magna', conceived in embryo as early as 1603 and proposed in more permanent form in 1620, soon became the puritan ideal of a completely reformed and Christianised world, "the ultimate millennial goal", derived largely from the eschatological writings of Joseph Mede, William Twisse, Thomas Goodwin, Johan Alsted and others, Charles Webster, *The Great Instauration: Science, Medicine and Reform, 1626-1660* (1975), 17-27. Following the Restoration reality took hold again, millennial expectations receded for the most part, and hopes of a "great instauration" became focussed, as Burnet indicated, on a newly created earth rather than a wholly converted world.
3. *Ibid.,* 130, 138. The ecliptic is the sun's apparent annual path among the stars, "the great circle of the celestial sphere which is the apparent orbit of the sun", *OED.*
4. Thomas Burnet, *A Treatise Concerning the State of Departed Souls Before, and At, and After the Resurrection* (tr. J. Dennis, 1730), 321. Walker gives a brief history of the *Treatise* or *De Statu Mortuorum* in *The Decline of Hell,* 158-9.

approval of most biblical scholars in the seventeenth and eighteenth centuries, attempting as they did to relate the affirmations of Scripture to the knowledge arising from scientific discovery and reflection. Thus the divine purpose in creation would ultimately be fulfilled in re-creation and the universe would continue in the divine plan unencumbered by evil and human weakness. It was, truly, a prospect almost too good to contemplate. Mortalists would only have disagreed with Burnet's lingering millenarian proviso that the new earth was to be the home of the redeemed for only a thousand years.[1]

With theology, history, the biblical text, and now, for those who wanted it, cosmology on their side mortalists were quite sure of their ground. Locke had argued that the body was necessary to human identity, sensibility and comprehension.[2] He had also argued the necessity of the resurrection of the dead and the translation of the living saints at Christ's coming "to make all those who are Christ's capable to enter his eternal kingdom of life".[3] Thus at the end, or more correctly, perhaps, at the beginning, the righteous who had been created in the first place to "subsist" corporeally on earth as "sensible intelligent beings", would be restored "to the like state of sensibility in another world".[4] The future life was one of corporeal reality. Henry Layton's "restitution of all things" involved the "dissolution of the earth" as it now stands[5] and the creation of a new earth. Layton claimed that in terms of eternal rewards, the idea of the soul's ascent to heaven at death, "if it can be capable of a mansion there", is illogical, since a soul "coming at the resurrection to be put into its body again", thereby to be "made an inhabitant of a new earth" would certainly be disappointed, if not "a loser by that change".[6]

Joseph Hallett III, a noted Unitarian biblical scholar and a hesitant believer in the soul's immortality, took time to examine the biblical data concerning the new earth, thereby demonstrating, among other things, that substantial grounds for agreement could still be found between mortalists and immortalists. Hallett confesses in his *Free and Impartial Study of the Holy Scriptures* that he is "not satisfied" with the arguments "commonly urged from reason to prove the immateriality of the soul".[7] He also argues that belief in the soul's immortality is not a matter of serious consequence in any case since man's ultimate destiny lay not in the life of the soul in heaven after death but rather in an eternal existence "on the new earth for ever".[8] Mortalists would certainly have concurred with

1. Burnet's earlier translator, Matthias Earbery, had taken him to task for dipping "too freely into the millenarian scheme" and straying "into the land of fairies"; Burnet, *Of the State of the Dead and Those that are to Rise* (tr. Matthias Earbery,1727), 7.
2. Locke, *Essay Concerning Humane Understanding*, 180-1.
3. Locke, *Paraphrase on First Corinthians*, 100.
4. *Ibid.,* 311.
5. [Layton], *Second Part of a Treatise*, 149.
6. *Ibid.,* 111.
7. Hallett, *A Free and Impartial Study*, 211, 215.
8. *Ibid.,* 192, 214.

that, even if they had more defined thoughts about the soul. Hallett follows earlier expositors in asserting that the fires mentioned in II Peter 3 merely change and refine the present earth.[1] He then says that the redeemed saints "are to live upon an earth . . . made new and fit to receive them", emphasising that "without bodies they would not be fit to live on earth".[2] Once again, the resurrection and a new body are necessary pre-requisites to eternal life.

Hallett also had well-defined views about heaven, a word which in Scripture "never once . . . signifies the place in which good men shall dwell after the Judgement day". Hallett says he is "positive" about this because he has "examined every place in the New Testament in which heaven is mentioned". The word heaven, he maintains, "signifies the throne of God, the place where Christ and the angels now dwell", declaring that "when the apostles speak of good men after the day of Judgement they never call it heaven".[3] So Hallett can ask with reference to the traditionalists, "Where can the heaven be of which they speak?" And he can say in terms of the prevailing cosmology, "In the boundless space that surrounds us we know of nothing but suns, or fixed stars, earths, moons and comets".[4] Already we hear the argument that belief in heaven as traditionally understood is contrary to reason and to the known facts of science, as well as being unbiblical. No, the redeemed would "inhabit the earth" in accordance with the consistent testimony of Scripture and the promise of Christ himself.[5] So Hallett anticipates the life of the saints in their resurrection bodies in a restored and renovated earth:

> We are then to conceive good men as living in bodies, but become spiritual, glorious, and immortal, upon a new earth, where they will feel no more heat, or cold, pain, or weakness, toil, or weariness; where they will meet with no enemies, storms or dangers, and where they shall spend all their duration in love and in happiness.[6]

It was an expectation which mortalists of all shades of opinion could readily endorse. David Hartley, similarly impressed by "a very wonderful agreement between philosophical discoveries and the Scriptures", asked the rhetorical question, "Is it not probable that this earth . . . will continue to be the habitation of the blessed?", but advised caution in the contemplation of these "things of another world", since we can now only think of them as "children do concerning the pleasures, privileges and occupations of manhood".[7]

1. *Ibid.*, 194.
2. *Ibid.*, 198.
3. *Ibid.*
4. *Ibid.*, 200.
5. *Ibid.*
6. *Ibid.*, 202.
7. Hartley, *Observations*, II, 399. Hartley found many "hints" of the concurrence between contemporary understanding of the natural world and Scripture in the works of William Whiston. Whiston's *New Theory of the Earth*, first published in

We may appropriately leave the last word to Edmund Law who, as a prominent Cambridge scholar, lived at or near the centre of mid-eighteenth-century English intellectual life and whose own views of truth, if sometimes thought unorthodox, were nonetheless shaped by "deductions of reason" applied to both "revelation" and "natural religion".[1] Remarking that man's understanding of the world in its natural state had "of late increased" and that the "present world" itself had "generally improved" Law, the convinced mortalist, says:

> The more we know of the world, the more we view its order, beauty, symmetry; the uniform laws which it is governed by; the just arrangement and mutual subserviency of all its parts . . . the more we see the glory and perfection of its architect, and are more fully satisfied that He designed its several inhabitants for happiness in general.[2]

Such observations of the present world, Law then states, enable us "to argue from it to *another*"[3] and to conclude that it too will proceed on a similar basis, "consisting of like inhabitants and conducted by the same hand, . . . thus the whole Creation for ever beautifying in its Maker's eye, and drawing nearer to Him".[4] Life for the inhabitants of the world to come will thus continue to improve in "growing happiness through all eternity".[5] Having arrived "at those blessed mansions", men will exercise and enjoy "each good moral habit and intellectual accomplishment", dependent on "that God who is to be both our guide thither and our great reward there". In His hands "we always are, and always ought to wish ourselves".[6]

Such was to be the ultimate realisation of the mortalist vision. Immortality and eternal life were to be realised at the end, at Christ's return, following the last judgment and the final conquest of death, evil, human weakness and suffering and Satanic malice. In Layton's words, this was to be "the happy state which the new raised people" would enjoy after the resurrection, or the "primitive

---

1696, did not examine in any detail the world to come, dealing mainly, as its title-page indicated, with the present world "from its original to the consummation of all things", i.e, "the creation of the world in six days, the universal deluge, and the general conflagration", all of which Whiston set out to demonstrate were "perfectly agreeable to reason and philosophy". He did allow, however, that the final conflagration would not destroy the earth completely, but put it into "a new state, proper to receive saints and martyrs for its inhabitants" for a thousand years, William Whiston, *A New Theory of the Earth* (1696), 212.

1. Law, *Considerations*, 250 -1.
2. *Ibid.*, 249-50.
3. Emphasis in the original.
4. *Ibid.*, 250.
5. *Ibid.*
6. *Ibid.*, 251.

excellency of the whole creation restored",[1] as George Hammon put it. It was Milton's paradise, regained and finally restored. It was the ultimate hope which mortalist believers saw as the final reality, to them the more biblical alternative to the immortality of the soul, and it continually called them forward as they lived out their present life in what was all too often a very tangible vale of tears. It fortified their denial of the soul's natural immortality, providing a focus to the life of faith they were called to live in the present condemned and decaying world. And it reminded them constantly that Christian faith was rooted and grounded in the complete and efficacious work of Christ, whose resurrection at the beginning guaranteed their own at the end. At a distance of three hundred years, more or less, it is still possible to capture the strength of their conviction and to sense the certainty of their hope.

1. [Layton], *Second Part of a Treatise,* 111; Hammon, *Syons Redemption* in *A Discovery,* 154.

Appendix I
The Mortalist Works of Henry Layton
(1622-1705)

Between 1691 and 1704 Henry Layton produced at least fourteen works[1] defending the thnetopsychist view of man, which the *Dictionary of National Biography*, misleadingly – as many are of considerable length – referred to as "pamphlets". Most were responses to works by writers favouring the traditional view of the soul's natural immortality. Layton's works were published anonymously, without date or place,[2] and were printed privately for limited circulation.[3] They were subsequently collected and issued posthumously, again anonymously, in 1706 by "A Lover of Truth", in two volumes under the general title *A Search after Souls*. Most of the copies of this collection were suppressed, but a few have survived, as have copies of an earlier, more limited collection. Layton's works appear below in bold type and the authors and works he opposed appear in italics. The information is based largely on the 1706 two-volume collection *A Search after Souls* at Dr. Williams's Library, London, after comparison with those held in The British Library and the Bodleian and Regents Park College Libraries, Oxford.

The Dr. Williams's Library holding is the most comprehensive extant collection of Layton's works. It appears that an attempt was made to present the material in this collection in chronological order, although a few anomalies remain. If the chronology is more or less correct, then the only works the date of which present a problem are the *Observations Upon Mr. Wadsworth's Book of the Soul's Immortality*, and both parts of the treatise *a Search after Souls and Spiritual Operations in Man* (nos. 3 and 6, not to be confused with the title of the 1706 collection). The *Observations* is placed first in the 1706 collection and would therefore be presumed to have an early 1690s date. The *DNB*, however, tentatively suggests [1699?]. The *Observations* is placed later in the earlier and more limited British Library, Bodleian and Regents Park College collections,[4] although these do not appear to have been arranged chronologically. Following

---

1. If the two letters of Layton contained in no. 7 below are regarded as separate works, which in effect they are, and the additional title in Note 1 is included, the total is sixteen.
2. With the exception of no's 7 and 14 below, which are dated 1703.
3. At a point in the 1690s, probably c.1697, Layton sent a manuscript to London for printing, but could not find a publisher willing to undertake the work. Both the *DNB* and the *ODNB* suggest that Layton's views aroused considerable antipathy in their day.
4. See Note 2, below.

the 1706 collection, the earlier date is retained below, although without compelling evidence.

The *ODNB* gives a 1698(?) date for both parts of *A Search after Souls*, seeing them as a reply to Timothy Manlove's *Immortality of the Soul Asserted* (1697). This is unlikely, however, as no. 5, *Observations upon a Short Treatise* (1697?), was Layton's reply to Manlove. Internal evidence establishes the date of many of the pieces. A few, in addition to no. 1, remain tentative, but may be considered accurate to within a year, or two at most.

[Henry Layton], A Search after Souls: or, The Immortality of a Humane Soul, Theologically, Philosophically, and Rationally Considered. With the Opinions of Ancient and Modern Authors. By a Lover of Truth, Vol. I, 1706.

1. Observations upon Mr. Wadsworth's Book of The Souls Immortality, and his Confutation of the Opinion of the Souls Inactivity to the Time of General Resurrection (1670), [1692?]
Contra: Thomas Wadsworth, *Antipsychothanasia, or, The Immortality of the Soul Explained and Proved by Scripture and Reason,* 1670.[1]

2. Observations upon Dr. Charlton's Treatise; Intituled, The Immortality of the Humane Soul, demonstrated by the Light of Nature (1657), n.d. [2]
Contra: Walter Charleton, *The Immortality of the Human Soul, Demonstrated by the Light of Nature,* 1657.

3. A Second Part of a Treatise Intituled A Search after Souls [1692,?].[3]

4. Observations upon a Sermon Intituled, A Confutation of Atheism from the Faculties of the Soul, alias, Matter and Motion cannot think: Preached April 4, 1692. By way of Refutation, [1692].
Contra: Richard Bentley, *Matter and Motion cannot Think: or A Confutation of Atheism from the Faculties of the Soul,* 1692.[4]

5. Observations upon a Short Treatise, Written by Mr. Timothy Manlove: Intituled, The Immortality of the Soul Asserted; and Printed in Octavo at London, 1697. [1697?]
Contra: Timothy Manlove, *The Immortality of the Soul Asserted, and Practically Improved,* 1697.

1. The sub-title, *A Confutation of the Irrational and Irreligious Opinion of the Soul's Dying with the Body,* indicates how well established thnetopsychism was by the middle of the century.
2. *Ad cal.* with no. 1, and consequently sometimes overlooked.
3. Written after no. 6.
4. Bentley's Boyle lectures (1692) including this sermon, were more specifically levelled at Hobbes, whom Bentley regarded as an atheist disguised as a theist.

6. **A Search After Souls and Spiritual Operations in Man** [1691].[1]

[Henry Layton], **A Search after Souls: or, The Immortality of a Humane Soul, Theologically, Philosophically, and Rationally Considered, With the Opinions of Ancient and Modern Authors** ,Vol. II, 1706.

7. **Arguments and Replies in a Dispute concerning the Nature of the Humane Soul,** 1703[2].
Contains the following three letters:
Reply to a letter Dated Aug. 15, 1702
The Second Answering Letter, Dated London, Sept. 14, 1702[3]
A Reply to a Letter Dated Septemb. 14, 1702[4]

8. **[Continuation of Observations on Mr. Wadsworth's "Book of the Souls Immortality"],** [1703?].[5]

9. **Observations upon a Treatise Intituled Vindiciae Mentis. Printed Lond. 1702** [1703?]
Contra: *Vindiciae Mentis. An Essay of the Being and Nature of Mind, Wherein the Distinction of Mind and Body . . may be made concerning the Life and Immortality of our Souls,* 1702.

10. **Observations upon a Treatise intitled Psychologia: or, An Account of the Nature of the Rational Soul (in Two Parts),** [1703]
Contra: John Broughton, *Psychologia: or An Account of the Nature of the Rational Soul,* 1703.[6]

11. **Observations upon Mr. Broughton's Psychologia, Part Second,** [1703]

12. **Observations upon a Treatise Intituled, A Vindication of the Separate Existence of the Soul, from a Late Author's Second Thoughts, by Mr. John Turner, Lecturer of Christ Church, London,** [1703?]
Contra: John Turner, *A Briefe Vindication of the Separate Existence and Immortality of the Soul from a late Author's Second Thoughts . . .* 1702.[7]

13. **Observations upon a Treatise intitled, A Discourse concerning the Happiness of Good Men in the next World. Part I Containing the Proofs of the Immortality of the Soul, and Immortal Life. By Dr. Sherlock, London, 1704,** [1704].

1. This appears to have been Layton's first mortalist work, and takes issue with the views, *inter alia,* of Richard Baxter, Francis Bacon, Henry More, and Descartes.
2. The title/title page is missing in the DWL collection.
3. Written to Layton.
4. The first two of the above are responses to letters attributed to Henry Dodwell, The Elder.
5. Untitled and *ad cal.* with no. 7, but clearly merits its own identity.
6. Principally directed against John Locke and William Coward.
7. Turner also published *A Farther Vindication of the Soul's Separate Existence, and Immortality. . . ,* 1703.

Contra: William Sherlock, *A discourse concerning the happiness of good men, and the punishment of the wicked, in the next world,* 1704.

14. Observations upon Dr. Nicholls's Book, intituled, A Conference with a Theist: Being a Proof of the Immortality of the Soul. And in Answer to the Objections made against that Doctrine, in a Book Intitul'd, Second Thoughts concerning Human Soul[1] . . . London, 1703, 1703.
Contra: William Nicholls, *A Conference with a Theist,*1696.

Additional Notes

1. The *DNB* lists one further work, **An Argument concerning the Humane Souls Seperate** [*sic*] **Subsistence,** [1699?], missing from the 1706 collection.

2. The British Library, Bodleian Library and Regents Park College Library collections all contain only some of the above, in the following order: 4, 5, 6, 3, 1, 2, all pre-1700, suggesting that an earlier, limited collection had been put together. The Bodleian has an additional collection containing the following: 7, 8, 14, 10, bound with other works not by Layton; and no. 13 in another volume, also bound with other works.

3. The Bodleian copy of no. 7 includes the title, which is missing from the DWL copy.

4. The *DNB* states that the DWL 1706 collection is a "re-issue", meaning a collection of the published works to 1706, and not a re-print.

5. In addition to the collection noted above, the British Library holds many of Layton's works as separate items.

6. The Regents Park College collection lacks a title page, but bears John Locke's autograph on the inner cover, with the note "ex dono Authoris".

---

1. By William Coward.

Appendix II
The Mortalist Interpretation of Controverted Biblical Texts

The mortalist case rested heavily on the testimony of Scripture derived from a broad study of the biblical text in its entirety. Mortalists were highly suspicious of doctrinal conclusions formulated on less than all the evidence available. It was the weight of the textual evidence as a whole that was regarded as the norm for correct exegesis, "the strong current or stream of Scripture texts", in Henry Layton's words, that "ought to be accepted" as the basis of doctrine and belief and that was to be the indispensable guide in the determination of truth.[1]

While this maxim held for every doctrine and the pursuit of all biblical truth, it applied particularly to mortalist doctrine for, as mortalists themselves recognised, there were certain scriptural texts which were frequently quoted against them in support of the traditional doctrine of the soul's immortality and as evidence of mortalism's own flawed interpretation of Scripture. Mortalists believed that such texts were misinterpreted, taken out of context, misapplied or, in particular, used without regard to the testimony of Scripture as a whole. Peter Peckard was aware of the difficulties and wanted to know if what he and other mortalists considered as debatable or unclear texts of the Bible should be given precedence over those that were quite clear and asked, "or shall these give way and be explained by those which cannot be mistaken?"[2]. The answer to that question, he believed, was self-evident. So when Peckard declares "Scripture expressly asserteth the mortality of man and the restitution to life from that mortality by Jesus Christ",[3] he means Scripture in its entirety, read thoroughly and interpreted correctly according to accepted principles of exegesis.

Overton, Hammon, Milton and Layton may be taken as representative mortalists who recognised some of the difficulties and who responded to the texts most frequently cited in support of the soul's immortality. Milton deals with nine such texts, Overton with twenty-one in *Man Wholly Mortal*, including four that Milton does not mention. Hammon discusses the relevant passages in at least two works, and Layton concentrates on five New Testament passages. Other writers were also aware of the difficulties and responded

1. [Henry Layton], *Arguments and Replies in a Dispute concerning the Nature of the Humane Soul* (1703), 69.
2. Peckard, *Observations*, 37.
3. *Ibid.*, 4.

accordingly, although it must be said not always with the clarity that might have been expected. The following references, in the order in which they appear in the Bible, were the most frequently quoted texts supporting the immortalist position and are explained from the thnetopsychist standpoint of a theology derived from the whole of Scripture.

1. **Ecclesiastes 12: 7**: *". . . the spirit shall return unto God who gave it."*

Overton explains that in biblical usage the spirit is not equatable with the soul, but generally means breath, and that here, specifically, "by Spirit is meant Life". [1] If 'spirit' is the same as 'soul' then a further problem arises. Citing Ecclesiastes 3:19, "For that which befalleth the sons of men befalleth beasts; even one thing befalleth them: as the one dieth, so dieth the other; yea, they have all one breath; so that a man hath no preeminence above a beast", Overton says that beasts have the same spirit (breath) as man. If spirit means soul then animals must also have a soul as man is supposed to have one, a conclusion unacceptable to both mortalists and immortalists. [2] Milton also holds that spirit means breath and cannot here mean soul, since the text speaks in general terms of the human experience of death and not only of the death of the righteous, and "must be understood with considerable latitude" for "the wicked do not return to God at death". [3]

2. **Matthew 10: 28**: *"And fear not them which kill the body, but are not able to kill the soul: but rather fear him which is able to destroy both soul and body in hell."*

George Hammon believed that this was the strongest text supporting the traditional view, since it seemed to imply that there did indeed exist "a soul which cannot be killed". [4] Referring to Luke, "the most exact writer", ch. 12: 4, 5, Hammon says the passage proves that man can only destroy the body, but God can "destroy both the body which is mortal, and also cast the whole man into hell when it is immortal after the Resurrection". [5] We recall that Hammon had already by this time published against the commonly held doctrine of hell, so that "this in short is the meaning of the words . . . after the Resurrection none can destroy it (the whole man) but God". [6]

Milton deals directly with the text itself, drawing a similar conclusion by interpreting the terms 'body' and 'soul' more comprehensively:

. . . properly speaking, the body cannot be killed, as being in itself a thing inanimate; the body therefore, as is common in Scripture, must be taken

---

1. *MM*, 30.
2. *Ibid.*
3. Milton, 'Christian Doctrine', in *Prose Works*, IV, 278.
4. Hammon, 'A Discourse Touching the Mortality of the Soul', *ad cal.* with *Truth and Innocency Prevailing*, 41.
5. *Ibid.*
6. *Ibid.*

for the whole human compound, or for the animal and temporal life; the soul for that spiritual life with which we shall be clothed after the end of the world, as appears from the remainder of the verse, and from 1 Cor. xv. 44.[1]

3. Luke 16:19 ff: *The Parable of the Rich Man and Lazarus*

Mortalists consistently pointed out the parabolic nature of this passage, maintaining that it was therefore not an acceptable basis for conclusions about doctrine and thus rejecting it as having any relevance to the debate. Samuel Richardson argues that this story "is not any proof of any torments in hell, because it is a parable, not a history ", and is "no more a proof of punishment after this life than Judges 9:8 is a proof that trees did walk and speak".[2] Layton similarly says, "We take it not for proof, because it was but a parable, spoken to a quite other intent, and without design to teach any thing concerning the State of Man after death".[3] Overton likewise insists, "There was never such a man as Dives or Lazarus, or ever such a thing happened, no more than Jotham's trees did walk and talk".[4]

4. Luke 23: 43: *"And Jesus said unto him, Verily I say unto thee, Today shalt thou be with me in paradise."*

George Hammon takes up this text on more than one occasion, but does not need to use the argument from punctuation, which Milton calls on.[5] Even as the text stood, it could not be taken literally, since Christ Himself did not ascend to paradise that same day, nor was it certain that the thief to whom the promise was made actually died that day. Hammon feels that it is more likely that he died the following day because "Christ was not dead Himself till after the ninth hour".[6] With reference to the actual wording of the text, Hammon declares:

> All that may be safely gathered from these words is that Christ gave him a promise of Paradise that day, not that Christ and the Thief were to be both together in Heaven that same day, for Christ did not ascend in many days after; and it cannot be proved that the Malefactor was dead that day.[7]

The promise was made in order to give the thief assurance of salvation,

---

1. Milton, 'Christian Doctrine', in *Prose Works,* IV, 279.
2. [Richardson], *Torments of Hell,* 22-3.
3. [Layton], *Observations upon a Short Treatise, Written by Mr. Timothy Manlove,* 43.
4. *MM,* 31.
5. Hammon, 'Discourse' in *Truth and Innocency,* 44-46; Milton, 'Christian Doctrine', in *Prose Works,* IV, 281. The argument contends that in the original, unpunctuated Greek the adverb *semeron,* "today", can be taken equally to apply to the preceding clause.
6. Hammon, 'Discourse' in *Truth and Innocency,* 45.
7. Hammon, *Syons Redemption,* 86.

as if he should have said to him, thou desired me to remember thee
when I come into my Kingdome, but to put thee out of doubt, I will
tell thee at present, (or today) to thy comfort, thou shalt be with me
in Paradise.

    Doth it follow therefore because Christ giveth him a promise that day
of heaven, that therefore he must be in heaven the same day . . . so then
that day was but the day of promise, but the day of enjoyment is yet to
come; namely, when the Lord Jesus shall be revealed. . . .[1]

More to the point, in Hammon's view, was the fact that Christ did not speak
in dualistic terms, but in clear thnetopsychist language:

Moreover, consider Christ did not tell the thief that his SOUL should be
with him in Paradise; but saith, *thou shalt be with me,* not thy SOUL, but
thou. . . man, shalt be with me.[2]

    5. **II Corinthians 5: 6, 8:** *"Therefore we are always confident, knowing
that, whilst we are at home in the body, we are absent from the Lord: . . .
We are confident, I say, and willing rather to be absent from the body,
and to be present with the Lord."*

Hammon, again, comes straight to the point in what is a good example of a
text interpreted in context. "The Apostle in this place doth not so much as
hint at such a thing as the soul being immortal, or distinct from the body,
but speaks of the happy estate and condition of the godly at that time when
mortality shall be swallowed up of life (verse 4),. . . . meaning by the state of
a resurrection.[3]

    And then, with reference to verses 9 and 10 which speak of judgement
and final rewards, he concludes that the text can only apply to these future
eschatological events:

our being present with the Lord is not to be till the day of Judgment,
which day of Judgment, will not be until after the Resurrection, so that
Paul in this place . . . makes no distance of time between the putting off
this body, and the putting on immortality (viz. the Resurrection) which
sheweth, that there is no time to the dead; so that this text speaks not
against man being wholly mortal.[4]

    Overton also insists that this passage must be interpreted in the light of Paul's
other eschatological declarations which, he says, clearly show that believers are
present with the Lord only after the resurrection.[5]

1. Hammon, 'Discourse' in *Truth and Innocency,* 46.
2. *Ibid.,* 45-6.
3. *Ibid.,* 42.
4. *Ibid.*
5. *MM,* 23.

6. **II Corinthians 12: 2, 4:** *"I knew a man in Christ above fourteen*
years ago, (whether in the body, I cannot tell; or whether out of the body
I cannot tell: God knoweth;) such an one caught up to the third heaven. . . .
How that he was caught up into paradise, and heard unspeakable words,
which it is not lawful for a man to utter."

Overton deals with this passage by first pointing out that Christ Himself, the
believer's example, had not ascended immediately to heaven at death, implying
that believers could not anticipate a better future than their Lord. On the basis
of Scripture, he argues that Christ eventually returned to heaven "to prepare
a place" for His disciples to inhabit. And " if it were then to prepare, it was
not then in *esse*, [and] there could be none in it before itself was in being". So
"the place of glory for the dead saints is not yet". Moreover, on the testimony
of Scripture as a whole, "it shall not actually be till the dissolution of heavens
and earth".[1]

7. **Philippians 1:23:** *"For I am in a strait betwixt two, having a desire*
to depart, and to be with Christ; which is far better."

Overton argues that to interpret this text as meaning that death releases the
soul to heaven is to make Paul contradict himself. He "did not preach one
thing to the Philippians and the contrary to the Corinthians". This text is "not
contrary" to human mortality, "for though there be long time to the living till
the Resurrection, there is none to the dead".[2]

Milton enlarges on this point and presents the usual thnetopsychist
interpretation:

> But to say nothing of the uncertain and disputed sense of the word
> *analusai*, which signifies anything rather than *dissolution*, it may be
> answered that although Paul desired to obtain immediate possession of
> heavenly perfection and glory, in like manner as every one is desirous of
> attaining as soon as possible to that, whatever it may be, which he regards
> as the ultimate object of his being, it by no means follows that, when
> the soul of each individual leaves the body, it is received immediately
> either into heaven or hell. For he *had a desire to be with Christ;* that is,
> at his appearing, which all the believers hoped and expected was then at
> hand. In the same manner one who is going on a voyage desires to set sail
> and to arrive at the destined port, (such is the order in which his wishes
> arrange themselves) omitting all notice of the intermediate passage. If,
> however, it be true that there is no time without motion, which Aristotle
> illustrates by the example of those who were fabled to have slept in the
> temple of the heroes, and who, on awaking, imagined that the moment

---

1. *Ibid.*, 29.
2. *Ibid.*, 21. Overton further says "Being only commensurate with time, or length of
   dayes; not to be cannot possibly be capable thereof ", *ibid.*

in which they awoke had succeeded without an interval to that in which they fell asleep; how much more must intervening time be annihilated to the departed, so that to them to die and to be with Christ will seem to take place at the same moment? Christ himself, however, expressly indicates the time at which we shall be with him; John xiv 3. "if I go and prepare a place for you, I will come again and receive you unto myself; that where I am, there ye may be also.[1]

8. **I Peter 3:19, 20:** *"By which also he went and preached unto the spirits in prison; Which sometime were disobedient, when once the long-suffering of God waited in the days of Noah, while the ark was a preparing, wherein few, that is, eight souls were saved by water."*

In relation to this text Hammon declares, "the meaning of this place is no other, but that the spirit of Christ did preach to the old world in Noah's days, or Christ by the same spirit (wherewith he was quickned), preached in the days of Noah to those that are now dead or in prison",[2] the word prison to be understood metaphorically of those confined by the constraints of sinful humanity and bound over to future judgement, but who are now literally dead.

Milton reaches a similar conclusion, pointing out that the Syriac version translates the phrase 'in prison' *in sepulchro*, "in the grave", which means the same as prison "for the grave is the common guardian of all till the day of judgment".[3] Then appealing again to context, he adds,

What therefore the apostle says more fully, iv. 5, 6. 'who shall give account to him that is ready to judge the quick and the dead; for, for this cause was the gospel preached also to them that are dead,' he expresses in this place by a metaphor, 'the spirits that are in guard [*in sepulchro*];' it follows, therefore, that the spirits are dead.[4]

9. **Revelation 6: 9, 10:** *"And when he had opened the fifth seal, I saw under the altar the souls of them that were slain for the word of God, and for the testimony which they held: And they cried with a loud voice, saying, How long, O Lord, holy and true, dost thou not judge and avenge our blood on them that dwell on the earth?"*

Context again is held to be essential to the correct understanding of this passage. Milton disposes of it from that standpoint, concluding that there is no support here for a soul separated from the body:

in the Scripture idiom the soul is generally often put for the whole animate body, and in this passage it is used for the souls of those who were not

1. Milton, 'Christian Doctrine' in *Prose Works*, IV, 279-80.
2. Hammon, 'Discourse' in *Truth and Innocency*, 47.
3. Milton, 'Christian Doctrine', in *Prose Works*, IV, 281.
4. *Ibid.*

yet born; unless indeed the fifth seal was already opened in the time of John: in the same manner as in the parable of Dives and Lazarus, Luke xvi. though Christ, for the sake of the lesson to be conveyed, speaks of that as present which was not to take place till after the day of judgment, and describes the dead as placed in two distinct states, he by no means intimates any separation of the soul from the body.[1]

So here the soul again indicates the whole person and the parable of the rich man and Lazarus is taken as a precedent for future events spoken of in terms of the present.

Hammon also recognises the symbolic nature of the entire passage but says of the souls in question, "If they cry, then they are not in heaven . . . because when they come there, all crying and trouble shall vanish away". [2] By the souls crying under the altar, Hammon says, "we are to understand the blood of the Saints crying for vengeance", for after the red horse of Revelation 6 had taken peace from the earth, under the symbol of the black horse in that same chapter "John saw the blood of the just ones lying under the Alter [sic] Table; that is, the place where they were made a sacrifice, or where they offered up their blood or lives a sacrifice for Christs sake, and the testimony of a good conscience; and that (viz. blood) cryed for vengeance".[3] That which is obviously symbolic cannot be interpreted literally.

Other texts were also brought by immortalists in defence of their position and against that of mortalists, and were similarly dealt with. Overton, for example, responded to I Kings 17: 21, 22 and Genesis 35:18, and Milton to Psalm 49:15 reminding us once again of the fundamental thnetophychist argument that the word soul, particularly in the Old Testament, is "variously used upon various occasions",[4] that is to say, is translated in different ways, but always retaining its essential meaning of the whole person as an integrated, living being. The most comprehensive study of the various Hebrew and Greek words on which much of the debate centred was that by Edmund Law in 1755. It appeared as an appendix to the third edition of Law's *Considerations on the Theory of Religion* and led Law to conclude, "No man can prove from Scripture that the human soul is a principle which lives, and acts, or thinks independent of the body".[5]

1. *Ibid.*
2. Hammon, 'Discourse' in *Truth and Innocency*, 46.
3. *Ibid.*, 47.
4. *MM*, 23.
5. Law, *Considerations*, 3rd edn (1755), 401.

Appendix III
The Eighteenth-Century Sussex Baptists

Chapter six might suggest that by the mid-eighteenth century mortalism in England was espoused only by a few senior Anglican academics and influential Nonconformists, either Presbyterian or Unitarian. Chapter four (cf. p 93) might lead to the conclusion that Baptist interest in mortalist doctrine was in the main spent by 1660 or shortly thereafter, certainly by 1679 with the publication of the *Orthodox Creed: or, A Protestant Confession of Faith*. A document among the State Papers in the National Archives demonstrates how premature any such conclusion would be. Catalogued as a "List of Baptist Preachers in Sussex, 1745",[1] the document seems to be part of a report on dissenting clergy in Sussex who might qualify for charitable financial assistance. It lists the 21 Baptist ministers across the county, including Horsham, Chichester, Lewes, Cuckfield, Billingshurst and Worthing. The report states that Baptists were "very increased" of late, particularly around Horsham itself, and that the 21 names reported were "not thought to be above a third part of them".[2]

It adds that the Sussex Baptists were "sometimes called Soul Sleepers and Kiffinites, from one Kiffin, a London Alderman, and a preacher among them".[3] Clearly there were still mortalists in Sussex (and perhaps Kent) in the mid eighteenth century; their mortalism defining their identity among those outside their own ranks. The identity of "one Kiffin" is not quite as obvious. There are two possibilities. William Kiffin (1616-1701) of Devonshire Square, London, was influential, but as a Particular Baptist, unlikely to associate with the General Baptists of Horsham and Sussex. Matthew Caffyn (1620-1715) was a leading Sussex and Kent General Baptist for several decades and a mortalist (see chapter four). Whitley describes Caffyn's influence in General Baptist churches in Kent and Sussex surviving well into the eighteenth century. Raymond Brown notes that Caffyn's church at Horsham had meeting places "in and around Horsham" and that the churches in Kent and Sussex "stood by" Caffyn for many years.[4] It seems likely that Matthew Caffyn is the Sussex leader referred to in the State

1. "List of Baptist Preachers in Sussex, 1745", National Archives, SP/36/71.
2. Ibid., fols. 189, 190.
3. Ibid., fol. 189r.
4. Whitley, *History of British Baptists*, 172; Brown, *English Baptists of the Eighteenth Century*, 16, 22.

Papers, particularly as he was also well known in London at the time.

It is also possible, even probable, that the anonymous compiler of the 1745 document, perhaps unfamiliar with the details of Baptist history, inadvertently confused Caffyn with Kiffin, and that the "Soul Sleepers" in Sussex were probably known as Caffynites rather than Kiffinites, an easy mistake, particularly if the report or part of it was initially communicated verbally. Kent and Sussex Baptists were in any case already known by that name from the seventeenth century. In 1828 an article entitled "Heresy in Kent and Sussex a Century Back" in *The Christian Reformer, or Unitarian Magazine* still referred to the early eighteenth-century "Cafinites" [sic] of Sussex and Kent, describing Matthew "Cafin" as a "remarkable person", whose "errors" (including his repudiation of man's immortal soul) had spread into "many churches in Kent, Sussex and London".[5]

In 1710 Caffyn ordained his son, Matthew, Jun., as one of two pastors, or "preaching elders" to succeed him and shortly thereafter, in 1717, Horsham had become "the most considerable church in those parts", credited with having 350 hearers.[6] The elder Caffyn was, however, responsible for introducing heterodox doctrine into the church at Horsham and well beyond during the seventeenth century, causing much disquiet in the wider Baptist community for decades.

In 1745, and probably for some years after that, as well as for much of the seventeenth century, significant numbers of Soul Sleepers were to be found in Baptist churches in Kent and Sussex, supporting the charge laid against Caffyn in the 1701 work *The Vail Turned Aside*[7] of spreading Socinianism and mortalism throughout London and the south-east. Whether or not Edmund Law was aware of the Kent and Sussex Caffynites when in 1749 he defended mortalism before an august body of Cambridge academics for his Doctor of Divinity degree may never be known, but the continuing appeal of mortalist thought across a broad theological spectrum in mid-eighteenth-century England now appears certain.

5. "Heresy in Kent and Sussex a Century Back", in *The Christian Reformer, or Unitarian Magazine*, (vol. xiv, No. clviii, Feb 1828), 65. This refers in some detail to the rare 1701 work written by Christopher Cooper, and elsewhere given the title *The Vail Turned Aside* (see Whitley, *BB*, I, 13-701) but concentrates on Caffyn's Socinianism. See also p. 88.

6. RCHME notes for Christopher Stell's series of books on Nonconformist chapels and meeting-houses, National Monuments Records, Swindon.

7. This work, of which no copy has been located, is mwntioned on p.88 as a "pamphlet", after a reference in C.E. Whiting, *Studies in English Puritanism* (1931), 89-90, one of few sources to notice the work. The 1828 article, "Heresy in Kent and Sussex a Century Back" quotes from p. 122, indicating a more substantial work, *The Christian Reformer*, 68. *The Term Catalogues*, like Whitley, attribute the work to Christopher Cooper of Ashford but gives 1703 for publication, and the title *The Veil turn'd aside, or Heresy Unmask'd*, and a long sub-title including "the late errors of Socinus and others of our days", *The Term Catalogues 1668-1709* (ed. E. Arbor), III (1697-1709), 377.

Bibliography

The place of publication, unless otherwise stated, is London.

Primary Works

Adams, Thomas, *A Commentary or Exposition upon the Divine Second Epistle Generall, written by the Blessed Apostle St. Peter*, 1633.

Alexander, John, *A Paraphrase upon the Fifteenth Chapter of the First Epistle to the Corinthians*, 1766.

Baillie, Robert, *A Dissuasive from the Errours of the Time*, 1645.

Barrow, Isaac, *Sermons and Fragments attributed to Isaac Barrow*, ed., J. P. Lee, 1834.

_____ *The Works of the Learned Isaac Barrow, D.D.*, 3 vols., 1683-87.

Baxter, Richard, *The Life of Faith*, 1670.

_____ *The Reasons of the Christian Religion*, 1667.

_____ *The Unreasonableness of Infidelity*, 1655.

Beconsall, Thomas, *The Doctrine of a General Resurrection: Wherein the Identity of the Rising Body is asserted, against the Socinians and Scepticks*, Oxford,1697.

[Benson, George], *A Paraphrase and Notes on St. Paul's First Epistle to the Thessalonians*, 1732

_____ *A Paraphrase and Notes on the First Epistle of St. Peter*, 1742.

Biddle, John, *Brevis Disquisitio; or, A Brief Enquiry Touching a Better Way Then is commonly made use of, to refute Papists, and reduce Protestants to certainty and Unity in Religion*, 1653.

[_____] *The Spirit of Persecution Again Broken Loose*, 1655.

Blackburne, Francis, *The Confessional, or, A Full and Free Enquiry into the Right, Utility, Edification and Success of Establishing Systematical Confessions of Faith and Doctrine in Protestant Churches*, 1766, 2nd edn,1767.

[_____] *No Proof in the Scriptures of an Intermediate State of Happiness or Misery between Death and the Resurrection*, 1756.

[_____] *Remarks on Dr. Warburton's account of the Sentiments of the Early Jews Concerning the Soul*, 1757.

_____ *A Short Historical View of the Controversy Concerning An Intermediate State and The Separate Existence of the Soul Between Death and the General Resurrection*, 1765, 2nd edn, 1772.

Blackburne, F., ed., *The Works, Theological and Miscellaneous, of Francis Blackburne*, 7 vols., 1804-5.

Blount, Charles, *Anima Mundi*, 1679.

_____ *The Oracles of Reason*, 1693.

[Bold, Samuel], *A Discourse Concerning the Resurrection of the Same Body*, 1705.

_____ *Meditations Concerning Death*, 1696.

_____ *Observations on the Animadversions . . . on a Late Book Entituled, The Reasonableness of Christianity, As delivered in the Scriptures*, 1698.

_____ *A Short Discourse of the True Knowledge of Christ Jesus. . . .with some Animadversions on Mr. Edwards's Reflections on the Reasonableness of Christianity, and on his Book, Entituled Socinianism Unmasked*, 1697.

_____ *Some Considerations on the Principal Objections and Arguments . . . against Mr. Lock's Essay of Humane Understanding*, 1699.

Bourn, Samuel, *A Letter Concerning the Christian Doctrine of Future Punishment*, 1759.

_____ *A Series of Discourses on the Principles and Evidences of Natural Religion and the Christian Revelation*, 2 vols., 1760.

Braght, T. J. von, *Het Bloedig Tooneel, of Mastelaers Spiegel der Doops-Gesinde of Weereloofe Christenen*, Amsterdam, 1685.

Bramhall, John, *The Catching of Leviathan*, 1658.

Brayne, John, *The Unknown Being of the Spirit, Soul, and Body Anatomized. Wherein very many Scriptures falsely translated, and corruptly interpreted, are clearly explained*, 1654.

A Brief Confession or Declaration of Faith, 1660.

Broughton, Hugh, *An Explication of the Article . . .of Our Lorde's Soule Going from His Body to Paradise*, 1605.

Broughton, John, *Psychologia: or An Account of the Nature of the Rational Soul*, 1703.

Browne, Thomas, *Religio Medici*, 7th edn, 1672.

Bull, George, *Some Important Points of Primitive Christianity Maintained and Defended in Several Sermons and Other Discourses*, 2 vols., 1713.

Bullinger, Henry, *Fiftie godlie and learned Sermons . . . containing the chiefe and principall points of Christian Religion*, tr., H. I., 2nd edn, 1584.

_____ *An Holsome Antidotus or counter-poysen agaynst the pestylent heresye and secte of the Anabaptistes*, tr., J. Veron, [1548].

Burnet, Thomas, *De Statu Mortuorum et Resurgentium*, 1720.

_____ *Of the State of the Dead and of Those that are to Rise*, tr. M. Earberry, 1727.

_____ *The Theory of the Earth, Containing an Account of the Original of the Earth, and of all the General Changes which it hath already undergone, or is to undergo 'Till the Consummation of all Things*, 2nd edn, 1691.

_____ *A Treatise Concerning the State of Departed Souls Before, At, and After the Resurrection*, tr. J. Dennis, 1730.

Caffyn, Matthew, *The Deceived and Deceiving Quakers Discovered*, 1656.

Calvin, John, *An excellent treatise of the Immortalytie of the Soule*, tr., T. Stocker, 1581.

Calvin's Tracts, tr., H. Beveridge, 3 vols., Edinburgh, 1851.

_____ *Institutes of the Christian Religion*, tr., H. Beveridge, 2 vols., Grand Rapids, MI, 1964.

_____ *Psychopannychia*, Geneva, 1545.

_____ Sermons . . . on the Epistles of St. Paul to Timothy and Titus, tr., L. Tomson, 1579.

_____ A short instruction for to arme all good Christian people agaynst the pestiferous errours of the common secte of Anabaptistes, [1549].

_____ De statu animarum post mortem liber, quo asseritur vivere apud Christum non dormire animos sanctos, qui fide Christi decedunt: Assertio, Strassburg, 1542.

A Catalogue of the severall Sects and Opinions in England and other Nations. With a briefe Rehearsall of their false and dangerous Tenents, 1646.

Chappelow, Leonard, Two Sermons Concerning the State of the Soul On its immediate Separation from the Body, Cambridge, 1765.

Chishull, Edmund, A Charge of Heresy Maintained Against Mr. Dodwell's late Epistolary Discourse concerning the Mortality of the Soul, 1706.

Clark, George, A Vindication of the Honour of God and the Rights of Men, 1789.

[_____] A Vindication of the Honour of God: in a Scriptural Refutation of the Doctrines of Eternal Misery and Universal Salvation, 1792.

Clarke, Samuel, A Letter to Mr. Dodwell, Wherein all the Arguments in his Epistolary Discourse against the Immortality of the Soul are particularly answered, 1706.

A Confession of Faith, Put forth by the Elders and Brethren of many Congregations of Christians (Baptized upon Profession of their Faith) in London and the Country, 1677.

The Confession of Faith, Together with the Larger and Lesser Catechisms. Composed by the Reverend Assembly of Divines Sitting at Westminster, 1658.

The Confession of Faith of those Churches which are commonly (though falsly) called Anabaptists, 1644.

A Confession of Faith of several congregations of Christ in the county of Somerset, and some churches in the counties near against, 1656.

[Cooper, Christopher], The Vail Turned Aside, 1701.

[Coward, William], Farther Thoughts Concerning Human Soul, in Defence of Second Thoughts, 1703.

C[oward], W[illiam], The Grand Essay: or a Vindication of Reason and Religion, 1704.

_____ The Just Scrutiny: or a Serious Enquiry into the Modern Notions of the Soul, [1705].

Coward, William, Ophthalmiatria, 1706.

[Coward, William], Second Thoughts Concerning Human Soul, Demonstrating the Notion of Human Soul As believ'd to be a Spiritual Immortal substance, united to Human Body, To be a Plain Heathenish Invention, And not consonant to the Principles of Philosophy, Reason, or Religion, 1702, 2nd edn,1704.

Crosby, Thomas, The History of the English Baptists, 4 vols., 1738-40.

Dent, Arthur, The Ruine of Rome: or An Exposition upon the whole Revelation, 1603.

Dodwell, Henry, An Epistolary Discourse, Proving from the Scriptures and the First Fathers, that the Soul is a Principle Naturally Mortal; but Immortalized Actually by the Pleasure of God, to Punishment, or to Reward by its Union with the Divine Baptismal Spirit, 1706.

_____ A Preliminary Defence of the Epistolary Discourse Concerning the Distinction *between Soul and Spirit*, 1707.

_____ *The Natural Mortality of Humane Souls Clearly Demonstrated from The Holy Scriptures and the concurrent Testimonies of the Primitive Writers*, 1708.

_____ *The Scripture Account of the Eternal Rewards or Punishments of all that hear of the Gospel, without an Immortality necessarily resulting from the Nature of the Souls themselves that are concerned in those Rewards or Punishments*, 1708.

Edwards, John, *Some Thoughts Concerning the Several Causes and Occasions of Atheism, Especially in the Present Age*, 1695.

_____ *Socinianism Unmasked*, 1696.

Edwards, Thomas, *The First and Second Part of Gangraena: or A Catalogue and Discovery of many of the Errors, Heresies, Blasphemies and pernicious Practices of the Sectaries of this time, vented and acted in England in these four last years*, 3rd edn, 1646.

_____ *The Third Part of Gangraena, or A new and higher Discovery of the Errors, Heresies, Blasphemies, and insolent Proceedings of the Sectaries of these Times*, 1646.

The Faith and Practise of Thirty Congregations, Gathered According to the Primitive Pattern, 1651.

Flavel, John, *Pneumatologia. A Treatise of the Soul of Man*, 1685.

Fleming, Caleb, *A Survey of the Search After Souls*, 1758.

Fox, John, *The Acts and Monuments of John Foxe*, ed., S. R. Cattley, 8 vols., 1837.

Frith, John, *A Boke made by John Frith prisoner in the Tower of London*, 1533.

_____ *A Disputation of Purgatory* in *The Works of the English Reformers: William Tyndale and John Frith*, ed., T. Russell, 3 vols., 1831.

_____ *John Frith's Judgment upon Master William Tracy's Testament* in *The Works of the English Reformers: William Tyndale and John Frith*, ed., T. Russell, 3 vols., 1831.

Gansfort, Wessel, *Farrago Rerum Theologicarum*, Wittenberg, 1522.

[Hall, Thomas], *The Pulpit Guarded with XX Arguments Proving the Unlawfulness, Sinfulness and Danger of Suffering Private Persons to take upon them Publicke Preaching*, 1651.

_____ *Vindiciae Literarum*, 1655.

Hallett, Joseph III, *A Collection of Notes on some Texts of Scripture, and of Discourses*, 1729.

_____ *A Free and Impartial Study of the Holy Scriptures*, 1729.

Hammon, George, *A Discourse Touching the Mortality of the Soul*, [1660].

_____ *A Discovery of the Latitude of the loss of the Earthly Paradise by Original Sin*, 1655.

_____ *The Resurrection of the Body Proved*, [1660].

_____ *Syons Redemption Discovered*, 1655.

_____ *Syons Redemption, and Original Sin Vindicated*, 1658.

_____ *Truth and Innocency, Prevailing against Error and Insolency*, [1660].

Hartley, David, *Observations on Man, his Frame, his Duty, and his Expectations*, 2 vols., 1749.

[Henrick, William], *Ontologos . . . An Essay to Prove that the Soul of Man is not, neither Can it be, Immortal*, Dublin, 1721.

Hobbes, Thomas, *An Answer to a Book Published by Dr. Bramhall called The Catching of the Leviathan*, 1682.

_____ *Leviathan*, 1651.

H[odson], W[illiam], *Credo Resurrectionem Carnis*, [1636].

Hody, Humphrey, *The Resurrection of the (same) Body Asserted*, 1694.

Holland, Hezekiah, *An Exposition or Epitome of the Most Choice Commentaries Upon the Revelation of Saint John*, 1650.

Homes, Nathaniel, *The Resurrection Revealed: or The Dawning of the Day-star about to rise*, 1653.

Hugh, William, *The Troubled Man's Medicine*, 1546.

Keach, Benjamin, *The French Impostour Detected*, 1702.

Killingworth Grantham, *The Immortality of the Soul Proved from Scripture . . . an Answer to the Rev. Mr. Sam. Bourne's Reasons against it*, 1761.

Latimer, Hugh, *Sermons by Hugh Latimer*, ed., G. E. Corrie, Cambridge, 1844.

Law, Edmund, *Considerations on the State of the World with Regard to the Theory of Religion*, 1745.

_____ *Considerations on the Theory of Religion*, 3rd edit., Cambridge, 1755; 4th ed.,1759.

_____ *Considerations on the Theory of Religion*, ed., G. H. Law, 1820

_____ *The Nature and End of Death under the Christian Covenant*, 1755.

Lawson, Thomas, *An Untaught Teacher Witnessed Against*, 1655.

[Layton, Henry], *Arguments and Replies in a Dispute concerning the Nature of the Humane Soul*, 1703.

[_____] *Observations upon Mr. Wadsworth's Book of The Soul's Immortality, and his Confutation of the Opinion of the Soul's Inactivity to the Time of General Resurrection*, [1692?].

[_____] *Observations upon a Sermon Intituled, A Confutation of Atheism from the Faculties of the Soul, alias, Matter and Motion cannot think: Preached April 4, 1692. By way of Refutation*, [1692].

[_____] *Observations upon a Treatise intitled, A Discourse concerning the Happiness of Good Men in the next World*, [1704].

[_____] *Observations upon a Treatise Intitled Psychologia: or, An Account of the Nature of the Rational Soul*, [1703].

[_____] *Observations upon a Short Treatise, Written by Mr. Timothy Manlove: Intituled, The Immortality of the Soul Asserted . . .*, [1697?]

[_____] *A Reply to a letter Dated Sept. 14, 1702*, [1703?].

[_____] *A Search after Souls: or The Immortality of a Humane Soul, Theologically, Philosophically, and Rationally Considered. With the Opinion of Ancient and Modern Authors*, 2 vols., 1706.

[_____] *A Search after Souls and Spiritual Operations in Man*, [1691].

[_____] *A Second Part of a Treatise Intituled A Search after Souls* [1692?].

Lloyd, Evan, *A Muzzle for a Mad Dog: or, Animadversions On some late Scandalous Papers call'd Rehearsers*, 1707.

Locke, John, *An Essay concerning Humane Understanding*, 2nd edn, 1694.

_____ *A Paraphrase and Notes on the Epistles of St. Paul*, 1707.

_____ *A Paraphrase and Notes on the Epistles of St. Paul to the Galatians, 1 and 2*

Corinthians, Romans, Ephesians, ed., A. W. Wainwright, 2 vols., Oxford, 1987.
[_____] *The Reasonableness of Christianity, as delivered in the Scriptures*, 1695.
[Lushington, Thomas], *The Expiation of a Sinner*, 1646.
Luther, Martin, *Luther's Works*, eds., J. Pelikan and H. T. Lehmann, 55 vols., St. Louis, MO, 1958-86.
The Materiality and Mortality of the Soul of Man, And its Sameness with the Body, Asserted and Prov'd from the Holy Scriptures of the Old and New Testament, 1729.
Mede, Joseph, *A Paraphrase and Exposition of the Prophecies of St. Peter, concerning the Day of Christ's Second Coming*, 1642.
_____ *The Works of the Pious and Profoundly Learned Joseph Mede, B.D.*, ed., J. Worthington, 4th edn, 1677.
Milton, John, *Complete Prose Works of John Milton*, ed., D. M. Woolfe, 8 vols., New Haven and London, 1953-82.
_____ *The Prose Works of John Milton*, ed., J. A. St. John, 5 vols., 1853
_____ *Milton's Poems*, ed., B. A. Wright, 1969.
Monck, Thomas; Wright, Joseph; Hammon, George; Jeffery, William; Stanley, Francis; Reynolds, William; Smith, Francis, *Sions Groans for her Distressed, or Sober Endeavours to Prevent Innocent Blood, and to Stablish the Nation in the Best of Settlements. Grounded upon Scripture, Reason, and Authority*, 1661.
More, Henry, *The Immortality of the Soul*, 1659.
[_____] *A Explanation of The Grand Mystery of Godliness*, 1660.
[_____] *Antipsuchopannychia, or A Confutation of the Sleep of the Soul after Death*, 1642.
More, Thomas, *A dyalogue of syr Thomas More knyghte*, 1529.
Napier, John, *A Plain Discovery of the Whole Revelation of Saint John*, 5th edn, 1645.
Newton, Isaac, *Observations Upon the Prophecies of Daniel, and the Apocalypse of St. John*, 1733.
An Orthodox Confession: or, A Protestant Confession of Faith, 1679.
O[verton], R[ichard], *Mans Mortalitie: or, A Treatise Wherein 'tis proved, both Theologically and Philosophically, that whole Man (as a Rationall Creature) is a Compound wholly mortall, contrary to that common distinction of Soule and Body*, Amsterdam, 1644.
[_____] *Man Wholly Mortal, or, A Treatise Wherein Tis proved, both Theologically and Philosophically, That as whole man sinned, so whole man died; contrary to that common distinction of Soul and Body*, 1655.
Pagitt, Ephraim, *Heresiography, or A description of the Hereticks and Sectaries of these Latter Times*, 3rd edn,1649.
Pareus, David, *A Commentary Upon the Divine Revelation of the Apostle and Evangelist John*, tr., E. Arnold, Amsterdam, 1644.
_____ *In Divinam Apocalypsin. S. Apostoli et Evangelistae Johannis Commentarius*, Heidelberg, 1618.
Parker, Thomas, *The Visions and Prophecies of Daniel Expounded*, 1646.
[Payne, John], *Royall Exchange*, Haarlem, 1597.
Peckard, Peter, *Farther Observations on the Doctrine of an Intermediate State*, 1757.

_____ *Observations on the Doctrine of an Intermediate State between Death and the Resurrection,* 1756.

_____ *Observations on Mr. Fleming's Survey,* 1759.

Perronet, Vincent, *A Vindication of Mr. Locke, from the Charge of giving Encouragement to Scepticism and Infidelity,* 1736.

[Pitts, Joseph], *Immortality Preternatural to Human Souls,* 1708.

Porter, Edmund, *Theos Anthropophros, or God Incarnate. Shewing that Jesus Christ is the Onely, and the Most High God,* 1655.

Priestley, Joseph, *Disquisitions Relating to Matter and Spirit,* 1777.

_____ *Doctrines of Heathen Philosophy, Compared to those of Revelation,* 1804.

_____ *An History of the Corruptions of Christianity,* 2 vols., 1782.

_____ *Hartley's Theory of the Human Mind,* 1775.

A Relation of Severall Heresies . . . Discovering the Originall Ring-leaders, and the Time when They Began to Spread: as also their Dangerous Opinions, and Tenents, 1646.

Reynolds, Edward, *A Treatise of the Passions and Faculties of the Soul of Man,* 1640.

[Richardson, Samuel], *Of the Torments of Hell,* 1658.

Richardson, Samuel, *The Life of Faith,* 1643.

_____ *The Saints Desire,* 1647.

R[obinson], J[ohn], *Philosophical and Scriptural Inquiries into the Nature and Constitution of Mankind,* 1757.

Ross, Alexander, *Leviathan Drawn out with a Hook: or Animadversions Upon Mr. Hobbs his Leviathan,* 1653.

_____ *Medicus Medicatus,* 1645.

_____ *Pansebeia, or, A View of all Religions in the World,* 1653; 2nd edn,1655.

_____ *The Philosophicall Touch-stone,* 1645.

Scott, Joseph Nicol, *Sermons Preached in Defence of All Religion, Whether Natural or Revealed,* 1743.

Seager, John, *A Discoverie of the World to Come According to the Scriptures,* 1650.

Sixteen Articles of Faith and Order unanimously asserted to by the Messengers met at Warwick, the 3rd Day of the 3rd Month,1655. 1655.

Spanheim, Friedrich, *Englands Warning by Germanies Woe,* 1646.

[Stillingfleet, Edward], *The Bishop of Worcester's Answer to Mr. Locke's Second Letter,* 1698.

Taylor, Jeremy, *The Great Exemplar,* 1653.

_____ *The Rule and Exercise of Holy Dying,* 1651.

Taylor, John, *The Scripture Doctrine of Original Sin,* 1740.

The Testament of Master Wylliam Tracie esquier expounded both by William Tyndale and Jhon [sic] Frith, Antwerp, 1535.

Tillotson, John, *The Works of Dr. John Tillotson,* 2 vols., 1712.

Tottie, John, *Sermons Preached before the University of Oxford,* 1775.

Tracy, William, *The Testament of William Tracy* in *The Works of the English Reformers: William Tyndale and John Frith,* ed., T. Russell, 3 vols., 1831.

A True Relation of The Commissions and Warrants for the Condemnation and Burning of Bartholomew Legatt and Thomas Withman, 1651.

Tyndale, William, *An Answer unto Sir Thomas More's Dialogue* in *The Works of the English Reformers: William Tyndale and John Frith*, ed., T. Russell, 3 vols., 1831.
_____ *The New Testament, 1526*, ed., W. R. Cooper, 2000.
_____ *The New Testament diligently corrected and compared with the Greek*, Antwerp, 1534.
Wadsworth, Thomas, *Antipsychothanasia, or, The Immortality of the Soul Explained and Proved by Scripture and Reason*, 1670.
Wake, William, *The State of the Church and Clergy of England*, 1703.
Warburton, William, *The Divine Legation of Moses Demonstrated, on the Principles of a Religious Deist, From the Omission of the Doctrine of a Future State of and Punishment in the Jewish Dispensation*, 3 vols., 1738.
A Warning Against Popish Doctrines: or Observations on the Rev. Mr. Thomas Broughton's Defence of an Inherent Immortality in Man; Shewing it to be a Doctrine of Human Invention, 1767.
Watts, Isaac, *Death and Heaven; or, The last Enemy Conquered, and Separate Spirits made perfect*, Edinburgh, 1749.
Whiston, William, *The Eternity of Hell Torments Considered: or, A Collection of Texts of Scripture, and Testimonies of the three first Centuries relating to them*, 1740.
_____ *Historical Memoirs of the Life and Writings of Dr. Samuel Clarke*, 3rd edn, 1748.
_____ *A New Theory of the Earth . . . Wherein The Creation of the World in Six Days, The Universal Deluge, And the General Conflagration As laid down in the Holy Scriptures, Are shown to the perfectly agreeable to Reason and Philosophy*, 1696.
[_____] *Sermons and Essays Upon Several Subjects*, 1709.
Wither, George (tr.), *The Nature of Man. A Learned and usefull Tract writtten in Greek by Nemesius . . . one of the most ancient Fathers of the Church*, 1636.
[Writer, Clement], *An Apologetical Narration, or a Just and Necessary Vindication of Clement Writer*, (n.d.).
Writer, Clement, *Fides Divina*, 1657.
[Writer, Clement], *The Jus Divinum of Presbyterie*, 2nd edn, 1655.
Wycliffe, John, *Select English Works of John Wyclif*, ed., T. Arnold, 3 vols., Oxford, 1869-71.

Secondary Works

Allen, D.C., *Doubt's Boundless Sea*, Baltimore, 1964.
Aries, P., *The Hour of Our Death*, 1981.
Baines, A.H.J., *The Signatories of the Orthodox Confession of 1679*, 1960.
Bainton, R.H., *Here I Stand: A Life of Martin Luther*, New York, 1950.
Balke, W., *Calvin and the Anabaptist Radicals*, tr., W. Heynen, 1981.
Ball, B.W., *The English Connection: The Puritan Roots of Seventh-day Adventist Belief*, 1981.
_____ *A Great Expectation: Eschatological Thought in English Protestantism to 1660*, Leiden, 1975.

The British Reformers from Wickliff to Jewell and Fox, 15 vols, 1827-31.

Brown, R., *The English Baptists of the Eighteenth Century*, 1986.

Burns, N.T., *Christian Mortalism from Tyndale to Milton*, Cambridge, Mass., 1972.

Burrage, C., *The Early English Dissenters in the Light of Recent Research*, 2 vols, Cambridge, 1912.

Canright, D.M., *A History of the Doctrine of the Soul*, Battle Creek, MI., 1870.

Capp, B.S., *The Fifth Monarchy Men*, 1972.

Cardwell, E., *Synodalia*, 2 vols., Oxford, 1842.

Champion, J.A.I., *The Pillars of Priestcraft Shaken*, Cambridge, 1992.

Collinson, P., *The Elizabethan Puritan Movement*, 1967.

Cross, Claire, *Church and People 1450-1660*, 1979.

Cullmann, O., *Immortality of the Soul, or Resurrection of the Dead?*, 1958.

Daniell, D., *William Tyndale, A Biography*, New Haven and London, 2001.

Davies, M., *Cranmer's Godly Order: The Destruction of Catholicism Through Liturgical Change*, New York, 1976.

Davis, J.F., *Heresy and Reformation in the South-East of England, 1520-1559*, 1983.

De Beer, E.S. (ed.), *The Correspondence of John Locke*, 8 vols., Oxford, 1976-89.

Dickens, A.G., *The English Reformation*, 1964.

Dobranski, S.B. and Rumrich, J.P.(eds.), *Milton and Heresy*, Cambridge, 1998.

Duffy, E., *The Stripping of the Altars: Traditional Religion in England c.1400-c.1580*, New Haven and London, 1992.

Firth, C.H. and Rait, R.S.(eds.), *Acts and Ordinances of the Interregnum, 1642-1660*, 3 vols., 1911.

Firth, K.R., *The Apocalyptic Tradition in Reformation Britain, 1530 -1645*, Oxford, 1979.

Fisch, H., *Jerusalem and Albion*, New York, 1964.

Frank, J., *The Levellers*, Cambridge, Mass., 1955.

Froom, L.E., *The Conditionalist Faith of our Fathers*, 2 vols., Washington, D. C., 1965.

Gaarder, J., *Sophie's World*, 1996.

Gladstone, W.E., *Studies Subsidiary to the Works of Bishop Butler*, 1896.

Gordon, A., *Cheshire Classis Minutes 1691-1745*, 1919.

_____ *Heads of Unitarian History*, 1895.

Haller, W., *The Rise of Puritanism*, New York, 1957.

Hardwick, C., *A History of the Articles of Religion*, 1851.

Harrison, D.(ed.), *The First and Second Prayer Books of Edward VI*, London and Toronto, 1977.

Harrison, J. and Laslett, P., *The Library of John Locke*, Oxford, 1971.

Higgins-Biddle, J C. (ed.), *John Locke: The Reasonableness of Christianity as delivered in the Scriptures*, Oxford, 1999.

Hill. C., *Antichrist in Seventeenth-Century England*, 1971.

_____ *The Century of Revolution, 1603-1714*, Edinburgh, 1961.

_____ *The World Turned Upside Down*, 1975.

Howell, T.B. and Howell T.J. (eds.), *A Complete Collection of State Trials*, 34 vols, 1816-28.

[Hunter, J.] (ed.), *Letters of Eminent Men Addressed to Ralph Thoresby, F.R.S.*, 2 vols., 1832.

Hunter, W.B.(ed.), *A Milton Encyclopedia*, 9 vols., Lewisburg and London, 1978-83.

Keeble, N.H. and Nuttall, G.F., *Calendar of the Correspondence of Richard Baxter*, 2 vols., Oxford, 1991.

Kerr, H.T., *A Compend of Luther's Theology*, Philadelphia, 1943.

King, P. (ed.), *Thomas Hobbes, Critical Assessments*, 4 vols, London and New York, 2000.

Lane, A.N.S., *John Calvin: Student of the Church Fathers*, Edinburgh, 1999.

Lamont, W.M., *Godly Rule*, 1969.

Lumpkin, W.L., *Baptist Confessions of Faith*, 1959.

MacCulloch, D., *Reformation: Europe's House Divided, 1490 -1700*, 2004.

McGrath, A., *A Life of John Calvin: A Study in the Shaping of Western Culture*, 1990.

_____ *In the Beginning; The Story of the King James Bible*, London, Sydney, Auckland, 2001.

McLachlan, H.J., *Sir Isaac Newton, Theological Manuscripts*, Liverpool, 1950.

_____ *Socinianism in Seventeenth-century England*, Oxford, 1951.

Mackinnon, J., *Calvin and the Reformation*, 1936.

MacPherson, C.B., *The Political Theory of Possessive Individualism*, Oxford, 1962.

Martinich, A.P., *A Hobbes Dictionary*, Cambridge, Mass., and Oxford, 1995.

Marshall, P., *Beliefs and the Dead in Reformation England*, Oxford, 2002.

Masson, D., *The Life of John Milton*, 6 vols., 1871-1880.

Matthews, A.G. (ed.), *Walker Revised*, Oxford, 1948.

Mergal, A.M. and Williams, G.H., (eds.), *Spiritual and Anabaptist Writers*, Philadelphia, 1957.

Miller, P., *Errand into the Wilderness*, Cambridge, Mass., 1956.

Mills, A.J., *Earlier Life-Truth Exponents*, 1925.

More, A.L., *The Parousia in the New Testament*, Leiden, 1966.

More, P.E. and Cross, F.L., *Anglicanism*, 1962.

Mosheim, J.L. von, *Institutes of Ecclesiastical History*, tr., J. Murdoch, ed., H. Soames, 4 vols., 1841.

Murray, I.H., *The Puritan Hope: A Study in Revival and the Interpretation of Prophecy*, Edinburgh, 1975.

Nuovo,V., *John Locke, Writings on Religion*, Oxford, 2002.

Parker, J. (ed.), *The First Prayer-Book . . .of King Edward VI [1549]*, Oxford and London, 1883.

Parker, T.M., *The English Reformation to 1558*, 1950.

Patrides, C.A., *Milton and the Christian Tradition*, Oxford, 1966.

Phillipson, N. and Skinner, Q. (eds.), *Political Discourse in Early Modern Britain*, Cambridge, 1993.

Porter, H.C., *Puritanism in Tudor England*, 1970.

Reid, W.S., *John Calvin: His Influence in the Western World*, Grand Rapids, MI, 1982.

Robertson, J.M., *A Short History of Free Thought Ancient and Modern,* 2 vols., 1914-15.

Robinson, H., (ed.), *Original Letters Relative to the English Reformation*, Cambridge, 2 vols., 1847.

Robinson, H. Wheeler, *The Christian Doctrine of Man*, 1926.

Rowse, A.L., *Milton the Puritan*, 1977.

Rupp, E.G. and Drewery, B., *Martin Luther*, 1970.

Russell, T. (ed.), *The Works of the English Reformers: William Tyndale and John Frith*, 3 vols., 1831.

Saurat, D., *Milton, Man and Thinker*, New York, 1925.

Schaff, P., *The Creeds of Christendom*, 3 vols., 6th edn, 1931.

Scott, Jonathan, *England's troubles*, Cambridge, 2000.

Sell, Alan, *John Locke and the Eighteenth-Century Divines*, Cardiff, 1997.

Sewell, A., *A Study in Milton's Christian Doctrine*, 1967.

Shaw, W. A., *History of the English Church 1640-1660*, 2 vols., 1900.

Smith, N., *Perfection Proclaimed*, Oxford, 1989.

Stewart, M.A. (ed.), *English Philosophy in the Age of Locke*, Oxford, 2000.

Stickelberger, E., *Calvin: A Life*, London, 1961.

Strauss, L., *Natural Right and History*, Chicago, 1953.

Tavard, G.H., *The Starting Point of Calvin's Theology*, Grand Rapids, MI and Cambridge, 2000.

Thomas, K., *Man and the Natural World*, 1983.

Travis, S.H. , *I Believe in the Second Coming of Jesus*, 1982.

Tedeschi, J.A.(ed.), *Italian Reformation Studies in Honour of Laelius Socinus*, Florence, 1965.

Temple, W., *Nature, Man and God*, 1934.

Underwood, A.C., *A History of the English Baptists*, 1947.

Walker, D.P., *The Decline of Hell*, Chicago, 1964.

Walch, J.G. (ed.), *Martin Luther's Sammtlichte Schriften*, 1904.

Webster, C., *The Great Instauration: Science, Medicine and Reform, 1626-1660*, 1975.

Werrell, R.S., *The Theology of William Tyndale*, Cambridge, 2006.

Wendel, F., *Calvin*, 1965.

White, B.R., *The English Baptists of the Seventeenth Century*, 1983.

White, Edward, *Life in Christ*, 1846.

Whiting, C.E., *Studies in English Puritanism*, 1931.

Whitley, W.T., *The Baptists of London*, [1928].

_____ *A Baptist Bibliography*, 2 vols., 1916, 1922.

_____ *A History of British Baptists*, 1923.

Wilks, M., (ed.), *Prophecy and Eschatology*, Oxford, 1994.

Williams, G.H., *The Radical Reformation*, 3rd edn, Kirksville, MO, 1992.

Wilbur, E.M., *A History of Unitarianism In Transylvania, England, and America*, Cambridge, Mass., 1952.

_____ *A History of Unitarianism. Socinianism and its Antecedents*, Cambridge, Mass., 1945.

Williamson, G., *Seventeenth Century Contexts*, Chicago, 1961.

Workman, H.B., *John Wyclif: A Study of the English Mediaeval Church*, 1966.

General Works of Reference

A Biographical Dictionary of British Radicals, 3 vols., 1982-84.
Calendar of State Papers, Domestic.
Dictionary of Anonymous and Pseudonymous English Literature, 7 vols., 1926-34.
The Dictionary of National Biography, 63 vols., 1885-1900.
The Mennonite Encyclopedia, 5 vols., 1955-90.
The New Catholic Encyclopedia, 2nd edn, 15 vols., 2003.
The Oxford Companion to British History, 1997.
The Oxford Dictionary of the Christian Church, 3rd edn, 1997.
The Oxford Dictionary of National Biography, 60 vols., 2004.
The Oxford English Dictionary.
Short-Title Catalogue . . . 1641-1700, 3 vols., 1972.

Journals and Articles

Acontius, Jacob, *Stratagems of Satan*, tr., C.D.O'Malley, California State Library, Occasional Papers, English Series, 5, pt II , San Francisco, 1940.

Craig, J and Litzenberger, C., 'Wills as Religious Propaganda: The Testament of William Tracy', *Journal of Ecclesiastical History*, 44, 1993.

Geach, P., 'The Religion of Thomas Hobbes', *Religious Studies*, vol. XVII, Dec., 1981.

Henry, N.H., 'Milton and Hobbes :Mortalism and the Intermediate State', *Studies in Philology*, 48, 1951.

Horie, H., 'The Lutheran Influence on the Elizabethan Settlement', *The Historical Journal*, 34, 1991.

Johnston, D., 'Hobbes's Mortalism', *History of Political Thought*, X, 1989.

Letwin, S.R., 'Hobbes and Christianity', *Daedalus*, 105, Winter, 1974.

Temple, W., 'The Idea of Immortality in Relation to Religion and Ethics', *The Congregational Quarterly*, X, 1932.

Williamson, G., 'Milton and the Mortalist Heresy', *Studies in Philology*, 32, 1935.

Wolfe, D.M., 'Unsigned Pamphlets of Richard Overton, 1641-1649', *Huntington Library Quarterly*, XXI, 1957-8.

Young, B.W., 'The Soul-Sleeping System: Politics and Heresy in Eighteenth-Century England', *Journal of Ecclesiastical History*, 45, 1994.

Zagorin, P., 'The Authorship of *Mans Mortalitie*', *The Library*, 5th Series, V, 1950-1.

Index of Biblical References

The Old Testament

Genesis, book of,	31, 100, 142	72:8	180
1	117	88:11-13	118
1:20, 24	152	96:10	179
2:7	74, 108, 112, 117-118, 137, 152, 171	103:15,16	101
2:17	124	105	152
9:5	145, 152	115:17	118
14:21	145	146	59, 101, 118
17:14	152	150:6	152
35:18	207	Proverbs 11:25	152
36:6	145	13:3	152
37:21	152	Ecclesiastes, book of	30, 56
Exodus 1:5	145	1:4	179
4:19	152	3	101, 121n, 132, 202
12:16	152	7:12	121n
Leviticus 4:2	152	9:4-6	101
Deuteronomy 18	70	9:5	30, 121n
20:16	152	9:10	30
31:16	152	12:7	86, 118n, 202
Numbers 5:2	152	Isaiah, book of	178
31:28	152	26:19	63, 91
Judges 9:8	203	33:20-24	184
I Kings 11:43	152	45	190
17:21,22	207	45:17,18	190
I Chronicles 5:21	145	45:18	179
16:30	179	53	70
Job 7:21	152	65:17-25	176
14	108	66:22-23	176
14:1,2	101	Jeremiah 25:29	145
14:11,12	152	Daniel, book of	34, 142n, 177, 179
19	53	2	178
19:25	63	2:35	179n
Psalms, book of	31, 117	2:44,45	178n
6:5	118	12:2	63
49:15	118n, 207	Malachi, book of	70

The New Testament

Matthew 5	176	5:1-20	118n
9:24	57n	5:6,8	204
10:28	118n, 202	5:10	92
25:1,31	187	9:10	204
25:34	63	12:2,4	205
25:46	124n	Ephesians 2	188
26:38	152	2:7,8	188n
Luke 12:4,5	202	Colossians 3:4	89, 92
16:19	203	Philippians 1:23	118n, 205
21:31	187	I Thessalonians, Epistle to	146
23:43	118n, 203	4	49, 122n
23:46	118n	4:13	152
24:51	92	4:13-18	57n, 146
John, Gospel of	70	4:16	63
3:13	101	II Thessalonians 1:4-9	88
5:25	63	Hebrews 9:27	92
5:28,29	122	10:39	78
11:11-13	57n, 152	11	52
11:25	63	11:10	181
14:3	206	11:40	52n
18:36	185	I Timothy 6:14,16	101
Acts 1:3	92	6:16	108
1:9-11	92	II Timothy 4:1	92
1:11	183	4:8	89
2:43	152	James 4:14	101
24:15	91	I Peter 1:3	146
Romans 2:6	63	1:4	89
I Corinthians, Epistle to	123n	3:19	118n
15	30, 32n, 49, 53, 59, 63,	3:19,20	206
	122-123, 165, 189	4:5,6	206
15:6	152	II Peter, Epistle of	178
15:18,19,22	122	2:14	152
15:20,21	124	3	177, 191, 193
15:21,22	92	3:10	177
15:22	63, 125	3:10-13	176
15:35-38	122	Jude v.7	124n
15:40-55	121	Revelation, book of	34, 111n, 142n,
15:42-44	92, 123		176-177
15:44	203	5:10	180
15:45	152	6	207
15:49	92	6:9,10	118n, 206
15:53	122	21:1-5	176
15:54	109	21:2,10	182
II Corinthians, Epistle to	122		
5:1-4	122		

Index of Names

Excludes names of biblical characters and names of authors
when cited only in footnote references.

Acontius, Jacob, 63
Adams, Thomas, 178
Alexander, John, 165
Allen, D.C., 28n
Alsted, Johan, 192n
Amsdorf, Nicholas von, 29
Anaxagoras, 132
Andrews, Thomas, 44n
Aquinas, Thomas, 73n, 115n
Aries, P., 57n
Aristotle, 12, 27, 205
Arius, 70n, 159
Arminius, 159
Athanasius, 130, 159
Mrs Attaway, 84n
Augustine, 41, 51, 87

Bacon, Francis, 192n, 199n
Bader, Augustine, 33-34
Baillie, Robert, 82-83
Bainham, James, 47
Baines, A.H.J., 88n
Balke, W., 39n, 41
Barrow, Isaac, 15, 96n, 97n, 150
Batty, John, 84
Baxter, Richard, 10, 87, 88n, 131-132,
    199n
Beconsall, Thomas, 123n
Benoit, Andrew, 40
Benson, George, 14, 128, 145-147
Bentley, Richard, 120, 131, 198
Beveridge, H., 67n
Biddle, John, 25, 78-80
Blackburne, Francis 13, 29, 32, 61-
    62, 98, 106, 127, 131n, 132, 150,
    158-165, 174-75

Blount, Charles, 120-121
Blunt, Richard, 87n
Bodley, Thomas, 63
Bold, Samuel, 14, 127-130, 158n
Bourn, Samuel, III, 145, 166-167
Bowling, William, 69, 86, 88
Bramhall, John, 105-107
Brayne, John, 76-77, 87
Broughton, Hugh, 72-73, 85n
Broughton, John, 130n, 132, 134, 136,
    150, 199
Brown, R., 208
Browne, Thomas, 14-15, 69, 74-78,
    79n, 81
Brunfels, Otto, 40n
Bucer, Martin, 41n
Budny, Simon, 37
Bull, George, 127-128, 150n
Bullinger, Henry, 29, 35, 38, 60, 64,
    67
Burnet, Thomas, 120, 142-144, 191-
    193
Burns, N.T., 15-17, 20-21, 27, 47-49,
    51n, 59, 66, 71, 80, 84, 86, 98n,
    99n, 107, 109n, 114, 115n, 157n
Burrage, C., 70
Butler, Joseph, 120

Caffyn, Matthew, 88-89, 91-93, 208-
    209
Calvin, John, 23, 29, 33-35, 37-42, 56,
    64-68, 115n, 159
Canne, John, 99
Capito, Wolfgang, 41n
Capon, John, 47
Cardano, Girolamo, 27-28

Carlstadt, Andreas, 26, 28-29, 32-35
Cerinthus, 70n
Champion, J.A.I., 121
Chandler, Samuel, 167
Chappelow, Leonard, 127n, 150
Charles I, 95
Charles II, 92, 110
Charleton, Walter, 132, 198
Chishull, Edmund, 139-141
Chrysostom, 41
Clark, George, 14, 168-169
Clarke, Samuel, 137-143
Colbrand, Michael, 55
Collier, Thomas, 91
Collinson, Patrick, 86
Cooper, Christopher, 61n, 209n
Copernicus, 191
Corbet, Richard, 78
Coward, William, 127-129, 135-138, 149, 150n, 156, 158n, 199n
Craig, J., 53n, 54n, 55
Cranmer, Thomas, 37n, 56-57, 59, 67, 72
Crellius (Krell), Johannes, 79, 125n, 142n
Cromwell, Oliver, 85
Crosby, Thomas, 70, 109
Cross, F.L., 94n, 95, 96n
Cyprian 41

Daniell, D. 16-17, 48n
Davis, Joan, 55
Dawson, Benjamin, 165
Dent, Arthur, 177, 182, 185, 187
Descartes, R., 199n
Dickens, A.G., 25, 44, 46, 60, 67, 68
Digby, Kenelm, Sir, 75n
Doddridge, Phillip, 120
Dodwell, Henry (the Elder), 15, 138-142, 199n
Duffy, E., 45, 46n
Du Perron, Cardinal, 29

Earbery, Matthias, 144, 193n
Edward VI, 55-56, 61, 65, 67
Edwards, John, 129
Edwards, Jonathan, 168
Edwards, Thomas, 83-84, 86-87, 98-99

Elizabeth I, 43, 62, 66
Emmes, 87n
Eusebius, 82n

Fairfax, Thomas, 85
Fisch, H., 95, 114
Fisher, John, 51-52
Fleming, Caleb, 138, 149, 156-157, 163
Forsett, John, 47
Foxe, John, 46n, 63
Frith, John, 18, 43, 47-48, 51-55, 56n, 58, 61-62, 69, 94, 97, 149
Froom, L.E., 14-15, 35n, 44-45, 70n, 79, 98, 109n, 131n, 137, 143n, 144n, 157n, 163
Fulke, William, 85

Gaarder, Jostein, 13
Geach, P., 103-105
Goddard, Peter, 150n, 160
Goodwin, Thomas, 192n

Hall, Thomas, 21, 82
Haller, W., 67, 114
Hallett, Joseph III, 15, 145n, 193-194
Hamilton, Patrick, 46
Hammon, George, 14-15, 69, 88, 91-92, 97, 109-114, 195, 201-207
Hardwick, C., 60
Harrison, D., 59n
Hartley, David, 16, 147n, 170, 194
Henrick, William, 144n
Henry VIII, 55
Henry, N., 61, 104n, 115n
Herman of Gerbehaye, 40
Heynen, W., 33n
Higgins-Biddle, J. C., 190n
Hill, C., 46, 84n
Hobbes, Thomas, 12-15, 18, 21, 69, 76, 97, 103-109, 114, 127, 149, 150n, 170, 182-185, 187, 190, 198n
Hodson, William, 10
Hody, Humphrey, 82n, 191
Holland, Hezekiah, 111-112
Homes, Nathaniel, 14-15
Hooper, John, 60-61
Hoppy, Edward, 55

Horie, H., 59n, 62n
Hugh, William, 47-48
Hunter, W. B., 115n
Hut (Huth), John (Hans), 34, 39

Irenaeus, 41

James I, 70
Jenney, William, 84n
Jerome, 41, 87
John XXII, Pope, 26-27
Johnston, D., 103n
Josephus, 142
Joye, George, 16, 18, 50, 56
Justin Martyr, 140n, 141n

Keach, Benjamin, 136, 138
Kiffin, William, 208-209
Killingworth, Grantham, 167n
Krell see Crellius

Lamb, Thomas, 84, 87n
Lane, A.N.S., 39n, 41n, 42n
Latimer, Hugh, 18, 48, 55-56, 58, 60,
    149
Laud, William, 70, 95
Law, Edmund, 11, 120, 127, 150-154,
    156, 158-161, 163-165, 174, 195,
    207, 209
Lawson, Thomas, 89
Layton, Francis, 131
Layton, Henry, 127-138, 141, 149,
    156n, 158n, 176, 193, 195, 197-
    201, 203
Legatt, Bartholomew, 70n
Leland, John, 14
Leo X, Pope, 28
Leslie, James, 138n
Letwin, S.R., 103-104
Litzenberger, C., 53n, 54n, 55
Lloyd, Evan, 138
Locke, John, 12-13, 16, 18, 76, 97, 119-
    129, 137, 142n, 145-146, 149-150,
    160, 186-190, 193, 199n, 200
Lushington, Thomas, 14, 78-81, 94
Luther, Martin, 23, 25-34, 44, 48,
    50-52, 54-56, 83, 96, 115n, 159,
    174

MacCulloch, D., 17
Macedonius, 70n
McGrath, A., 23n, 25, 56, 67
McClachlan, H.J., 79n, 142n
Magus, Simon, 70n
Manelfe, Peter, 38n
Manes, 70n
Manlove, Timothy, 132, 198-199
Margaret of, Navarre, 35n
Marshall, P., 16, 18, 44n, 48, 51, 52n,
    56, 176
Martinich, A.P., 104-105, 183n
Mary Tudor, 60-61
Masson, D., 17, 114
Mede, Joseph, 115n, 177-179, 182,
    185, 192n
Miller, P., 186n
Mills, A.J., 14-15, 109n, 131n, 144n,
    157n
Milton, John, 9, 13, 15-18, 69, 95,
    103n, 104n, 109-110, 114-119, 127-
    128, 149-150, 185-186, 190, 196,
    201-203, 205-207
Monck, Thomas, 110
Moon, Thomas, 46
Montague, Henry, 178
More, Henry, 21-22, 199n
More, P.E., 94n, 95, 96n
More, Thomas, 16, 30, 48-49, 51-52
von Mosheim, J.L., 82n, 92, 174n

Napier, John, 176-177, 182-187, 190
Neile, Richard, 70
Nemesius of Emesa, 73-74
Newton, Isaac 142-143
Nicholls, William, 132, 136, 200
Nuovo, V., 119, 120n, 122, 124-125,
    126n

Origen, 41, 47, 82, 174
Overton, Richard, 18, 21, 69, 72, 74,
    76, 84, 87, 97-98, 100-103, 109,
    112, 114, 118, 127, 149, 182n, 201-
    205, 207

Pagitt, Ephraim, 82-83
Paley, William, 151

Pareus, David, 177
Parker, Samuel, 130
Parker, Thomas, 179
Patrides, C.A. 75n, 186
Paul, Gregory, 37, 39
Payne, John, 25, 71
Peckard, Peter, 61-62, 127, 150, 154, 155-161, 163, 165, 201
Photinus, 70n
Pieters, Jan, 63
Pitts, Joseph, 141-142
Plato, 41, 132, 137-138, 158, 172
Pocquet, Anthony, 35, 40, 63
Pomponazzi, Pietro, 27-28
Porter, Edmund, 79
Priestley, Joseph, 10, 13, 16n, 80, 97, 104n, 169, 170-174
Pythagoras, 132, 137

Rainoldes, Richard, 43
Renato, Camillo, 35n, 36-37, 39
Reynolds, Edward, 94-95
Richardson, Samuel, 85-86, 88, 203
Ridley, Nicholas, 60
Roberts, Robert, 104n
Robinson, John, 165
Ross, Alexander, 76, 81-83, 107
Rowse, A.L., 117n
Rutton, Matthias, 111

Sattler, Michael, 34
Saurat, D. 17, 114
Schaff, P., 62
Schiemer, Leonhard, 34
Schlaffer, John (Hans), 34
Scott, J., 83n, 84n
Scott, Joseph Nichol, 128, 147-148
Scott, Thomas, 147
Seager, John, 179, 180-182, 187
Secker, Thomas, 154
Sell, A., 120, 124
Servetus, Michael, 38-39, 40, 42
Sewell, A., 116
Seymour, Thomas, 55
Shakespeare, William, 57n
Shepherd, William, 55
Sherlock, William, 132, 200

Sidebotham, Thomas, 84
Smith, Nigel, 77n
Smith, William, 131n
Socinus, Faustus, 35, 37-38, 78, 125n, 142n, 209n
Socinus, Laelius, 35n, 36-37, 39, 78, 125n
Socrates, 137
Spanheim, Friedrich, 25
Spilsbury, John, 85
Spittelmaier, Ambrose, 34
Stall, Christopher, 209n
Stegmann, Joachim, 25, 80
Sterry, Peter, 14
Stillingfleet, Edward, 120-123, 187n
Stocker, Thomas, 66-67
Sumner, C.R. 115n

Tavard, G.H., 20n, 34, 39, 41
Taylor, Jeremy, 95-96
Taylor, John, 153n
Temple, William, 15n, 22
Tertullian, 41, 87
Terwoort, Hendrik, 63
Tewkesbury, John, 46
Thieffry, Quintin, 35n
Thomas, K., 103n
Thomason, George, 98n
Thoresby, Ralph, 131n
Tillotson, John, 14, 120n, 124n
Tottie, John, 14, 150, 166
Tracy, William, 17-18, 48, 52-55, 62, 69
Turner, John, 136, 199
Twisse, William, 192n
Tymmes, Joan, 55
Tyndale, William, 16-18, 23n, 25, 30, 43-44, 47-52, 54-58, 61-62, 69, 94, 97, 118, 149

Underwood, A.C., 85

Valentinus, 79n
Veron, John, 64

Wadsworth, Thomas, 132, 198
Wainwright, A.W., 12n, 119, 120n, 122n, 129n, 187n, 189n
Wake, William, 59

Walker, D.P., 15, 143n, 192n
Warburton, William, 14-15, 162-163
Watts, Isaac, 14-15, 120
Wendel, F., 39n
Werrell, R., 17
Wesley, John, 120
Westerburg, Gerhard, 33
Whiston, William, 142-143, 147, 150,
    194n, 195n
Whitby, Daniel, 130
White, B.R., 91
White, Thomas, 106
Whitley, W.T., 61n, 85, 87n, 88, 98,
    99n, 208, 209
Wightman, Edward, 69-73, 76, 78

William and Mary, 138
Williams, G.H. 19, 23, 29n, 34-40, 60,
    63-65
Williamson, G., 98n, 114n
Wingrove, William, 46
Wishart, George, 47
Wither, George, 73-74, 77
Wolfe, D.M. 114n
Workman, H.B., 44n, 45
Writer, Clement, 14-15, 69, 86-88,
    99n, 114
Wycliffe, John, 9, 13, 43-46, 174

Young, B.W., 158n

Zwingli, Ulrich, 29, 35

General Index

Includes place and county names. Topics (e.g. soul, body, death, mortality,
immortality, resurrection), that appear repeatedly throughout the text and concepts
mentioned only in titles of cited works are excluded.

Abingdon, 145
Acts of Uniformity, 161
Adamites, 72n
Amsterdam, 98n, 99
Anabaptists/ism, 20n, 26, 34, 38n,
    40, 48n, 63-64, 70, 82, 84, 86
    Dutch, 25, 63-64, 71
    English, 46, 59-63, 65, 71, 78, 87n,
    114
    German, 25
    Italian, 36
    Swiss, 35
Anabaptist Council of Venice, 36,
    38n
Anabaptist martyrs, 60
angels, 45, 49, 51, 63, 91, 105, 143,
    154, 167, 183, 185, 194
Anglican/ism, 13, 29, 43, 61, 63, 67,
    76, 94-96, 127, 137, 142, 149-150,
    161, 165, 208
annihilationists/ism, 16, 20-21, 48n,
    66, 83n, 121, 168, 172

anthropology, 12, 16, 22, 95, 125
Antichrist 22, 111, 167, 179
anti-clericalism, 46, 109
antinomianism, 188n
anti-paedobaptist, 38n
anti-Trinitarianism, 34, 37, 38n, 72n,
    78-79
Antwerp, 52n
apocalyptic/ism, 39, 111, 186
Apostles' Creed, 72-73, 85
Arabia/Arabians, 82, 107, 174
Arianism 70, 142, 147, 169
Aristotelian/ism, 12, 27, 32, 94, 113
Armagh, diocese of, 105
Arminian/ism 86, 110n, 145
Articles of Religion (Anglican), 15n
    Forty-Two (1553), 59-60, 62, 161-
    162
    Six (1539), 55n
    Ten (1536), 55
    Thirty-Nine (1563), 61-62, 158,
    160-161

Ashford, 61n, 209n
atheism, 87-88, 104, 106, 109, 170, 175, 198n
atonement, 37, 146, 169
Augsburg, 34
Augustinianism, 42
Austria, 34
Avignon, 26

Babylon, kingdom of, 178
Babylonian captivity, 178
baptism, 70, 139, 141, 188
Baptist/s, 13, 60, 61n, 63, 70, 72, 79, 81, 85-86, 90, 94, 97-99, 109-111, 112-113, 128, 167n, 174n, 208-209
  General, 84-93, 99, 109-111, 113-114, 115n, 142, 174n, 208-209
  Particular, 85, 87n, 89, 90-91, 110n, 208
Baptist confessions of faith, 89-90, 93, 110n
  General Baptist Confession (1660), 110
  General Baptist Orthodox Creed (1679), 110n
  Particular Baptist Confession (1677), 110n
Basle, 63, 68
Baughton, 111
Bedfordshire, 93n
Bible/biblical (see also Scripture), 11, 16, 28, 36, 41, 43, 52, 61, 69, 73, 87, 89, 92, 99, 101-102, 116-117, 120, 122, 137, 140, 146, 152, 169, 171-172, 179, 193, 201-202
  as revelation, 12, 72-73, 76, 126, 157
  Authorised Version, 23, 146
  authority of, 16, 28, 33, 50, 183
  Geneva 23n, 67
  incorrect interpretation of, 77, 87-88, 104, 105n, 147, 171, 181, 201
  inspiration of, 169
  interpretation of, 11-12, 25, 32, 36, 41, 81, 100-101, 106, 116, 118, 148n, 158, 201

meaning of, 152, 154, 160, 184
New Testament (see also Tyndale's New Testament), 22, 31, 44, 48, 50, 55, 67, 104, 119, 121,146, 152, 162, 166-169, 171-172, 194, 201
Old Testament, 31, 104, 119, 121, 152, 169, 171-172, 178, 207
  Syriac version, 206
  teaching of, 11, 49, 101
Biddenden, 88, 110
Billingshurst, 208
Birmingham, 145
Bodleian Library, 82n, 165n, 197-198, 200
Book of Common Prayer, 105
Boyle lectures, 198n
brain, 133-135
British Library, 56n, 98n, 197-98, 200
Broadclyst, 179
Buckinghamshire, 88, 93
Burford, 43
Burgh, 165
Burton-on-Trent, 69
Bury St Edmunds, 44n
Bushey, 132

Caffynites, 93, 209
Calvinist/ism, 61-62, 67, 90, 104n, 110n, 129, 143, 145, 175
Cambridge, 11, 72, 83, 85, 159, 209
Cambridge Platonists, 191
Canterbury, 70, 154
Canterbury, diocese of, 65
Carlisle, diocese of, 150-151
Catholic/ism, Roman, 10, 22, 26, 34, 54, 104, 106, 158n, 167
  medieval, 42, 46n, 48n, 80
Catholic theology/doctrine, 26-28, 41-42, 50, 62, 80-81, 87, 93, 104-106, 158n, 159, 163-164
character of God, 119, 166, 168
Chichester, 132, 208
Christ, ascension of, 205
  death of, 53, 92, 106, 120n, 129, 146, 153, 155

humanity of, 71
incarnation/advent, 57, 129, 155,
    179-180
kingdom of, 34, 58, 88, 92, 115,
    151, 178-180, 187-189, 193, 204
mediation of, 155-157
nature of, 167n, 169
resurrection of, 9, 11-12, 30, 49,
    53, 58, 91, 104, 109, 113, 120n,
    129, 141, 146-147, 153, 179, 196
second coming of, 32, 34-35, 48,
    57, 63, 78, 87-92, 100, 103, 118-
    119, 124, 135, 144, 147, 151-152,
    175-179, 182-187, 189, 193, 195,
    204, 206
work of, 12, 35, 49n, 105, 125,
    129-130, 154-156, 183, 185, 196
Christadelphians, 104n
Christendom, 22, 163
Christian/s (excludes references to
    Christian mortalism), 34n, 42-43,
    45n, 49-50, 70, 72-73, 104, 107, 139,
    165, 168, 179, 183, 190-192n, 196
dogma/teaching, 16, 22, 32, 77, 79,
    103, 116, 119-120, 135, 137, 154-
    155, 158-159, 162-163
early, 70, 108, 139, 143, 159, 166,
    174
English, 10, 12-13, 23, 43, 66-70,
    128
thought, 108, 113, 187
Christianity/Christian faith, 34n, 50,
    70, 105, 109, 126, 132, 138, 143,
    147, 151-152, 161-164, 170n, 174
Christology, 35n, 37, 70-71, 86, 89,
    93, 125
Church, Catholic (see also
    Catholicism), 26, 28, 44, 105, 162
Christian 45, 105, 107, 159, 160, 180
English, 54, 59, 67-68, 81, 105
medieval, 19, 27-28, 42, 137-138,
    174
triumphant, 71, 88
Western, 27, 87
Church Fathers, 41-42, 111, 132,
    143, 174

Church of England, 58-59, 61-62, 67,
    69-70, 72, 95, 104, 113, 136, 158n,
    159, 161
civilisation, 151-152
College of Surgeons, 135
Cologne, 48n
Commonwealth, 86
Conditional Immortality Mission,
    14n
conditionalism, 11, 22, 45, 80, 97n,
    101, 124, 139-140, 143n, 182
Confessions of Faith, 158-161, 164
    Augsburg (1530), 62n
    Savoy (1658), 110n
    Scottish (1560), 47, 60, 62
    Second Helvetic (1566), 60
    Westminster (1647), 10, 77n, 89,
    110n
    Wurttemberg (1552), 62n
conscience, 158, 162
consciousness, 12, 19, 27, 32, 34, 39,
    40, 58, 125, 144-145, 151, 153,
    156-157, 166, 174
Continent/Europe, 19, 23, 25-26, 28-
    30, 33, 36, 38-39, 40-43, 61, 63-64,
    66, 71, 75, 78-79, 81, 88, 142n,
    150, 177-178, 190
Convocation, 55, 65
cosmology, 186n, 191-194
Councils, church,
    Fifth Lateran (1512-1517), 26, 28,
    32, 36-37
    Florence (1438-1445), 26-27
    Vienne (1311-1312), 26
Coventry and Lichfield, diocese of,
    70
Cranbrook, 86, 88, 110
Creation, 75, 77, 84, 90, 100-101,
    108, 112, 116-117, 124, 139n, 142,
    145, 166, 179, 190-191, 193, 195
Creeds, 16, 158-159, 161, 164
    Nicea and Chalcedon 93n
Cuckfield, 208

Daniel, book of, 34, 142n, 177
deism, 120, 167

demonology, 108
destruction of Jerusalem, 187
Devil/Satan, 45n, 91, 119, 143, 167
Devon, 77, 179
Dissenters, 129, 145, 147, 208
Dr. Williams's Library, 197, 199n, 200
doctrinal error, 28, 34, 93, 100
doctrine (excluding references to mortalist and immortalist doctrine), 22, 25-29, 32, 39, 44, 50-51, 55, 67, 71, 77, 80-81, 85, 95, 101, 103, 105, 116, 119, 126, 133, 135, 143, 147, 154, 158, 161, 163, 166-167, 174, 191, 201-203, 209
Dorset, 129
Dort, 170
Down and Connor, diocese of, 95
dualism, 73-74, 120-121, 171-172, 204

Ebionites, 70n
Emesa, 73
Engelen, 40
England, 9, 13-14, 19, 21-22, 25, 28, 30, 34, 36n, 41-43, 46, 48n, 51, 52n, 53n, 54, 57, 61, 64-67, 72, 75, 78, 150, 174, 208-209
English Church in Geneva, 68n
English Independent Church in Holland, 82, 99
Enlightenment, the, 120
epistemology, 38, 120
Erastianism, 109
eschatology, 14-15, 17, 26, 32, 38-39, 41-44, 51-52, 59, 68, 76, 78, 84n, 85-86, 88-90, 92-93, 95, 98, 104-105, 112, 115, 119, 124-125, 128, 143, 154-155, 172, 174-177, 180-181, 189-192, 204
Essex, 60-61, 77, 139, 177
eternal life, 11-13, 17, 22, 30, 32, 35, 43, 48, 52-53, 57-58, 65, 78, 89-90, 95, 102, 104, 106, 119, 120n, 123, 125, 130, 138, 146, 153, 155, 160, 168-169, 176, 182-184, 186, 188-

189, 194-195
eternal torment, see hell
Europe, see Continent
Evangelical/ism, 51, 120, 155
experience, 133-134, 153, 173, 176

Fall, the, 91, 94, 101, 124, 130, 162, 177, 184
Familists/ism, 66, 72n
Ferrara, 36
Fifth Monarchy Men, 115n, 183n
Fletton, 154
Flood, the, 177-178, 184-185, 191, 195n
France, 35, 40
Frankfurt, 33, 68
freewill, 110n, 139n
French Church in Norwich, 147
fundamentalism, 46
futurism, 177n

Gerbehaye, 40
Geneva, 40, 67-68, 159
Germany, 19, 33, 47, 174
Gloucester, diocese of, 60
Gloucestershire, 17, 44, 47, 52, 53n, 55
Grays Inn, 131
Greece, 9n
Greece, kingdom of, 178

Haarlem, 25, 71
Halifax, 55
heaven, 17, 27, 43-47, 49, 52, 55-56, 58, 71, 78, 80, 82-83, 88-89, 91-92, 99-100, 102, 104-106, 118, 131, 144, 156, 175-176, 179, 181-184, 191, 193-194, 203-205, 207
hell, 10n, 15, 17, 28, 36, 45-46, 49, 52, 56, 72-73, 77, 80, 82-86, 91, 93, 97n, 99-100, 102, 104-108, 111, 119, 120n, 124, 143-144, 147-148, 150, 166, 167n, 168, 182-183, 202-203, 205
Hemel Hempstead, 77
heresy/heretics, 11, 17-18, 26, 30n, 34, 39, 44, 46-47, 53, 60-61, 63, 66,

69, 70-73, 79, 81-83, 88, 95, 104,
   107, 127n, 138-139, 150, 158-159
heresy trials, 51-52, 70
hermeneutics, 38, 42
Hertfordshire, 88, 93n
Hetheringtonians, 72n
Highweek, 77
historicism, 177
history, Christian, 11, 14, 70, 107,
   146, 158-159, 163, 173, 177n
   world, 35, 39, 129, 152, 157, 177-
   178, 180, 185
Hitchenchurch, 46
Holland, see Netherlands
Holy Spirit/Ghost, 57, 70, 78, 90,
   105, 139-141
hope, 10-13, 18, 21, 23, 33, 38, 43-
   44, 48-49, 51-54, 56-59, 87, 96,
   100, 102, 106, 113-114, 119, 125,
   128, 135, 141, 144, 146-147, 152-
   154, 156, 172, 180, 185, 196
Horsham, 88, 208-209
House of Commons, 135, 149, 158
House of Lords, 80
human existence, 9, 12, 22, 27, 37,
   100, 120, 122, 129, 131, 134, 137,
   153, 169
human nature (see also man, nature
   of), 156, 169-170, 175
humanism, 34n, 41

Independents, 13, 76-77, 82, 99
indulgences, 27, 33, 45n
Inquisition, 38
intermediate state, 27, 31, 44, 58, 62,
   104n, 119n, 139, 147n, 150n, 154,
   156, 160, 162, 174, 176, 181
Interregnum, 61, 85-86, 115
invocation of saints, 29, 44-45, 81,
   142n, 160n
Isle of Purbeck, 129
Italian Evangelical Rationalists, 30,
   33-34, 35n, 36-37, 94
Italy, 12, 19, 27, 36-37

Jesuits, 72n
Judgement, Day of/Last, 10n, 20n,

26-27, 29, 34-36, 39-40, 47, 51-52,
   56n, 57-58, 60, 63-64, 67, 77-78,
   82-83, 88-93, 102, 106, 111, 119,
   138, 143, 159, 177, 180, 183n,
   184-185, 187-188, 194-195, 204,
   206-207
justification, 37

Kent, 60-61, 69, 84-86, 88, 91, 93,
   110-111, 113-114, 208-209
kingdom of darkness, 105, 188
kingdom of God/heaven (see also
   Christ, kingdom of), 58, 175, 178,
   180, 183-189
Kings Norton, 82

last day/s, 10-11, 31-32, 34, 44n, 45,
   49, 53, 57-58, 60, 66, 73-74, 78,
   82, 89, 92, 102, 106, 112-113, 124,
   130, 139, 146, 160, 166, 172, 179-
   180, 185-186, 191
latitudinarian/ism, 150, 158-159
Leicestershire, 90
Levellers, 87, 99
Lewes, 208
Libertines, 35
Lichfield, 69, 72
Lincoln, diocese of, 46, 65
Lincolnshire, 90
Lithuania, 36-37
Little Poland, 37
Lollards/Lollardy, 25, 43, 46-47, 54,
   86, 154
London, 23, 25, 59n, 63-64, 84, 86,
   88, 90-91, 98n, 99, 135, 149, 167,
   197, 208-209
Lowestoft-with-Kissingland, 142
Ludney, 46
Lutheran/ism, 17, 25, 29n, 48, 52-53,
   55-56, 62, 115n
Lymington, 77

Maidstone, 110
man, nature of, 11, 18, 36, 72, 81,
   90, 96, 100, 102, 117, 120-122,
   125-126, 130, 133, 151, 153-156,
   172, 182n

Man of Sin, 111
Mariolatry, 81
Marian exiles, 68
Marian persecution, 60
Mass, 33, 45n
materialism, 17-18, 95, 100, 104, 107, 114, 133n, 137
Medo-Persia, 178
Mendlesham, 55
Middle Ages, 73n, 174
Midland Association (Baptist), 90
Milan, 27
millenarian/ism, 84n, 91, 99n, 111-112, 115, 167n, 176n, 181, 192n, 193
millennium, 111-112, 119, 193, 195n
mind, 20, 53, 94, 112, 125n, 133-134, 147n, 170-171
Minor Church in Poland, 38
monism, 17, 18n, 121

natural religion/theology, 28, 97n, 195
Navarre, 35, 40
necromancy, 145
Netherlands, 35, 40, 54n, 63
new earth/world, 84n, 175-186, 189-95
New Jerusalem, 84n, 111, 182
Newland St. Lawrence, 77
Ninety-Five Theses, 27
Nonconformist/ity, 68, 89n, 113, 137, 145, 149, 165, 208, 209n
Northampton, 135
Norwich, 147, 166, 167n
Norwich, diocese of, 46, 94, 137
Norwich Old Meeting, 147

Oates, 142n
obedience, 130, 157, 169, 189
observation, 133-134
Old Jewry, 167
original sin, 126, 151, 157, 182, 184
Oxford, 78-79, 89n, 98n, 103n, 150, 166, 197
Oxford martyrs, 55
Oxfordshire, 43, 93n

pagan/ism, 22, 50, 126, 142n, 158, 174
Papacy, 26, 27n, 29, 42, 111
Papal Bull, Exsurge Domine, 28
papistry/popery, 26, 62, 73, 80, 158, 161-162
paradise, 28, 35, 88, 93, 124, 182, 185, 192, 196, 203-204
Paris, 40
Parliament, 82, 106, 110, 158
personal identity, 76, 120, 122-123, 125-126, 172-173, 193
Peterborough, 150, 154
philosophy, 12-13, 16, 26-28, 32, 44, 50, 73, 87, 94, 100, 107, 112, 114n, 118, 120-121, 124-127, 131, 135, 137, 153, 155, 174, 195n
physiology, 134
Platonism/neo-Platonism, 27-28, 41, 73, 113, 137, 140, 155, 158, 174
Poland, 35-36, 79
political theory, 104n
Popish plot, 93n
Prayer Book, First (1549), 56-57, 59, 62n
Prayer Book, Second (1552), 59n, 62n
prayer/s for the dead, 27, 45-47, 142n
predestinarianism, 19
Presbyterian/ism, 10n, 13, 21, 81-83, 86, 94n, 115n, 145, 162, 165-167, 169, 179, 208
preterism, 177n
procreation, 100-102, 118, 137
prophecy, 34, 70, 111, 175, 177-178, 182
Protestant/ism, 10, 22, 36, 42, 52, 62, 80, 97n, 104, 106-107, 137, 158n, 160, 162-164
  Continental, 36, 41-42
  English, 18, 41-42, 46, 52n, 54-55, 56n, 68, 84, 86, 176-177
psychology, 16, 94n, 117
psychopannychist/ism, 15-16, 19-22, 27, 29-40, 45, 47-48, 53-67, 71, 77, 81, 95-96, 107-108, 110n, 128,

135-136, 139-140, 142-144, 147n,
150, 191
psychosomnolence, 19, 33-34, 37n, 39
punishment of the wicked, 15n, 45,
73, 80, 86, 91, 106, 111, 119, 130n,
143, 147, 161-162, 167-168, 184
purgatory, 10, 26-29, 33, 44-49,
51-52, 56, 81-82, 100, 105-106,
160n,174
Puritan/ism, 11, 67-68, 72-73, 85,
111, 114n, 177, 192n

Quakers, 89

Racovians, 38, 104n
radicals/ism, 19, 26, 30, 32-35, 38-
39, 42, 61, 65, 94, 98, 112, 115,
120
Rakov, 79
rationalism, 12, 16, 34n
Rawdon, 131
reason, 13, 27, 33, 36, 76, 86, 94,
97n, 100-102, 107, 109, 116, 126,
133-134, 136-137, 161-162, 166-
168, 170, 183-184, 193-195
redemption, 104, 130, 146, 153-157,
162, 182-183, 185, 190
Reformation, 9-12, 16, 18-19, 25-27,
30, 35, 37-41, 50, 54, 55n, 83n, 87,
115n, 158-159, 163, 174
Continental, 9, 33-34, 38
English, 11, 18-19, 23n, 25, 42-43,
50, 56, 59, 61-62, 78, 94, 97, 149,
174
German, 32
Radical, 19, 33-34, 37-38, 42
Reformers, English, 17, 42, 47-48,
50, 149
Protestant, 27, 29-30, 41, 120, 159,
164
Reformed faith, 41, 68n
Regents Park College Library, 197-
198, 200
religious liberty, 110
Restoration, 92, 113, 115, 192n
revelation, 12, 22, 27, 50, 72-73, 76,
97n, 102, 104, 116, 126, 128,130,

132-134, 137, 147, 155-157, 161,
166-167, 175, 185, 195
Revelation, book of, 107, 111, 142n,
176-177
Rhaetia, Republic, 36
Rochester, 51-52
Rome/Roman Church (see also
Catholicism, Catholic Church), 22,
27, 29, 41, 100, 105, 113, 115n,
158-159, 161-162, 164
Roman Empire, 178

Salisbury, 47
salvation, 17, 49, 53, 91, 99, 102,
104-105, 113, 120n, 160, 182, 184,
188, 190, 204
sanctification, 37
Satan, 9n, 69, 195 (see also Devil)
Saxony, 33
Scotland, 46-47
Scripture (see also Bible), 103, 105-
106, 109-110, 113, 123, 132, 167,
176, 183, 190, 205
authority of, 25, 42, 50, 56, 70, 87,
108, 116, 119, 133, 158-159
interpretation of, 36, 81, 97n, 101,
133, 148n, 201
incorrect interpretation of, 50, 100,
147-148, 150n, 156, 162, 171, 181,
189
meaning of, 32, 59, 78, 85, 91,
104, 108, 111-112, 124n, 145, 153,
182, 184, 203, 205-207
study of, 120n, 124, 129, 152
teaching of, 11-12, 16, 30, 49, 51-
53, 60, 62, 84, 93, 107-108, 118,
130, 133-134, 140, 144, 146, 154-
156, 159, 166, 168, 169n, 170, 175,
179, 183, 189, 191, 194, 201-202
Seekers, 70, 72n, 77, 86-87
Selsey, 132
separatist/ism, 86, 90
Shapwick, 129
sin, 53, 60, 99n, 130, 184, 206
Smithfield, 46, 54n, 63
Socinian/ism, 26, 35n, 38, 70, 78-81,

88, 94, 104, 125n, 129n, 169, 209
sola-fideism, 19
Somatists, 10
Somerset, 77, 91
soteriology, 34-35, 37, 48n, 52, 130, 155
soul sleep, 11-12, 14n, 15, 17, 19-20, 25, 29, 30-36, 40, 42-43, 45-48, 50, 56-58, 59-61, 63-67, 68n, 70-71, 72n, 82-83, 112, 136, 143, 151,161-164, 208-209
South Shoebury, 177
Southwater, 88
spirit, 40, 77-78, 81, 92, 113, 117, 133, 141n, 145, 152, 160, 162, 170, 202
Spiritualists, 34-35, 40, 63
St. David's, diocese of, 128
State Papers, 208
Steeple, 129
Strangers Church, London, 63
Strasbourg, 40-41, 68
subscription, 158-162
Suffolk, 53n, 55, 142, 165
Sussex, 53n, 55, 60-61, 84, 88, 93, 208-209
Sutton Vallence, 111
Switzerland, 19, 34, 36, 47

thnetopsychist/ism, 13, 15-16, 19-21, 29-30, 33-37, 39-40, 48n, 53-55, 59-61, 65-67, 71, 75-77, 79-81, 83n, 102, 106-107, 109-115, 117-119, 121-122, 124-126, 128, 132, 134-136, 138, 140, 142, 144-145, 150-151, 156-157, 164-165, 168-170, 174, 197, 204-205
thought, pre-Christian, 112, 132, 137, 174
Toddington, 52
transubstantiation, 44, 143
Transylvania, 36-37
Trinitarians/ism, 38
Trinity, 70, 105, 143, 158, 180
truth, 56, 71, 100, 131, 133, 153n,

154-156, 160, 175-176, 181, 185-186, 195, 197, 201
Tyndale's New Testament (1526 and 1534), 16, 23n, 25, 48n, 50-51, 54, 56, 57n

Unitarian/ism, 13, 35, 38, 79-80, 165n, 168-169, 193, 208
Universalism, 169-170
universe, 119, 177, 186, 190-193
universities (includes references to individual colleges at Cambridge and Oxford), 27-28, 87
  Aberdeen, 146
  Bologna, 27
  Cambridge, 11, 95, 96n, 97n, 120, 142, 150-151, 154, 157-158, 160, 177, 195
  Ferrara, 27
  Glasgow, 82, 167
  Heidelberg, 177
  Oxford, 78-79, 94, 127, 131, 135, 138-139, 150n, 154, 166, 191
  Padua, 27-28, 32, 37, 94
  Paris, 26
  Sienna, 32

Venetian Republic, 37
Virgin Mary, 34, 40, 46

Waldenses, 174
Walthamstow, 85, 139
Western thought, 67, 109
Westminster Assembly, 82, 94n
Whigs, 155
Wittenberg, 33, 48n
Worcester, diocese of, 55, 60, 122
Worcester/Worcestershire, 64, 86, 150, 166
Worms, 48n
Worthing, 55, 208

Yaxley, 154
York, 150
Yorkshire, 53n, 131

Zurich, 35, 68

Printed in the United States
141733LV00002B/56/A

9 780227 172605